Designing and Developing Secure Azure Solutions

Michael Howard
Heinrich Gantenbein
Simone Curzi

Designing and Developing Secure Azure Solutions

Published with the authorization of Microsoft Corporation by:
Pearson Education, Inc.

ISBN-13: 978-0-13-790875-2
ISBN-10: 0-13-790875-X
Library of Congress Control Number: 2022947556

1 2022

Trademarks

Microsoft and the trademarks listed at http://www.microsoft.com on the "Trademarks" webpage are trademarks of the Microsoft group of companies. All other marks are property of their respective owners.

Warning and Disclaimer

Special Sales

For information about buying this title in bulk quantities, or for special sales opportunities (which may include electronic versions; custom cover designs; and content particular to your business, training goals, marketing focus, or branding interests), please contact our corporate sales department at corpsales@pearsoned.com or (800) 382-3419.

For government sales inquiries, please contact governmentsales@pearsoned.com.

For questions about sales outside the U.S., please contact intlcs@pearson.com.

CREDITS

Editor-in-Chief:
Brett Bartow

Executive Editor:
Loretta Yates

Sponsoring Editor:
Charvi Aora

Development Editor:
Kate Shoup

Managing Editor:
Sandra Schroeder

Senior Project Editor:
Tracey Croom

Copy Editor:
Kim Wimpsett

Indexer:
Ken Johnson

Proofreader:
Barbara Mack

Technical Editors:
Jonathan Davis, Mike Becker, Rick Alba, Altaz Valani, Hasan Yasar

Editorial Assistant:
Cindy Teeters

Cover Designer:
Twist Creative, Seattle

Compositor:
codeMantra

Art:
Cover illustration:
Valex/Shutterstock

Figure 10-37:
Gordon Lyon

Pearson's Commitment to Diversity, Equity, and Inclusion

Pearson is dedicated to creating bias-free content that reflects the diversity of all learners. We embrace the many dimensions of diversity, including but not limited to race, ethnicity, gender, socioeconomic status, ability, age, sexual orientation, and religious or political beliefs.

Education is a powerful force for equity and change in our world. It has the potential to deliver opportunities that improve lives and enable economic mobility. As we work with authors to create content for every product and service, we acknowledge our responsibility to demonstrate inclusivity and incorporate diverse scholarship so that everyone can achieve their potential through learning. As the world's leading learning company, we have a duty to help drive change and live up to our purpose to help more people create a better life for themselves and to create a better world.

Our ambition is to purposefully contribute to a world where:

- Everyone has an equitable and lifelong opportunity to succeed through learning.
- Our educational products and services are inclusive and represent the rich diversity of learners.
- Our educational content accurately reflects the histories and experiences of the learners we serve.
- Our educational content prompts deeper discussions with learners and motivates them to expand their own learning (and worldview).

While we work hard to present unbiased content, we want to hear from you about any concerns or needs with this Pearson product so that we can investigate and address them.

- Please contact us with concerns about any potential bias at https://www.pearson.com/report-bias.html.

Contents at a glance

Contents

PART I   SECURITY PRINCIPLES

Chapter 1   Secure development lifecycle processes   3

Chapter 2   Secure design   23

Chapter 4   Threat modeling   79

Chapter 5   Identity, authentication, and authorization   123

PART II SECURE IMPLEMENTATION

Chapter 14   CI/CD security   435

Chapter 15   Network security   443

Acknowledgments

This book covers a diverse and complex set of security-related topics. When writing a book like this, we as authors must make sure our facts are straight and our guidance is correct. We can do this only by asking questions of and obtaining assistance from people in the Azure product groups and people who are experts in their respective fields. To this end, we'd like to graciously acknowledge the help and assistance from the following people at Microsoft:

Amar Gowda, Amaury Chamayou, Anthony Nevico, Antoine Delignat-Lavaud, Barry Dorrans, Ben Co, Ben Hanson, Ben Oberhaus, Bhuvaneshwari Krishnamurthi, Dan Simon, David Nunez Tejerina, Dhruv Iyer, Eric Beauchesne, Eustace Asanghanwa, Hannah Hayward, Jack Richins, Jakub Szymaszek, Jenny Hunter, Joachim Hammer, Jon Lange, John Lambert, Josh Brown-White, Ken St. Cyr, Kozeta Garrett, Luciano Raso, Mark Simos, Michael McReynolds, Michael Withrow, Mirek Sztajno, Nicholas Kondamudi, Niels Ferguson, Panagiotis Antonopoulos, Pieter Vanhove, Prasad Nelabhotla, Rafael Pazos Rodriguez, Robert Jarret, Rohit Nayak, Run Cai, Sameer Verkhedkar, Shubhra Sinha, Srđan Božović, Steven Gott, Sylvan Clebsch, Taylor Bianchi, Thomas Weiss, Vikas Bhatia, and Yuri Diogenes

Other Microsoft colleagues acted in a consulting capacity, spending hours helping with some of the more complex parts of the book. They are:

Kyle Marsh, Mark Morowczynski, and Bailey Bercik (for identity); Dave Thaler, Graham Berry, and Vikas Bhatia (for confidential computing); and Hervey Wilson (for Key Vault)

We also got feedback from people outside of Microsoft for their specific expertise:

Arun Prabhakar (Boston Consulting Group), Avi Douglen (Bounce Security), Brook S. E. Schoenfield (True Positives, LLC), Dave Kaplan (AMD), David Litchfield (Apple), Donna McCally (HITRUST), Izar Tarandach (Squarespace), Lotfi Ben Othmane (Iowa State University), Mark Bode (AMD), Mark Cox (RedHat), Mark Curphey (Crash Override), Matthew Coles (Dell Technologies), Michael F. Angelo (Micro Focus), Mike Dietz and Robert Seacord (Woven Planet), and Shane Gashette and Steve Christey Coley (MITRE)

We'd like to thank our technical reviewers, who scrutinized every aspect of our drafts. The technical reviewers were:

Altaz Valani (Security Compass), Hasan Yasar (Software Engineering Institute, Carnegie Mellon), Jonathan Davis (Microsoft), Mike Becker (Microsoft), and Rick Alba (Microsoft)

This book would not have been possible without the folks at Pearson/Microsoft Press: Loretta Yates for saying "yes"; Charvi Arora, who kept us marching forward to hit our dates; and finally, Kate Shoup, who did a magnificent job editing our text and yet maintaining our tone and technical intent.

Finally, we'd like to thank Scott Guthrie for writing the foreword and for leading the magnificent team that is Microsoft Azure.

Michael Howard
Austin, Texas

Heinrich Gantenbein
St. Paul, Minnesota

Simone Curzi
Perugia, Italy

About the Authors

Michael Howard

Michael Howard is a 30-year Microsoft veteran and is currently a Principal Security Program Manager in the Azure Data Platform team, working on security engineering. He is one of the original architects of the Microsoft Security Development Lifecycle and has helped diverse customers such as government, military, education, finance, and healthcare secure their Azure workloads. He was the application security lead for the Rio 2016 Olympic games, which were hosted on Azure.

Heinrich Gantenbein

Heinrich Gantenbein is a Senior Principal Consultant on Cybersecurity in Microsoft's Industry Solutions Delivery. With 30+ years of experience in software engineering and more than 30 years of experience in consulting, he brings a wealth of practical know-how to his role. Heinrich specializes in Azure security, threat modeling, and DevSecOps.

Simone Curzi

Simone Curzi is a Principal Consultant from Microsoft's Industry Solutions Delivery. He has 20+ years of experience covering various technical roles in Microsoft and has fully devoted himself to security for more than 10 years. A renowned threat modeling and Microsoft Security Development Lifecycle expert, Simone is a regular speaker at international conferences such as Microsoft Ready, Microsoft Spark, (ISC)^2 Security Congress, Carnegie Mellon's SEI DevOps Days, and Security Compass Equilibrium. Simone is also author of an open source threat modeling tool, Threats Manager Studio.

Foreword

In the last decade we have witnessed a dramatic shift in the way organizations have harnessed technology to completely reinvent and transform how they do business. Recent global challenges and unpredictable far-reaching events have only accelerated that change, and organizations have had to pivot and adapt to meet their customer and employee needs and ensure business resilience.

This digital transformation has been made possible in part by technology advancements and hyperscale cloud providers like Microsoft Azure that provide organizations with the agility to realize new efficiencies and capabilities. However, as we continue through this era of unprecedented transformation, including migration to the cloud, we are also experiencing new threats and requirements to ensure security and privacy.

When people think of security, they often think of endpoint protection, firewalls, and anti-malware tools, which are critically important, but architects and developers can't ignore application security during design and development. This book — *Designing and Developing Secure Azure Solutions* — is a necessary resource to understanding the essential elements of end-to-end secure software design and development on Azure. It addresses two areas I care about deeply – the security of Azure and software development.

The Microsoft Cloud has many reliability and security benefits compared to on-premises solutions, but architects and developers cannot ignore fundamental security practices when they deploy on Azure. Cloud-based solutions have a shared responsibility model, and some of the security onus is on the tenant as well as the cloud provider. *Designing and Developing Secure Azure Solutions* provides a holistic and approachable resource for anyone building secure workloads running on Azure. Readers working on Azure solutions will gain a contemporary understanding of secure development, design, and implementation.

The authors Michael, Heinrich, and Simone have decades of application security experience between them. They have worked with governments and companies — large and small — enabling each to design, develop, deploy, and manage secured solutions on Azure. I know the authors to be dedicated to helping anyone designing and developing on Azure achieve the reliability, scalability, and security demanded by their organizations and end users.

This book is an essential guide for every architect and developer deploying secure, business-critical solutions on Azure.

Scott Guthrie
Executive Vice President
Cloud + AI Group, Microsoft

Introduction

In mid-2021, during a recording of the *Azure Security Podcast*, Azure security expert and author Yuri Diogenes asked Michael if he planned to write an update to his book, *The Security Development Lifecycle*. Without hesitation, Michael responded, "No!"

But that wasn't the end of the matter.

The question Yuri asked planted a seed. Over the next few weeks, the three of us—Michael, Heinrich, and Simone—assembled a plan to write this book. Between us, we have worked with hundreds of customers to help them deploy business-critical solutions on Azure with confidence. This book is the culmination of that real-world experience.

The reason we wrote this book was not only to help you understand how to design and develop secure solutions running on Azure but to offer you pragmatic advice. The Venn diagram shown in Figure I-1 reflects how we see this book.

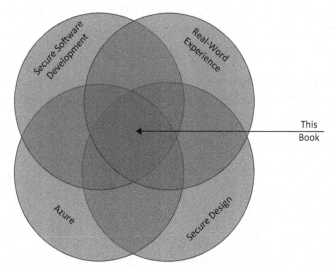

FIGURE I-1 The Intersection of this book's areas of coverage.

We do not cover some areas within Azure; otherwise, this book would be quite a tome. Most notably, we do not cover topics such as the following:

- **Privileged access workstations (PAWs)**   A PAW is a workstation designed for administrative tasks only. It does not have access to email, general web browsing, and other productivity tasks. PAWs are used by elevated accounts to perform actions in high-risk environments, such as production, account administration, and more. You can learn more about PAWs here: *https://azsec.tech/irb*.

- **Conditional access and multifactor authentication (MFA)**   These are often handled by an identity team, and the infrastructure should already be in place. With that said, conditional access and MFA are critical to securing an Azure-based solution. Learn more here: *https://azsec.tech/59d*.

- **Privacy**   This is a book on security. Although security and privacy do overlap, security is mainly about fortifying a system and its data against unauthorized use, while privacy is about handling personal data. You can have security without privacy, but you cannot have privacy without security.

We've kept things relatively brief by including lots of links to outside information rather than covering some topics in depth in this book.

Organization of this book

This book is not designed to be read from cover to cover. You can do that, of course, but we have tried to make the chapters as independent as possible so they can be read individually. With that said, there are cross-references between chapters, and you might sometimes need to read a section of a different chapter to get the big picture.

The book also covers multiple ways to achieve a task, such as the following:

- Using the Azure Portal (although it's not common to use the Azure Portal in production systems because deploying in the real world usually uses a pipeline to push resources)

- Using the Azure command-line Interface (CLI)

- Using PowerShell code

- Using more complete code examples in different languages such as C#, Python, JavaScript, and more

 Tip We have uploaded code samples and snippets to our GitHub repository at *https://github.com/AzureDevSecurityBook/,* so please make a point of visiting regularly.

Who should read this book

Just who is this book for? It's for anyone deploying solutions on Azure—whether they're architects, developers, or testers—who might not know a great deal about security but who want to make sure their design and code are as secure as possible. We cover a lot of ground in the book, but we also cover many complex topics in depth.

One final point: if you use the NIST Cybersecurity Framework (NIST CSF), then you're familiar with its core components: identify, protect, detect, respond, and recover. The material in this book focuses primarily on the protect component and some aspects of the detect component. Rolling out industry-grade solutions on Azure requires your organization to cover the other four components of the NIST CSF. You can read more about the NIST CSF in Chapter 8, "Compliance and risk programs," and on the NIST website, at *https://azsec.tech/81t*.

Thanks for reading!

Conventions and features in this book

This book presents information using conventions designed to make the information readable and easy to follow:

- Boxed elements with labels such as "Note" provide additional information

- Text that you type (apart from code blocks) appears in bold

- A plus sign (+) between two key names means that you must press those keys at the same time. For example, "Press Alt+Tab" means that you hold down the Alt key while you press the Tab key

- A vertical bar between two or more menu items (e.g. File | Close), means that you should select the first menu or menu item, then the next, and so on

System requirements

Examples and scenarios in the book require access to a Microsoft Azure subscription and a computer that can connect to Azure. You can learn more about a trial subscription at this site:

azure.microsoft.com/en-us/free

GitHub Repo

The book's GitHub repository includes sample code and code snippets, and the authors will update this over time. The repo is *github.com/AzureDevSecurityBook/*.

The download content will also be available on the book's product page: *MicrosoftPressStore.com/SecureAzureSolutions/downloads*

Errata, updates, & book support

We've made every effort to ensure the accuracy of this book and its companion content. You can access updates to this book—in the form of a list of submitted errata and their related corrections—at:

MicrosoftPressStore.com/SecureAzureSolutions/errata

If you discover an error that is not already listed, please submit it to us at the same page.

For additional book support and information, please visit *MicrosoftPressStore.com/ Support.*

Please note that product support for Microsoft software and hardware is not offered through the previous addresses. For help with Microsoft software or hardware, go to *support.microsoft.com.*

Stay in touch

Let's keep the conversation going! We're on Twitter: *twitter.com/MicrosoftPress*

## PART I

Security principles

## CHAPTER 1

Secure development lifecycle processes

After completing this chapter, you will be able to:

- Understand some of the processes required to build more secure software.

- Grow a security culture within your organization.

- Explain the purpose of different types of environments for development work to production and how they require nuanced security controls.

Developers are the number-one source of compromises

The number-one source of compromises isn't hackers, attackers, or other nefarious actors. Rather, the number-one source of compromises is us—the software development community. Indeed, according to a 2020 analysis by Contrast Security, almost 50 percent of all compromises are due to vulnerabilities within applications—vulnerabilities that were ultimately created by software developers. You can read a synopsis of the report here: https://azsec.tech/lvz.

As software developers, we can't do much about attacks. They will happen no matter what. But what we can do is improve the security of our code. The simple fact is that the design of our system and the quality of our code can be the difference between a failed attack and a successful one. We must change the way we design and develop software to foster better security in as seamless a way as possible, with as little friction as possible. The key word here is *friction*. Security is often seen as a tax that developers must pay that inhibits delivery. It just gets in the way. We must include processes and tasks that increase security, are as frictionless as possible, and are viewed as simply one more critical aspect of getting the job done.

Tools are important, of course. But they should not be used blindly or seen as the sole source of your solution's security. Besides, no matter how much tooling or automation you use in your development practices, at the end of the day, it is humans who build software, and your security posture depends on humans, too. As the adage goes, "A fool with a tool is still a fool." So, we must invest not just in the latest shiny security tools but also in human security capital and processes.

Introducing the Microsoft Security Development Lifecycle

The Microsoft Security Development Lifecycle (SDL) started life in the early 2000s and has been adopted and adapted over the years. There is a saying, "There is nothing new under the sun," and that is true about the SDL. But the SDL *is* different in the amount of supporting documentation, tooling, research, and thought leadership that Microsoft has made publicly available.

So, what is the SDL? The SDL is a set of practices to improve software security. It has two overarching goals:

- Reducing the number of vulnerabilities in your code

- Reducing the severity of the vulnerabilities you miss

These two goals introduce some tension to your security strategy. That is, you want to build the most secure software possible while acknowledging that you will miss things and that attacks evolve over time. What was secure and correct today may be vulnerable tomorrow.

Quality ≠ security

We have heard people say, "If you improve quality, then security will improve, too." While this statement sounds plausible, there is no evidence to back it up. None. Software quality programs rarely find security issues because security issues are different from quality issues. Moreover, as we discuss later in the book, security is often defined as "extra" functionality.

For example, suppose you have an application that performs only the following database operations:

- Adding a new user (*creating* in CRUD)

- Reading a user's details (*reading* in CRUD)

- Editing a user's details (*updating* in CRUD)

- Deleting a user (*deleting* in CRUD)

- Printing the user's details

You build some tests meant to succeed or fail (on purpose!) and then verify those successes and failures. If all the tests meant to check for success succeed and all the tests meant to check for failure dutifully fail, you might conclude the application has no defects. However, this is not the case. If, for example, the application has an SQL injection vulnerability that allows a tester (or attacker) to read all users or delete a database table, the application will still pass all the success tests and fail all the failure tests. The moral of this story is you *must* add security discipline to your software development processes.

Securing features vs. security features

The Microsoft SDL focuses on securing your software, not just on adding more security features. Security features are important, but you can't just throw every security product at your solution and call it secure. The features you add to your solutions must be secured, too. This philosophical perspective represents an important mind-shift for many people who think they can buy a product and call it done—especially when so many companies sell their wares as a silver bullet.

> **Important** In short, you must focus on the discipline of software engineering security. You can't abdicate that responsibility to a product.

SDL components

The main Microsoft SDL tasks and requirements are as follows:

- Security training

- Defining your bug bar

- Attack surface analysis

- Threat modeling

- Defining your toolchain

- Avoiding banned functionality

- Using static analysis tools

- Using dynamic analysis tools

- Security code review

- Having an incident response plan

- Performing penetration tests

Let's look at each of these in more detail.

Security training

Security training is a must. But by security training, we don't mean "don't reuse passwords!" training; we mean "application development security" training.

For a long time, Microsoft required all *technical* staff members to attend general security training, and employees can still do this if they want. But these days, we use a leaner training model that's more area specific. For example, we require engineering staff to take security-related classes that relate to their role rather than a more general course of training.

For example, if a developer writes Node.js server-side JavaScript code for a web application, then that developer must understand cross-site scripting (XSS) issues, secure use of cookies, and other web- and HTTP-related security issues and defenses. If that same application communicates with an SQL database, then having a solid understanding of SQL injection, least privilege database connections, and securely storing connection string information is also important. However, odds are this developer does not need to understand potential memory corruption issues while using strcpy() in C. So, they could simply read, watch a video, or complete some online training about the topics of importance to them.

Note There are multiple modes of training, so you should choose the mode that works best for you as a developer, architect, or tester. Still, never underestimate the value of a short video that gets right to the core of the issue at hand!

From an Agile perspective, no one should be permitted to work on a sprint until they have a baseline level of security knowledge. Be sure everyone on the engineering team is educated about the company's requirements regarding building secure software. If your company does not have a list of recommended secure application design and development resources, you should build one. You might even consider making this book required reading for all your engineering staff.

Real-world experience: "Required reading"

When Michael wrote *Writing Secure Code* with David LeBlanc, Bill Gates read the book and deemed the second edition "required reading" at Microsoft. This quickly raised the collective security IQ across the company.

Defining your bug bar

Not all security bugs are created equal; defining some way to calculate the severity of your security bugs is critical. There are many ways to calculate severity calculations, but the method *du jour* is the Common Vulnerability Scoring System (CVSS). According to NIST, the CVSS is "an open framework for communicating the characteristics and severity of software vulnerabilities." The CVSS communicates the risk associated with a particular vulnerability using a numerical score that ranges from 1 (low) to 10 (critical).

> **Tip** First.org provides a list of CVSS examples to help you learn how to score vulnerabilities. You can find it here: https://azsec.tech/wt7.

Chapter 8, "Compliance and risk programs," covers CVSS in detail. For now, the important thing is to define what the CVSS risk scores mean to you. For example, suppose you're about to push some code into production, but you discover it contains a security vulnerability with a CVSS score of 7.3. What should you do? If that same vulnerability had a CVSS score of 1.7, it would be a low-risk bug—not one that should prevent you from pushing the code into production, but rather something you should probably fix at some point. A score of 7.3 presents more of a dilemma. Should you push to production and quickly fix the bug afterward? Or should you postpone deployment for a day or two to make the fix and test it beforehand? It's a hard call to make, but generally erring on the side of caution is best.

> **Note** While CVSS is commonly used, there is some pressure to use other methods in Agile development. However, none has emerged to topple CVSS. There is an excellent write-up of the topic here: https://azsec.tech/1zh.

To assess risk, Microsoft has historically taken a bug bar approach. A bug bar contains a set of conditions and the relative damage potential of each. Many of these conditions relate to attack surface (see the next section) because the more exposed a potential vulnerability is, the more severe it could be. You can see a sample Microsoft bug bar here: https://azsec.tech/dsx.

The idea behind a bug bar is you assess only the conditions within the environment to arrive at an overall "T-shirt size." Microsoft uses the following T-shirt sizes both internally and for external patches:

- **Critical** A critical vulnerability is one whose exploitation could allow code execution without user interaction.

- **Important** An important vulnerability is one whose exploitation could result in compromise of the confidentiality, integrity, or availability of user data, or of the integrity or availability of processing resources.

- **Moderate**   The impact of a moderate-rated vulnerability can be mitigated to a significant degree by requiring authentication applying the associated component to nondefault configurations only.

- **Low**   The impact of a low-rated vulnerability is comprehensively mitigated by the characteristics of the affected component. Microsoft recommends that customers evaluate whether to apply the security update to the affected systems.

Figure 1-1 and Figure 1-2 show the core components of a bug bar. Note that the chart shown in Figure 1-1 leads to the one shown in Figure 1-2; we did this to make the bug bar more legible.

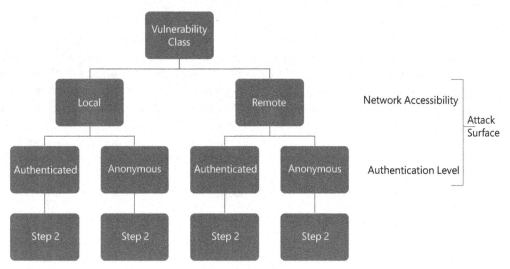

FIGURE 1-1   The first step of a sample bug bar, focusing on the vulnerability class and the level of authentication.

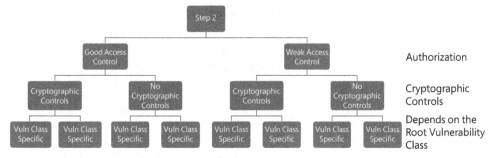

FIGURE 1-2   The second step of a sample bug bar, focusing on authorization and cryptographic controls, and then the final node depends on the vulnerability class.

The top node, Vulnerability Class, is one of the STRIDE categories. We explain these in detail in Chapter 4, "Threat modeling." Briefly, STRIDE is an acronym for a set of key attacker objectives, which are as follows:

- **Spoofing**   Impersonating something else, such as a user or a computer

- **Tampering**   Changing data or code without proper authorization

- **Repudiation**   Reversing a transaction

- **Information disclosure**   Viewing data without proper authorization

- **Denial of service**   Degrading or preventing service

- **Elevation of privilege**   Gaining privilege you normally would not have

As an example, suppose you have a sensitive file in an Azure blob storage account, and you want to calculate the potential risk posed if an attacker reads the data. Walking down the bug bar shown in Figure 1-1 and Figure 1-2 from top to bottom, the (pathologically bad) scenario is as follows:

- **Vulnerability class**   Information disclosure

- **Client authentication**   None (that is, the blob is set to anonymous access)

- **Access control/authorization**   None (that is, there is no Shared Access Signature [SAS] token or data plane role-based access control [RBAC] mechanisms)

- **Data encryption**   None

- **Data sensitivity**   High

> **Important** The last item, data sensitivity, is specific to the information disclosure vulnerability class, because for information disclosure, the concern is data sensitivity.

This series of catastrophic conditions is certainly an example of a critical issue (i.e., T-shirt size). In fact, you have to wonder, how did it even happen? Regardless, you must fix it quickly.

In an Agile environment, you need some way to calculate vulnerability severity before you start building code. If you don't have one, then you must define one quickly—and make sure everyone understands how to use it. The aforementioned Microsoft bug bar example at https://azsec.tech/dsx covers specific issues that could influence the severity of a particular vulnerability, making it a good resource for developing your own approach for calculating vulnerabilities.

Now consider a different scenario with these parameters:

- **Vulnerability class**   Information disclosure

- **Client authentication**   Azure Active Directory authentication

- **Access control/authorization**   Data plane RBAC that restricts access to a small set of trusted users

- **Data encryption** Client-side encryption with keys managed in Key Vault and an RBAC policy that restricts who can access the keys

- **Data sensitivity** High

Although the data sensitivity in this scenario is still high, this is a low-severity scenario and in fact is good design. Of course, there is no such thing as no risk. There is always risk. But in this scenario, the risk is acceptable.

Attack surface analysis

Chapter 9, "Secure coding," covers attack surface analysis in greater detail. For now, it's enough to know that it's a way to determine how exposed your application is to attackers.

Obviously, your goal is to reduce the attack surface as much as possible. The two main axes for determining attack surface are as follows:

- Network accessibility

- Level of authentication

Reducing attack surface poses an interesting problem in the cloud because, by default, platform as a service (PaaS) offerings are accessible to the internet. This is why technology such as private endpoints exist: to help isolate and reduce the service's network accessibility. Adding appropriate authentication and authorization also reduces how exposed a service endpoint is to attackers. An endpoint (for example, a REST endpoint) that is accessible to the internet with no authentication or authorization has a significantly higher attack surface than the same endpoint that is accessible only from a subset of IP addresses and requires authentication to access.

Whether you use Agile development methods or not, you should always ask yourself what the appropriate attack surface is for all your endpoints. You must also determine what the network, authentication, and authorization policies should be and how they will be enforced. Microsoft offers an attack surface analysis tool called Attack Surface Analyzer that can give you an idea of how the Windows platform measures attack surfaces, which you can learn about here: https://azsec.tech/p0r. In an Azure environment, this is still useful when deploying your code into IaaS Windows VMs.

> **Important** You should strive to keep your attack surface as low as possible—and then drive it even lower!

Threat modeling

This book contains an entire chapter on threat modeling (Chapter 4), so we won't discuss it in detail here. Suffice it to say that threat modeling is a critically important secure design practice. When building an application in an Agile environment, you must develop a threat model as soon as is feasible and adjust it as needed as you add new functionality to the app. This enables you to ensure the appropriate mitigations are in place.

Defining your toolchain

The toolchain is a set of tools used for software development. It includes everything from the editor to your compilers, linkers, libraries, and bug-tracking tools. When using Agile methods in software development, you must define your toolchain and which options to use to support security. This section covers several of these tools. Technically, the toolchain also includes static and dynamic analysis tools, but we will discuss those a little later in this chapter.

> **Tip** You might need someone who understands this space to decide which toolchain versions to use, as this can require specialized knowledge.

For the most part, editors are a personal preference and have very little impact on security. However, some editors have better support for security-related plug-ins, such as linting tools. One example is Microsoft's DevSkim (https://azsec.tech/4lt), which works with Visual Studio and Visual Studio Code. Speaking of Visual Studio, it also has numerous lightweight tools based on the Rosyln compiler platform (https://azsec.tech/wj8) that plug in to the editor. Examples include the following:

- Roslynator (https://azsec.tech/ia0)

- SonarAnalyzer (https://azsec.tech/0ws)

- GitHub Advanced Security (https://github.com/advanced-security/)

Compilers and linkers are often updated to add new security defenses. (This is especially true for C and C++ compilers.) For example, .NET 6 and later includes new memory-corruption defenses named W^X (short for Write XOR eXecute) in the underlying infrastructure and libraries. You get this for free by simply using the newer version. (For more information about some of the newer .NET 6 defenses, see https://azsec.tech/ec3.

> **Important** If there is an option to use a compiler version that includes security defenses either by default or by using a compiler or linker flag, then you should use it. This includes frameworks and libraries. You should always err on the side of using tools that emit more secure code. (Chapter 9 discusses secure coding in more detail.)

The bug-tracking process is another important part of the toolchain. All security issues must be marked as `Type=Security Issue` or indicated in some other way to denote that the issue must be treated as important. This practice also allows you to track your security vulnerability trend over time. Ideally it trends down!

Avoiding banned functionality

Some functionality is just bad—not just insecure, but outright bad—and should never be used. Examples include weak cryptographic algorithms, insecure methods, and insecure libraries.

Examples of banned cryptographic algorithms with known practical weaknesses include the following:

- MD4, MD5, SHA-1

- RC4, DES, 3DES, Rijndael

- Electronic Code Book (ECB) block cipher mode

Table 1-1 lists other examples of banned functionality.

TABLE 1-1 Examples of banned functionality

Function Category	Banned Functionality
JavaScript functions and methods	eval execScript setTimeout that uses a string as the first argument (it's OK to use this method with a direct function reference) setInterval that uses a string as the first argument (see setTimeout) setImmediate that uses a string as the first argument (see setTimeout)
Java functions and methods	java.lang.System.runFinalizersOnExit java.lang.Runtime.runFinalizersOnExit
C functions	strcpy, strcat strncpy, strncat gets sprint vsprintf memcpy Too many more to mention!

Tip You can catch banned functions in C by using the banned.h header, which is available at Michael's GitHub repo, located here: https://github.com/x509cert/banned.

Also, any function that creates weak pseudorandom numbers should be banned when the output is used for cryptographic purposes. For example:

- **C** rand()

- **Java** java.lang.Math.random()

- **C#** System.Random()

- **Python** random.randint() from the random library

The list of banned functionalities should also include libraries that support insecure behavior. For example, old versions of .NET were susceptible to XML DTD denial-of-service bombs. In response, .NET versions 3.5 and later added a `ProhibitDtd` property on various XML classes, which, when set to true, mitigates DTD bomb attacks completely and elegantly.

DTD bomb attacks

An XML DTD bomb is an XML document that has a self-referencing document type definition (DTD). Here's an example:

```
<?xml version="1.0"?>
<!DOCTYPE lolz [
  <!ENTITY lol "lol">
  <!ENTITY lol2 "&lol;&lol;&lol;&lol;&lol;&lol;&lol;&lol;&lol;&lol;">
  <!ENTITY lol3 "&lol2;&lol2;&lol2;&lol2;&lol2;&lol2;&lol2;&lol2;&lol2;&lol2;">
  <!ENTITY lol4 "&lol3;&lol3;&lol3;&lol3;&lol3;&lol3;&lol3;&lol3;&lol3;&lol3;">
  <!ENTITY lol5 "&lol4;&lol4;&lol4;&lol4;&lol4;&lol4;&lol4;&lol4;&lol4;&lol4;">
  <!ENTITY lol6 "&lol5;&lol5;&lol5;&lol5;&lol5;&lol5;&lol5;&lol5;&lol5;&lol5;">
  <!ENTITY lol7 "&lol6;&lol6;&lol6;&lol6;&lol6;&lol6;&lol6;&lol6;&lol6;&lol6;">
  <!ENTITY lol8 "&lol7;&lol7;&lol7;&lol7;&lol7;&lol7;&lol7;&lol7;&lol7;&lol7;">
  <!ENTITY lol9 "&lol8;&lol8;&lol8;&lol8;&lol8;&lol8;&lol8;&lol8;&lol8;&lol8;">
]>
<lolz>&lol9;</lolz>
```

When the XML parser reads &lol9, this expands to 10 references to &lol8, and each of these references 10 &lol7. You can see where this is going! You can read more here: https://azsec.tech/9yq.

For any development process, including Agile, it's a good practice to maintain a list of banned functionalities and recommended replacements and to keep it up to date as new vulnerabilities emerge. Here are a few resources to get you started:

- **Vulners** https://vulners.com/
- **API Security** https://apisecurity.io/

Real-world experience: Banning functionality

You can't just ban something. You need a viable replacement, too. For example, Microsoft wanted to ban the C `memcpy()` runtime for some time but could not do so until the `memcpy_s()` runtime became widely available.

Using static analysis tools

Static analysis tools—or more correctly, static application security testing (SAST) tools—are a cornerstone of Agile methods. You should use these tools, use them early, and use them often. These tools provide scalability and a base level of correctness. Essentially, they analyze your source code and data flows to find vulnerabilities. Or at least, the better ones work this way! Some are just glorified string searches or grep tools.

> **Note** For some issues, grepping is fine. For example, if you search some code for MD4, then the odds are good that anything found is a weak hash algorithm. You don't need to do a data-flow analysis for something like that.

One way to use static analysis tools is at the developer's desktop as they compile code. These tools are usually built into the IDE or environment and should be run often. They are usually relatively lightweight, and although they don't perform complex data-flow analysis, they can often find issues quickly. Figure 1-3 shows some sample C code and the results of running the analysis tools built into Visual Studio. Notice in the output that the tool has detected five issues, and that for three of them, it has included explanations.

```
CodeBugs.cpp
CodeBugs                                        (Global Scope)                              AddTail(LinkedList * node, i

 92   LinkedList* AddTail(LinkedList* node, int value)
 93   {
 94       // finds the last node
 95       while (node->next ≠ nullptr)
 96       {
 97           node = node->next;
 98       }
 99
100       // appends the new node
101       LinkedList* newNode = AllocateNode();
102       newNode->data = value;
103       newNode->next = 0;
104       node->next = newNode;
105
106       return newNode;
```

```
Error List
Entire Solution ▾   ⊗ 0 Errors   ▲ 5 Warnings   ⓘ 0 Messages      Build + Intelli ▾

   Code  Description                                                          Line   File            Project
 ▲ C6230 Implicit cast between semantically different integer types.           43    CodeBugs.cpp    CodeBugs
 ▲       Assignment '=' used when equality '==' probably intended.             56    CodeBugs.cpp    CodeBugs
◢▲ C6001 Using uninitialized memory 'i'.                                       83    CodeBugs.cpp    CodeBugs
   Detailed Explanation
   77: 'i' is not initialized
   79: Skip this branch, (assume 'n==0' is false)
   83: 'i' is used, but may not have been initialized
▸▲ C6001 Using uninitialized memory 'j'.                                       83    CodeBugs.cpp    CodeBugs
◢▲ C6011 Dereferencing NULL pointer 'newNode'.                                102    CodeBugs.cpp    CodeBugs
   Detailed Explanation
   101: 'newNode' may be NULL
   102: 'newNode' is dereferenced, but may still be NULL
```

FIGURE 1-3   Output from the static analysis of a C program using the /analyze compiler switch in Visual Studio.

> ## Real-world experience: Static analysis on planet Earth
>
> John Carmack, cofounder of id Software and lead developer of *Doom*, *Quake*, and *Wolfenstein*, makes some pertinent points about the value of static analysis tools in this video: https://azsec.tech/a64.

The bane of all software developers is static analysis tools that create numerous false positives (that is, items flagged by the tool as bugs that aren't really bugs) and that flag low-severity issues. When you use these tools, you must keep track of the issues they detect, as well as which issues are real and which are not. If the tool seems to flag more nonreal vulnerabilities than is reasonable, you might want to constrain the list of issues you flag or talk to the tool vendor.

To determine which bugs you want your static analysis tool to flag and which ones you don't, ask yourself these three questions:

- **Do I care about this bug class?** For example, some tools will alert you if you use the wrong case for a variable name. Do you want it to do this? Do you really want to receive hundreds of warnings about camel case versus Pascal case? Probably not!

- **How severe is the bug?** You want to receive warnings about a bug that could result in a catastrophic error causing data loss, but you might not care so much about a bug that causes some truncated error text in a dialog box.

- **How confident am I that the bug is real?** This is the important one. To answer this, you might need to ask the tool developer how *they* determine whether a bug is real. Inter-function data-flow analysis will usually uncover issues with a higher confidence level than a simple string search.

With these answers in mind, you can determine which warnings to heed. For example, suppose your tool detects 170 distinct issues; 65 of them are not correct or high risk, 70 are low risk, and 10 are low confidence. That means you're really left with only 25 warnings to consider. You might add more warnings over time; it's best to start small and not aggravate the developers!

> **Note** You can run lightweight analysis tools at developers' desktops as part of the developers' build process, but a central analysis team could use heavier tools. This team could then triage results and file individual bugs with developers.

Real-world experience: Effective use of static analysis tools

Do not give your developers a massive list of untriaged, potentially low-quality issues found during static analysis. Doing so will make the developers despise the tools and make you "public enemy #1." Instead, start with a small number of high-severity and high-confidence warnings. Then, over time, add new warnings to your analysis and reports. With this said, there is no harm in running tools with all warnings enabled and having application development security experts review the results and hand-pick any serious issues to send to the development backlog.

Using dynamic analysis tools

In Agile environments, dynamic analysis tools are just as important as static analysis tools, and both must be used early and often—if not continuously—so you can find and fix issues quickly. After all, it is better to find one bug a day and fix it than to wait a month, find 45 bugs, and realize you probably can't mitigate them all! *Fuzz testing*, described in more detail in Chapter 9, is a form of dynamic testing, in that you launch tests against a running system.

> **Note** A more accurate name for dynamic analysis tools is *dynamic application security testing* (DAST).

Where static analysis tools analyze source code, dynamic analysis tools analyze running systems. And where static analysis tools attempt to understand and find logic issues, dynamic tools attempt to discover behavioral flaws. Still, there is potential overlap between static and dynamic analysis tools. For example, both can detect SQL injection vulnerabilities. However, they do so using different analysis techniques. OWASP maintains a list of dynamic analysis tools here: https://azsec.tech/nh1.

> **Note** Many tools that contain the word *scanner* in their name are dynamic tools.

Interestingly, dynamic tools have few positives. This is because if a system exhibits an error while being tested, then it's a *real* error—the sort of error that an attacker might be able to capitalize on. Static analysis tools miss a lot of these types of errors because they just look at the code without knowing how the code is deployed.

There is one category of dynamic analysis tool, used to detect configuration vulnerabilities, that is not required by the SDL, because these types of tools look at patches and general security posture. This category includes tools in the Microsoft Defender suite of tools. These tools are important but outside the realm of software architects and developers.

> **Real-world experience: Analysis tools are "just-in-time learning"**
>
> This might sound funny, but we want to elaborate on the point we just made about running these tools often. If you write some code and then run an analysis tool and find a bug, your "bug IQ" goes up! You now know not to use the construct that led to the bug, and you likely won't make the same mistake in the future.

Real-world experience: Selecting static and dynamic analysis tools

Notice that we have not provided a list of common static and dynamic analysis tools. This was on purpose, because:

- There are many of these tools.

- There is no one tool that fits all.

So, rather than providing a list, we've offered some guidelines to help you select appropriate tooling. Let's start with static analysis tools. Ask yourself these questions:

- Does the tool work with my development languages?

- Does it provide a good list of vulnerability types?

- Does the tool have few false positives?

- Does the tool work on my development platforms?

For dynamic analysis tools, simply ask yourself whether the tool supports your deployment environment. And for all tools, consider whether the tool provides details about code coverage and actionable reports when it detects issues.

Security code review

Tools are great because they allow you to scale as well as enforce a minimum-security baseline. However, you must augment tools with human code review. There is no replacement for a knowledgeable human performing a security code review, even if the process is slow.

The general process is as follows. First, identify any ingress points, such as REST API endpoints and web sockets. Then, follow the data as it traverses through the code. This is called *flow analysis*. There are two types: control-flow analysis and data-flow analysis.

You should be able to see the endpoints in the threat model. If they are not in the threat model, then the threat model should be updated. Also, take note of endpoints at the high end of a trust boundary, because these are likely the highest risk.

Control-flow analysis

First, let's perform manual control-flow analysis. This is the mechanism used to step through logical conditions in code. The process works as follows:

1. Starting at an ingress point, study the code and identify each branch condition. These could be loops, if statements, or exception handling blocks.

2. Identify the conditions under which each block will be executed and ask yourself the following questions:

- Are they correct?

- Are all conditions covered?

- Are security decisions made in this branch?

- Are the conditions under which each block will be executed correct?

- Does a security decision fail securely (fail-closed)?

3. Move to the next input and repeat.

Data-flow analysis

The questions in the preceding section will help you find many bugs and vulnerabilities. Now you're ready to use a technique called *data-flow analysis* to find bugs associated with poor input handling. Data-flow analysis is the mechanism used to trace data from points of input to points of output. We're not looking at control flow here; rather, we're looking at how incoming data is handled by the code. The process works as follows:

1. For each ingress point, determine how much you trust the input source. When in doubt, give it no trust. Refer to the threat model if needed.

2. Trace the flow of data to each possible output, noting along the way any attempts at data validation.

3. Move to the next input and repeat.

When you are finished, you should have a list of all the functions that each piece of input data touches, as well as the eventual outputs where they all end up. Pay particular attention to areas where data is parsed and could end up in multiple output locations. Also pay attention to intermediary output locations. For instance, the input might end up in a database and then later be placed in web page content.

In an Agile environment, security code review is important. Thankfully, because Agile models tend to produce small amounts of code rapidly, it is easier to review a code diff than an entire source code file. With that said, at some point, the entire code base should be manually reviewed.

Having an incident response plan

For most companies, responding to a security incident in any project is usually handled by a central team rather than the project's development team. Even so, there needs to be someone on the development team who is on point if an issue is found—in other words, someone who answers that 3 a.m. phone call. Your central response team needs a list of everyone to talk to for each of your applications in the event of a compromise. If your company does have an incident response plan in place, be sure someone in your team understands the process. If it doesn't, you need to make one. This page can show you how: https://azsec.tech/dva.

Performing penetration tests

A penetration test (*pentest*) is a test performed by a skilled individual to find weaknesses in your application in an attempt to break it. Many compliance programs require pentests.

Regarding pentests, there are two things you should be aware of:

- **A pentest is only as good as the pentester** One highly skilled individual is often better than four mediocre people who have little experience. So, if you hire a pentest organization, make sure the people performing the work are skilled.

- **Pentests are not for what you think they are for** This may sound like heresy, but too many companies assume that the purpose of a pentest is to find security bugs so they can fix them. This is a costly mistake. In fact, a successful pentest is one that finds nothing, because you took all the right security measures ahead of time. Besides, waiting for a pentest to detect an issue is folly, because if an issue is found, what are the chances you can fix it quickly enough?

Your job is to build solutions that make the pentesters' lives miserable! If you build your solutions securely and a good pentester turns up nothing serious, then everyone has done their job. Of course, the pentesters will find *something*, no matter how insignificant, because they must! That being said, as good as a pentester may be, they will not find everything.

Agile methods generally don't call out when a pentest should be completed because they are usually out of band from the development process. At some point, though, a build should made accessible to pentesters, and they should spend the amount of time allotted to find issues and report what they discover.

> **Tip** The Payment Card Industry (PCI) offers guidance about pentesting at https://azsec.tech/0q2.

Real-world experience: Technical security debt

We have found that when people adopt practices to improve security, the first thing that usually happens is they discover their code and design have a lot of security issues. The issues were always there, but now they have found some (but not all!). This is a great example of technical security debt.

You must reduce technical security debt as soon as possible, without breaking the code. Be especially careful when making design changes because of issues you found in a threat model; you always run the risk of regression. Large code changes can also introduce regressions. Once you have your technical debt under control, you can focus on putting processes and tools in place to prevent new vulnerabilities from emerging in your system.

When management sees a spike in security bugs, they will wonder if this new security initiative is cost effective! Just remember, the bugs were always there. It just took new security-related education, processes, and tools to find them.

SDL tasks by sprint

You won't do all the SDL tasks every sprint, but you do need to do them at some point. Here's a high-level overview of what to do, and when:

- **Security training** All developers must understand security issues relating to the code they will work on in each sprint. Working on database code? Understand SQL injection and injection in general. Working on cryptographic code? Understand what the cryptographic requirements are, where keys are stored, and so on.

- **Defining your bug bar** This should be done before the project begins—perhaps as part of sprint zero. Sprint zero is a step before the first sprint during which developers perform tasks such as setting up the development environment, task tracking tools, and threat modeling.

- **Attack surface analysis** This can be ongoing if tools are used. What constitutes the attack surface should be understood ahead of time.

- **Threat modeling** A core threat model should be in place prior to code work, perhaps in sprint zero. If significant changes are made to the design, then the updates should be incorporated into the threat model in each sprint. The amount of work to update a threat model with the relatively small changes in a sprint is low.

- **Defining your toolchain** This should be done before work starts. Once the toolchain is in place, the tooling should be consistent sprint over sprint.

- **Avoiding banned functionality** This should be defined prior to the outset, possibly as part of sprint zero. It should be enforced in every sprint.

- **Using static analysis tools** These tools are used every sprint—possibly daily at developer workstations and every few days if there's a central set of tools. Tools used by developers and in your continuous integration/continuous delivery (CI/CD) pipelines should enforce a minimum quality gate. These tools should be configured to detect high-severity and high-confidence issues only.

> ## Real-world experience: Quality gates
>
> Windows Vista was the first Windows version to have a code check-in quality gate. These quality gate tools focused on highly specific checks such as certain kinds of memory corruption issues, banned functionality, profane language, IPv4 code dependencies (that is, an IP address is not just four octets), and others.

- **Using dynamic analysis tools** These are used every sprint, as long as there is something functional to test, which should always be the case.

- **Security code review** This should occur with every pull request by at least one other person who is not the code author.

- **Having an incident response plan**   A central team will likely perform this, so it is therefore not really of concern to the development team.

- **Performing penetration tests**   This depends on your requirements. For example, PCI DSS 3.2.1 requires at least annual penetration tests.

The human element

The number-one issue facing the software industry is hiring and retaining good engineering staff across all the development disciplines who understand security. The best way to remedy this is to grow your expertise internally. There will always be someone who has a passion for security but who does not have "security" in their title. Work with that person (or people) to help them learn more about security and make an impact across the company. Never underestimate the value of a domain expert learning about security in your environment. The world needs more well-rounded security people!

We often refer to these people as *security champions*. A key role of security champions is to stay abreast of new security issues as they are found in the industry, to learn from them, and to change processes and tooling as needed to find, fix, or prevent similar issues in your code. Security champions are also go-to people when an architect or developer has security-related questions. SAFECode has an excellent document about security champions, located here: https://azsec.tech/mib.

> **Note** Perhaps that new security champion is you! You have this book in your hands after all!

Summary

Security is not just about tools and features. It is also designing, developing, and testing solutions to make them more secure.

You must adopt multiple techniques to improve your security posture. However, you must do so in a way that is relatively frictionless, so you use the tools as much as possible but also raise the collective security IQ of your organization.

Adopting the techniques laid out in this chapter will demonstrably improve the security of your product. When you first start out, you will find many security issues—most of which you never knew you had. This is called technical security debt, and you must remove it as soon as you can.

Over time, you will have fewer security issues. Still, security is fluid, so learn from new research and vulnerabilities and adapt accordingly. Changing your development processes to accommodate more security discipline is paramount, but you have to ship, too, so be practical.

## CHAPTER 2

Secure design

After completing this chapter, you will be able to:

- Begin integrating security when developing cloud solutions with your organization's DevOps processes.

- Apply a basic zero-trust approach in a development context.

- Identify areas of improvement in secure design for developing solutions on the cloud.

- Adopt fundamental security design principles for developing Azure solutions.

The cloud, DevOps, and security

The cloud has revolutionized how we develop solutions. Organizations adopt the cloud for its flexibility and agility, which has forced development teams to evolve how they implement solutions to fulfill the cloud's promises. For this reason, it is almost a necessity to adopt DevOps and Agile when developing solutions for the cloud.

Agile is a philosophy more than a single methodology to develop software. It is a set of principles and techniques to improve the software development process by increasing the ability to adapt to the changes and to provide value at an accelerated speed. Examples of Agile frameworks are Scrum and Extreme Programming. The main characteristics of Agile development are discussed here: https://agilemanifesto.org/.

DevOps is a set of practices designed to accelerate the software and systems development lifecycle by linking development with IT operations activities. It embeds and empowers principles such as continuous integration (CI) and continuous delivery (CD) to shorten the time required to deliver updates to production systems. In its purest implementation, DevOps allows code to go into production every day, possibly even multiple times per day.

One main principle of DevOps is to use automation to accelerate everyday tasks like building, testing, and deployment, to make them more predictable and repeatable. One tenet of iterative and Agile processes like Scrum is to provide value with every iteration. If done properly, these methods lead to the early creation of limited but functioning products with rapid incremental improvements.

It is common to use specialized security tools to analyze code automatically. You can find a description of some common categories in Chapter 1, "Secure development lifecycle processes." These tools evaluate the code developed for a solution, searching for common security problems or known vulnerabilities. Sometimes, you might supplement these automated tests with manual ones, such as security code reviews or penetration testing. These approaches are complementary, because they focus on different categories of issues. It is not unusual for one of these approaches to identify problems that the others have missed.

> **Note** These tools generally do not cover security issues related to the design of the solution. Penetration testing might identify some of them, but it is performed only occasionally, often later in the project, and the coverage is never complete. Thus, you must take care of the security of the design. This chapter collects some of the most important concepts related to this topic.

With all these tools to ensure the security of your solution, it is only normal to wonder if you need them all. As you may guess, the usual answer applies: it depends. The general recommendation is to include them all. If your solution has limited sensitivity and is not exposed, you could classify it as a low risk for the organization and its users. This might allow you to opt out of some of these practices. In our experience, secure design represents one of the most essential and effective practices, and you should not disregard it.

IaaS vs. PaaS vs. SaaS, and the shared responsibility

One of the first steps you must take when designing a solution is to decide which cloud security model to adopt. This decision is crucial, because it determines what you can do, what you are responsible for, and the cloud provider's responsibilities.

The Shared Responsibility Model is common to all cloud service providers (CSPs), including Microsoft. While it is possible to identify some common characteristics, summarized by the Cloud Security Alliance (CSA) at https://azsec.tech/cu0, there are some differences to note. For this book, we focus on Azure.

Per the Azure Shared Responsibility Model shown in Figure 2-1, we can say that the responsibility varies depending on the types of services used. Microsoft categorizes Azure services into three main categories:

- Infrastructure as a service (IaaS) includes all services providing bare-bones resources. For example, in this category are virtual machines (VMs), networking, and simple storage like virtual disks.

- Platform as a service (PaaS) contains all services built upon bare-bones resources and provides capabilities that you can use to develop your solutions. For example, App Services (which allow the development of web applications and APIs), Azure SQL, and Azure Data Lake Storage are in this category.

- Software as a service (SaaS) contains complete solutions you can use as is or extend with your specific capabilities. Microsoft 365 and Power BI fall under this category.

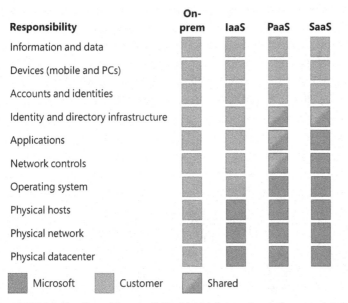

FIGURE 2-1 The Shared Responsibility Model. Source: https://azsec.tech/o6w.

Nothing prevents you from creating solutions spanning multiple types of resources. It is quite common to adopt IaaS and PaaS services simultaneously. It is also common to extend SaaS solutions with IaaS or PaaS.

You may wonder if, given a choice, it would be best to adopt a solution based purely on IaaS rather than PaaS or even SaaS. This is a build versus buy dilemma that you can solve only by understanding how much the organization values control over quality and how much it fears vendor lock-in. The reasoning is that something you build for yourself, starting from your specific requirements, gives you the most control over the final result but cannot be as tested and streamlined as something used by hundreds or thousands of other users around the globe. Moreover, a solution built over IaaS would be easily transferrable elsewhere, which may not be accurate for solutions based on PaaS or SaaS. But let's consider only security as a deciding factor. It is typically better to use SaaS over PaaS, and PaaS over IaaS, simply because it's easier to secure a system where our responsibilities are limited.

At this point, a legitimate question may be, what is the difference, if any, between having a solution on IaaS instead of having it on-prem? There are various pros and cons to any option, even if we focus only on security. You may know that Microsoft implements comprehensive security policies for its datacenters. These policies encompass physical security and how Microsoft's administrators access your systems and data. The general principle is that no Microsoft administrator has access to your data, save for a few exceptions, because everything is typically handled automatically. Microsoft has put in place multiple security controls to minimize the need for a Microsoft employee to access your data. In cases where you might want to allow access, Microsoft enables you to specify whether to do so. For example, when you open a support case, you can choose to allow or deny access to advanced diagnostic information containing sensitive data.

If you adopt Azure Customer Lockbox, you define an escalation path that allows Microsoft Support engineers to ask you for additional access when required. If you decide not to adopt Azure Customer Lockbox, Microsoft Support engineers will still be able to get the access they need to address the support cases you raise, but the escalation path to get it is entirely internal to Microsoft. This can affect support because the required information is unavailable and there is no path to access it. This approach safeguards your data because it considers its protection as the first requirement.

> **Note** You can find out more about Azure Customer Lockbox here: http://azsec.tech/o4z.

An advantage of Azure IaaS over on-prem solutions is that it facilitates compliance. This advantage is because of Microsoft's focus on getting certified for every applicable law and standard, including GDPR and ISO/IEC 27018 for privacy, and ISO/IEC 27001 and CIS Benchmark for security. The main resource to learn about Azure compliance is the Azure Trust Center (https://azsec.tech/hen). Microsoft publishes the complete list of supported regulations and standards at https://azsec.tech/7v8. This is a helpful resource if you need to evaluate Azure for compliance before adoption or to demonstrate the compliance of your solutions built over Azure. The Microsoft Azure Trust Center also enables you to download and inspect compliance reports prepared for Microsoft by third-party certification entities.

> **Note** Chapter 8, "Compliance and risk programs," expands on the importance of compliance and how Azure can help you to achieve it.

Given the number of Microsoft's controls, you may already be convinced that the security offered by Azure's datacenters is at least on par with what you have on-prem, if not superior. But there are other reasons to move to the cloud, too. For example, as you saw in Figure 2-1, with IaaS, the responsibility of maintaining hosts for VMs is on Microsoft. This represents a significant advantage over the on-prem scenario. Microsoft also applies security fixes over the hosting environment for you. Vulnerabilities like the recently infamous Log4Shell can create massive problems for organizations, most of which are not prepared to apply fixes quickly. You can read more about this vulnerability here: https://azsec.tech/9tz. All this is to say, it might make sense to have crucial components of your infrastructure, like the hosting environment, managed and patched by Microsoft.

> **Note** During the initial phases of Azure, Microsoft discovered that if it applied security fixes after publishing the bulletins, attackers still had time to exploit the related vulnerabilities. For this reason, it has started publishing the bulletins only after having patched the infrastructure.

Of course, you may still be concerned or even scared of sharing your environment with many others, some of whom possibly have malicious intentions. To address these concerns, you can adopt features like Azure Dedicated Hosts and Azure Confidential Computing to address these concerns.

> **Note** For more information about Azure Dedicated Hosts, see https://azsec.tech/zpt. To learn about Azure Confidential Computing, see https://azsec.tech/fjz. This topic is also discussed in Chapter 11, "Confidential computing."

Shared responsibility means precisely that: you are responsible for selecting the right services and using them correctly, while Microsoft is responsible for ensuring they are secure by developing and operating them using the best practices available, including the Microsoft SDL.

So, the question is, how can you design and develop secure solutions on Azure? To get the answer to this question, you must read the rest of the book!

Zero trust for developers

NIST SP 800-207, titled "Zero Trust Architecture," defines *zero trust* as a "cybersecurity paradigm focused on resource protection and the premise that trust is never granted implicitly but must be continually evaluated." And then, it continues defining zero-trust architecture as "an end-to-end approach to enterprise resource and data security that encompasses identity (person and non-person entities), credentials, access management, operations, endpoints, hosting environments, and the interconnecting infrastructure." You can download NIST SP 800-207 here: https://azsec.tech/4rc.

Zero trust is a consequence of the failure of traditional defense approaches based on establishing a perimeter, granting implicit trust to anything inside it. The perimeter defense model assumes you can create an impenetrable separation between internal resources and the external world. Unfortunately, there is nothing further from the truth.

Perimeter defenses cannot provide perfect security. For instance, every firewall has known and unknown vulnerabilities that attackers can exploit. A 2020 survey by Ponemon Institute revealed that 60 percent of respondents found legacy firewalls unable to prevent attacks against critical business and cloud-based applications. You can read about it here: https://azsec.tech/336. Moreover, current business practices like bring your own device (BYOD) undermine the assumption that internal resources can be trusted. Thus, there is the need to adopt a different approach, which is zero trust.

> **Note** A 2003 study by Seny Kamara, Sonia Fahmy, Eugene Schultz, Florian Kerschbaum, and Michael Frantzen, titled "Analysis of Vulnerabilities in Internet Firewalls," analyzes several leading firewalls to determine a possible taxonomy for the vulnerabilities. You can download it from here: https://azsec.tech/vvc.

When dealing with cloud solutions, the situation gets even worse, because the cloud is, by defini-tion, characterized by an absence of walls. Not only is a cloud solution hosted in a virtual environment on the internet, but other customers of the CSP might have access to the same resources you are using. Therefore, adopting a zero-trust approach becomes even more vital for cloud solutions.

So, what is zero trust? In a nutshell, it is an approach based on the following principles:

- **Authenticate your counterparts**   Authentication should be independent of location. For instance, you cannot rely on an IP address or a MAC address because malicious actors can eas-ily forge them. Authentication with certificates and private keys or other strong credentials is preferred. If you are calling a service, you must authenticate to get access. You also must verify the service's credentials because a malicious actor could impersonate it. For users, multifactor authentication (MFA) is a recognized approach to providing good security.

- **Require a stronger authentication when accessing more sensitive services or data**   For example, suppose you are implementing a web portal for a bank that contains a public area, a marketing area with no sensitive information, and a home banking area. The public area would require no authentication because it is public. In contrast, the marketing area would need to identify the customer to provide relevant messages. Finally, the home banking area would require the strongest form of authentication, like MFA. So, the user might be required to re-authenticate when moving from the marketing area to the home banking area.

- **Apply the principle of least privilege**   Wikipedia defines the principle of least privilege as the requirement that "every module (such as a process, a user, or a program, depending on the subject) must be able to access only the information and resources that are necessary for its legitimate purpose." Applying this principle means assigning the rights strictly required to perform specific duties and limiting access based on them.

> **Note** A good way to apply the principle of least privilege might be to use a privileged iden-tity management (PIM) solution like Azure AD PIM. For more information on Azure AD PIM, see https://azsec.tech/dil. Azure AD PIM is also covered in Chapter 5, "Identity, authentica-tion, and authorization."

- **Apply policy-based authorization**   You can implement this approach by evaluating access rights using not only the identity and location of the caller, but also other parameters such as the integrity of the client and recent user behaviors. To achieve this in Azure, you can use Azure AD Conditional Access (https://azsec.tech/cvl) and Microsoft Defender for Identity (https://azsec.tech/aem).

- **Limit the duration of access rights**   Access rights to resources should last for the duration of the session and then be re-evaluated for each new session. Repeating access evaluation is fundamental to removing assigned rights shortly after the system has identified a user or a device as insecure. Azure AD PIM represents an approach to achieve this goal, because it can be configured to automatically remove the access rights a few hours after the assignment.

- **Limit the scope of access rights**   Access rights granted for one resource should not extend to a different resource. Otherwise, access control may not be as effective as expected, allowing an attacker to extend control over more resources.

- **Micro-segment the network**   Traditional approaches to security discriminate between what is inside an organization's intranet and what is on the internet. However, this is so broad that an attacker can compromise any system on the intranet and use it as a beachhead to extend their reach. If we micro-segment our networks, then we can minimize the attacker's reach because each segment contains only a few resources and cannot be accessed from other segments. Micro-segmentation is a recognized tool for achieving zero trust. However, it also represents a significant management burden. Therefore, it might not be easy to implement broadly across your organization.

- **Encrypt data in transit**   This applies even for data in transit internally. Protocols like Transport Layer Security (TLS) address confidentiality and integrity concerns and provide strong authentication for the called service.

- **Monitor and scan services, clients, and resources, and how they interact**   This enables you to identify possible problems and improve your security posture. Monitoring alone is not enough if you do nothing when you detect a problem; you must clearly define what should be done to address each problem you might face. On a related note, you must put into effect a continuous learning process so you can better understand how attacks happen and how to prevent them, and keep up with the increasing sophistication of attacks.

Microsoft extends these principles by linking zero trust with the assume-breach approach. According to a strategy brief published by the Microsoft Cyber Defense Operations Center, assume breach means that "despite all the protections in place, we assume systems will fail or people will make errors, and an adversary may penetrate our infrastructure and services. This posture places us in an 'always ready' position to rapidly detect a compromise and take appropriate actions." You can read the strategy brief in its entirety here: https://azsec.tech/oy7.

The assume-breach approach plays a vital role in securing your solution. If you assume your counterparty may have been breached, you adopt multiple controls to check all interactions. For example, it would not be enough to authenticate, even with strong authentication; you would also need to demonstrate the client's integrity.

In any case, when we talk about zero trust for developers, we mean:

- **Designing your solution to support the concepts behind zero trust**   For example, each component must verify the caller's and callee's identity and then check authorization for each request.

- **Protecting the development environment using zero-trust principles**   This involves hardening and protecting developers' machines. Otherwise, if an attacker were to successfully compromise one of them, they could inject malicious code into the solution, steal privileged credentials, or even steal production data.

- **Secure CI/CD pipelines following zero-trust principles** For instance, the service accounts used to these pipelines should have only the rights required to build the code and deploy the generated artifacts. Moreover, only a few select DevOps team members should be allowed to edit the pipelines, and they should do so using trusted workstations.

These scenarios represent what zero trust for developers typically means. However, we believe that for software development, it should go beyond that. For example, while user input is one of the most critical aspects of software security, zero trust does not consider it. To quote Michael Howard and David LeBlanc from their book, *Writing Secure Code*, "All input is evil." Unfortunately, the mitigations typically included as part of a zero-trust architecture do not consider the input sent to the various services. Rather, they focus on other categories such as authentication and authorization. But in our view, all input should be proven malicious until proven benign. Consequently, you should validate everything you receive with strict rules and reject all requests found not compliant. You could also encode input to ensure that your code can't execute scripts and embedded commands injected by a malicious user.

Many security attacks are based on the injection of commands as part of input. Cross-site scripting (XSS) attacks and SQL injection are good examples. Encoding is an effective approach to protect against some of them. Moreover, if you limit your monitoring to what the infrastructure provides out of the box, you might miss attacks specific to the solution under development. Therefore, you must include services like web application firewalls (WAFs), which can detect, alert you to, and even block some of these attacks.

> **Note** OWASP publishes guidance for preventing cross-site scripting by way of encoding in https://azsec.tech/e33. Similarly, it publishes guidance for preventing SQL injection in https://azsec.tech/bf5.

> **Note** Azure Application Gateway with WAF is an example of a service that includes a WAF. For more information on Azure Application Gateway with WAF, see https://azsec.tech/5f6.

Still, relying on tools like WAFs might not be enough. Some automated tools implement WAF-evasion techniques. For example, tools like SQLMap exploit SQL injection issues. These tools apply techniques like those discussed by OWASP in https://azsec.tech/gl1. Experts might also conduct manual attacks to go undetected.

> **Important** SQLMap and similar security tools can be used only to perform authorized security testing and penetration testing. Using these tools when not authorized constitutes a felony and may be prosecuted.

For this reason, it is crucial to design and implement your solution defensively. In other words, you must apply the defense-in-depth security principle. This scenario, says ISO/IEC 62443 1-1, essentially consists of "the application of multiple countermeasures in a layered or stepwise manner to achieve security objectives. The methodology involves layering heterogeneous security technologies in the common attack vectors to ensure that attacks missed by one technology are caught by another." In lay-person's terms, applying defense in depth means accepting that every security control we put in place will ultimately fail. Therefore, we cannot rely on any one of them; rather, we must combine different controls to increase effectiveness. To address this, we must design the solution securely, thinking about what can go wrong and including the mitigations required to achieve the desired level of security.

Thinking about secure design

So far in this chapter, you have learned the importance of zero trust for developers. You have also learned that applying zero-trust principles by the book might not be enough—that you must consider the specifics of your solution to provide a complete answer. This requires rethinking how you design your solutions to make them secure. In other words, you must ensure that the solution is secure by de-sign. Wikipedia defines secure by design as a design approach in which "security is considered and built into the system at every layer and starts with a robust architecture design."

Thinking about security early in the development lifecycle means *shifting left*. We typically draw development processes as a flow going left to right, so shifting left means anticipating security issues early on.

Fixing an issue, such as a security issue, earlier rather than later can yield significant savings. Accord-ing to one older study from NIST, fixing a design issue in production code costs about 30 times more than repairing it during the design phase. You can read the study here: https://azsec.tech/wzz. One might argue about the applicability of this study, as we build software differently nowadays; indeed, the specifics of it probably aren't relevant anymore. Nevertheless, it is self-evident that postponing security considerations until the end of the development process has many downsides. For example:

- It is too late to make significant changes, so your options are limited.

- Often, you will have already spent most of the available budget by then, further limiting what you can do.

- The additional activities needed to address the security issue delay the deployment in production.

As a result, you do less than you should, so the solution is less secure than expected, making it easier prey for malicious actors.

At this point, you might be wondering what losses your organization could face as a consequence of a breach. To calculate it, you could adopt a quantitative risk analysis methodology like FAIR. However, this might be overkill for our purposes. If you need an order of magnitude, you can rely on the 2021 Cost of Data Breach Report from IBM Security and the Ponemon Institute, which states that the aver-age total cost of a data breach is $4.24 million. Mega breaches, in which more than 50 million records are affected, raise these costs to a whopping $401 million.

With numbers like these, it's easy to understand why it is essential to shift left security as much as possible. But how? The answer is to focus on security during the design process. One way to do this is to learn some security design principles and patterns. These represent an excellent place to start and can guide you in creating better solutions. They are covered in more detail in the next several sections of this chapter and in Chapter 3, "Security patterns." Sometimes, though, that's not enough, in which case you will need to adopt a more structured approach to analyze and design your solution securely. This approach is called *threat modeling*. You'll learn more about threat modeling in Chapter 4, "Threat modeling."

Security design principles applied to Azure

The story of the development of security design principles begins in 1975, when two computer scientists, Jerome Saltzer and Michael Schroeder, defined the first set of principles in a paper titled "The Protection of Information in Computer Systems." You can download it here: https://azsec.tech/732. While old, this paper is still relevant, because it introduces some essential security concepts. By applying these principles, you can significantly improve your security posture. The following pages list these principles, integrated with a few other security tenets, to explain what they are and how they are relevant for the most modern solutions based on Azure. The principles are sorted alphabetically.

Attack surface reduction

Understanding the concept of attack surface is essential for security. NIST defines the attack surface of a solution as the "set of points on the boundary of a system, a system element, or an environment where an attacker can try to enter, cause an effect on, or extract data from, that system, system element, or environment." In other words, it focuses on how exposed the system is to attackers.

The concept behind attack surface reduction is that if an attack surface for a given system is too large, then attackers have more opportunities to compromise it. Therefore, an excellent way to increase security is by reducing the attack surface, which typically means removing unnecessary features and closing any unnecessary entry points.

Microsoft has adopted this principle since the early 2000s, with the introduction of Windows Server 2003. With this version, you had to enable many features before using them. Enabling a feature meant installing it; the default installation didn't even include the binaries for these features. This was in contrast to Windows 2000 Server, which installed everything by default.

What changed in the years between 2000 and 2003? In 2002, Bill Gates, then Microsoft's CEO, sent to all employees a famous email titled "Trustworthy Computing." You can read the email here: https://azsec.tech/60i. This email represented an epochal cultural change for Microsoft and for security at large. It was so important because it made security everyone's responsibility, and it set for the entire organization the goal of becoming a trustworthy business. This was a game-changer—not just for Microsoft, but for many other companies, too. It resulted in a security improvement process that continues evolving even today. One of the most visible results of this initiative has been the principle of attack surface reduction. Indeed, you can see this principle in effect everywhere in Azure. All services are disabled by default, and all ports are closed. You must expressly enable them if you need to in order to achieve your goals.

You must also apply this principle to your solutions. We have seen many situations in which development teams have designed and implemented solutions without considering the principle of attack surface reduction. For example, suppose your deployment process provides interfaces for development-to-production environments. If these interfaces include a page granting access to all tables in your database, it would be an invaluable tool for developers—and for attackers.

One example we saw firsthand was a solution designed to support various configurations. The problem was that the installation process didn't discriminate between different usage scenarios; it installed everything, everywhere. Then it logically disabled certain features, depending on the settings. In a nutshell, that company made the same mistake Microsoft did with Windows 2000 Server.

> **Note** The only secure code is the code that does not exist; therefore, you must remove everything unnecessary.

Be aware that back doors and hidden functionalities represent a violation of the attack surface reduction principle. Thus, you should not implement them. This is especially critical because these functionalities tend to receive limited testing, if any.

Complete mediation

The complete mediation principle is about executing authorization controls for each request. It explicitly forbids saving an authorization token somewhere, which somebody may steal, and then allowing access based on this token.

Saltzer and Schroeder define complete mediation like this:

"Every access to every object must be checked for authority. This principle, when systematically applied, is the primary underpinning of the protection system. It forces a system-wide view of access control, which in addition to normal operation includes initialization, recovery, shutdown, and maintenance. It implies that a foolproof method of identifying the source of every request must be devised. It also requires that proposals to gain performance by remembering the result of an authority check be examined skeptically. If a change in authority occurs, such remembered results must be systematically updated."

The complete mediation principle tries to address the issue of the assumed right to access resources located in a specific area simply because one has access to that area. A classic example of this situation is accessing web pages exposed via random names. If you grant access to these pages simply because the caller knows their names, then a user who stores the links somewhere public as a convenient way to retrieve them later could defeat the protection. In other words, the simple fact that someone knows the name does not mean they should be able to access these pages.

To apply this with Azure, the first recommendation is, as usual, to use the Azure infrastructure as much as possible. Azure AD, for instance, may play a significant role. When you perform a successful authentication with Azure AD, it issues a token containing information about the user, including its grants, which indicate what that user can do with the application. Thus, the token helps address both the authentication of the user and the authorization of the user. This behavior provides value because if a user's credentials are incorrect or they do not have any right to access the application, they do not receive any tokens.

But this is not complete mediation. With complete mediation, when you try to access any resource exposed by your solution, you get it not because you have a valid token but because that token provides the level of access required. This behavior is provided out of the box by all resources and services that are part of Azure, but you may have to implement it for the code you write, like APIs or pages for web applications.

> **Note** You can read more about complete mediation here: https://azsec.tech/ydn.

Defense in depth

The section on zero trust for developers introduced the principle of defense in depth, so we won't rehash all that here. Still, it may be helpful to remind you of the definition of defense in depth, from ISO/IEC 62443 1-1, which is "the application of multiple countermeasures in a layered or stepwise manner to achieve security objectives. The methodology involves layering heterogeneous security technologies in the common attack vectors to ensure that attacks missed by one technology are caught by another."

We do want to highlight here how you can use this principle to improve the security of your solutions. To address the fact that every security control can fail—and it will—you must combine multiple security controls. But how?

Think, for example, of demilitarized zones (DMZs), an old concept typical of traditional on-prem architecture and still in use for some cloud architectures. Wikipedia defines DMZs as follows:

"A physical or logical subnetwork that contains and exposes an organization's external-facing services to an untrusted, usually larger, network such as the internet. The purpose of a DMZ is to add an additional layer of security to an organization's local area network (LAN): an external network node can access only what is exposed in the DMZ, while the rest of the organization's network is firewalled."

When implemented on-prem, DMZs are typically based on two firewalls—one protecting the communications between the systems in the DMZ and internet, and the second one dedicated to protecting the communications between the DMZ and the intranet. (See Figure 2-2.) In many situations, the two firewalls are from the same company, are the same model, and typically even have the same patches applied.

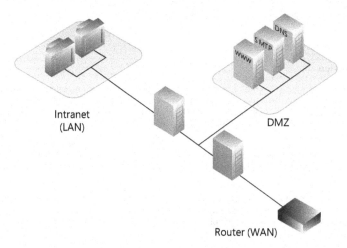

FIGURE 2-2 Diagram of a typical network employing DMZ using dual firewalls. Source: https://azsec.tech/nnb.

Does this configuration satisfy the defense-in-depth principle? If you answered no, you are correct. Of course, you have two different layers, represented by the two firewalls, but once an attacker compromises the first one, compromising the second is a trivial exercise.

Let's now consider a second example, more specific to Azure. This example, shown in Figure 2-3, has an instance of Azure Storage, where users store files, and an Azure Function, which retrieves the file and processes it.

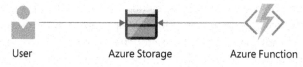

FIGURE 2-3 A simple solution where a user saves files to Azure Storage.

As you know, a malicious user could upload an empty file in an attempt to cause a crash in the Azure Function and then perform some nefarious action. To prevent this, the Azure Function performs a simple file validation. If the file is empty, the Azure Function automatically removes it before processing. After a while, you might realize that this is not enough, so you add another validation for the file. Now, our Azure Function checks to see if the received JSON file is compliant with strict rules, which define field by field what is known to be good. Here, the same question applies: do these two checks, when combined, satisfy the defense-in-depth principle?

Again, even if the second approach is better than the first, the answer is no. You have two very similar controls, and even more importantly, the second includes the first. So, you need something different. In our experience, the best approach for achieving defense in depth is to combine different types of security controls. Table 2-1 shows a partial list of controls. There are other types of security controls that you could consider using, but they are less prevalent in daily practice.

TABLE 2-1 Some common types of security controls

Name	Description
Preventive or preventative	Preventive controls reduce the probability or impact of the threat event, effectively buying you time and forcing the attacker to make attempts that you can detect. These controls are designed to prevent successful attacks. Nevertheless, they could be bypassed by skilled and determined attackers. A typical example is encrypting data in transit to prevent information disclosure.
Detective	Detective controls enable you to detect an attack while it is in progress, but they do not stop the attack. A typical example is the monitoring capabilities provided out of the box by Azure Services.
Corrective or responsive	Corrective controls respond to attacks while they are in progress and may even stop these attacks. Their primary intent is typically to reduce the damage. A typical example is the distributed denial-of-service (DDoS) protection, which automatically identifies and disables malicious IPs.
Recovery	You might rely on recovery controls to recover from damage that occurs as a result of an attack. Examples of recovery controls include backup and restore capabilities.
Deterrent	Deterrent controls are mostly there to convince potential attackers that the cost of attacking may be higher than the potential gain. An example is the implementation of auditing capabilities against malicious insiders.

If you consider the previous two examples with this new knowledge, you should be able to identify a better way to secure them.

For the first example, which relates to DMZs, you could consider additional preventive measures, such as adopting conditional access to block clients or accounts identified as potential risks. This approach would require Microsoft Defender for Identity, Microsoft Defender for Endpoints, and Intune. Together, these tools can provide a pretty accurate evaluation of the risk represented by the users and their devices. Another idea might be to change the type of control altogether. For example, you could monitor requests blocked by the firewalls (a detective control) and block for some time the offending IP address when the number of errors is higher than the threshold you set. In addition, you could set up your system to raise an alert if this happens too often. This control would be both corrective (because it blocks attacks in progress) and detective (because it involves raising an alert). Therefore, this approach would represent an exemplary application of the defense-in-depth principle.

The second example, which pertains to users uploading a file on Azure Storage, could be similarly improved by adding a different preventive control—for instance, strict access rules to ensure users can access only a dedicated folder inside the Azure Storage. While this approach would provide a significant improvement, you could do even better by adding a different type of control. For example, you could introduce a detective control by setting up your system to raise an alert when a malformed file is received. Or you could introduce a corrective control that blocks the sender for some time to delay attacks in progress.

Sometimes, solutions provide multiple kinds of security controls at the same time. For example, Azure Application Gateway with WAF and Microsoft Defender for Endpoints are both detective controls (because they allow for the detection of abnormal situations that might represent attacks in progress) and preventive controls (because they can block attempts). Microsoft Defender for Endpoints can also block accounts identified as potentially compromised. Therefore, it also represents a corrective control.

At this point, you might wonder when you should stop searching for additional controls to implement. Of course, the security of your solution increases with the number of controls. At the same time, implementation and operation costs increase as new controls are added. So, you want to achieve a balance between costs you may face due to potential attacks and costs you face by implementing and operating the additional mitigations. Figure 2-4 shows this sweet spot, where the overall cost is minimized.

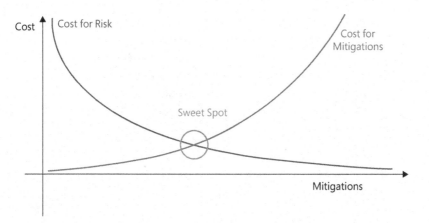

FIGURE 2-4   Optimizing the residual risk. Source: https://azsec.tech/f48

At this point, you should ideally stop. In reality, you may stop even earlier than that. It may be enough to reach a point where the potential losses are deemed as acceptable, even if it is not the best you can achieve. At that point, you would not need to add more mitigations because you have already achieved your security goals.

Economy of mechanisms

The economy of mechanism principle is about simplicity. That is, the more complex a system is, the harder it becomes to understand it. And the harder it becomes to understand it, the harder it is to avoid mistakes and pitfalls that a malicious actor might exploit to compromise it.

Saltzer and Schroeder describe it like this:

"Keep the design as simple and small as possible. This well-known principle applies to any aspect of a system, but it deserves emphasis for protection mechanisms for this reason: design and implementation errors that result in unwanted access paths will not be noticed during normal use (since normal use usually does not include attempts to exercise improper access paths). As a result, techniques such as line-by-line inspection of software and physical examination of hardware that implements protection mechanisms are necessary. For such techniques to be successful, a small and simple design is essential."

The first consideration of the economy of mechanisms principle is that you must design your solutions to be as simple as possible. Otherwise, you might open attack paths, which could go undetected for some time due to the complexity of the solution. This makes root-cause analysis next to impossible.

> **Note** With complex solutions, identifying and understanding attacks become more challenging, which means there is a higher chance for attacks to succeed and go undetected for an extended time.

The economy of mechanisms principle can also be a good guide for choosing the best types of cloud services to use. If you rely on PaaS or, even better, SaaS, part of the complexity is abstracted away, enabling you to focus on what matters the most: the solution itself. For instance, services like Azure Functions and Azure SQL Serverless abstract the location where the code is executed or the data is stored; all this is managed by the infrastructure. So, many activities are more straightforward, meaning you make even fewer configuration mistakes, and your solution is therefore more secure. Of course, the downside is that you forfeit some control.

> **Note** You can read more about economy of mechanisms here: https://azsec.tech/0p2.

Fail-safe defaults

Saltzer and Schroeder's original paper on security design principles introduces the term *fail-safe defaults*. Saltzer and Schroeder describe these as the need to "base access decisions on permission rather than exclusions." In other words, this principle is about granting access because you know a request is secure instead of denying it when you know it is not secure. It is complicated to identify in advance what should be prevented. Most assuredly, you will miss something. So, it is much safer if you carefully define what *is* allowed and reject everything else.

This principle is called fail-safe defaults because, if you apply it, you may end up rejecting valid requests because your definition of what is safe is too restrictive. Usually, being too restrictive does not compromise security. But if you are *way* too restrictive—to the point that legitimate users cannot perform legitimate work—it could cause a service availability issue with security implications. Still, both these scenarios are better than neglecting this principle and defining what is not secure rather than what *is* secure, which could cause your solution to accept malicious input as secure.

> **Note** Usually, it is much safer to be too restrictive than to be too permissive.

Fail safe and fail secure

Fail safe and fail secure are two more security design principles missing from Saltzer and Schroeder's paper. According to NIST, *fail safe* is "a mode of termination of system functions that prevents damage." And by *fail secure*, again according to NIST, we mean "a mode of termination of system functions that prevents loss of secure state when a failure occurs or is detected in the system (but the failure still might cause damage to some system resource or system entity)." So, both these principles concern what happens when there is a failure.

According to the defense-in-depth principle, every mitigation put in place will fail. Therefore, to secure your solution, you need a plan to minimize or even eliminate the damage that will result when a failure occurs. That is what the fail-safe principle is all about. One must also accept that it is impossible to avoid all possible damage from a failure. At a certain point, some damage will occur. The focus of fail secure is to ensure that failures do not cause the solution to be insecure, even if they cause some damage.

Suppose your solution depends on an external service, and some attacker manages to put that service offline. In that case, you could automatically disable the functions that depend on the service. Of course, this could have a substantial impact on your solution. You might even be unable to provide essential services. But worst case, you could still provide a minimal set of services, like informing your users that you are facing technical difficulties.

Let's consider a practical example. Suppose your solution needs to connect with an external service using HTTPS and that the certification authority (CA) that has issued the certificate for that service publishes a certificate revocation list (CRL) in a specific location. Now suppose that the CRL location becomes unavailable, and your cached copy of the CRL expires, meaning you can no longer rely on it. What should the application do?

Because a malicious actor may have stolen the certificate, your application should no longer trust the external service. Therefore, it should stop all activities requiring interaction with that external service while keeping everything else active. It should also notify users of technical issues and, at the same time, raise an alert so that those who operate the solution can promptly work to troubleshoot and solve the problem. Of course, you would incur some damage due to the temporary unavailability of some functions provided by your solution. Still, you will have done a great job safeguarding your solution's security by adopting the fail secure principle!

As a second example, suppose the previous external service receives messages from your system and there is no strict requirement for immediate processing. So, you store them on a local database while the external service is unavailable. When the external service becomes available again, you can retrieve the unsent messages from the database and send them to the external service. This scenario is an example of the fail-safe principle, because your system's security would not be at stake, and you would not face any loss.

Least common mechanism

The least common mechanism is a security principle that states that you should, to quote NIST, "avoid having multiple subjects sharing mechanisms to grant access to a resource." This might happen if multiple services share the same communication channels; a malicious actor could affect all those systems by attacking one of them.

Here's an example. Suppose you have a queue shared by many services. If a flood attack targets one of them, the other services might experience degradation, too. Another example would be using the same web app to serve both privileged and unprivileged users. Because this web app would contain the code for both categories of users, a malicious user might be able to exploit some vulnerability and execute the code requiring higher privileges.

You can mitigate all these issues by isolating the affected systems. That is, instead of having a single queue shared between services, you can define multiple distinct queues. Or, instead of having a single web app for privileged and unprivileged users, you could create two different web apps—one for each type of user—and ensure that neither can affect the other.

Cloud infrastructures like Azure have another critical scenario in which the least common mechanism plays a significant role: VM hosting. The fact is that all services—IaaS, PaaS, and SaaS—are virtualized. So, the cloud usually deploys applications in random locations. That means you do not know your "neighbors"—meaning you might be using the same machine as your competitor or, worse, a malicious actor!

According to the least common mechanism, this may be bad. But what should you do? More importantly, should you do anything at all? Both these questions are fundamental, and we are not the only ones who are asking them. Indeed, Microsoft has introduced several controls to mitigate these risks.

One such control is the fast application of security patches. Microsoft applies security fixes to infrastructure without even waiting for its security bulletin to be published. After all, it does not make sense to wait unnecessarily, and accelerating the deployment of these fixes reduces the chances of someone attacking the platform. (Of course, this does not necessarily protect your IaaS infrastructure, because it is your responsibility to patch it, but that is another story.)

In addition to quick patching, there are other controls in place, too. For example, hardening host machines makes them much more difficult to compromise. In addition, Microsoft maintains bounty programs to stimulate security. Under these programs, researchers actively search for vulnerabilities in Microsoft's products, including Hyper-V, the virtualization engine used to provide most of the services on Azure.

Relying on Microsoft's patching process and other controls is not your only option to mitigate the risk of having a malicious neighbor. To further limit this risk, you can rely on Azure Dedicated Hosts. With Azure Dedicated Hosts, you have a physical machine dedicated to you, guaranteeing that you will have no external neighbors.

The combination of these two approaches—one provided out of the box with Azure and the other provided by way of a service made available by Azure to improve your security—represents a great way to noticeably reduce your risk.

Regarding the section question—should you adopt additional controls to reduce the risk?—as is usually the case, the answer is, it depends. Ask yourself: if you don't implement these additional controls, will the risk level be acceptable? Remember, absolute security is not an achievable goal. So, you should strive for *just enough* security. Anything more represents an unnecessary cost. How do you know when you have just enough security? A good threat model can help you answer this question. You will learn more about this in Chapter 4.

Least privilege

Least privilege is a fundamental security concept. As explained by Wikipedia, least privilege means that "every module (such as a process, a user, or a program, depending on the subject) must be able to access only the information and resources that are necessary for its legitimate purpose." You have already encountered this principle, in the section "Zero trust for developers."

As discussed, the principle of the defense in depth indicates that every protection you put in place will eventually fail. There is no guarantee that you can fully protect user accounts, so you must assume that they will ultimately be compromised. But this doesn't mean you cannot protect your solutions. On the contrary, you can do much to make life harder for attackers, and even stop most of them. The least privilege principle provides one of the most powerful weapons in your arsenal to achieve this.

The idea behind the least privilege principle is that not all users are equal. Some users receive privileges—sometimes powerful ones—while others don't. If an attacker manages to impersonate a legitimate user with substantial rights, they inherit those rights and can wreak havoc. On the other hand, if the attacker compromises an account with fewer privileges that can perform only basic activities, their options would be much more limited. So, the idea is to ensure that each user receives only the permissions they need to perform their job, for just the amount of time they need them, and nothing more.

In Azure, you can achieve this by using capabilities provided by Azure AD, like Azure AD Access Reviews. This service allows for regular reviews of accounts to ensure their rights are not assigned longer than necessary. Another helpful tool is Azure AD Privileged Identity Management (PIM), which grants permissions when required and automatically revokes them when they are no longer needed.

> **Note** For more information on Azure AD Access Reviews, see https://azsec.tech/ty8. To learn more about Azure AD PIM, visit https://azsec.tech/dil.

Simply by adopting the least privilege principle, your organization will mitigate many possible issues. However, this does not mean you cannot improve your situation even more. For example, you still must assign administrative rights to only a few users. One of the most common approaches is to give each of these users two different accounts—one with minimal (if any) assigned privileges, and the other with all the necessary administrative rights. This way, each of these users can use their account with administrative rights only when strictly required and then use the less-privileged account the rest of the time to reduce the risk of compromise.

If you take this approach, you should separate the two accounts such that you would not be able to use the less-privileged account to perform actions allowed by the more-privileged one, and vice versa. For example, you might set up the unprivileged account to access external resources like commercial websites but block the privileged one from accessing them. To further limit exposure, you should operate the two accounts on different machines, using the privileged account only on hardened devices, like privileged access workstations (PAWs).

> **Note** For information about PAWs and how to create one, see https://azsec.tech/hgw and https://azsec.tech/gr9.

The requirement to duplicate accounts and machines does not typically apply to all users. Instead, most organizations apply it only to the most privileged users in the organization. Moreover, it is possible to virtualize these PAWs and even have two VMs in the same physical machine: the first for all privileged activities and the second for everything else. This way, the inconveniences would be limited.

You may ask yourself why this principle matters to you, since you develop only cloud applications. Managing Azure AD is someone else's concern, so why bother? The fact is that your solution requires the assignment of privileges for its own management. Some applications, like multitenant SaaS solutions, also require you to endow some users with the privileges required to manage their tenants. It is your responsibility to design these rights to satisfy the least privilege principle.

Leveraging existing components

Leveraging existing components is one of these principles not included in Saltzer and Schroeder's paper. Perhaps the best way to describe it is to share with you a personal story. The first project I did as a Microsoft consultant required developing a cache. At the time, there was no open source, and Microsoft's venerable and now-defunct Patterns and Practices initiative was still years into the future. So, our team developed a cache. When the project was finished, our team started work on another project—one that also required a cache. Did we reuse the one we developed for the previous project? No. We had the rights to reuse it, but our lead developer was not happy with it. So, we invested other resources to develop something new.

> **Note** If you do not know about the Patterns and Practices initiative, you can check its story at https://azsec.tech/xx8.

This story is interesting from a historical perspective, because it illustrates how we used to work more than 20 years ago. It is also a clear example of how important it is to leverage open source from a business point of view. But from a security point of view, it is nothing short of a nightmare. Repeatedly creating the components you use has important security implications, because you do not give them time to consolidate and mature. Think about it: would you create an app to replace Notepad, if you need its capabilities? Of course not! The effort required to implement and test it at comparable levels would make that endeavor too expensive, not to mention a total waste of your time.

This scenario has led to the development of the leveraging existing components principle, which requires you to adopt existing components whenever available and applicable instead of building your own.

This principle is interesting for a variety of reasons. First, using third-party components like open source code is an excellent choice—maybe. The fact is not all open source projects are equal. Some of these projects have many contributors and long histories replete with improvements, and a few particularly successful ones have been adopted by millions of users. These virtuous examples of open source projects enjoy occasional scrutiny by security experts, and some even maintain bug bounties. But this is not true for the vast majority of open source projects. Most are maintained by a single developer, adopted by a few users, and sporadically updated. Security experts rarely scrutinize these projects because they would not receive any recognition by identifying their vulnerabilities. Therefore, adopting these types of open source components is not necessarily a better choice than repurposing your own code. On the contrary, some of these neglected projects represent even greater risk.

A second consideration is that on Azure, due to the leveraging existing components principle, one should prefer SaaS over PaaS, and PaaS over IaaS. This is because using an IaaS solution means implementing most of it yourself, while with PaaS and SaaS, Azure provides an increasing number of components and amount of logic for you.

Open design

According to Saltzer and Schroeder, adopting the open design principle means ensuring that the design of a solution is not secret. They explain:

"The mechanisms should not depend on the ignorance of potential attackers, but rather on the possession of specific, more easily protected, keys or passwords. This decoupling of protection mechanisms from protection keys permits the mechanisms to be examined by many reviewers without concern that the review may itself compromise the safeguards.

In addition, any skeptical user may be allowed to convince himself that the system he is about to use is adequate for his purpose. Finally, it is simply not realistic to attempt to maintain secrecy for any system which receives wide distribution."

> **Note** You might be familiar with a similar principle, Kerckhoff's principle, named after a 19th century linguist and cryptographer named Auguste Kerckhoff. This principle stated that "a cryptosystem should be secure, even if everything about the system, except the key, is public knowledge."

The open design principle is the worst enemy of anyone who seeks to achieve security by obscurity. If you assume your solution is secure because nobody knows how to compromise it, then it becomes *insecure* when someone finally figures out how to do so. And you can rest assured that someone will, because whatever approach you've taken to secure your solution, you can be certain that others have done the same in the past or will do in the future. So, it is safer to secure your solution using algorithms and patterns that are widely known and deemed secure.

Obscurity has other downsides, too. For example, as observed by Saltzer and Schroeder, it does not allow reviewers to check your solution. It also does not allow your stakeholders to verify what you are doing and could delay your response when an incident does occur. The truth is, most of the time, obscurity is used not for security reasons but to protect the intellectual property of your solution. The bottom line is, relying on obscurity could impair security and should generally be avoided whenever possible.

> **Note** You should not consider security as an absolute—something you attain and never risk losing. On the contrary, what is known as secure today is doomed to become insecure later. Cryptography is full of these examples, like DES, RC4, MD5, and SHA1. You must continuously re-evaluate your solution to ensure it stays secure.

All that being said, there might be times when hiding your design could make sense, because it could somewhat delay an attacker. As noted earlier in Table 2-1, the primary goal of preventive or preventative controls is to buy you time to allow other controls to kick in. So, obscurity may still have some role. Still, it is most assuredly counterproductive if you base your entire security strategy on it.

Open design vs. open source

Open design and open source are not necessarily linked. That is, an open design does not imply that your solution is open source. On a related note, you might create an open design solution whose source is so complex that it is difficult to analyze, in some ways negating its "openness." Indeed, you might even do this on purpose by using a technique such as source code obfuscation, which makes it difficult to examine code. For more information on source code obfuscation, see https://azsec.tech/mui.

Both open source and open design can increase the quality and security of your solution, but of course, the open design security principle focuses on the latter. Indeed, open design should be almost considered a requirement to achieve security. With regard to the effect of open source on security, as discussed in the section "Leveraging existing components," its impact will be limited in most cases, save for the select few open source projects that have been adopted by millions of users and are constantly scrutinized by security experts.

Psychological acceptability

Saltzer and Schroeder define the psychological acceptability principle as the need to design human interfaces "for ease of use, so that users routinely and automatically apply the protection mechanisms correctly. Also, to the extent that the user's mental image of his protection goals matches the mechanisms he must use, mistakes will be minimized. If he must translate his image of his protection needs into a radically different specification language, he will make errors."

This principle is commonly understood to mean that imposing lightweight and straightforward security requirements on users might be more acceptable than imposing overly complex tasks. Other factors like routine could also play a role, however, causing users to prefer worse approaches. Change is often considered an unacceptable effort—even if it is for the better. Indeed, the primary takeaway from this security principle is that you should never assume users will accept changes you propose that are for the better. Even simple changes, like the implementation of MFA, may require you to train, convince, and support users during the various phases of adoption. If you must introduce even more significant changes for the sake of security, it may be necessary to adopt a change management framework, like the Prosci ADKAR Model. This model is designed to help people to understand how change happens and to plan their change management journey. It includes five phases, from which the model derives its name: awareness, desire, knowledge, ability, and reinforcement.

> **Note** We are not endorsing Prosci *per se*; we are simply aware of it because it has been adopted throughout Microsoft.

Be aware that this principle applies not only to unprivileged users but also to administrators. If, for example, you propose that administrators use two different accounts to increase security, each account dedicated to a set of distinct tasks and systems, you may face strong resistance and low adoption. Therefore, you might want to define a more acceptable solution, even if it means forfeiting some security, and work with administrators to facilitate its adoption.

Separation of duties

Separation of duties is one of the principles not included in Saltzer and Schroeder's paper. According to NIST, separation of duties is "the principle that no user should be given enough privileges to misuse the system on their own. For example, the person authorizing a paycheck should not also be the one who can prepare them." There are various ways to implement this principle, including two tools provided by Azure itself to do so.

The first tool is role-based access control (RBAC) by Azure AD. RBAC enables you to specify exactly who can configure the various resources and who can access the data. For example, suppose you assign the Contributor role for an Azure Storage instance to a group of users. In this case, members of that group of users can review and modify the Azure Storage instance's configuration, but they cannot access the data. Now suppose you assign the Storage Blob Data Contributor role for the same Azure Storage to another group of users. This allows those users to access the data without granting them any rights to configure the instance. You can then achieve separation of duties for the Azure Storage instance by separating these two groups so that no user belongs to both. This way, users who can manage the Azure Storage instance cannot access the data it contains, and vice versa.

Separation of duties in Azure

As discussed during the introduction to the Shared Responsibility Model, Azure Customer Lockbox represents an example of separation of duties. It allows you to get control of the escalation process that support engineers may use to get access to your data when it is necessary to address a support request. For more information on Azure Customer Lockbox, see http://azsec.tech/o4z.

Azure AD PIM is another tool for achieving separation of duties with Azure. It allows you to require approval from another person before granting rights. Azure AD PIM represents an effective way to prevent possible misuses—not only because of its support of authorization processes, but also because it requires the specification of a business reason, which Azure AD PIM can track.

Note As someone who develops cloud solutions, you can rely on the capabilities provided by Azure. Still, it is your responsibility to design your solution to support the separation of duties principle. For this reason, it is so crucial that you understand it.

Single point of failure

A single point of failure is one of the principles not included in Saltzer and Schroeder's paper. Wikipedia defines a single point of failure as "a part of a system that, if it fails, will stop the entire system from working."

The most natural way to address the single point of failure issue is to use redundancy to achieve high availability. However, this is no easy task. Too frequently, when one part of the system crashes, the entire system enters a corrupted state, which prevents the redundant systems from kicking in. Therefore, it's vital to provide redundancy and high availability at the infrastructural level.

Many Azure services provide high availability out of the box. However, even if a particular service does not automatically provide high availability, you can still achieve it by adopting one of the supported configurations. For example, Azure VMs use availability sets, which provide redundancy within the same datacenter. They also use availability zones, which provide redundancy within different datacenters located in the same region. Moreover, Azure VM Scale Sets (VMSS) offer a more advanced way to achieve redundancy for a load-balanced set of VMs scattered across various availability zones. All these approaches provide a means by which to enable, disable, provision, deprovision, and update VMs without causing the user to experience any visible downtime, reaching 99.99 percent availability.

> **Note** For information on availability sets, see https://azsec.tech/xd4. To learn more about availability zones, see https://azsec.tech/pa6.

Azure Storage, a service that is both an IaaS and a PaaS (for example, because it supports data lake capabilities), supports different redundancy levels as discussed in Table 2-2.

TABLE 2-2   Redundancy levels for Azure Storage

Name	Description
Locally redundant storage (LRS)	Provides redundancy within the same datacenter by storing three copies of the data in as many racks. Provides a limited safeguard but is also the least expensive of the available modes.
Geo-redundant storage (GRS)	Builds on LRS by adding a synchronous copy of the data to a single location in the secondary region. This propagation triggers the creation of two other copies using LRS in the secondary region, resulting in six copies.
Zone-redundant storage (ZRS)	Provides redundancy within the same region by storing a copy in each datacenter, offering 99.9999999999% (12 nines) availability. Azure automatically handles any problems that arise, switching access to one of the copies if the main one fails.
Geo-zone-redundant storage (GZRS)	Builds on ZRS by adding a synchronous copy of the data to a single location in the secondary region. This propagation triggers the creation of two other copies using ZRS in the secondary region, resulting in six copies.

Azure App Services, a PaaS service, can be designed with redundancy in mind, deploying various instances in different regions and then using a load balancing solution like Traffic Manager to dispatch requests between them. For more on Traffic Manager, see https://azsec.tech/qda. A fault-tolerant solution reconfigures the load balancer to move traffic away from the faulty instances. Another complementary option is to deploy zone redundancy in various availability zones. This second approach requires App Service Plan v2 or v3. SaaS solutions like Exchange Online are natively configured with high availability and do not require any action from your side. These are just examples of how you can configure services for fault tolerance and high availability. The bottom line is that a cloud infrastructure like Azure can be instrumental in avoiding a single point of failure scenario in your solution.

Weakest link

Weakest link is another principle not included in Saltzer and Schroeder's paper. The concept of the weakest link relates to the observation that, to quote the Cybersecurity & Infrastructure Security Agency (CISA), "attackers are more likely to attack a weak spot in a software system than to penetrate a heavily fortified component."

You can interpret this observation in different ways. A first, more superficial but still valid, read is that you should prioritize mitigations for the most exploitable vulnerabilities. A clear example is highly hyped vulnerabilities in software you rely on, because many attackers will try to compromise systems by leveraging them. For instance, even amateur attackers, like the so-called script kiddies, could try this using proof of concepts found on the internet.

In its Security Intelligence Report Volume 21, published in June 2016, Microsoft published a study that highlighted the importance of prioritizing mitigation efforts to address the most exploitable vulnerabilities. The study focused on some of the nastiest types of vulnerabilities, such as those involving remote code executions and elevation of privilege. In 2010, attackers could exploit 28 percent of these vulnerabilities within 30 days of the patch being applied; thanks to the new approach, though, that number dropped to 4 percent in 2015. You can download the study here: https://azsec.tech/sek.

A second consideration is that if the attacker is not determined to compromise you specifically, it may be possible to divert their attention by making the job harder. This approach is highly effective for categories of attackers like the aforementioned script kiddies, who can use only readily available scripts, and cybercriminals looking to maximize their return on the effort they expend. It would be less effective against hacktivists and state-sponsored attackers, who are more likely to persist in their attacks against you, specifically.

Be aware that this concept might not work very well in practice. Every attacker has a specific skill set. For example, some might have a strong development background, while others may be good at social engineering. Therefore, your assumptions about what makes it harder to compromise your system could be correct or not, depending on who is attacking you and what routes they choose. For this reason, Microsoft experts typically do not speculate about potential attackers, preferring to focus instead on actual attack paths and their potential damage.

Once, while re-engineering an existing solution, we identified multiple vulnerabilities in the design and the overall infrastructure. During a meeting to discuss these issues with the project's architects, they said there were too many "weak links" to address them all. So, they accepted the risk and addressed none of them. Fortunately, we were able to show how mistaken they were. This is to say that the weakest links principle does not mean you can ignore your issues if you have too many of them, because whatever you do, your solution would still be vulnerable. Instead, you should focus on the most critical issues you *can* address. Then, if the result is still unacceptable, it might be best to start over.

Summary

This chapter discussed secure design and explained why it is so important. It started by introducing fundamental concepts like zero trust for developers. It then covered various security design principles and how they apply when you develop Azure solutions.

You have seen how the Azure infrastructure provides many capabilities you can rely on to simplify your work and create more secure solutions. You have also begun to grasp the role these services can play and what problems they can address. By applying the secure design practices discussed in this chapter (and throughout the rest of the book), you can quickly identify those problems in your software and determine how to address them.

Secure design can play a crucial role in improving security and lowering associated costs because it is an excellent incarnation of the shift-left principle of DevOps. However, we have only scratched the surface on this topic. You'll learn more about this in Chapter 3, which introduces some key patterns for securing Azure solutions, and Chapter 4, which shows you how to design a secure cloud solution using threat modeling.

Security patterns

After completing this chapter, you will be able to:

- Adopt the proposed patterns to improve how you securely design your solutions.

- Identify even more Azure security patterns, further improving your understanding of Azure.

What is a pattern?

Design patterns are not new to information technology, but they still play a fundamental role. Design patterns were conceived by a British-American architect of Austrian origins named Christopher Alexander. In 1977, Alexander wrote a book about recurring solutions to common problems related to building physical structures. However, this book became influential beyond its original field. Indeed, Alexander's work inspired four computer scientists and researchers—Erich Gamma, Richard Helm, Ralph Johnson, and John Vlissides—to apply the same concepts to software design. The result was a book titled *Design Patterns: Elements of Reusable Object-Oriented Software*, which is still widely used today.

In his book, Christopher Alexander defines patterns as follows:

> "Each pattern describes a problem which occurs over and over again in our environment, and then describes the core of the solution to that problem, in such a way that you can use this solution a million times over, without ever doing it the same way twice."

The point here is that patterns represent a structured approach to address common problems. They are a way to collect and share know-how that has consistently provided value to many disciplines, including software design. Given that this book relates to the development of secure solutions on Azure, we focus here on design patterns in that context.

Our take on Azure security patterns

Azure uses design patterns extensively. You can find them almost everywhere such as when dealing with data protection at rest, implementing user authentication, and too many other scenarios to include here. Instead of reinventing the wheel, Azure adopts the same patterns and sometimes even the same services to provide critical capabilities and address common problems.

It is essential to know Azure's security patterns because they represent the best way to address common security problems. They may even enable you to design secure solutions without adopting more sophisticated approaches, like threat modeling, discussed in Chapter 4, "Threat modeling." This chapter introduces some of these patterns and includes the following information about each one:

- The name of the pattern

- The intent of and motivation behind the pattern

- A description of the pattern

- Examples of the pattern's implementation in Azure

- Related security principles (discussed in Chapter 2, "Secure design")

- Related patterns

Furthermore, the patterns are split into categories to simplify their identification:

- **Authentication** These patterns deal with the authentication of the counterparts of an interaction.

- **Authorization** These patterns focus on controlling access to resources.

- **Secrets management** These patterns deal with how the solution manages the secrets.

- **Sensitive information management** These patterns focus on how to manage sensitive information.

- **Availability** These patterns deal with ensuring that resources are accessible by legitimate users.

In the following pages, we describe a few patterns, sorting them by alphabetical order within each category. This is not an exhaustive list by any means. It simply includes some of the most common patterns we have seen in our practice that focus solely on solution design. This chapter does not cover implementation and deployment patterns, like those related to the supply chain. Considerations that relate to those patterns are covered elsewhere in the book, in Chapter 9, "Secure coding" and Chapter 14, "CI/CD security." By discussing some of the most important patterns here and clearly stating why you need to adopt them, we aim to provide you with a consistent view.

> **Note** For a more complete list of patterns, see https://azsec.tech/kph.

Once you know about patterns and their importance in Azure, you might be able to identify other patterns in the services you use. This understanding of design decisions empowers you to design better solutions by adopting the same concepts and by using Azure Services correctly.

The Azure Well-Architected Framework

Microsoft has published a set of guidelines on implementing sound architectures on Azure. These guidelines are available as part of the Azure Well-Architected Framework, which is available here: https://azsec.tech/dm8. These guidelines cover multiple aspects of implementing architectures, including reliability, security, cost optimization, operational excellence, performance efficiency, workloads, and services. For our purposes, the section on security is the most interesting. It covers topics like governance, landing zones, identity and access management, and much more. Many concepts within the Azure Well-Architected Framework can be mapped to the design patterns discussed in this chapter, but it goes well beyond our scope. Therefore, our recommendation is to take a look at it.

Authentication pattern

Authentication is an essential property of any solution. It pertains to identifying your counterpart in a conversation with some certainty.

We typically refer to the degree of certainty as the *authentication strength*. For example, suppose someone declares who they are without providing any proof. This would not be an authentication, but rather an identification. If they do a little better and provide a password, this would be weak authentication. Of course, you can impose restrictions to ensure an attacker cannot easily guess user passwords, but this has a limited effect on security.

Authentication typically involves the use of one, two, or all of the following parameters:

- **Something you know** This might be a password.

- **Something you have** This could be your phone or a physical token.

- **Something you are** This might be biometric information.

If you base authentication only on the password—that is, something you know—you have single-factor authorization, which can easily be compromised. To increase security, you should pair it with a second factor—for example, your username and password (things you know) and your phone (something you have). The idea here is that although an attacker might easily compromise any one of them, compromising them both at the same time would be much more challenging. Finally, you could add the third factor—something you are—to improve security even more. This approach is typically called *multifactor authentication* (MFA) because it relies on more than one factor.

> **Note** Chapter 5, "Identity, authentication, and authorization," contains more information about this topic.

Authentication does not represent a value per se, but it is instrumental in securing your application and data.

This section focuses on one common pattern for securing your solution through authentication: using a centralized identify provider for authentication.

Use a centralized identity provider for authentication

Intent and motivation

The cloud is a convenient platform for hosting applications—so much so that you might host many applications on it, all of which require authentication. It is only natural for organizations to seek a centralized approach for managing identity to access all different services with a single set of credentials. This requirement is not only for simplicity but also to retain control and visibility.

Centralizing identity allows for the adoption of tools like user and entity behavior analytics (UEBA). These tools enable you to determine whether any account or system represents a potential risk for the organization by analyzing its behavior, often adopting artificial intelligence (AI) algorithms able to identify changes in usage patterns.

Another advantage of centralized identity systems is they provide a single location for managing identities and grants. They also allow you to integrate identity management with HR processes—for example, to remove or disable a user's account as soon as that user ceases their relationship with the organization. Finally, these identity systems enable you to review assigned rights and remove them when necessary.

Description

Azure AD represents a complete and unified approach to identity management on Azure. It provides fundamental capabilities, like managed identities and access reviews, and can be extended with additional services to increase security. These services include:

- **Azure AD Identity Protection**   This service determines which identities are at risk by analyzing signals from many sources, such as threat intelligence, leaked credentials, and Microsoft Defender for Cloud Apps (Microsoft's Cloud Access Service Broker, or CASB).

- **Microsoft Defender for Cloud Apps**   You can use this service to control and limit the adoption of applications and to detect the presence of shadow IT in your organization.

- **Microsoft Defender for Endpoints**   This is a user and entity behavior analytics (UEBA) solution that can be integrated with Windows 10, Windows 11, and various devices.

- **Azure AD Privileged Identity Management (PIM)**   This service enables you to assign access rights when required, eventually requiring approval from a third party before executing the assignment.

Azure AD also provides zero-trust security for the implementation of identities through the use of conditional access. This defines policies to prevent access to services by users who are not trusted enough. For example, suppose Azure AD Identity Protection has identified a potential security risk related to a particular user. It can then force that user to authenticate with MFA when accessing sensitive resources.

> **Note** Azure AD is not your only option for identity management. You could use a third-party tool instead. Indeed, there are various reasons to use a third-party identity provider. For example, your organization might have already adopted one for your on-premises environment or to support different clouds, like AWS or GCP.

Examples

- Adopt conditional access to require MFA for privileged users such as the solution administrators.

- Use Azure AD to define custom application roles to control how the solution is used. You can find out more about these here: https://azsec.tech/0g6.

- Although some services—like Azure SQL Database, SQL Managed Instances, Cosmos DB, and Azure Storage—provide different ways to authenticate, including using Azure AD credentials, you should use Azure AD credentials whenever possible, because they can be better controlled from a central location. Using Azure AD credentials also enables the adoption of the whole set of capabilities offered to secure these identities.

Related security principles

- Zero trust

- Complete mediation

- Defense in depth

- Economy of mechanisms

- Least privilege

- Leveraging existing components

Related patterns

- Adopt just-in-time administration

- Use role-based access control (RBAC)

- Use managed identities

Authorization patterns

Authorization is another fundamental property of any secure solution. It comes after authentication. Authorization focuses on allowing users to perform actions they are entitled to perform and on preventing them from performing actions they are not entitled to perform. This section focuses on some common patterns for securing your solution through authorization.

We mentioned that authentication does not represent a value per se, but it is instrumental in securing your application and data. The same applies to authorization.

Adopt just-in-time administration

Intent and motivation

Accounts are not all equal. Some have considerable privileges assigned to them, making them a juicy target for malicious actors. For example, highly privileged administrators, like those assigned the roles of Global Administrator or User Administrator, are powerful, and it would cause significant damage to the organization if their user accounts were abused. For this reason, the most common recommendation is to apply the principle of least privilege by assigning the various roles only to those users who require them for a legitimate business reason and only when there is no other alternative that would allow for the assignment of fewer rights. For example, suppose one user needs to read security reports because she works on the security team. In that case, you should assign her the Security Reader role instead of Secure Administrator or Global Administrator.

This approach is a critical best practice, so there is a good chance your organization already applies it. Still, too many organizations struggle to adopt this approach due to the many roles defined in Azure AD and Azure Services. That is to say, sometimes the "best" role for a user—the one that most closely meets that user's needs—is not the most secure one. This pattern ensures that no unnecessary rights are assigned that could be exploited by an attacker or a malicious insider. Still, the rights that are assigned could be enough to cause significant losses.

A study by IBM Security and ObservelT, published in 2020, found that the average cost of a security breach caused by an insider was $11.45 million. The study also found that, on average, the companies interviewed during the course of the study experienced 3.2 such incidents per year. Finally, the study determined that it's possible to reduce these losses by about $ 3 million by adopting a privileged access management (PAM) tool.

> **Note** You can download the study mentioned here from https://azsec.tech/56t. For a discussion of the study, see https://azsec.tech/au8.

The idea behind PAM tools is that users do not need privileges 24×7. Rather, they need them for only a limited time. So, a privileged account represents a potential risk only when someone uses it to perform necessary actions. Outside that period, a PAM tool can revoke the rights, such that the user in question has no assigned privileges. PAM tools also deter malicious use because they require users to specify a business reason to obtain a particular privilege. They can also be used to require the approval for a third party to assign a particular right, in accordance with the separation of duties principle.

Description

Azure AD PIM is the primary tool within Azure for just-in-time administration. This tool extends how you assign roles to users or groups. With plain Azure AD, you assign roles globally or within a specific context, depending on the scope of the role. The role is then assigned forever. With Azure AD PIM, you can mark a role as eligible and then assign policies to that role. An eligible role remains dormant until it is activated. Activation can be subject to approval and could require additional authentication with MFA as well as the specification of a business reason. Activation can also be temporary and automatically removed after a set time.

> **Tip** Azure AD PIM is not something you implement for the purposes of application development. It is part of a broader initiative that is typically the responsibility of those who manage your Azure AD tenant. If you decide you need Azure AD PIM to limit the exposure of privileged accounts for your application, you might want to ask the owners of the tenant to adopt it. If your organization has already adopted it, you can ask to define the rules you require for your application.

Example

Sometimes developers need access to production data to troubleshoot problems. While this is understandable, you should try to avoid it. That being said, in an emergency, you might not be able to avoid this, as developers will need to access this data to quickly identify a solution. The best way to handle these types of situations is to plan for them. In this effort, Azure AD PIM may play a significant role by enabling you to define an authorization process that requires a valid reason and approval by a third party.

Related security principles

- Attack surface reduction
- Defense in depth
- Least privilege
- Leveraging existing components
- Separation of duties

Related patterns

- Use a centralized identity provider for authentication

- Use role-based access control (RBAC)

Assign roles to groups

Intent and motivation

Let's face it: determining what access rights are required is not always a trivial matter. In many cases, identifying the right blend of rights is a matter of trial and error. It's very tempting to assign full rights and call it a day!

This behavior is a consequence of many factors, not least of which is the number of built-in roles provided with Azure. There are currently more than 80 built-in roles for Azure AD and more than 240 built-in roles for Azure services! No wonder it is so difficult to find the right roles to assign.

Still, it is imperative to identify a feasible approach to guarantee that users are assigned the most limited rights possible. Focusing on feasibility might be the difference between having an academic requirement and effectively making a difference.

Description

The critical point here is to apply least privilege without sacrificing manageability. One way to achieve this is by using groups. The idea is to define whatever usage scenarios you need and then create groups to support them. Once that's done, you can assign the required roles to each group and then assign users to groups as needed.

This approach is helpful for two reasons:

- It minimizes management because it aligns groups according to how the organization works.

- It enables you to minimize the number of role assignments. This is essential because Azure restricts you to 2,000 role assignments per subscription. For more on this, see https://azsec.tech/ad8.

Common exceptions to this rule are service principals and managed identities, which are typically assigned the required roles directly.

> **Tip** Designing a suitable authorization model is a matter of business requirements, which must be agreed upon in advance among business, architecture, and operations stakeholders, per the organization's current policies and with requirements from security and operation. Many aspects are common to all projects, but the details will depend on your solution.

Example

If you have a data lake, you might want to guarantee different levels of visibility, depending on your area. You can address this requirement by assigning the required permissions. The easiest way to do this is to define a group for each category of users—like HR, research, and marketing—and then assign the required rights to various branches in the data lake, based on the desired visibility. You can even reuse the same groups for many applications simply by assigning additional rights to them when required.

Related security principles

- Least privilege

Related patterns

- Use a centralized identity provider for authentication

- Use role-based access control (RBAC)

Isolate from the internet

Intent and motivation

Chapter 2 showed that zero trust has been designed to address the many shortcomings of walled-in defenses. For example, suppose that for your security, you rely only on controls blocking external users from accessing the internals of your solution. In that case, you could be compromised as soon as someone figures out how to circumvent your layer of protection.

So, the answer would be to *not* rely on firewalls and similar protections, right? Wrong! The defense-in-depth principle states that every single control you can put in place can be circumvented. This principle doesn't imply, however, that you should give up your hopes of protecting your solution or that you should ditch controls like firewalls because they can't fully protect you on their own. It simply means that you need to integrate them with other controls to make your solution more secure. The bottom line is that network isolation still plays a significant role in Azure.

Description

So, how can you protect your solution using network defenses? The first step is to identify the parts of your solution that you must expose to the internet, as well as the parts of your solution that must remain internal. Then, you need to focus on these parts that should not be exposed to ensure that no unauthorized entities can reach them from the internet.

There are a couple of ways to achieve that:

- **Define firewall rules** Most services can define firewall rules. Once these rules are defined, you can use them to block access from the internet. This approach is simple and requires minimal configuration. But it has a downside: your resource or service is exposed. In other words, the firewall rules blocking unwanted traffic are your only protection against external malicious actors.

- **Define private endpoints** As with firewall rules, most services can define private endpoints. With private endpoints, there is no exposure over the internet, because the endpoint gets a private IP address. You can then connect to the private endpoint using private links. Configuring private endpoints and private links requires more work than configuring firewall rules, but it is more secure.

> **Note** Chapter 15, "Network security," includes additional information and details on implementing this pattern and on networking in general.

Examples

- If you have a web application or a web API that is internal to your organization and you do not want to expose it on the internet, you can host it with App Service Environment (ASE). An ASE is a high-performance isolated environment to host your web applications and APIs. ASE is the only way to deploy web applications and APIs based on App Service to a VNet.

- You can configure Azure SQL with firewall rules to prevent direct access from the internet as a whole but still allow access from specific IP addresses. If you instead want to prevent all access from the internet, you might want to use a private endpoint.

Related security principles

- Attack surface reduction

- Defense in depth

Related patterns

- Create secure channels

- Isolate with an identity perimeter

Isolate with an identity perimeter

Intent and motivation

You learned from the preceding pattern, isolate from the internet, that network isolation is a key mitigation that you should not disregard. The same goes for identity. Both should be applied simultaneously, per the defense-in-depth principle.

> **Note** This pattern is specular and complementary to the previous one.

Description

Identity can represent a perimeter that a user must cross to access protected resources. In this way, it is similar to networking. With networking, you can use rules to allow specific IP addresses to access your solution but not others. Similarly, you can use identity authentication and authorization to control who can access your resources and what they can do with them.

These approaches are both different and complementary, providing different capabilities due to their respective limitations. For example, with IP filtering, you can allow requests from specific geographies or buildings and deny everything else. With authentication and authorization, you can define rules for a specific user or account and establish its rights with regard to your solution or its components.

Example

Azure Front Door, App Gateway, and API Management Gateway are three network virtual appliances (NVAs) that you can configure to provide network perimeter defenses via private networking. The private networking approach is often considered enough for many solutions, but is that really so? As usual, the defense-in-depth principle says no. Rather, the recommendation is to add an identity perimeter defense as an additional layered defense. Adding an identity perimeter is typically achieved with TLS mutual authentication. With this approach, the NVA presents its client certificate to the back end. In turn, the back end verifies the certificate and its validity to ensure that the connection comes from the expected NVA and not from a malicious or accidental source.

Related security principles

- Zero trust

- Defense in depth

Related patterns

- Use a centralized identity provider for authentication

- Isolate from the internet

Use role-based access control (RBAC)

Intent and motivation

Managing authorization can be complicated. There are many resources and applications, and each of them defines multiple actions that must be authorized. With thousands of actions that can be authorized, you need some way to group and manage them. Moreover, you need a mechanism for use with custom solutions. The idea is that by taking a widely used approach, you can have a more reliable and secure method for authorization than what you could have with a custom authorization process.

Description

Azure RBAC is a common approach that you can use for Azure AD and Azure Services. It provides a structured way to assign users prebuilt sets of rights designed to address everyday needs. Azure AD currently provides more than 120 built-in roles you can choose from. For example, the Reader role allows the user to read the configuration of a service but typically not its data. In contrast, the Contributor role allows the user to change the configuration of a service or create new resources, depending on where the role is assigned. You can also create custom roles, but these are rarely necessary and often create management issues.

A fundamental advantage of using Azure RBAC is that it allows for a centralized view of all the rights assigned to users. This is essential in the event of a compromise because it enables you to browse for affected user accounts to grasp the security implications of their compromise. If you instead use credentials local to the resources and assign rights without using RBAC, you must inspect each resource to obtain the same information. Using RBAC also enables the execution of access reviews to periodically verify that the granted access is still required. And adopting Azure AD credentials and RBAC allows you to leverage a growing set of tools to analyze identities, like Azure AD Identity Protection and Sentinel.

> **Tip** Azure RBAC is not the only approach to authorization. Sometimes you might need something different, like a custom database representing your authorization matrix. Before searching for an alternative solution, however, you should determine whether you can leverage Azure RBAC to achieve the desired result.

Roles for applications

You might want to apply something similar to RBAC for your applications. For example, if you are creating a web portal and you want some users to provide content, it would be great if you could define a role called Editor and then have that role sent back to the application as part of the authentication token.

Of course, you could use an Azure group to do that, but this might not provide you with the right granularity. For example, maybe you want to have multiple distinct groups of users with the Editor role, one for each structure in your company. This is where defining a role would come in handy because it allows you to create as many groups as you want and then assign the role to all of them. Your application could then check if the role is present, not whether the user belongs to one of the groups.

Azure provides this capability through the app roles. App roles can be assigned to users and groups and are sent to the application when a user accesses it. App roles can also be assigned to client applications to access your application. App roles are a great way to structure access control for applications, using a secure approach that is integrated with the platform. You can find additional information about app roles here: https://azsec.tech/0g6.

Example

Suppose you need to create a multilevel authorization hierarchy. Your organization has multiple departments, including one called the Commercial department. The top level of this department is Global Commercial, which controls various regions. For example, as shown in Figure 3-1, there's a region called ATZ, another called Europe, and others. Several countries comprise each region. So, for instance, ATZ includes the USA, Canada, Mexico, and other countries. Each user in Global Commercial has complete visibility; each user associated with a particular region can see everything within that region; and users associated with a particular country can see only the information pertaining to that country.

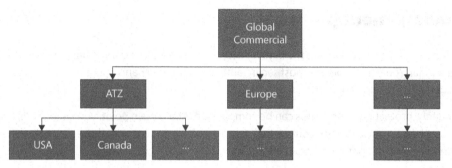

FIGURE 3-1 The hierarchy of the Commercial department.

How might you handle this scenario with Azure RBAC? At a minimum, you would need to rely on a database to represent the hierarchy and on custom code to enforce it. But you can do better. For example, you could do the following (see Figure 3-2):

1. Create a group for each country, a group for each region, and a group for the "global" level.

2. Make the group for a particular region a member of each country group within that region.

3. Make the global group a member of each region group.

4. Use RBAC to assign the required rights to each country and region group, as well as to the global group. This way, each region group will inherit the rights of the country groups within it, and the global group will inherit the rights of each region group.

FIGURE 3-2 How the groups must be nested: Global Commercial is a member of ATZ, which is a member of both USA and Canada.

Related security principles

■ Leveraging existing components

Related patterns

■ Use a centralized identity provider for authentication

■ Assign roles to groups

Secrets management patterns

Secrets are important because they are the keys for accessing services and data. Protecting secrets is therefore essential. You could have the most secure authentication mechanism, but if you do not protect the credentials, then you could be compromised.

Unfortunately, protecting your secrets can be complicated. At a certain point, you need them, and that is exactly when a malicious actor could attack you. Therefore, this is one of those situations where sticking with known secure patterns is most important.

Use managed identities

Intent and motivation

Most applications contain multiple components and require some type of interaction among them. This communication typically involves some form of credentials or sensitive information.

For example, suppose you connect to a database. In that case, you need a connection string specifying the name of the server or of the cluster exposing the database and the credentials to access it. Here is the problem: how can you store these credentials securely?

One obvious answer is to store them in configuration files. Unfortunately, this is not secure, because someone could steal them. Of course, you could encrypt the files, but then you have the problem of protecting the encryption key, and so on.

Alternatively, with an IaaS, you could use Data Protection API to encrypt the configuration file. Unfortunately, this approach has a couple of drawbacks, too. First, DPAPI provides only partial security because users with enough rights access secrets protected by DPAPI. Second, it does not protect the secrets in memory.

If you base your solution on App Services, you could use the application settings. These provide some protection and eliminate the need to store secrets in configuration files. Still, they do not protect the secrets in memory. And again, users who have enough rights can read the secrets—for example from the Azure Portal.

Description

A better way to store secrets is to use managed identities. These are service accounts that are entirely managed by Azure AD.

With managed identities, you have no access to the password, and your application doesn't either. The platform automatically injects it when you send out a request using the managed identity.

Not all possible callers on Azure support managed identities, nor do all possible callees. For a list of callers and callees that do, see https://azsec.tech/hia. This list is updated continuously, so you'll want to check it often. For example, Azure Cosmos DB didn't support managed identities until recently.

> **Note** See https://azsec.tech/laf and https://azsec.tech/akg for information on using RBAC and managed identities with Cosmos DB.

Managed identities can be system-assigned or user-assigned. The main difference is that system-assigned managed identities are dedicated to the service, while user-assigned managed identities can be shared with various services. Therefore, if you want to minimize management and have many instances of the same application, you can simply assign the same user-assigned managed identity to all of them.

> **Tip** There is one scenario in which system-assigned managed identities are preferable to user-assigned managed identities: for root cause analysis after an incident. That's because system-assigned managed identities are specific to an instance of a service, which makes it easier to identify the instance affected by the attack.

You can assign managed identities to virtual machines (VMs). This doesn't mean that all applications hosted by the VM can automatically access resources using the assigned managed identity, however. You must write code to leverage this possibility. This typically involves sending a request to the Azure Instance Metadata Service to obtain a token for the required resource. See https://azsec.tech/dff for details on using managed identities with Azure VMs.

> **Note** The URL to call to obtain a token from the Azure Instance Metadata Service is http://169.254.169.254/metadata/identity/oauth2/token. The Azure infrastructure automatically injects the assigned managed identity, without ever exposing them, even in the message metadata.

Examples

- Suppose your code can use managed identities and needs to access a resource that supports managed identities. In this case, you should not store the credentials anywhere. Instead, it would be best to directly use the managed identity to access said resource.

- If your code supports managed identities but not the resource, check whether the resource at least supports managed identities for administrative purposes. If so, you might still be able to use managed identities to retrieve some credentials that grant access to the data from the resource. Therefore, it might be possible to have an initialization phase to gather the credentials from the service with your managed identity via the control plane and then use them for any ensuing calls. For example, Microsoft recommended this approach for accessing Cosmos DB data before it introduced support for managed identities.

Note You might prefer this option to the alternative, which is to store the credentials in Azure Key Vault, because it reduces the exposure of the credentials and simplifies management.

Related security principles

- Attack surface reduction

- Economy of mechanisms

- Leveraging existing components

Related patterns

- Use a centralized identity provider for authentication

- Protect secrets with Azure Key Vault

Protect secrets with Azure Key Vault

Intent and motivation

As discussed with the previous pattern, you need some place to store your secrets. For example, you might need to store a private key associated with a certificate instead of a username and password. A typical example is a bring-your-own-key (BYOK) scenario, where you provide a key to be used in some way, like for encrypting an SQL Database using Transparent Data Encryption (TDE).

You cannot always use managed identities to achieve this. For example, a compute service or called resource might not support managed identities. Or if you have an off-the-shelf application hosted in IaaS, it might not have been modified to support managed identities, and therefore it cannot use them. For example, it sometimes takes Microsoft some time to implement support for managed identities in open source solutions, like Redis Cache, that are incorporated as Azure Services.

So, what to do?

Description

Whatever your situation, if you cannot use managed identities to access a resource directly, the best approach is to use Azure Key Vault—a secure and centralized storage for secrets and encryption keys. Azure Key Vault is more secure than the alternatives because it can be isolated and made inaccessible from the internet, even if your application needs to be exposed using private links. You can rely on various services to secure Azure Key Vault, like Microsoft Defender for Key Vault, which—among its other capabilities—can help identify anomalous interactions. It is also more secure than many alternatives because the Premium SKU provides hardware security module (HSM) capabilities to prevent attackers from stealing private keys.

Leveraging Azure Key Vault is not enough to make your solution secure. For example, as discussed in our coverage of the prefer managed identity principle, if you host code in an environment supporting managed identities, like a VM or an App Service, you should use a managed identity to call Azure Key Vault. If you need a key to access Key Vault, you have the problem of protecting that key, which becomes very difficult. With VMs, you can use DPAPI, but this is not possible with a PaaS solution, because they might be occasionally moved to other servers by the Azure infrastructure, rendering your secrets inaccessible.

Another critical decision you need to make is how many Azure Key Vault instances to use. Microsoft recommends dedicating multiple instances for your application—one for each environment. Our recommendation is to have even more of them, particularly for production environments. If your application has multiple layers, you might dedicate an Azure Key Vault to each of them to ensure that an attacker can get hold of only a few secrets in the event of a compromise. (See Figure 3-3.)

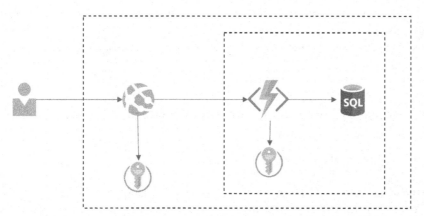

FIGURE 3-3 An example of a system with two Key Vaults: one for the front end and one for the back end.

This approach might seem radical and sometimes unnecessary. After all, having multiple Azure Key Vaults results in a more complex solution, introducing additional management burdens and increasing the possibility of mistakes by expanding the attack surface. So, the approach you decide to adopt depends on the characteristics of your solution.

Azure Key Vault for microservices

Microservices architectures present an interesting scenario. They are characterized by many small applications interacting with each other. If you had to apply a Key Vault for each microservice, the system would quickly become unmanageable. In this case, it might be best to avoid the fragmentation of the AKVs and dedicate just a single instance. Remember, per the economy of mechanisms principle, simpler is typically better.

Be aware that you might achieve significant compartmentalization even without dedicated instances. This is typically achieved by leveraging authorization. Azure Key Vault supports two authorization models: access policies and RBAC. With access policies, you assign access rights to whole categories of objects, like secrets or private keys. This means you cannot discriminate between secrets; you can read all of them or none of them. In contrast, with RBAC, you can assign roles even at a single object level. You can then have a single instance, because the object-level RBAC role assignment provides the granularity needed to determine what anyone can access.

Important The ability to assign access rights so granularly is excellent, but it has one significant downside: Azure supports up to 2,000 role assignments per subscription. So, it might be best to adopt RBAC (because it provides the greatest flexibility and control), but use it sparingly.

As discussed with our coverage of the use RBAC principle, you should use RBAC because it enables you to verify and manage role assignments centrally. Moreover, this comprehensive visibility enables you to adopt tools to identify potential risks and processes to manage role assignments more or less automatically.

Note Chapter 10, "Cryptography in Azure," has more details on Azure Key Vault.

Examples

Azure Key Vault is great for storing secrets to access resources that don't support managed identities, like Azure Cache for Redis. Azure Key Vault is also effective for storing secrets that you cannot replace with managed identities, like connection strings or private keys. When you store private keys, you should choose the Premium SKU to leverage its HSM capabilities. The Standard SKU is enough for all other scenarios.

Related security principles

- Fail secure
- Least privilege
- Leveraging existing components

Related patterns

- Use role-based access control (RBAC)

- Use managed identities

- Use bring your own key (BYOK)

Sensitive information management patterns

Secrets are important, but the information they protect is even more critical. There are many options for securing your data, but not all options are born equal, and it can be tricky to choose the right ones. Consider, for example, data protection at rest: all storage options from Azure allow or even enforce encryption of data at rest. For example, Azure encrypts Azure Managed Disks automatically. You have only a few options to determine how they are protected and who provides the encryption key. But do you need this type of encryption? Of course, the answer is yes, but things aren't so simple. You have to satisfy multiple needs for encryption, and this sort of protection addresses just a few of them. Again, relying on patterns is important to correctly address the most significant problems.

Create secure channels

Intent and motivation

Communications are usually the main risk for a solution. If you have a closed box that does not receive any input and does not provide any output, it is fully protected and will not be attacked. Unfortunately, such an isolated system makes sense only as an intellectual exercise.

All practical applications of technology are connected to *something*. It could be the internet, a local network, or even just a power outlet. Even devices that aren't connected to anything, because they use a battery and have their Wi-Fi connectivity disabled, still send out information through screens or simply through the electromagnetic field emitted by their electronics.

In Chapter 2, you learned that the Azure security model assigns customers partial responsibility for the security of the solutions it hosts. But whatever model you choose—IaaS, PaaS, or SaaS—it is Microsoft's responsibility to protect the physical devices. Good news, then: you do not need to be concerned about power connections and electromagnetic fields! Still, all the other concerns are well within your scope.

Description

What does it mean to create secure channels? Or better, how can you determine whether a channel is secure? There are a few requirements that must be satisfied:

- **Confidentiality** The channel must preserve data confidentiality. Transmission over the internet moves through many systems, and each of these systems could potentially read and disclose the contents of the communication. To preserve confidentiality, you must wrap the content such that unauthorized parties cannot read it, typically through encryption.

- **Authentication** The channel must authenticate with certainty all parties that are privy to the communication. In most situations, the main concern is the authentication of the caller, but this should not be the case. You also need to ensure that the called service authenticates itself. Fortunately, the adoption of TLS provides the authentication of the service implicitly. Still, you might need to ensure that your callers perform additional checks on the provided certificate—for example, checking whether the certificate has been issued by the expected certification authority.

- **Integrity** You must confirm the integrity of transmitted information. In other words, those who receive it must check whether it has been modified by some third party while in transit. Transmission protocols usually split big messages into multiple packets. Therefore, some of these packets may be lost in transit or received in a different order than expected. To preserve integrity, you must ensure that what is received matches what has been sent.

Azure addresses some of these requirements by imposing channel encryption for most communications. With channel cryptography, like TLS, you can provide confidentiality, integrity and server authentication. But you still have to address client authentication, which is optional in TLS..

There are various ways to authenticate the client—too many to include them all here. But it might be helpful to talk about one of them in particular: client certificates. These establish a strong connection that prevents man-in-the-middle attacks. If you don't use client certificates, an attacker can intercept a communication, terminate the TLS channel at its end, and create a new, false one directed toward the server. If you do use client certificates with TLS, however, this would not be possible because the man in the middle would not present your certificate to the target server. (Admittedly, we rarely use client certificates because they involve a high cost.)

Another approach is to create secure channels and isolate them from the internet. You can then use these secure channels to prevent the exposure of your resources and services over the internet. You can typically achieve this by using VPNs or ExpressRoute.

The likelihood of interception

How likely is it that an attacker will intercept your traffic? After all, the internet is vast, with billions of messages sent every second. Intercepting *your* traffic isn't like finding a needle in a haystack; it's harder! So, how big of a problem is it, really?

The truth is, there are a couple situations in which the chances of your traffic being intercepted raise significantly:

- The attacker might just be in the right place at the right moment, and you might unknowingly send your traffic their way. This could happen if you use an easily intercepted channel, like Wi-Fi, when the attacker is near you. This type of attack occurs more frequently than you might imagine—particularly in specific situations, like at security conferences.

- You might unknowingly send your traffic through malicious nodes. A typical example of this situation is when you use Tor or some free VPN. Malicious actors host many of these resources, and they use them to tap into your traffic and potentially perform malicious actions.

Examples

- Configure end-to-end TLS with Azure Application Gateway to ensure that TLS encryption is provided internally between Application Gateway and the target service or resource.

- Use a point-to-site VPN to connect a single workstation to resources on Azure to avoid exposing them over the internet.

- Use a site-to-site VPN to connect a site, which could be your office, to cloud resources not exposed over the internet. This typically requires the installation of VPN gateways to collect the traffic on both sides.

- Use ExpressRoute to connect a site similarly to the site-to-site VPN. The main difference is that ExpressRoute is based on a dedicated infrastructure, so the connection is typically faster and more reliable.

Related security principles

- Defense in depth

Related patterns

- Encrypt data client-side

- Use bring your own key (BYOK)

Encrypt data client-side

Intent and motivation

As discussed at the beginning of this section, Azure uses encryption to protect all storage. This is obviously a great feature, but does it address all your needs? To answer this question, you must first identify exactly what needs this sort of encryption *does* address.

The encryption at rest provided by Azure for most storage options falls under the category of transparent encryption. In other words, it ensures that if you access the storage using one of the sanctioned channels, data will be available in unencrypted form. If you access the storage using any other means, however, the data will unreadable. For example, if you try to access the data by stealing the virtual or physical disks, you will wind up with encrypted content that is not readable, even if you have the required rights.

So, transparent encryption increases the isolation of the customer data from Microsoft management environments. More specifically, it makes it more difficult for Microsoft's administrators to get to your data. However, there are other needs that transparent encryption does not address. For example, data in memory remains unencrypted.

Data can assume three states, and you have to protect all three of them:

- **At rest**   This is when the data is stored somewhere.
- **In transit**   This happens when you transmit the data between two locations.
- **In memory**   This is when the data is temporarily stored in computer memory, ready for processing.

Transparent encryption only protects data at rest. When you use transparent encryption, the data is unencrypted in memory for both the database or storage server and the client. So, you typically protect data in transit by adopting TLS, which Azure enables by default.

Still, if a malicious actor manages to get hold of some authentication material, that person could access the data stored in some repository. Of course, there are a few conditions for this to happen. For example, the malicious actor must have access to the repository. But when these conditions are met, the malicious actor can read the data. This is a scenario that, in most cases, could be safely considered "already mitigated." Still, if your solution requires a higher level of security assurances, you need to consider something else, like client-side encryption.

Description

The idea behind client-side encryption is that you encrypt the data on the client before sending it to the storage system. This ensures that the data is encrypted from that point on, including in the repository memory. Of course, the application must decrypt the data to consume it. At that point, the data would be potentially at risk.

If your storage system is a database server, things become interesting. Because the client-side encrypted data is not readable by the logic executed on the database server, it would be impossible to perform typical activities like searching its content. Still, with some implementation of client-side encryption, like Cosmos DB and SQL Server Always Encrypted, it is possible to perform limited comparisons.

The implementation of client-side encryption is possible when the platform supports it, and it might still be achievable as a custom activity. But in that case, it should be treated as a delicate task, requiring thorough testing and in-depth validation by experts, because it is possible to make fatal mistakes. And even under the best conditions, client-side encryption can have a significant impact on the performance of the system, due to computational costs and because it may be impossible to index data to improve search speed.

 TIP When you implement client-side encryption, a typical pattern is to consider adopting Azure Key Vault for storing the cryptographic keys.

Examples

- Cosmos DB and SQL Server Always Encrypted provides a way to encrypt data client-side. It includes a mode called *deterministic encryption*, which allows to search for records having some specific value. For example, if you encrypt a tax code with deterministic encryption, you can get all rows in a table where a field has the same tax code.

> **Note** The very characteristic that makes deterministic encryption worthwhile is also its main weakness. For example, an attacker could group all the records associated with the same tax code, which could provide them with enough information to identify a person from the other metadata. For this reason, consider *randomized encryption* as the first option and revert to deterministic encryption if necessary.

- Some libraries that provide programmatic access to Azure Storage implement the necessary logic to perform client-side encryption for Azure Storage. For examples of this with .NET, Java, and Python code, see https://azsec.tech/ci5.

Related security principles

- Defense in depth

- Fail secure

- Leveraging existing components

Related patterns

- Protect secrets with Azure Key Vault

Use bring your own key (BYOK)

Intent and motivation

Data encryption has multiple roles. One of the least commonly considered is crypto-shredding. Crypto-shredding involves deliberately deleting or overwriting encryption keys used to secure sensitive data. In this way, you can ensure that nobody can read the data you no longer need, or you can block data exfiltration in an emergency. With crypto-shredding, you can make it impossible for anyone to access your data.

Description

One of the best ways to do this is to use BYOK. With this approach, Azure Key Vault stores the key, which is under your control. So, to crypto-shred your data, you simply purge your key from its Key Vault. When you do, all that data becomes immediately unrecoverable.

> **More on BYOK**
>
> One of the primary purposes of BYOK is to increase users' control over their keys. The idea is that by introducing their own keys, users make it harder for the cloud service provider to access their data. Unfortunately, that's not why BYOK is useful. If you do not trust Microsoft with your data, why should you trust it to handle your key securely? You are storing it in its systems. In other words, if you assume that a malicious administrator could access your data, you should also assume that person could access your keys, too. Fortunately, Azure includes many other controls to prevent this from happening, including strong physical controls and various isolation layers that require escalation paths under the control of the customer to access the data.

Of course, this is a two-edged sword, because a malicious actor could leverage this approach to cause a denial of service. Some SaaS solutions like Microsoft 365 implement mechanisms to prevent losses due to the destruction of the BYOK. One such feature is called Availability Key and is discussed here: https://azsec.tech/89t.

Example

If you have an Azure SQL or Azure Storage and have used BYOK to encrypt them at rest, you can re-move the key from Azure Storage to crypto-shred the content.

Related security principles

- Defense in depth

- Leveraging existing components

- Separation of duties

Related patterns

- Protect secrets with Azure Key Vault

Availability pattern

Availability is often considered a given. You expect your solution to be there when needed and provide its services to every user. Unfortunately, it is not so automatic to achieve this, and you have to work hard to guarantee that your solution is up and running.

In the cloud, the situation is even worse, if possible. When you develop a complex system integrating many services, you rely on all of them to be available. The unavailability of any service may cause your solution to be partially or entirely unavailable. When each of these systems is managed at least in part by a third party, you lack control over the maintenance activities. Therefore, you have to design your solution to be more resilient than you used to do with on-prem solutions.

> **Important** It would be a mistake to think that this problem is specific to the cloud or to Azure. On the contrary, the pervasive adoption of automation you have with these platforms has dramatically reduced the prevalence of the incidents compared to on-prem. Still, incidents are a possibility and maintenance a necessity. The new approach gives you this awareness and the tools to design and implement your solutions in a resilient way to meet your availability requirements.

Let's see what you can do to improve the availability of your solution.

Design for denial of service

Intent and motivation

Denial-of-service (DoS) attacks are common occurrences. They happen when someone creates the conditions for your solution to fail by bombarding it with more requests than it can handle or by sending artfully crafted messages causing your solution to crash. In any case, these attacks cause the unavailability of your service. A variant of DoS attacks is called *distributed DoS* (DDoS). DDoS attacks are characterized by the generation of the attack from multiple points, sometimes in the order of the thousands or tens of thousands.

DoS and DDoS are some of the easiest attacks to execute. Some organizations even provide DDoS attacks as a service. You tell them who the target is, you pay them, and they do the rest! Very convenient and powerful.

You can address this problem in various ways, but the easiest is to simply add more resources to your application. One of the characteristics of the cloud is elasticity, which means you can allocate resources dynamically, as you need them. However, although this is easy and fast, it can be expensive and unfeasible in the long run. Here is where this pattern becomes useful.

Description

All public cloud platforms, including Azure, offer a base level of protection from DoS attacks. Azure also offers Azure DDoS Protection Standard (https://azsec.tech/s1h), designed to protect public IP addresses from potentially massive DDoS attacks.

The documentation for this service uses some specific wording that you should be aware of:

"Azure DDoS Protection Standard, combined with application design best practices, provides enhanced DDoS mitigation."

Note that it says *enhanced*, not *complete*. In other words, as with any other anti-DDoS system, Azure cannot represent your only line of defense against DDoS attacks. These systems complement a more comprehensive strategy, which starts with the design of your solution. For this reason, you should not design a system without thinking about how your architecture might respond to a DDoS attack.

Consider this real-life example: a customer with nearly 100 public IP addresses protected by the Azure DDoS Protection Standard service suffered severe service degradation. This was due to a DDoS attack, but it went undetected because the attack was "low and slow." That is, it fell below the triggering threshold for Azure DDoS Protection Standard, so none of the service's mitigation policies were triggered. As a result, the combined traffic flow across all IP addresses overloaded the back-end NVAs, which forced them to drop part of the traffic. The security anti-pattern in this design takes data from multiple untrusted sources and concentrates that traffic on a single, internal endpoint. In this case, all that data was concentrated on a single VM running the NVA, which is where the impact of the attack became evident. The customer quickly applied the NVA's built-in auto-scaling capabilities to bring more network bandwidth and compute online. In this scenario, a range of one to three NVAs mitigated the attack.

> **Note** To see Microsoft documentation on including DoS and DDoS protection support in your designs, see https://azsec.tech/xin.

One final note: many Azure services can throttle requests. For example, Azure Key Vault allows 4,000 secret transactions (for example, reading an SQL connection string) per 10 seconds. If your code goes beyond this threshold, further requests are throttled and return a 429 ("Too Many Requests") response. To remedy this, cache data if possible. In the Key Vault example, you could cache the connection string in memory for 15 minutes and read from Key Vault only four times per hour, which is way under the threshold. You can find a list of Azure subscription and service limits, quotas, and constraints at https://azsec.tech/9it.

Examples

- Many services can be configured with networking rules or private endpoint connections. One such service is Azure Storage. If you opt to adopt the networking rules, the service itself is still exposed and can receive requests; you just have a high-speed mechanism to reject the requests because they are not from an acceptable IP address. While fast, this mechanism can still be overwhelmed or bypassed—for example, by an IP spoofing attack. Therefore, it is typically better to use private endpoints.

- Consider the availability requirements of your solution. If you have strict availability requirements that do not allow for partial unavailability, it's best to design the solution accordingly. For example, you could use a content delivery network (CDN) to serve the static content and a distributed and redundant architecture to provide the service to the relevant geographies.

Related security principles

- Attack surface reduction

- Defense in depth

- Single point of failure

- Weakest link

Related patterns

- Isolate from the internet

- Isolate with an identity perimeter

Summary

This chapter introduced Azure security patterns. It started with a discussion of why the concept of patterns is so essential. It then introduced a few of the most common patterns to secure your solution on Azure.

This list is limited, and you might be able to identify one or two significant ones that are missing. The intent here is not to be comprehensive but to introduce you to an approach for building secure software on Azure based on the adoption of renowned patterns.

The next chapter goes beyond this to introduce a different way of thinking about security and designing secure solutions: threat modeling.

## CHAPTER 4

Threat modeling

After completing this chapter, you will be able to:

- Explain why threat modeling provides a unique value for improving the security of any solution.

- Describe the Microsoft STRIDE threat modeling approach.

- Select a threat modeling tool that aligns with your specific requirements.

- Execute a simple threat modeling exercise using Threats Manager Studio.

TL;DR

Threat modeling is a critical skill, and over time, you will get better at it. But it's a big topic—so this is a big chapter. But trust us: even if we tried to summarize everything we think is critical about threat modeling in this chapter, it would still be quite long. But don't be scared by the size! This chapter will give you all the information you need, whether you are a threat modeling expert or a complete novice.

The chapter has eight sections:

- What is threat modeling?

- The four main phases of threat modeling

- STRIDE's threat-classification approach

- The trouble with threat modeling

- Searching for a better threat modeling process

- A better way to perform threat modeling: The five factors

- Threat modeling tools

- How to threat model: A real-life example

Tip If you are just starting out with threat modeling, we recommend you follow along through this chapter. If you are already knowledgeable, you might want to start at the section "The trouble with threat modeling" and then skip straight to "Threat modeling tools."

What is threat modeling?

The "Threat Modeling Manifesto" (http://www.threatmodelingmanifesto.org/) defines threat modeling as a security practice for analyzing "representations of a system to highlight concerns about security and privacy characteristics." In other words, it is a way to evaluate the security of a given solution and assist its secure design.

As an assessment, threat modeling aims to identify security issues and determine how to address them. As a security design process, it allows you to design solutions from the ground up to be secure, because it prompts you to consider all the possible attacks and embed the necessary controls to prevent them.

Both these uses for threat modeling highlight two uniquely combined characteristics—the focus on the solution's design and on identifying the most appropriate security controls (what to do)—and linking them with the threats themselves (why the controls are required). This combination yields two desirable results:

■ It enables you to perform threat modeling very early during the development process. You will see how important this is to maximize effectiveness while reducing costs in the following pages.

■ It removes most uncertainties about why you need to implement the proposed mitigations.

Other approaches to security, like those based on best practices, cannot provide the same benefits. Consider, for example, a control library like Azure Security Benchmark. It is a set of general controls for Azure as a whole and a reference tool for creating service-specific guidance, called Baselines. Microsoft designed Azure Security Benchmark and Azure Security Baselines to address common security attacks related to relevant systems. Each control included has a purpose. The problem is you might not know what it is. You cannot discriminate between must-haves and nice-to-haves because there is no clear link between the proposed controls and their reason for being. So, faced with doubt, you might feel the need to implement them all.

> **Note** You can find out more about Azure Security Benchmark here: https://azsec.tech/i5c. To download it, along with the associated Baselines, see https://azsec.tech/fyc.

Other control libraries, like Center of Internet Security (CIS) Benchmarks, provide a rationale for their recommendations. CIS Benchmarks are collections of controls to be put in place to secure specific products, like Windows, Linux, Oracle, or even Azure. Still, it might be difficult to determine the exact blend of mitigations you need, because you do not have a map that enables you to understand the consequences of the various mitigations for your specific scenario, which could introduce limitations. So, you want what is strictly required, and nothing more. In any case, these libraries are intrinsically incomplete, because they correspond to someone else's scenarios, not necessarily yours.

> **Note** CIS Benchmarks is available here: https://azsec.tech/uki.

A solution that uses barcodes is an excellent example. Suppose that when you designed the solution, you considered only best practices and guidance like CIS Benchmarks and Azure Security Baselines. This presents a problem because you might miss barcodes as an attack vector. Malicious actors could force your users to scan barcodes containing URLs pointing to malicious payloads, like scripts, which your application would execute, causing all sorts of nasty things.

> **Note** The fact that you can overcome these issues with threat modeling doesn't mean that you should ignore libraries like CIS Benchmarks and the Azure Security Benchmark. On the contrary, these libraries are essential for quickly addressing the most common issues. They have a proven track record of improving a solution's security when you can't or don't want to apply approaches like threat modeling. Still, they have their limits—most importantly, the fact that they are not specific to your solution. Therefore, they might not be enough when the system is so critical that something more is required.

There are various ways to perform threat modeling, and they are all so different that it can be challenging to precisely define the threat modeling process. This book refers to a variant of Microsoft's STRIDE approach, specifically extended to improve DevOps integration. This chapter is intended to provide introductory guidance only; for more information, we suggest the following books, listed here in order of publication:

- Adam Shostack. *Threat Modeling: Designing for Security*, 1st edition, Wiley, February 2014

- Brook S. E. Schoenfield. *Securing Systems*, 1st edition, CRC Press, May 2015

- Izar Tarandach and Matthew J. Coles. *Threat Modeling: A Practical Guide for Development Teams*, 1st edition, O'Reilly, December 2020

The four main phases of threat modeling

Threat modeling typically consists of four main phases. These phases align with the Four Questions Framework. This framework was conceived by Adam Shostack and is discussed in his book. The framework has also been embraced by the "Threat Modeling Manifesto."

> **Note** The "Threat Modeling Manifesto" is a document developed by a group of top threat modeling practitioners to describe what threat modeling is. It abstracts the characteristics of current methodologies by identifying common principles and values. You can read it here: https://www.threatmodelingmanifesto.org.

The phases are as follows:

1. **Analysis**   This phase corresponds to the "what are we working on?" question in the Four Questions Framework. It involves analyzing the system in scope, which typically (but not necessarily) results in a diagram that represents the system itself. Microsoft's approach favors the creation of data flow diagrams (DFDs), which focus on how data flows inside the system.

2. **Threat identification**   This phase—which matches up with the "what can go wrong?" question in Shostack's framework—involves identifying threats that represent possible attacks faced by the system under scrutiny. Each threat is typically a contextualized attack scenario.

3. **Mitigation identification**   This phase, which is linked to the "what are we going to do about it?" question, involves identifying mitigations that address any threats unearthed in the previous step. This step ensures that all mitigations have a reason for being.

4. **Validation**   In this step, you validate the work done in the previous steps and, eventually, its integration or correction. It corresponds to the question, "Did we do a good enough job?"

As mentioned, DFDs (see Figure 4-1) play a significant role in many threat modeling processes, including Microsoft's. Therefore, it might be helpful to know a few basic things about them. DFDs decompose the system into parts called *processes* (which process data) and *data stores* (which store data). Processes and data stores are represented in DFDs as circles and as rectangles missing their vertical sides, respectively.

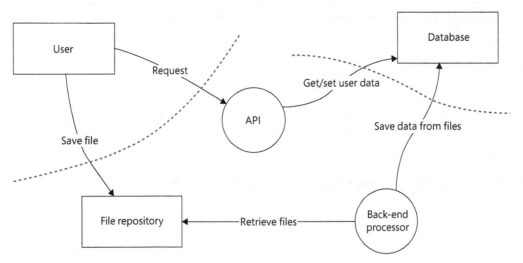

FIGURE 4-1 An example of a DFD.

> **Note** DFDs are not the only way to represent a system and its points of attack. You can also use UML, attack trees, process flow diagrams, or even simple tables in Excel files.

The difference between processes and data stores is not always clear-cut. You might occasionally have processes that contain some storage (like Azure Databricks, which mostly processes data but has a dedicated Azure Storage store) or data stores that contain business logic (like Azure SQL, whose main intent is to store and provide access to data but can also contain logic—for example, as stored procedures). A common trick to address ambiguity is to split the component in two. For example, an Azure SQL Database is a data store and a process that hosts stored procedures and the other logic.

DFDs also show external interactors, represented as rectangles. These represent everything that uses the system or is used by the system. For example, users and administrators, external services, and sometimes on-premises systems are external interactors. Because they are external to the system in scope, external interactors are considered black boxes. As such, you do not care about their inner workings. For example, it would be a mistake to show in a DFD an external interactor calling some service outside of the solution itself.

All these items interact via data exchanges called *data flows* or, more simply, *flows*. DFDs depict flows as directed arrows connecting the various entities. There are a few approaches to drawing these arrows. If you consider direction, the representation that is most faithful to the origins of DFDs is usually to illustrate how the data moves. For example, if you have a client calling Azure SQL to perform a query, the main flow would be from the database toward the client. This approach would not be practical from a security perspective, however, because what matters is who initiates the call. For instance, this knowledge is essential to determine the firewall rules required to allow that flow to happen. In other words, a scenario where a system you control calls some external resource should be considered less risky than a scenario where an external resource calls your system. Therefore, for our purposes, it is more important to determine who initiates the call than to determine how data flows.

A trust boundary is another component of a DFD. It is typically depicted as a dashed line or a box with a dashed border separating what is on one side from what is on the other side. Trust boundaries isolate areas at different levels of trust. For example, external interactors are at the lowest trust level in a threat model. So, trust boundaries must separate them from any component of the system they connect to. You should include at least one trust boundary in all your diagrams to contain all your processes and data stores to separate them from any external interactor. That trust boundary would represent your solution. Other trust boundaries might include:

- **Your tenant within Azure**   This includes all your subscriptions and their resources. By default, the tenant does not trust any external identity; you must establish a trust relationship explicitly. Therefore, the tenant is a clear trust boundary.

- **VNets**   Going more granularly, VNets define trust boundaries. There is a clear separation between what is internal and external to the VNet, so Azure blocks all traffic across VNets by default. You must authorize this traffic for it to be allowed.

- **Azure Services**   All Azure services require authentication and provide authorization mechanisms. Essentially, there is no implicit trust because you are located on Azure or in the same subscription, in line with the zero-trust principles introduced in Chapter 2, "Secure design." Nevertheless, you might want to avoid encasing all services within a dedicated trust boundary because that would make the system more complex to understand without adding much benefit. For this reason, we typically avoid including these trust boundaries.

- **Operating systems**   Operating systems discriminate between code executed in kernel mode and in user mode and grant higher privileges to the code executed in kernel mode. Because of this separation, kernel-mode code is more trusted than user-mode code. Therefore, you have a trust boundary between the two. With the identification of the trust boundary comes the need to introduce additional controls "at the borders" to ensure that what runs in user mode cannot affect what is executed in kernel mode. Still, you need to allow *some* controlled communications. Given that this happens through a trust boundary, these communications must follow a specific choreography designed to safeguard kernel mode.

It should now be clear why it is essential to identify trust boundaries: they highlight the need for additional security controls.

No trust boundaries?

You might be wondering if there are situations when there are no trust boundaries defined. The answer is no. Every system interacts with something external to it; therefore, every system has external interactors. And, as discussed, interactions between external interactors and the components of a solution must cross a trust boundary.

If you have a system that is completely isolated from external interactions, then that system does not provide value. It cannot collect or process data, and nobody can consult it. Therefore, such a system cannot exist. But even if it did, it would not be a valuable target for a threat model due to its complete isolation.

The bottom line is you cannot have a threat model without trust boundaries. So, if you see a DFD without any, you should ask yourself where they should go.

Identifying all external interactors and the related trust boundaries is one of the most crucial steps of diagramming. Remember, you miss a potential attack vector if you omit an external interactor in your threat model. Therefore, it pays to put extra care into enumerating all external interactors.

A typical mistake that results in missing some external interactors is to focus too much on the main scenario of your solution without considering the whole picture. For example, are you considering how developers provide the code deployed in production? If not, you might miss potential supply chain attacks like the one that infamously affected SolarWinds and many other companies worldwide. You can read about the SolarWinds attack here: https://azsec.tech/21h. Or are you considering how the solution is operated in the production environment? If not, you could miss potential insider attacks. These attacks represent a significant risk; indeed, a study from IBM X-Force published in May 2021 showed that 40 percent of the incidents analyzed involved an employee with privileges. You can download the study from https://azsec.tech/nm5.

Be aware that the DFD is *not* the threat model. We cannot stress this enough. The DFD is merely the first of the four steps in the threat modeling process. We have seen situations where, due to inexperience, perhaps coupled with inadequate tooling, organizations believe that the DFD is the only essential part of the threat model. Nothing would be further from the truth. The value provided by the threat-model diagram, when done correctly, is to represent the system as it is understood, but the threat model is much more than that. You achieve the potential of a threat model when you use it to drive the implementation of mitigations and to make your risks acceptable. A diagram alone cannot provide that value because it does not identify the threats or the related mitigations.

STRIDE's threat-classification approach

Your DFD must be up to date and accurate. Microsoft's threat modeling process builds on this foundation by adopting STRIDE's threat classification approach. By extension, many refer to the Microsoft threat modeling process as the Microsoft STRIDE threat-model approach. STRIDE is an acronym derived from the six categories of threats:

- **Spoofing** This is when an attacker impersonates a user or a system. It happens when there is a problem with authentication. Spoofing is typically a means to achieve other goals, such as tampering, information disclosure, or denial of service.

- **Tampering** This occurs when an attacker changes data stored in your system. It happens when there is a problem with integrity. Tampering is a common goal for attackers.

- **Repudiation** This is when there is the possibility of denying that an event happened or denying being involved in it.

- **Information disclosure** This includes all the threats where an attacker can access data stored in your system. It happens when there is a confidentiality problem. Information disclosure is a common goal for attackers.

- **Denial of service (DoS)** These attacks happen when attackers prevent, in full or in part, access to the system by legitimate users. They correspond to availability problems. DoS is one of the most common goals for attackers.

- **Elevation of privilege** This category includes threats where an attacker manages to obtain more rights than they should. These attacks happen when there is a problem with authorization or with processes executed with high privileges. Elevation of privilege is typically a means to achieve other goals, such as tampering, information disclosure, or denial of service.

One way to think about STRIDE is that each element in STRIDE is an attacker's objective. Looking carefully at the preceding list, you might see the relationship with the classic confidentiality, integrity, and availability (CIA) trifecta. STRIDE is a more fine-grained version of CIA, but from an attacker's perspective. CIA represents the security properties that architects want in their designs. For example, an attacker wants to view data (information disclosure), and a defender uses confidentiality controls.

STRIDE has been applied to threat modeling in two ways: STRIDE-per-element and STRIDE-per-interaction. The idea behind STRIDE-per-element is that you can identify the required threats by considering each element of the system and then applying the information in Table 4-1.

TABLE 4-1 The STRIDE-per-element threat identification table

	Spoofing	Tampering	Repudiation	Information Disclosure	Denial of Service	Elevation of Privilege
External interactor	X		X			
Processes	X	X	X	X	X	X
Data store		X	X	X	X	
Flows		X		X	X	

Note A repudiation threat for the data store exists only if it contains audit data.

When you generate a STRIDE-per-element threat model, you identify threats by looking at the components of the target system. Then you can determine whether there are any associated threats of a specific category by looking at Table 4-1. For example, if you have an external interactor, it is subject to spoofing and repudiation. Therefore, you must identify at least one spoofing threat and one repudiation threat. It is your responsibility to identify them.

STRIDE-per-element has been in use for many years and is still actively used today. This is not the only approach, though. For example, a few years ago, Larry Osterman and Douglas McIver from Microsoft defined an approach called STRIDE-per-interaction. This approach adopts a more extensive analysis that focuses on the interaction between elements instead of on the elements themselves. So, you can now identify a threat by considering a more comprehensive set of information: the flow, its source, its target, and eventually any trust boundaries.

With this new approach in mind, Microsoft introduced automatic threat generation with Microsoft Threat Modeling Tool 2014. Since then, threat modeling has been a more guided experience, grounded in knowledge bases describing a set of entities specifying the various types of objects and the possible threats with rules to automatically identify them in a given diagram.

The trouble with threat modeling

The approaches to threat modeling discussed so far have shown their limits over the years. In 2007, Adam Shostack published a blog post that listed issues related to threat modeling practices in use at the time. You can read the blog post here: https://azsec.tech/1tx. Here are a few of the most important ones, with our comments about the current situation:

- **It can be challenging to become proficient at threat modeling because there are too many processes** These processes do not address the typical problems nonexperts face. They also involve specialized terminology. Both these problems make threat modeling hard to understand and master.

- **Threat modeling is disconnected from the development process** Shostack suggests that this is because threat modeling is not repeated during the development process to ensure that the results are still aligned with the design. Shostack identified this problem 15 years ago, but it still applies today. And now it is compounded by a new problem: the development team cannot easily consume the threat model. Ideally, there should be some process to seamlessly ingest the threat model's output within an existing DevOps process—namely in the backlog—so that developers can incorporate it into their day-to-day activities.

- **It is not clear how to validate the threat model to determine the quality and completeness of the results** Many practitioners are unsure when to stop or how to handle the outcomes.

- **The return on investment (ROI) might not be obvious** This point is crucial—so much that we are starting to see situations where business decision-makers do perceive the value of threat modeling for their initiatives. So, they consider it a compliance requirement that they have to satisfy only because if they did not, they would not be authorized to deploy their solutions.

- **It requires a specific mindset that you cannot improvise** This mindset involves thinking like the attacker. In this way, you would be better able to design the protection needed in a particular scenario. Adopting this mindset is challenging—not only because your job is very different from the attacker's but also because there is no such thing as "the attacker." Rather, there are multiple types of attackers. For example:

  - **Script kiddies** These attackers can use tools and scripts written by others but cannot achieve much (if anything) independently.

  - **Cyber criminals** These attackers are more competent and proficient. Still, you might be able to discourage them and send them in other directions if you convince them that the effort required to compromise your system is too great.

  - **Nation-states** These attackers are even more competent and determined and have a better toolset. Nation-states also tend to have better funding. They can spend this funding on research to identify previously unknown security issues, which they can then leverage for malicious purposes. Or they can spend it on exploits purchased from private companies. See https://azsec.tech/j29 for more information.

Moreover, attackers with solid backgrounds in development tend to favor attacks that require the development of malicious code. In contrast, attackers with more infrastructural knowledge generally avoid anything that requires them to develop code.

 Note With all these alternatives, thinking like a generic attacker—or more importantly, thinking like your attacker—is hard to achieve, and you frequently have to settle for less.

All these problems still exist. If anything, they are now even worse, due to Agile methodologies and the accelerated software lifecycles imposed by the cloud. These new development approaches require you to go beyond the everyday experience to address problems like these:

- STRIDE-per-element and STRIDE-per-interaction focus on identifying threats. While these are significant, you cannot neglect mitigations. Identifying mitigations is the ultimate reason for performing threat modeling. You must elevate mitigations to first-class citizens within the threat model, providing similar support to that for the threats. You need an approach to identify the correct mitigations and to apply them more or less automatically, similar to what you do with STRIDE-per-interaction for threats.

- With DevOps, identifying what you *must* do is more important than determining what you *can* do. The third step of the STRIDE threat modeling process tends to identify one or more options for each threat, but what you need is to identify the *right* options. A good example of a "right option" is one that allows you to apply the same mitigation to many different threats. For example, multifactor authentication (MFA) tends to apply to most situations where there is a risk of spoofing users. In this way, you can spend only once but reap the benefits multiple times. This represents an essential factor for deciding what mitigations to implement.

Improving your ROI

You must improve your ROI on threat modeling by reducing the costs associated with it and by increasing the perceived value. To improve the effectiveness of threat modeling as a part of DevOps, you can integrate it with your task- and bug-tracking programs of choice. That way, threat modeling activities can become part of the backlog more efficiently, and security activities can be prioritized and aligned with sprint goals, which is crucial.

Searching for a better threat modeling process

In this chapter, you have explored the STRIDE threat modeling approach and its limitations when applied to DevOps-based cloud projects. It is now time to discuss how to evolve the threat modeling process to better integrate with cloud and DevOps scenarios.

There is no single way to perform threat modeling. Different organizations have different approaches, and experts adopt different techniques to address problems based on their experiences. The current trend is to assign the responsibility of threat modeling to developers to capitalize on their intimate knowledge of the solution, increase their involvement in the security process, and address the now-chronic lack of security experts. The idea is to leverage security champions—a team member within each development who acts as both a proxy of the security team and an improvement incentive for the team as a whole.

Security champions are enthusiasts who are trained and nurtured by the security team to execute basic security tasks from within the development team. Both Forrester and Gartner consider security champions as a much-needed approach. And SAFECode, a leading organization focused on secure development, dedicated a whole month of blog posts to the topic in 2012, available here: https://azsec.tech/xwm. SAFECode has also published guidance on creating a program to adopt security champions, which you can download here: https://azsec.tech/mib.

> **Note** Sandy Carielli, a principal analyst at Forrest, writes about security champions here: https://azsec.tech/wli. Richard Addiscott and Brian Reed, both analysts at Gartner, offer guidance on adopting this approach here: https://azsec.tech/mlj.

With respect to threat modeling, the security champion facilitates the team's execution of the threat model. This process is fast but intense, involving the whole development team. The idea is to convene regular team meetings, each one lasting no more than a couple of hours, to brainstorm and identify just a few security issues and related mitigations, typically using Shostack's Four Questions Framework. The idea is to repeat this process in every sprint to gradually improve security over time.

This approach has demonstrated its efficiency and effectiveness with Agile projects, thanks in part to the small size of the initiative involved. But this approach shows its limits with more extensive projects, rapidly becoming impractical as the complexity increases. And of course, the result is highly dependent on the quality of the team and on the guidance provided by the security champion.

At this point, Agile purists might note that a big initiative implemented with DevOps would not qualify as Agile because of its size. Typically, Agile initiatives involve small teams composed of just a handful of members. Having too large of a team—say, 10 members—introduces significant extra effort and causes Agile ceremonies like sprint planning and daily scrums to become long and unproductive. Of course, Agile purists are correct. Still, the problem of the limited consistency of the results remains. Moreover, the fact that teams should be limited in size does not stop organizations in many industries from adopting DevOps and Agile methodologies for massive projects involving dozens of developers.

Another problem with this approach is that threat modeling becomes an intimate experience for the development team. This misses one of the most significant benefits of threat modeling, which is to facilitate the creation of a bridge between the various roles involved in developing a solution. If the focus is on the development team only and the deliverables are designed to satisfy the requirements of that team only, then threat modeling cannot satisfy the needs of other roles, like the product owner, the product manager, the operations team, the security team, and the CISO. Indeed, we need to create such a communication channel because its benefits would be huge; it can even facilitate a natural collaboration among the various roles to ship the solution to production as quickly as possible.

> **Note** We argue that you cannot miss this opportunity to leverage threat modeling as a common language for security. You need a better approach to fulfill these promises.

Development vs. security

In our experience, most problems between development and security teams relate to communi-cation. Both teams can see only their own issues and try to address them as quickly as they can. This creates a situation in which the security team imposes requirements on the development team—for example, filling out a questionnaire. This often appears to the development team as an additional and ill-timed burden. From their perspective, the request occurs too late in the development process and produces additional work that was both unforeseen and unplanned. Worse, to the development team, the questionnaire seems wholly detached from the actual solution under development because the security team designed it to cover scenarios that simply do not apply. Therefore, developers fail to perceive the importance of the questionnaire and the urgency of the changes it identifies as required.

A better way to perform threat modeling: The five factors

Important The considerations presented in this section reflect our opinions, developed through our experiences assisting Azure customers with threat modeling.

As discussed, you cannot adopt a collegial approach to threat modeling with large projects. Instead, you must structure the threat modeling initiative as any other activity. This should be the responsibility of a team member devoted to security, such as a security expert or a security champion, and involves meeting with subject matter experts like business stakeholders, architects, lead developers, operators, and anyone else whose presence is strictly required. These meetings are part of the information-gathering activities that fuel the analysis phase and thus the whole threat modeling initiative. This approach works better than holding meetings with all team members throughout the entire threat modeling process because it maximizes the ability of the most relevant members of the team to contribute (which would be somewhat negated if the team contained more than five or six members) while minimizing time requirements for everyone. Moreover, placing someone whose focus is security in charge of the threat model initiative yields better and more consistent results, because it allows that person to obtain more advanced training and to become more experienced over time. We have used this approach for years, with great success.

Note This approach does not preclude you from adopting a security champion program. On the contrary, it somewhat requires it, due to the chronic lack of threat modeling experts.

As you embark on any threat modeling initiative, for best results, you should keep these five factors in mind:

- **Integration**   We have already mentioned the importance of adopting a threat modeling process that integrates with your organization's DevOps processes. It is also essential to leverage threat modeling to facilitate communication between the development and security teams. Another scenario in which integration provides value relates to the integration of your monitoring system (like your SIEM) with the threat modeling tool. Such an integration could, for example, allow you to determine if certain types of attacks become more prevalent. You could then reassess the severity of the related threats, due to the increased probability that such attacks could occur.

- **Mitigation**   Ideally, you want an approach that focuses on mitigations—their prioritization and their implementation. This is essential to ensure that outcomes are actionable and that they provide value to development teams. You must also ensure that the approach integrates seamlessly with the tools the development team already uses. Their lives are already complicated; they do not need threat modeling to make things worse by requiring them to learn and use yet more tools.

- **Guidance**   Your threat modeling process must have an easy learning curve. Few people have the knowledge required to perform a threat model without assistance. Providing guidance, in the form of knowledge bases and documentation, is essential to ensure broad adoption.

- **Automation**   Using automation tools can enable you to more easily identify threats and mitigations as well as accelerate threat modeling. A common approach is to use knowledge bases to define typical elements of the scenario of interest and include the rules used to generate threats and mitigations. This approach allows you to automatically generate the typical artifacts required by analyzing information you provide about the system in scope.

- **Flexibility**   You need a flexible approach that you can adapt to your organization's needs. For example, you must be able to integrate your threat modeling activities with existing processes and tools, such as those for risk management. These include tools built specifically for your organization. This flexibility also enables you to leverage the knowledge of your IT department on the types of attacks it sees.

The best way to achieve these five factors is to select the right tools. For guidance, read on.

Threat modeling tools

Choosing the right threat modeling tool can be a daunting task because there are many options, and new tools emerge regularly. This has been especially true in the last couple of years, due to increased interest in threat modeling.

Although you are not required to use a dedicated threat modeling tool, it certainly helps. Since the advent of the cloud, designing and building complex applications that are tightly interconnected with dozens of other systems has become increasingly common. As of this writing, Azure alone offers more than 200 products and services, and if you connect with external resources—such as on-premises systems, social accounts, identity providers, APIs, or IoT devices—the list is virtually unlimited. With so much complexity, analyzing an average system without the help of a dedicated threat modeling tool might be an impossible feat.

So, you need a tool. But how do you decide which one? Your first consideration is whether to adopt a commercial threat modeling tool or a free one. Commercial threat modeling tools have various advantages over most of the free tools. For instance, they typically connect with systems like task- and bug-tracking tools. They also provide complete guidance, such as knowledge bases, which are regularly updated and improved. In contrast, free tools provide a lightweight, noncommittal entry point to threat modeling. These tools might be adequate for your needs, at least at first, and perhaps even as your threat modeling practice matures.

Our experience is primarily with free tools, so we have focused on these in this section. This enables us to provide opinions based on firsthand experience. It allows us to cover all the features of each tool—something we would be able to do with limited trial and community versions, like those provided for some commercial tools. This section presents six tools we have used in the past for your consideration. Be aware, however, that other tools not covered here might better fit your needs.

For each tool, we provide the following essential information:

- The URL where you can find it

- The project status (whether the tool maintained or stale)

- A brief description of the tool

- How well the tool supports each of the five factors (see the preceding section)

> **Note** Please do not interpret our decision to focus on free tools to mean we think commercial tools are ineffective or inferior. On the contrary, we know that some of these tools—such as ThreatModeler, IriusRisk, Foreseeti securiCAD, and Security Compass SD Elements—result from hundreds of years of collective knowledge and efforts. We value the contributions of these companies to the threat modeling practice and believe they are a precious asset for the entire security community.

Assessing the five factors

When assessing how well each tool supports each of the five factors, we use three grades: Absent, Limited, and Complete. We present this assessment in table form. For example, Table 4-2 shows our assessment for a tool called Threagile (covered in more detail later in this section).

TABLE 4-2 Evaluating the five factors for Threagile

Factor	Evaluation
Integration	Absent
Focus on mitigations	Absent
Guidance	Absent
Automation	Limited
Flexible approach	Limited

In this example, the assigned values might be different from what you would expect. For example, if you read the description of Threagile in the upcoming section about it, you might infer that it supports integration with GitHub, because you can easily upload a YAML file representing a threat model to GitHub, and you can use a GitHub action to insert a Threagile execution as part of a pipeline. However, it does not enable you to insert identified mitigations in the backlog—one of the key capabilities of the integration factor. Similar considerations apply to the other factors. In other words, when in doubt, refer to the definition of each factor in the preceding section.

CAIRIS

- **URL** https://cairis.org/

- **Project status** Actively maintained and supported. The current version at the time of this writing is 2.3.8, released in December 2020.

CAIRIS is a web-based threat modeling tool. Because it is a web application, it can be accessed by any authorized connected device. You can configure CAIRIS to allow two or more users to access the same threat model simultaneously.

CAIRIS defines threat models using multiple tables that contain entities like roles, assets, threat types, threats, and countermeasures. It supports the importation of objects from other systems such as XML files, but it is up to you to transform your data to a format that CAIRIS can accept.

> **Tip** With CAIRIS, you can import sample threat types from the MITRE Common Weakness Enumeration (CWE), the MITRE Common Attack Pattern Enumerations and Classifications (CAPEC), and the OWASP Top 10. These files are merely samples, however. They are more than four years old, include just a few items, and cannot be used for an actual threat model. Instead, you must write some sort of custom script or application to import current threat types from these sources.

The object model defined in CAIRIS is probably the richest you will find among all the tools included here. Nevertheless, with this richness comes a downside: the steepest learning curve. On a related note, CAIRIS has a complex interface, so becoming proficient with it takes some time. The tool's documentation helps somewhat, but still, it takes time to learn how the various concepts fit together and how everything works.

To create a threat model with CAIRIS, you fill various tables in a logical order. If you do not follow the correct order, the tool will prevent you from proceeding. CAIRIS then uses the information you entered to evaluate your risk and returns its assessment in the form of a qualitative scale of three values: Low, Medium, and High. It can then automatically create documentation in various formats, including diagrams. Beyond that, CAIRIS provides unique capabilities, such as managing project requirements, and includes coverage of privacy concepts—rare for a threat modeling tool. And it provides guidance on how to extend it.

Troubleshooting CAIRIS can be problematic. Because you must fill in many tables in a set order, it is all too easy to forget something along the way and receive the wrong result. In some cases, you will know the result is wrong; but in others, you might not, which can be problematic.

Here are a few more points about CAIRIS worth considering:

- From a DevOps integration perspective, CAIRIS supports only Trello, a Kanban-style project-management software.

- You can install CAIRIS locally, within a container, or as an Ubuntu virtual machine.

- CAIRIS generates reports in many formats, but they are all predefined. It is not possible to change the layout of the generated reports.

The five factors

TABLE 4-3 Evaluating the five factors for CAIRIS

Factor	Evaluation
Integration	Limited
Focus on mitigations	Limited
Guidance	Limited
Automation	Absent
Flexible approach	Limited

Microsoft Threat Modeling Tool

- **URL** https://azsec.tech/yiv

- **Project status** Regularly updated, but the updates are minor. This tool has not received a significant update since 2016.

The Microsoft Threat Modeling Tool is the official threat modeling offering from Microsoft. It implements STRIDE-per-element. Using this tool to create a new threat model involves selecting a template that contains all the entities and related threats you need. The tool includes three templates out of the box, one of which is dedicated to Azure. You can also find other templates online (although they are rare) and create your own if necessary. And if your threat model uses a template that becomes updated, the tool will automatically upgrade your threat model to the new version.

On the negative side, the Microsoft Threat Modeling Tool is somewhat constrained. For example:

- Although this tool enables you to define and use templates containing helpful knowledge bases to create threat models, it does not support add-ins.

- The file format is undocumented. It is possible to find third-party libraries and applications that allow you to open and use the document produced by the Microsoft Threat Modeling Tool in other document formats, but there is no guarantee that they will continue to work in the future. Therefore, this further limits your ability to integrate the Microsoft Threat Modeling Tool with other services and applications.

- The tool's object model is minimal and misses essential concepts like mitigations. For example, unlike most templates, which include a text field (typically called Justification) where you can enter mitigations, this tool's templates do not.

- Editing templates can be difficult because each one must contain all the required information. Therefore, templates tend to become unmanageable as they grow.

- You cannot integrate the template definition yourself. For example, if you introduce a new type of entity, your changes will be lost when you apply the latest template version to the threat model.

- Although the Microsoft Threat Modeling Tool allows you to generate HTML reports, you cannot change the layout of those reports.

- The Microsoft Threat Modeling Tool can be installed only on Windows desktop machines.

> **Note** The Microsoft Threat Modeling Tool is one of the most documented tools available. You can find information about this tool on Pluralsight, LinkedIn, Udemy, YouTube, and many other sites.

The five factors

TABLE 4-4 Evaluating the five factors for Microsoft Threat Modeling Tool

Factor	Evaluation
Integration	Absent
Focus on mitigations	Absent
Guidance	Complete
Automation	Limited
Flexible approach	Absent

OWASP Threat Dragon

- **URL** https://azsec.tech/ws7

- **Project status** Alive and regularly updated. The current version at the time of writing is 1.6.0, released in December 2021 and version 2.0 is in development.

OWASP Threat Dragon is a web-based threat modeling tool. There is also a desktop version, based on Proton, which you can install on Windows, macOS, and Linux machines.

OWASP Threat Dragon generates plain DFDs; you cannot use it to create specialized entities. Previous versions included drawing tools and allowed you to insert threats manually. Version 1.6.0, released in December 2021, includes a new threat-generation engine. You can use this new feature to select an entity or flow and then generate the associated threats by:

- Adding a custom threat

- Adding threats identified using STRIDE-per-element, which requires you to describe the threat for each identified category

- Adding threats using the context

> **Note** The third option, adding threats using the context, is based on work by the OWASP Automated Threats to Web Applications Project. For more information about this project, see https://azsec.tech/3ab.

OWASP Threat Dragon includes significant guidance, and its authors have demonstrated it at many events. Given its simplicity, it is an adequate tool. However, there are a few downsides:

- Users cannot yet extend the rules used to generate the threats.

- Although Threat Dragon enables you to generate PDF reports, you cannot change the layout of those reports.

- The web version of Threat Dragon saves files on GitHub, while the desktop version saves them locally.

- Threat Dragon stores mitigations in an unstructured text field within the threat, so it is impossible to perform analysis or processing on mitigations, like showing threats associated with a given mitigation.

- Threat Dragon cannot integrate with a DevOps task and bug-tracking system like Azure DevOps or Jira.

The five factors

TABLE 4-5 Evaluating the five factors for OWASP Threat Dragon

Factor	Evaluation
Integration	Absent
Focus on mitigations	Absent
Guidance	Complete
Automation	Limited
Flexible approach	Absent

pytm

- **URL** https://azsec.tech/t7e

- **Project status** Alive and is regularly updated. The current version at the time of this writing is 1.2.0, released in April 2021.

pytm is a project developed by Izar Tarandach, a renowned expert and author of *Threat Modeling: A Practical Guide for Development Teams*. This tool has been recently incorporated as an OWASP project.

The idea behind pytm is that you define your system by using Python code. Because it consists of code, you can host it on GitHub or other source code repositories. This approach allows for concurrent work and collaboration on the file. The file can be processed to generate DFDs, Unified Modeling Language (UML) sequence diagrams, or even full-fledged reports using a Markdown template.

pytm generates threats using knowledge bases defined as JSON files. These JSON files include generation rules as conditional expressions with a natural and straightforward language. pytm provides one such file that defines about 100 different threats. These provided threats also refer to development issues like SQL injection and buffer overflow. However, these issues are addressed much more efficiently and effectively by static application security testing (SAST) tools like the ones discussed in Chapter 12, "Container security."

pytm has significant guidance. Moreover, its authors have demonstrated it at many events. Given its simplicity, what is available can be considered adequate. However, there are some downsides:

- pytm stores mitigations in an unstructured text field within the threats. Therefore, it is impossible to perform analysis or processing on mitigations, like showing the threats associated with a given mitigation.

- pytm cannot integrate with a DevOps task and bug-tracking system, like Azure DevOps or Jira.

The five factors

TABLE 4-6 Evaluating the five factors for pytm

Factor	Evaluation
Integration	Absent
Focus on mitigations	Absent
Guidance	Complete
Automation	Limited
Flexible approach	Limited

Threagile

- **URL** https://threagile.io/

- **Project status** Relatively new. There is no official release so far. Development appears to have stopped in November 2020 besides a minimal update in November 2021.

Threagile is a threat modeling tool developed by Christian Schneider. The idea behind Threagile is that you define your system using a YAML file. You create it as an empty stub using the Threagile command-line tool. Then, you include all your information in the available locations. Threagile facilitates editing by providing auto-completion and syntax coloring to many editors. You can host the YAML files on GitHub or other source code repositories, allowing concurrent work and collaboration on the file. Threagile provides guided tools to enable you to add scenarios to the YAML threat model by answering several questions. For example, one of the options focuses on CI/CD pipelines.

When you execute Threagile on a YAML file, it generates various artifacts:

- A PDF report with a DFD, a description of the system, a list of threats and their status, and various aggregations to facilitate analysis. This report is thorough and easily spans 100 pages or more.

- Various diagrams, including the DFD of the system.

- An XLSX file containing the same information as the PDF document, in tabular form.

- Various JSON files with the same information to support automated processing.

The generated JSON file can be processed to create DFDs, UML sequence diagrams, or even full-fledged reports using a Markdown template.

Threagile generates threats using rules codified as compiled Go code. You can create your own rules by writing them in Go and then compiling them. The provided threats are heterogeneous. They also refer to development issues like SQL injection and buffer overflow. However, these issues are addressed much more efficiently and effectively by SAST tools like those discussed in Chapter 9, "Secure coding."

Threagile stores mitigations in an unstructured text field within the threats. Therefore, it is impossible to do any analysis or processing on mitigations, like showing the threats associated with a given mitigation.

You can include Threagile processing of the YAML file in a build pipeline in GitHub, thanks to a free action called run-threagile-action. However, Threagile cannot integrate with a DevOps task and bug-tracking system like Azure DevOps or Jira. For example, it requires you to manually update the status of the threats in the YAML file.

Threagile does not have much guidance apart from a couple of presentations done at events and published on YouTube. The documentation provided is not enough to facilitate the tool's adoption because the language is complex. However, the author does provide support via a community chat hosted on Gitter.

The five factors

TABLE 4-7 Evaluating the five factors for Threagile

Factor	Evaluation
Integration	Absent
Focus on mitigations	Absent
Guidance	Absent
Automation	Limited
Flexible approach	Limited

Threats Manager Studio

- **URL** https://threatsmanager.com

- **Project status** Alive and regularly updated. The current version at the time of writing is 1.5.2, released in January 2022.

> **Important** Threats Manager Studio is the pet project of one of the authors of this book, Simone Curzi. The other authors have also participated in various ways in its design and evolution.

Threats Manager Studio has been under development since early 2018 to address problems identified during day-by-day threat modeling practices using existing tooling that do not consider the specific needs of experts, including limited extensibility and an excessive focus on automation. Starting in 2019 it became actively used within Microsoft, and it was published as a free tool for everyone's use in November 2020. Threats Manager Studio is continuously updated and extended with new capabilities.

Threats Manager Studio is designed using the Microsoft Threat Modeling Tool as a reference. However, it improves on it in multiple ways:

- **It is open**   Capabilities are implemented as modules called *extensions*, loaded dynamically by the tool.

- **It supports the dynamic editing of metadata**   Threats Manager Studio provides minimal metadata for all the various objects so you can create your own metadata to support your processes. You can create new metadata definitions and export them into templates so others can leverage them.

- **Templates are a fragment of knowledge bases**   With this new approach, you need not choose a template when you start a threat model. Instead, you can import what you need when you need it. So, templates can be smaller, and their maintenance is much easier.

- **Users can define their own entities, threats, and mitigations**   Users have full control of the entities, threats, and mitigations used in their threat models. This means they can easily integrate what is provided by the selected knowledge bases as the need is identified.

- **It provides specialized execution modes**   These are designed to cover the specific needs of categories of users. For example, there is an Expert mode for users who need to create or edit templates, a Simplified mode for users who only need to create or edit threat models, and a Business Decision Maker mode for users, such as product owners, who need to evaluate risks and make decisions.

- **It introduces a Mitigations feature**   This is instrumental in prioritizing remediations, by way of a roadmap tool. It is also helpful for integrating with DevOps systems (initially only Azure DevOps) to create work items from mitigations and to update the status of the threat model as the implementation proceeds.

Threats Manager Studio also provides diagramming capabilities comparable with DFD implementations like those of the Microsoft Threat Modeling Tool and of OWASP Threat Dragon, but it uses a different language to address some of the typical ambiguities of DFDs.

At the time of this writing, these are the downsides to using Threats Manager Studio:

- It is available only as a Windows desktop application on Windows 10 or 11.

- It does not support concurrent editing.

- It provides only a single template focused on a minimal subset of Azure PaaS services.

- Adopting a custom graphical representation might represent compliance problems for some organizations.

- Documentation is available but only in partial form. Although it discusses most functionalities, some of the tool's latest features are not yet well covered.

The five factors

TABLE 4-8 The evaluation of the five factors for Threats Manager Studio

Factor	Evaluation
Integration	Complete
Focus on mitigations	Complete
Guidance	Limited
Automation	Complete
Flexible approach	Complete

How to threat model: A real-life example

There is no better way to learn about something than to do it. This section contains a sample exercise to step you through the threat modeling process. The intent is not to provide you with a complete experience but to give you an idea of how it works. To get the most out of this exercise, follow the steps shown here, and refer to the accompanying material at https://azsec.tech/4ux.

The scenario we have chosen for this exercise is a sample web application to book COVID vaccinations. The approach taken here represents just one possible way you could tackle threat modeling—not necessarily the best one for you or your organization. We have designed this approach based on the one we have adopted for our day-by-day practice, but we have simplified it to highlight the most significant concepts without indulging in too many details.

> **Note** This example has been designed to demonstrate the essential threat modeling concepts discussed throughout this chapter. While it might appear similar to real projects, this is purely coincidental.

This exercise simulates the steps of a real-life threat modeling job using Threats Manager Studio version 1.5.2, the latest available at the time of writing. Of course, you can use the latest version available; just be aware that the process will be similar, but you might find minor differences. Threats Manager Studio provides the whole set of features required to cover all the necessary steps. It also integrates with Azure DevOps—an essential capability for generating actionable results for the development team. So, let's begin!

> **Important** To complete this exercise, you need the main distribution of Threats Manager Studio along with the Automatic Threat Generation, Quality, and DevOps extension libraries. These are available here: https://azsec.tech/tms. For guidance on installing and configuring the tool, see https://azsec.tech/tqv.

Analyzing the solution: The first meeting

This exercise begins at the earliest stages of the product's development. As a threat modeler, you should reach out to the development team to gather relevant documentation and discuss the characteristics of the activity. After that, you should have a first meeting with the solution architects and other members of the development team to obtain the information you need about the solution in question.

Suppose that during our first meeting, we receive the diagram shown in Figure 4-2. Of course, this is not a security diagram. Too much is missing, such as how systems interact, how accounts authenticate, and where sensitive data is stored (if anywhere). Still, it is helpful for you to recognize technologies you might not know, like Kubernetes.

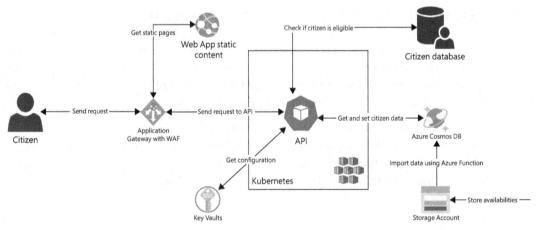

FIGURE 4-2 A diagram representing an application for booking COVID vaccinations.

Knowing what might go wrong with each solution component is essential to asking the right questions and identifying possible issues pertaining to whatever answers you receive. For this reason, it is crucial to have some background information about the solution before meeting with the development team and to investigate anything that is unfamiliar to you. Another technique you might employ is to have multiple sessions, with a few days between each one, to give yourself the time you need to understand what is missing and to ask meaningful questions.

 Important This lack of knowledge is a common situation for all threat modelers. The only way to address it is to do some research, preferably before meeting with team members. For this reason, it is essential to conduct a scoping call before the actual engagement. This meeting is an opportunity to ask about the services the team is using or is planning to use.

Suppose that at your first meeting with the architects and developers of the solution in question, you find out the following information:

- The team is building a solution to allow citizens to book COVID vaccine shots. It provides three primary capabilities: booking a COVID vaccination, seeing previous and current bookings, and changing any upcoming bookings.

- The application authenticates users by their tax ID number, name and surname, and birthdate. Although these pieces of information are sometimes public or inferred, they are the only option, because all citizens must use the solution. The country has a unified authentication system for granting access to the various public sites, but fewer than 50 percent of citizens use it.

- The availability of the solution is a critical concern. The solution should be able to sustain heavy traffic and still be responsive.

- The solution is a web application. The static content will be stored in Azure Storage and served using the static website hosting capability. An API implemented in a container and hosted within Azure Kubernetes Services will do the actual work. The team will ensure that the storage can be written only through the deployment pipeline.

- Users access the static content and the API through Azure Application Gateway with WAF.

- The API will access the Citizen DB, a repository containing data related to all citizens. Each citizen is represented by their tax ID number, name and surname, and birthdate, among the other data. To access the Citizen DB, the solution's API calls a web service, which requires basic authentication with credentials provided by its owners. Azure Key Vault protects these credentials.

- The API accesses a Cosmos DB, which contains all data related to bookings. As with the Citizen DB, the API accesses the Cosmos DB using authentication credentials stored in the same Azure Key Vault.

- The Cosmos DB contains information about appointment availability from various vaccination centers in the area. Each vaccination center uploads a list of available slots as CSV files into an Azure Storage account in the solution's back end. Vaccination centers use one of the two Storage Account Keys to authenticate and upload the files into the Storage Account.

- An Azure Function is automatically triggered when a file is uploaded. The file is then processed, and the Azure Function stores its content in the Cosmos DB. The Azure Function uses its system-assigned Managed Identity to access the resource in both cases.

Analyzing the solution: The second meeting

If you are a seasoned threat modeling expert, you would probably have identified various issues from the description in the preceding section. Even if you are not an expert, you might still see a few weaknesses. The most crucial part here, though, is understanding what you cannot analyze and focusing on that. For example, ask yourself if you are entirely comfortable with all the solution components. In this way, you might identify open points, like these:

- What is the application gateway with WAF, and what are its different operation modes? Does the solution have a secure configuration, or is it ineffective?

- Is the API checking if the requests it receives are from the application gateway?

- What is Kubernetes? What are the possible weaknesses for solutions based on it?

- Can you retrieve the secrets from Azure Key Vault securely?

- What are the Azure Storage keys used by the vaccination centers to connect to the back-end Azure Storage?

- Is there any way to improve the security of the citizens' authentication?

> **Note** This last question is the most important one of all.

This list is intentionally partial, and you might have already identified many additional questions. However, you might not yet have all the information you need to answer them all. In that case, you should do your research or ask the team.

As you try to understand the system better, try creating a diagram using the Azure PaaS Core template in Threats Manager Studio, available here: https://azsec.tech/9uy. When you open Threats Manager Studio, there is already a blank threat model created for you. To begin drawing your diagram in the blank threat model, click the **Create Diagram** button on the **Home** ribbon, and draw the diagram by dragging and dropping the various stencils in the **Item Templates** palette to the left of the diagram into the drawing pane (see Figure 4-3). To see the existing stencils, you first select a category from the options along the top of the palette (which in Figure 4-3 is Process) and then click the **Refresh** button near the category list.

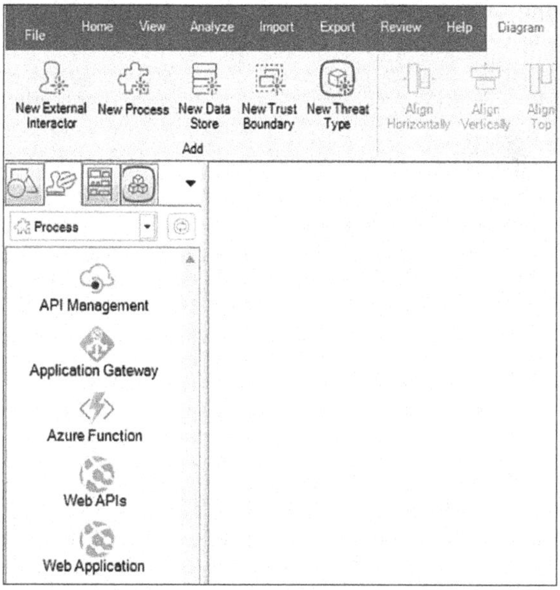

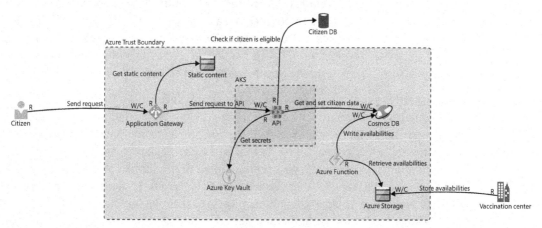

FIGURE 4-3 The Item Templates palette.

You can also use the basic stencils for External Interactor, Process, or Data Store to represent any missing stencils. Eventually, you can assign an item template. For example, to create the API in the diagram, you could drop a standard Process stencil, right-click it, click **Change Entity** in the context menu, and choose **API**. To create the flows, simply click and drag from the center of the initiator; then, when the mouse pointer becomes a hand, continue dragging the target object. Figure 4-4 shows a possible resulting diagram.

FIGURE 4-4 A threat-model diagram for the COVID booking solution.

💡 **Tip** For further information on using Threats Manager Studio to draw diagrams like the one shown here, see https://azsec.tech/s4c and https://azsec.tech/u4q.

The diagram shown in Figure 4-4 represents a transposition of the architectural diagram shown in Figure 4-2 but has a few notable differences:

- The flows are directed from the initiator toward the recipient. The *R* near the initiator indicates that the initiator can read data, while the *W/C* near the target means the initiator would send commands to the target or change its status.

- The borders highlight the trust boundaries defined in the solution. They separate areas at different levels of trust. Everything inside the Azure trust boundary is part of the solution, while everything outside of it is external. Citizens, the Citizen DB, and the vaccination centers are all external interactors.

- The diagram includes a couple of objects missing from the original one: the Azure Function to import the availability data and the vaccination centers. These objects were implied but not represented.

At the second meeting, you will refer to this diagram while asking the architects some of the same questions you asked yourself earlier. For the sake of this example, their answers, and certain steps you should take in response, are as follows:

- **What is the application gateway with WAF, and what are its different operation modes? Does the solution have a secure configuration, or is it ineffective?** The architects say the WAF is enabled in Detection mode. You research this mode at https://azsec.tech/8ds and discover that a WAF in Detection mode will not block attacks. When you press the architects to explain why they have taken this approach, they explain that it is necessary because they have had false positives blocking legitimate requests. In fact, they are even thinking of disabling the WAF altogether because it introduces delays.

- **Is the API checking if the requests it receives are from the application gateway?** According to the architects, the API is not checking anything. However, they do use the Application Gateway Ingress Controller, which manages the communication between the application gateway and the pod hosting the API. After reading up on the Application Gateway Ingress Controller at https://azsec.tech/9qe, you decide that this addresses the issue appropriately.

- **Can you retrieve the secrets from Azure Key Vault securely?** The architects are unanimous: of course you can! After all, they are using AKS, which is managed by Microsoft, which also manages Key Vault. So, everything is secure by definition! Unfortunately, things are not so simple. For instance, the APIs that access Key Vault use credentials stored in etcd, a configuration database that is part of Kubernetes, where secrets are Base64-encoded. The keyword here is *encoded*; there is no encryption. Therefore, an attacker who manages to get access to etcd would, by definition, be able to read the secrets. This is a problem you might need to consider for your threat model. A good way to address this problem could be to leverage Managed Identities using the Azure AD Pod Identity. For more information, see https://azsec.tech/dq9.

> **Note** At the time of writing, Azure AD Pod Identity has been deprecated and is in the process of being replaced with Azure AD Workload Identity. For more information, see Chapter 12.

You do not have to consult with the architects regarding all the questions you asked yourself earlier, however. You can answer some of them yourself by conducting your own research. For example:

- **What is Kubernetes? What are the possible weaknesses for solutions based on it?**
Kubernetes, more formally called Azure Kubernetes Services (AKS), is a very complex service. Microsoft manages AKS, and as such, it introduces some significant mitigations over the average unmanaged Kubernetes deployment. You decide to research AKS to analyze its security. Specifically, you check out a video of a recent presentation by Maor Kuriel from WhiteSource Software called *How to Build a Threat Model for Kubernetes Systems*, at https://azsec.tech/56r. This video references the CNCF Kubernetes threat model, discussed at https://azsec.tech/0ho, so you read that, too. In this way, you learn about the various possible attack vectors that could compromise the solution, including service tokens, compromised containers, network endpoints, denial of service, and RBAC issues. You understand that you need to include these attack vectors and possible mitigations to the threat model, taking them from the CNCF study. But you are dealing with AKS, not a bare-bones Kubernetes installation. Therefore, you must consider the mitigations that Microsoft already includes in AKS, detailed here: https://azsec.tech/29t. Chapter 12 includes various other considerations around AKS and container security.

- **What are the Azure Storage keys used by the vaccination centers to connect to the back-end Azure Storage?** Adopting Storage Account keys is often a bad move. In this case, they introduce two problems:

  - Storage Account keys are extremely powerful and provide complete control over the data stored in Azure Storage.

  - It is impossible to discriminate between vaccination centers. Therefore, it would not be possible to identify who caused the damage in the event of a mistake or misuse.

- **Is there any way to improve the security of the citizens' authentication?** This is an important question because, in this case, you cannot use one of the standard mitigations you usually use to improve authentication: MFA. Instead, you must rely on totally insecure authentication because the organization has already decided to use it for business reasons and the stakeholders have already accepted the consequences. So, the question becomes, what can you do to improve the situation, given these limitations? As with the previous question, this is not something you should ask the architects, but rather something you should try to answer as a threat modeler and security expert. The best approach is to refer to the security design principles introduced in Chapter 2. One of them is particularly useful here: defense in depth. Because you cannot adopt MFA as a preventive control, is there any other control you can consider? You will answer this question in the next section.

Identifying specific threats and mitigations

Although you can use Threats Manager Studio to automatically generate threats and mitigations for your threat model—and you will, in the next section—doing so is not enough. Adding the threats and mitigation you identified by asking the right questions is usually more important, and you will do that now.

Recall the threats and mitigations you have identified so far:

- Authentication is weak, meaning an attacker could impersonate a citizen.

- The solution could become unavailable because it is not configured for high availability.

- The API accesses all resources using credentials stored in an Azure Key Vault, and it accesses the Azure Key Vault later using credentials stored in etcd, which is not secure.

- Vaccination centers access Azure Storage using a Storage Account key, which is the wrong decision.

We cannot cover how to flesh out all four of these threats and add them to the threat model created earlier, as this would consume too many pages. So, we will focus on the first one—the authentication problem—and leave the rest to you as exercises.

To begin, you need to recognize that the authentication problem represents a vulnerability, not a threat. The difference is that a *vulnerability* is a problem in a system, while a threat describes how a malicious actor could exploit a vulnerability for some unwarranted gain. In general, you want to focus on threats, because they enable you to understand how someone could exploit the related vulnerabilities. If you focus only on vulnerabilities, you will never get to a point where you determine whether one actually puts you at risk.

So, what is the threat here? Before we answer that, let's review the three primary capabilities of the solution:

- Booking COVID vaccinations

- Seeing previous and current bookings

- Changing any upcoming bookings

The threat, then, is that if authentication is weak, an attacker could impersonate a citizen. The attacker could then determine and potentially disclose whether a particular citizen has booked and received a vaccination, which represents a significant privacy risk. The attacker could also cancel or change a booking, which would cause damage, because the vaccination center could deny the citizen their vaccination. Thus, there are two threats you must add to your threat model, both associated with the Citizen object (because they relate to its authentication).

To add a threat to your threat model diagram, follow these steps (see Figure 4-5):

1. Click the **Citizen** shape in the diagram.

   Notice that the column to the right of the diagram shows the details of the selected object. That column is called the **Item Editor**.

2. In the **Item Editor**, click the **Add** button below the **Threat Event** list.

3. In the **Select Threat Type** dialog, enter the following information about the threat (see Figure 4-5) and click **OK**:

- **Assign a New Threat Type**   Select this option button. You need to create a new threat because the existing threats do not fit.

> **Note**   In other situations, you might be able to assign an existing threat type. In that case, you would select the **Use Existing Threat Type** option button and then choose the threat type you want from the corresponding drop-down list.

- **Name**   Type a name for the new threat type—in this example, **Information Disclosure of Bookings**.

- **Description**   Optionally, type a description for the new threat type.

- **Severity**   Select **High** from the drop-down list.

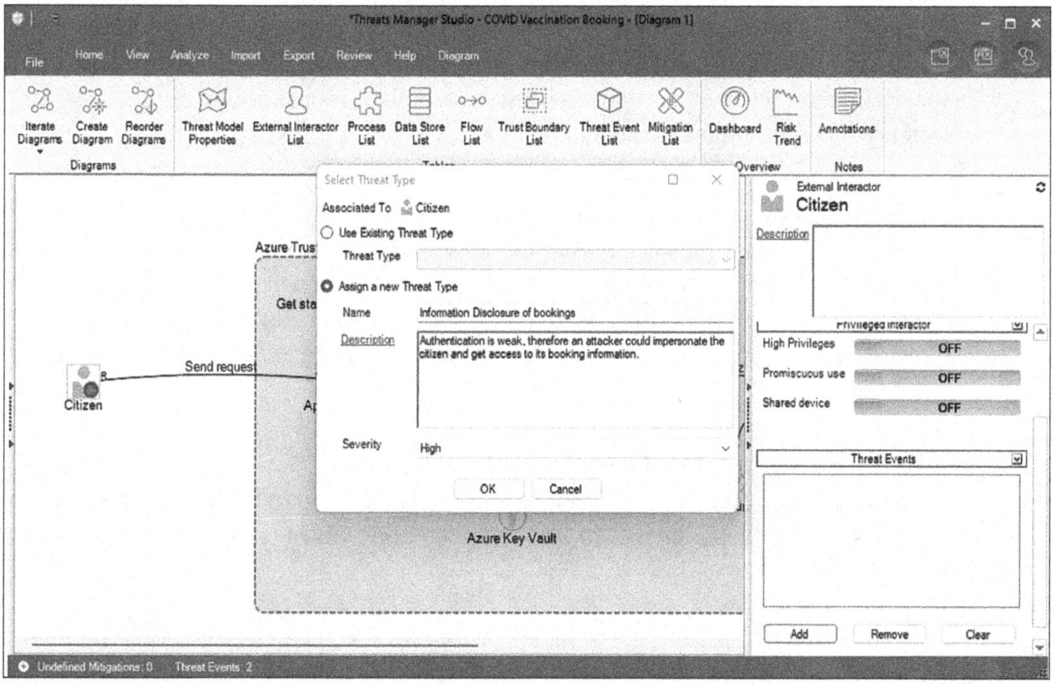

FIGURE 4-5 Creating a new threat.

Specifying the level of severity

As you have seen, when you specify the threat details, you must indicate its severity, which typically pertains to both its possible impact and the probability of its occurrence. The bug bar shown in Table 4-9 describes available options.

TABLE 4-9 Severity bug bar

Severity	Definition
Critical	Critical-level threats are related to the most important issues, both for the probability and potential impact. Critical threats have a high probability of causing a catastrophic failure of the solution and critical damage to the involved counterparts.
High	High-level threats are related to important issues both for their probability and potential impact. They have a significant probability of causing major damage to the solution and the involved counterparts.
Medium	Medium-level threats are related to average issues, both for their probability and the potential impact.
Low	Low-level threats are related to minor issues, both for their probability and their potential impact.
Info	You choose this threat level for mitigated threats that have a negligible probability of causing damage to the solution and involved counterparts.

> **Note** In reality, this bug bar is different from the one used in the current version of Threats Manager Studio. Whereas this bug bar associates severity with both impact and probability, that bug bar associates severity with impact only, which is wrong. See https://azsec.tech/kla for information on how to change the definition of the various severity options in your instance of Threats Manager Studio.

Given what you know about the solution, you are probably thinking you want to assign a severity of High or Critical to both identified threats. Our advice is to choose High. This is because although it is easy to attack a specific citizen, which makes it highly likely such an attack could occur, this is different from attacking the whole population. Moreover, while the attacker might be able to cause some damage to whatever citizen they attacked, this damage would not likely be catastrophic in nature.

> **Note** Ultimately, the level of severity you assign is arbitrary. You want to be prepared to defend your decision, but at the same time, if it differs from that of the architects, you must be open to their suggestions. Your work as a threat modeler must provide value to the stakeholders, not just to you.

Defining mitigations

Now you are ready to define mitigations for the threats you have identified. Recall that your clients have already rejected the use of MFA in favor of a less-secure method of authentication. However, just because they have dismissed this mitigation does not mean you should not include it in your threat model if you think it could play an important role. For the sake of example, let's add that mitigation now:

1. Click the **Citizen** shape in the diagram.

   Details about the selected object appear in the **Item Editor** to the right of the diagram.

2. In the **Threat Event** list, double-click the threat to which you want to add a mitigation—in this case, **Information Disclosure of Bookings**.

3. Click the **Add** button under the list of mitigations to open the **Associate a Mitigation to the Threat Event** dialog. (See Figure 4-6.)

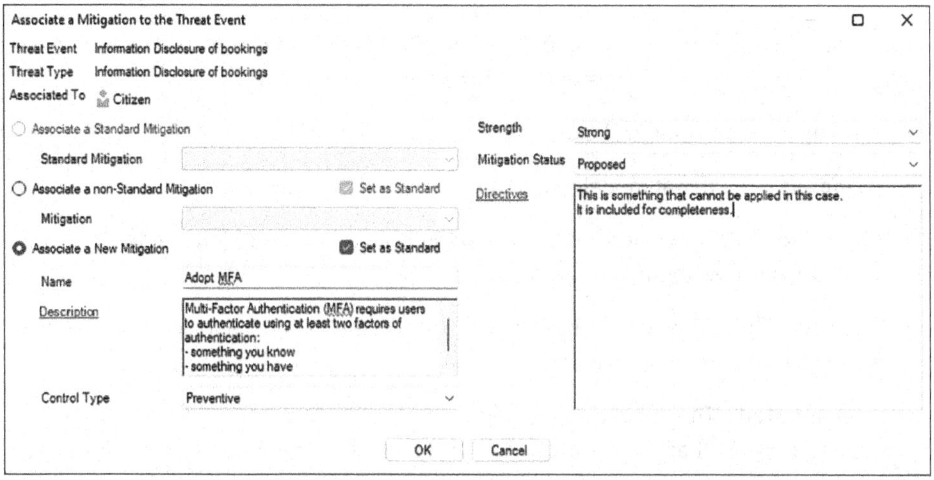

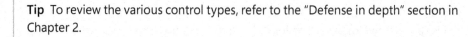

FIGURE 4-6 Creating a new mitigation.

4. You can choose to associate a standard mitigation, a nonstandard mitigation, or a new mitigation with the threat. For this exercise, select the **Associate a New Mitigation** option button.

5. Type a name for the new mitigation in the **Name** box and optionally a description in the **Description** box.

6. Open the **Control Type** drop-down list and choose a control type—in this case, **Preventive**.

> **Tip** To review the various control types, refer to the "Defense in depth" section in Chapter 2.

7. To indicate how effective the mitigation will be, open the **Strength** drop-down list and choose from the following options. Here, we have selected **Strong**.

- **Maximum**   The mitigation is as strong as it can possibly be and might be enough to address the threat.

- **Strong**   The mitigation is strong, but it might not be strong enough to address the threat.

- **Average**   The mitigation is of average strength. It might address the threat, but probably not enough.

- **Weak**   The mitigation is weak. Still, it will have a measurable impact on the threat.

- **Negligible**   The mitigation has no measurable impact on the threat.

8. To indicate the status of the mitigation, open the **Status** drop-down list and choose from the following options. Here, we have selected **Proposed**.

- **Existing**   The mitigation already exists.

- **Proposed**   The threat modeler has proposed the mitigation.

- **Approved**   The mitigation has been approved and is in the backlog, but there is no set date for when development will start.

- **Planned**   The mitigation has been planned, it is in the backlog, and an approximate date has been set for its implementation.

- **Implemented**   The mitigation has been implemented. You select this status when you are revising a system that has already been threat modeled. It allows you to identify mitigations implemented after a previous assessment.

9. Optionally, enter additional information about the recommendation in the **Directives** box.

Another possible mitigation for the authentication threat could be to add a registration procedure to the solution. So, the first time a citizen attempts to use the solution, they will be required to enter their personal information for identification purposes, like their tax ID number, name and surname, birth date, phone number, and (optionally) email address. From then on, anytime the citizen wants to use the solution, it will send a one-time password to the citizen's phone and email address (if configured). The citizen then uses their tax ID number as their username and the received one-time password to authenticate with the system. You can propose this mitigation using the same steps as before.

> **Note** These are just two of many possible mitigations. Another might involve requiring citizens to set their own passwords, but then you would need to safely store them (or better, their salted hashes!) somewhere. Typically, it is better to avoid storing information you do not need, so the other two mitigations might be better for our scenario.

Assumptions

This mitigation assumes that when a person registers with the solution, they will be a citizen, not an adversary. You want to track this assumption, and any others, by adding it to your threat model's assumption list. To access this list, click the **Threat Model Properties** button in Threats Manager Studio's **Home** ribbon.

Another typical assumption is that Azure Services are implemented securely because Microsoft is responsible for their security. This was discussed in Chapter 2, in the section "IaaS vs. PaaS vs. SaaS, and the shared responsibility." Typically, however, you cannot extend this assumption to third-party services if they are not precisely in scope for your analysis. For example, suppose an internal structure manages a third-party service on which you rely. You might assume this is secure because it is not something you can analyze as part of your threat model. But you cannot assume that a completely external service like the Citizen DB is secure, because it is a black box to you. So, you need to treat it as an external interactor.

Automatically identifying additional threats and mitigations

After you add all the threats you have identified using your ingenuity to your threat model, you can generate additional ones using an automated tool within Threats Manager Studio based on the template or templates you have imported. You should not underestimate the value of automatically generating threats and mitigations, because it prevents you from missing some of the more common ones. To do so, you simply click the **Generate Threat Events & Mitigations** button in the **Analyze** ribbon and click **OK** to confirm.

> **Tip** Some templates mark a few threats and mitigations as Top. This allows you to identify what typically matters the most. If you are working with a template that does this, the **Generate Threat Events & Mitigations** tool will ask you if you want to generate all threats and mitigations (click **Yes** in that case) or just the Top ones (click **No**). If your templates use the Top flag, the recommendation is to select **No** to generate only those threats; this typically saves up to two-thirds of the time normally required to create the threat model.

The automatic Generate Threat Events & Mitigations tool does not provide perfect results. You might find that some of the threats or mitigations it generates do not apply to your solution. For this reason, you should review the list of generated threats and mitigations and revise or remove any that do not apply before proceeding with your analysis. You do this using the Threat Event List and the Mitigation List, which you access from the **Home** ribbon.

Your next step is to assign a status to each mitigation. Fortunately, instead of doing this one mitigation at a time, you can assign a status to each type of mitigation; that status will then be applied to each mitigation of that type. By doing this for our example, you can reduce the number of objects you need to update from 131 to 47—an improvement of more than 64 percent. To do so, follow these steps:

1. Click the **Mitigation List** button in the **Home** ribbon.

2. Click the **Full Expand** button in the **Mitigation List** ribbon.

3. Right-click the first mitigation in the list and choose **Apply Status to all Instances** from the context menu that appears. (See Figure 4-7.)

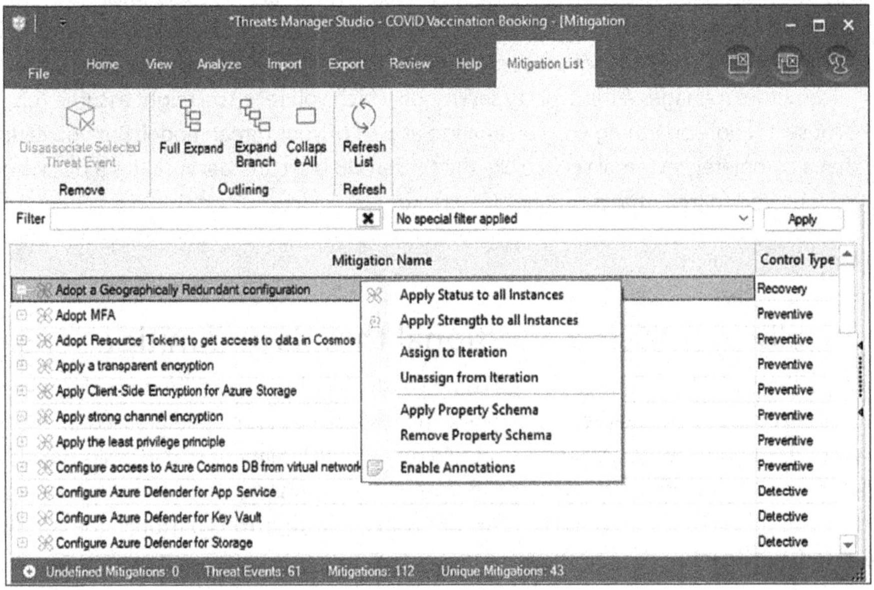

FIGURE 4-7 The context menu for the Mitigation List.

4. In the **Select the Status to Be Applied to All instances of This Mitigation** dialog, open the **Status** drop-down list and choose the status you want to apply. (If you are unsure, refer to the preceding section, "Defining mitigations," to review your status options.) Then click **OK**.

> **Note** If you want to assign the status to most, but not all, instances of a mitigation, you can easily do so. You just need to edit whichever mitigations should have a different status individually.

After that, you are ready to specify the severity of each of the threats identified by the Generate Threat Events & Mitigations tool. There is just one problem: threat events associated with mitigations whose status is Existing or Implemented will automatically have a lower severity than they do in your threat model, and you need to update the threat model to reflect this. Threats Manager Studio does not include a process to apply these changes automatically, but a feature in the tool's Quality Extension library does. This feature also allows you to approve each change before finalizing it.

To enable this feature, open the **File** menu and choose **Options**. Then, in the **Options** dialog, click **Quality**, select the **Enable Support for Calculated Severity** checkbox, and click **OK**. Then follow these steps:

1. In the **Review** ribbon, click the **Calculated Severity List** button.

   The list that appears shows all the threats whose assigned severity is different from the calculated one. See Figure 4-8.

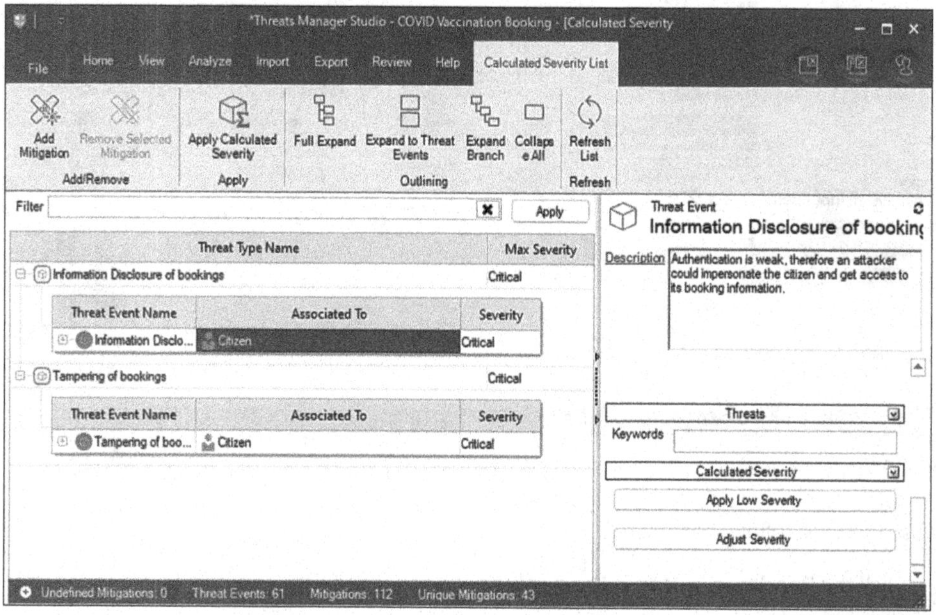

FIGURE 4-8 The Calculated Severity List showing two threat events with a calculated severity different from the assigned one.

2. Do one of the following:

   - For each threat with differing severity levels, apply the calculated severity by clicking the **Apply [Calculated Severity] Severity** button in the **Item Editor**. In Figure 4-8, the calculated severity is **Low**, so the button reads **Apply Low Severity**.

   - If the calculated severity is not right, you can adjust it by using the **Adjust Severity** button from the **Item Editor**.

   - To apply the calculated severity to all threats with differing severity levels, click the **Apply Calculated Severity** button in the **Calculated Severity List** ribbon. Then click the OK button to confirm.

Creating the roadmap

Threats Manager Studio offers a Roadmap tool, which you can use to define a possible distribution of recommended mitigations in three consecutive phases. Figure 4-9 shows an example.

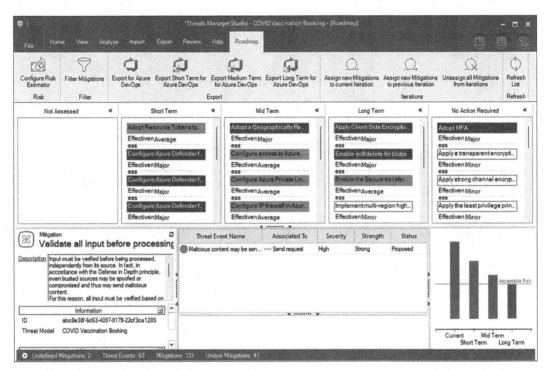

FIGURE 4-9 A sample roadmap.

To use this tool, follow these steps:

1. Click the **Roadmap** button in the **Analyze** ribbon.

   The roadmap that opens will have most of the defined mitigations listed in the **Not Assessed** column and a few others listed in the **No Action Required** column. All mitigations appear as blue rectangles with white text.

> **Note** The **No Action Required** column contains all the mitigations with a status of **Existing** or **Implemented**. They are already fully implemented, so nothing else is required.

Your next step is to evaluate the effectiveness of the mitigations and to define what represents an acceptable risk for the system. You do this using an estimator. At the time of this writing, there is only one estimator: the Bug Bar Residual Risk estimator.

2. Click the **Configure Risk Estimator** button in the **Roadmap** ribbon.

3. In the **Residual Risk Estimator Configuration** dialog (see Figure 4-10), enter the following information. Then click **OK**.

   - **Estimator**   Select **Big Bar Residual Risk Estimator**.

   - **Maximum Critical Severity Threat Events Count**   Set this to **0**.

- **Maximum High Severity Threat Events Count** Set this to **0**.

- **Maximum Medium Severity Threat Events Count** Set this to **10**.

- **Maximum Low Severity Threat Events Count** Set this to **50**.

- **Maximum Value** Set this to **100**. The values entered in the previous fields will be capped to the value specified here.

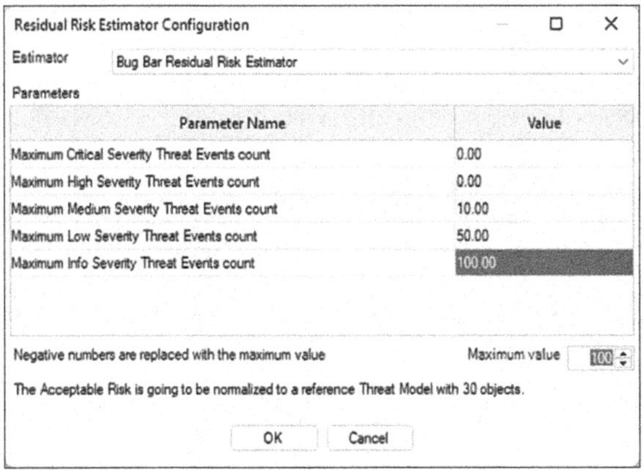

FIGURE 4-10 The Residual Risk Estimator Configuration dialog.

> **Note** After you configure the Residual Risk Estimator, the mitigations listed in the upper half of the Roadmap interface change color. Now each mitigation is color-coded based on its effectiveness. The effectiveness of each mitigation also appears in a label below its header.

4. In the main interface of the Roadmap tool, drag and drop each mitigation from the **Not Assessed** column into the desired target column.

The column you choose for each mitigation depends on various factors, such as its calculated effectiveness, its implementation, its operation cost, and whether it applies to one or more threats with Critical or High severity levels. The interface shows most of this information at a glance; it does not show the cost of the mitigation, however. The columns are as follows:

- **Short Term** This column is for the mitigations you propose to implement first, maybe in the first couple of sprints.

- **Mid Term** This column is for the mitigations you propose to implement after the ones in the Short Term column.

- **Long Term** This column is for the mitigations you propose to implement last.

- **No Action Required** Place in this column any mitigations you propose to ignore because they have already been fully implemented or because you do not want to recommend them.

As you drag and drop your mitigations, the chart in the bottom-right corner of the roadmap is updated to reflect how implementing each mitigation changes your estimated risk. For example, if you refer to Figure 4-9, you will see that the calculated risk for the Long Term phase is lower than the acceptable risk threshold (defined by the risk estimator parameters), and as a result, its column in the chart is green. This is a great result!

Using the dashboard

In addition to offering a roadmap to give you an overview of your mitigation plan, Threats Manager Studio also includes a dashboard, which reveals the solution's overall security posture. Figure 4-11 shows an example. To access the dashboard, simply click the **Dashboard** button in the **Home** ribbon.

FIGURE 4-11 The dashboard.

The dashboard provides a great tool on which to base discussions on the overall security of your solution with business stakeholders or to start a conversation with the security team. It provides many visual tools to communicate your security situation. Starting in the upper-left corner and moving clockwise, these tools are as follows:

- **Threat Types by Severity pie chart** This conveys the current security status.

- **Roadmap bar chart** This shows how the current situation could be improved.

- **Roadmap Threat Types by Severity pie charts**   This series of pie charts, which you view by clicking arrows on either side, shows the projected situation after the implementation of the short-term, mid-term, and long-term mitigations defined in the roadmap.

- **Highest Risks and Lowest Risks tables**   These tables list the threats that represent the highest and lowest risks, respectively.

- **Roadmap Details table**   This table shows the available mitigations for each phase of the roadmap.

- **Mitigations by Status pie chart**   This shows a distribution of mitigations by status.

Pushing selected mitigations into the backlog

The last step of this exercise involves interacting with DevOps systems to create work items in Azure DevOps that correspond to selected mitigations. In other words, you push these mitigations from Threats Manager Studio into the Azure DevOps backlog. This fundamental step makes your mitigations actionable and links the threat modeling experience with the DevOps process.

> **Note** For now, Threats Manager Studio supports only Azure DevOps. We assume you have a working knowledge of Azure DevOps. If necessary, you can refresh your knowledge here: https://azsec.tech/v3q.

To push selected mitigations from Threats Manager Studio into the Azure DevOps backlog, follow these steps:

1. Direct your web browser to Azure DevOps and locate the organization where the project to which you need to connect is published.

2. Create a personal access token, assign it Read and Write rights over work items, and create a copy of it. For more on personal access tokens, see https://azsec.tech/uon.

3. Open the Azure DevOps project and create a new Epic named **Threat Model**. You will use this as a parent work item in Threats Manager Studio.

> **Tip** Creating this parent work item as an Epic allows you to generate mitigation-related work items as features later. This is important because the implementation of the mitigations might span multiple sprints.

4. In Threats Manager Studio, click the **Connect** button in the **Analyze** ribbon.

5. In the **Connect to DevOps** dialog, choose **Azure DevOps Connector** from the **DevOps Connector** list.

6. In the **Server URL** box, enter the URL for the organization in the format https://dev.azure.com/ [organization_name].

7. Specify the personal access token you created earlier in the **Access Token** box.

8. Click the **Load** button. Threats Manager Studio loads a list of connected projects in Azure DevOps.

9. Select the desired project and click **OK**.

> **Note** Threats Manager Studio saves the personal access token in the Registry, in a location available only to you. It is also encrypted with DPAPI so that only you can read it.

After you successfully link the threat model to the DevOps project, Threats Manager Studio enables all the buttons for DevOps in the Analyze ribbon except the Mitigations Kanban button. You need to enable the Mitigations Kanban, which you will use to push selected mitigations into your Azure DevOps backlog.

10. Click the **Configure** button in the **Analyze** ribbon.

11. In the **DevOps Configuration** dialog, enter the following information, and click **Close**. See Figure 4-12.

   - **Parent**   Type the first three letters of the parent work item (in this case, **thr**). Then choose the full name of the parent work item from the list that appears—in our case, **Threat Model**.

> **Tip** If you cannot select the parent work item with your mouse, use the arrows on your keyboard.

   - **Parent Item Type**   This should automatically reflect the item type you assigned earlier (Epic).

   - **Item Type**   For this example, choose **Feature**.

   - **Tag**   Optionally, enter a tag, or leave this as is. The default is **ThreatModeling**.

   - **States**   Review the states in this table. Available states for the selected item type appear on the left, while the corresponding states supported by Threats Manager Studio appear on the right.

> **Tip** In most cases, the states are automatically determined. When this is not possible, the right column will contain a value of **Unknown**. Threats Manager Studio does not display mitigations having a status of Unknown in the Mitigations Kanban.

- **Fields** Optionally, edit this list using the **Add** and **Remove** buttons just below it. For more information, see https://azsec.tech/viu.

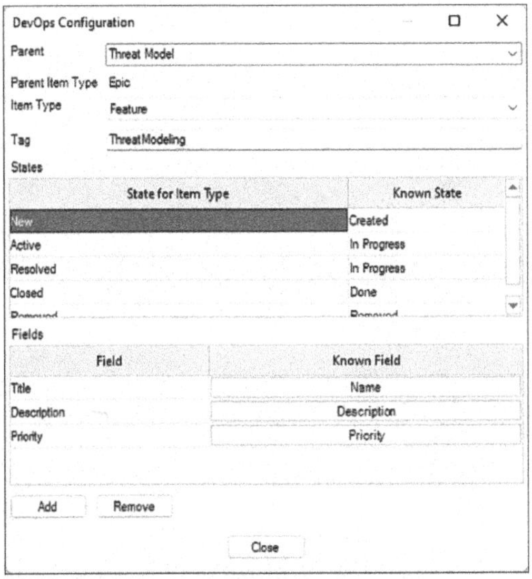

FIGURE 4-12 The DevOps Configuration dialog.

The Mitigations Kanban button is now enabled. Now you are ready to push the mitigations in your threat model to your Azure DevOps backlog.

12. Click the **Mitigations Kanban** button.
13. In the Mitigation Kanban interface, drag and drop a mitigation in the **Unknown** column to any other column—in this case, the **Created** column.
14. Switch to Azure DevOps and check your project. Notice that a feature with the same name as your mitigation has been created in the Threat Model Epic.
15. Open the mitigation (feature) in Azure DevOps and change its status to **Active** (to assign it to yourself), type a comment in the **Discussion** box, and click **Save & Close**.
16. Back in Threats Manager Studio, click the **Synchronize** button in the **DevOps** ribbon.

    The mitigation moves from the Created column to the In Progress column.
17. Click the mitigation.

Notice in the lower-left corner of the Mitigations Kanban interface that the mitigation's status has changed from **Proposed** to **Planned** and that the comment you entered in the Discussion box in step 15 now appears in the lower-right corner. (See Figure 4-13.)

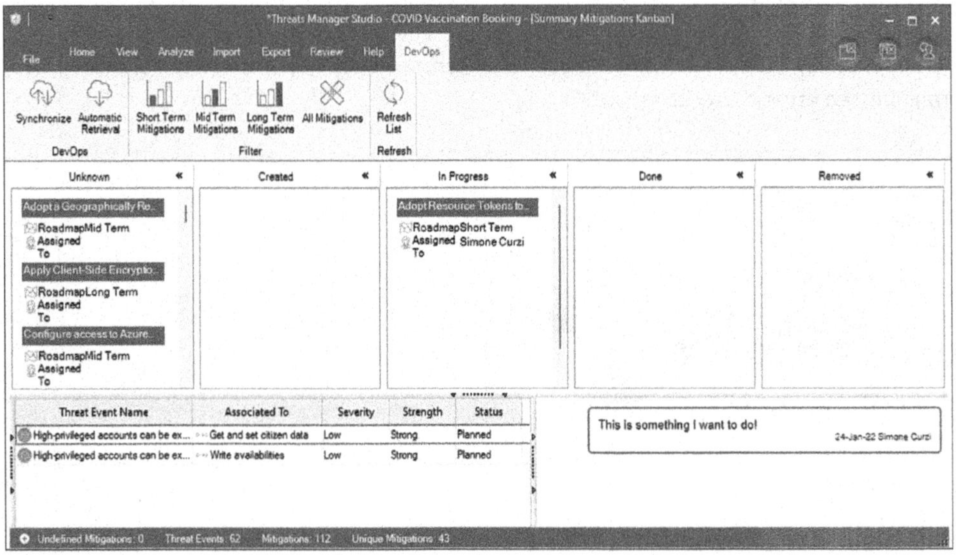

FIGURE 4-13 The Mitigations Kanban.

> **Tip** The Mitigations Kanban and DevOps synchronization are particularly powerful when linked to the Calculated Severity features. Together, they allow you to automatically update the status of each mitigation as the team implements it. At that point, updating the severity of the affected threats with the Calculated Severity List becomes an easy task.

> **Note** You have learned much about how to threat model using Threats Manager Studio, but there is still much to learn!

Summary

This chapter touched on a lot of different topics. It began with a discussion of threat modeling and analyzed Microsoft's STRIDE approach. It then asked and answered essential questions around threat modeling in harmony with DevOps (which is how most development teams implement cloud solutions). After that, it analyzed a few open source threat modeling tools to help you identify one that satisfies your requirements. Finally, it showed you how to threat model a real-life system using Threats Manager Studio.

This chapter concludes our series on the basic concepts of secure design. The next chapter discusses how to secure specific aspects of our solutions, starting with the concepts of identity, authentication, and authorization.

## CHAPTER 5

Identity, authentication, and authorization

After completing this chapter, you will be able to:

- Understand basic identity, authentication, and authorization concepts in Azure.

- Understand when best to use various identity, authentication, and authorization methods.

- Understand the basics of OpenID Connect and OAuth2.

- Understand the Microsoft identity platform.

- Understand security best practices when using the Microsoft identity platform.

Identity, authentication, and authorization through a security lens

Identity, authentication, and authorization are critical security controls. This chapter takes a deep dive into these topics from a design and development viewpoint, examining them through a security lens rather than a pure identity lens. Security is missing from most developer-oriented identity documentation. This documentation rarely describes the security implications of the various moving parts that make up the world of identity.

This chapter covers a great deal about identity that you might not need to know. This is because Microsoft offers a set of libraries—the Microsoft Authentication Library—that does most of the heavy lifting for you. However, developers are intellectually curious. We like to understand why things are the way they are and how they work. So, while we focus on pragmatics in this chapter, we do cover more ground to give you a better appreciation for how identity works.

> **Real-world experience: Identity and security**
>
> All three of us have had meetings with customer security teams during which the topic of discussion moves to Azure Active Directory (AD), user accounts, and authentication. At this point, the security team often taps out and asks for the identity team. Admittedly, identity is not a core security principle, but it is a critical part of your overall security posture. The best security teams place security and identity under a single, multidisciplined team, not two disjointed areas of expertise that do not talk to one another.

> **Important** The network is no longer the only security boundary. Identity is now an equally important boundary.

Authentication vs. authorization vs. identity

This chapter is broken into three main sections, covering identity, authentication, and authorization. This section briefly defines each of these.

Authentication (abbreviated as AuthN) is the act of something or someone—often called a *principal* in security parlance—proving who or what they are to something else. In other words, it is when a person, application, or device proves they are who or what they claim to be using some form of credential. This is something the principal knows (like a key or a password), something it has (like a cellphone or a hardware token), or something it is (a physical aspect of the principal, like an iris or fingerprint).

Authorization (abbreviated as AuthZ) is what principals, including users and apps, are allowed to do. Once a system or service authenticates the principal, permissions are used to enforce whatever authorization policy is in place. *Permissions* is a broad term that could include permissions (obviously), roles, access control lists, and privileges, depending on the environment or operating system. A permission might range from allowing a principal to view the contents of a file to allowing the principal to create new Azure resources.

Identity, sometimes spelled with a capital *I* in the context of security, is defined by *Merriam-Webster* as "the distinguishing character or personality of an individual." In this context, it represents the properties characterizing a digital persona associated with a user or process. In other words, the identity defines a user and includes information used to perform AuthN and AuthZ.

When discussing identity, you typically must consider how it is managed. Identity access management (IAM) is the set of policies and management used throughout the authentication and authorization lifecycle. This chapter does not cover policies, governance, and management, but it does focus on the security implications of the use of two protocols, OpenID Connect and OAuth2, for authentication and authorization.

Modern identity and access management

Modern identity is an umbrella term that covers authentication and authorization using modern and open protocols. A hallmark of modern identity is that authentication and authorization are often the work of another service, called an *identity provider*, and not something you, as an application designer or developer, need to worry about.

This offers many security advantages, including the fact that your code need not deal with user account information including passwords and authentication policies such as multifactor authentication (MFA) or detecting potentially suspect logins. It can also aid with compliance requirements, such as GDPR, which is covered in Chapter 8, "Compliance and risk programs."

Modern identity does not lock you in to a specific vendor. This is because its protocols are open standards such as OpenID Connect, OAuth2, and SAML, which are discussed in this chapter. Moreover, modern identity natively and securely supports the "new normal" work-from-home paradigm. The "access management" part of IAM refers to the governance, policies, and lifecycle of managing identities.

> **Tip** This book focuses on a developer audience. However, the topic of identity is so important to securing modern cloud applications that you cannot lose sight of the role of your security operations team (SecOps). Microsoft has created a must-read on this subject titled "Azure Active Directory Security Operations Guide for Applications," available at https://azsec.tech/secops.

Identity: OpenID Connect and OAuth2 fundamentals

Before we explain OpenID Connect and OAuth2, we need to discuss why they are important and what problem they solve. Today, OpenID Connect and OAuth2 are the cornerstone protocols used for modern identity solutions.

Suppose you use an app to send messages to people, and the app asks for your consent to read your contacts in your email service. In years gone by, you would have to give the app your username and password for your email service. Clearly, no one in their right mind would do that today, in part because we have better technology: OpenID Connect and OAuth2.

OAuth2 is designed to delegate access to resources using HTTP (over TLS) requests and responses without disclosing the user's credentials to any other service other than the authentication provider. In the case of Azure, this is Azure AD. In other words, you can grant access to an app without providing your credentials to the app. Instead, the app obtains a token that grants specific access to resources—again, without knowing your credentials. This token is valid only for a specific time, which could be up to 28 hours for Azure AD.

In our imaginary scenario, here is what happens:

1. The user (resource owner) opens their message-sending app (client) to send messages to various contacts.

2. The app sends a request to the authorization server to access contacts on behalf of the user.

3. The authorization server prompts the user for their credentials. This is because the app asked to act on behalf of the user, so the authorization server needs to know who the user is.

4. The authorization server prompts the user for the user's consent to allow the app to work on the user's behalf.

5. When that is successful, the authorization server generates a token allowing the client application the ability to read the user's contacts.

Figure 5-1 shows an abstract view of the process.

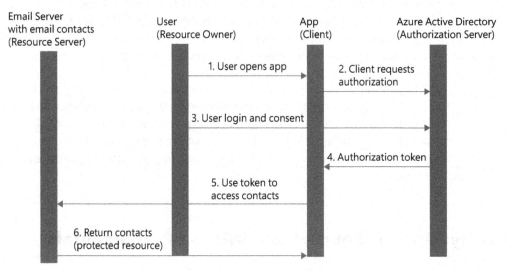

FIGURE 5-1 A generic view of how OAuth2 allows access to protected resources.

In this scenario, the user does not log into the app. Rather, the app asks for an access token, from which it cannot get the user's info. In fact, the app might not even care about the user logging in, as long as it can access the resource on behalf of the user.

> **Note** The user is called the *resource owner* in Figure 5-1 because the protected resource—in this case, the user's contacts—belong to the user. Also, *client* refers to the code that wants to access the protected resource. Many information systems refer to the client as the user, but this is not the case in the OAuth2 world.

> **Note** We are getting ahead of ourselves a little, but the end-to-end process shown in Figure 5-1 is a generic view of how OAuth2 works. The different roles interacting with each other over HTTPS is called a *flow*. OAuth2 has a small number of distinct flows that fit into different scenarios depending on the roles and environment. Some are simple, like implicit flow, and some more complex, like authorization code flow with PKCE.

The important part of this is that the email server and the app never see the user's credentials. Instead, when the authorization server—in this case, Azure AD—validates the user's credentials, it creates a token that includes information like the following:

- The user's ID
- When the token was issued
- When the token becomes valid and when it expires
- Who the token is intended for
- The scope of what is allowed (for example, read contacts)

The client application passes the token to the messaging service, which in turn passes it to the email service. The email service then validates the token is correct and returns the contacts to the messaging service. In this scenario, the messaging service never sees the user's credentials and is restricted to what operations it can do

You use OAuth2 every day

You can see this in action when you log in to https://portal.azure.com. When you enter your credentials, you will notice that the URL in the address bar is no longer the Azure Portal. Instead, it is something like https://login.microsoftonline.com/organizations/oauth2/v2.0/authorize. This is an OAuth2 endpoint for Azure AD.

After you correctly enter your credentials and Azure AD validates them (as well as applying any other login requirements, such as MFA or conditional access policies), you are redirected to the Azure Portal. At no point does the Azure Portal have your credentials. It does, however, have a token from Azure AD that allows the portal to access Azure resources on your behalf.

We are going to come straight out and say it: low-level OAuth2 is complex. *Incredibly* complex. In fact, it is so complex that you really should not concern yourself with the subtle nuances of the protocol. The OAuth2 rabbit hole goes deep quickly. So, rather than explain everything there is to know about OAuth2 and OpenID Connect, we will explain the protocols at a high level, point out potential security issues, and identify some best practices. As we go, we will also need to explain a few things:

- OpenID Connect and OAuth2

- Application registration

- Microsoft Authentication Library

- OAuth2 roles

- Flows

- Client types

- Tokens

- Scopes, permissions, and consent

- Anatomy of a JWT

- Using modern authentication in your Azure applications

OpenID Connect and OAuth2

When asked the question, "How do you authenticate users?" we have heard more than one person respond by answering, "We use OAuth2." That is not a correct answer, because OAuth2 is an authorization protocol, not an authentication protocol. For its part, OpenID Connect is an authentication layer on top of OAuth2. It is one of many authentication protocols available for applications. OAuth2 does not require your application to use OpenID Connect for authentication, but the two are often used together.

OAuth2 concerns itself with issuing and using tokens, which are time-gated blobs that represent claims. These claims can be used by services to determine whether a principal can perform actions or not. Incredibly, the format of these tokens is left to the implementor. The Microsoft identity platform uses the JSON Web Token (JWT) format, pronounced *jot*; it is commonly used for OAuth2. Technically, a JWT is a JSON Web Signature (JWS) that uses a digital signature to prevent tampering and prove authenticity. We will discuss JWTs in more detail later in the chapter.

 Important   OAuth2 tokens are treated as credentials and are therefore sensitive. So, TLS must be used by all communication channels employed to transfer the tokens.

Important   Because OAuth2 tokens can be any format, depending on the identity provider, the client should treat them as opaque and not look at the contents.

In their book *OAuth2 in Action*, authors Justin Richer and Antonio Sanso offer an excellent definition of OAuth2: "OAuth 2.0 is a delegation protocol, a means of letting someone who controls a resource allow a software application to access that resource on their behalf without impersonating them." We highly recommend this book if you want to obtain a deep understanding of the technical aspects of OAuth2.

What about SAML?

The Security Assertion Markup Language (SAML) is used to provide authentication for enterprise single sign-on environments. Rather than using JSON payloads (discussed later) like OpenID Connect, SAML uses XML payloads.

SAML authentication is frequently used with Active Directory Federation Services (AD FS), so it is often employed in enterprise applications. In contrast, OpenID Connect is commonly used for apps that are purely in the cloud, such as mobile apps, web apps, and web APIs. For the most part, Azure and Azure AD use OpenID Connect and OAuth2 rather than SAML. You can learn more about SAML and Azure AD at https://azsec.tech/saml.

Application registration

Before you can write any application code that uses OAuth2, you must register the application that will contain the code. You perform this process in Azure AD.

Now, we want to get this straight, because it can be a point of confusion: the phrase *app registration* is a misnomer. When you register an application, you are not dealing with code; rather, you are providing configuration information about the application so the application code can support OAuth2 correctly. In other words, when you register your app, it is configured to trust security tokens issued to it by the Microsoft identity platform. This is how an app tells Azure AD that the app will trust tokens from Azure AD.

When you register your app in Azure AD, the Microsoft identity platform assigns it certain values by default, while others can be configured based on the application's type. Two important app registration settings are:

- **Application (client) ID** This value, often a GUID, is assigned to your app by the Microsoft identity platform. The client ID uniquely identifies your app and is included in tokens issued by the platform. This ID is not a secret and does not need to be secured.

- **Redirect URI** The authorization server uses a redirect URI to direct the resource owner's user-agent (web browser or mobile app) to another destination after completing their interaction—for example, after the end user authenticates with the authorization server. Not all client types use redirect URIs.

Your app's registration also holds information about the authentication and authorization endpoints you will use in your code to obtain ID and access tokens. You can see these endpoints by clicking the Endpoints option when viewing an app registration.

Microsoft Authentication Library

The Microsoft Authentication Library (MSAL) enables developers to obtain tokens from the Microsoft identity platform to authenticate users and access secure web APIs. MSAL is used by Microsoft products such as Office 365. This might sound a little silly, but if you simply use MSAL, you are 90 percent on your way to building a client solution that takes advantage of modern identity, which is why we will use it in our sample application.

Tip The following website explains all the current authentication libraries and SDKs available for various Microsoft technologies, with a strong emphasis on MSAL: https://azsec.tech/libs.

With MSAL, all the hard work, bug fixes, and subtle protocol issues are handled for you. When the OAuth2 protocol is updated and new features are made available, MSAL is updated too, by people who understand OAuth2 well. For example, near the time of this writing, it was announced that OAuth2 will soon support proof of possession (PoP) to help protect against token replay. When this happens, MSAL will be updated accordingly.

MSAL can target many common programming languages and environments, including the following:

- Android
- Angular
- Go
- iOS and macOS
- Java
- JavaScript
- .NET
- Node
- Python
- React

MSAL targets clients or applications behaving as clients. For example, a web browser running Angular acts as a client when it accesses a server. Similarly, in the case of an Azure Function accessing Microsoft Graph, the function acts as a client.

 Note In OAuth2, a user is different from a client. A user is a human being, and a client is the software used by a human being or some other principal, such as a process.

Active Directory Authentication Library

An older library, Active Directory Authentication Library (ADAL), integrates with Azure AD only. However, ADAL has been deprecated in favor of MSAL. MSAL integrates with Azure AD, Microsoft personal accounts, and Azure AD Business to Customer (B2C), which can authenticate users using other identity providers such as Facebook, Google, and Twitter. So, you should not use ADAL, and if you do use ADAL, you must migrate to MSAL as soon as possible. You can read about the differences between ADAL and MSAL at https://azsec.tech/htc.

MSAL supports continuous access evaluation (CAE). What this means is if the user's situation changes—for example, malware is detected on their laptop—access to a protected resource can then be denied quickly. Here is another example: Suppose an employee logs in to their work laptop at home and accesses a protected resource. Then, the employee puts their laptop to sleep, packs it up, and takes it to a coffee shop, where they continue working while sipping on a latte. Because their situation changed, they might be prompted to log on again and maybe even satisfy a second authentication factor such as a phone app challenge.

MSAL also supports multiple application types—for example, web apps, mobile apps, native apps, daemons, and services. This is important because different application types have different security implications and use different OAuth2 flows, which we will explain in the "Flows" section.

Tip If you cannot use MSAL—for example, you use a programming language not supported by MSAL—you should use an actively maintained library instead. For options, see https://openid.net/developers/certified/.

Now, let's look at some sample JavaScript code. The following code creates an MSAL object. As you can see here, MSAL performs an immense amount of heavy lifting so you do not have to, in a small amount of code.

```
const msalConfig = {
    auth: {
        clientId: "d1361825-38d2-413a-9d2c-00e79a3a9221",
        authority: "https://login.microsoftonline.com/common",
        redirectUri: "https://localhost:4242",
}, <snip>
const myMSALObj = new msal.PublicClientApplication(msalConfig);
```

The `msalConfig` section shown here is important. (In this example, it is abbreviated.) It includes the following parameters:

- **clientId** This is the application (client) ID value in the Azure Portal for this application. You can find it in Azure AD by selecting App Registrations and then the name of the application.

> **Important** `clientId` is not a secret. We cannot stress this enough: the client ID does not need to be protected. This is different from a confidential client's credential, which *is* a secret and must be protected. We discuss confidential clients in the "Flows" section later in the chapter.

- **authority** This is the cloud instance. The associated URL is a discovery URL used by Azure AD to locate information about your application and will change depending on the types of users you are signing in. Here, the URL contains /common, which indicates a work, school, or personal Microsoft account. Other options are as follows:

  - **/organizations** This is for work and school accounts.

  - **/consumers** This is for personal Microsoft accounts (Xbox, Outlook.com, and so on).

  - **/<tenant>** This is the GUID for the tenant. It logs in users of a specific organization only.

- **redirectUri** This is the URI to return after the access token is issued. This example uses `local-host` as the redirect URI, which indicates that this code is not production ready. When the code is ready for production, this parameter is replaced with a real URI.

> **Tip** For a full explanation of `msalConfig`, see https://azsec.tech/cfg. (Note that much of this data is found when you create an application registration.) Also, a complete explanation of all the configuration options is available here: https://azsec.tech/kj2.

Real-world experience: Debugging OpenID Connect and OAuth2

We all know that sometimes things go wrong in code. Thankfully, MSAL—especially MSAL JS—has excellent debug logging. If things are not working as expected in your client MSAL code, open the Developer Tools page (press Ctrl+Shift+I in Edge) and click the Console tab. You will find any errors or warnings from MSAL in the console.

The preceding code also instantiates a `PublicClientApplication` class. This is because the code is JavaScript running in a browser. As such, it cannot securely store secrets, so it cannot be a confidential client. If you look at the MSAL JavaScript source code, you will notice there is no confidential client support, because supporting a confidential client is not possible.

After you create the MSAL object, you implement the following code to sign in the user:

```
const loginRequest = {
    scopes: ["User.Read"]
};
myMSALObj.loginPopup(loginRequest)
  .then(handleResponse)
  .catch(error => {
    console.error(error);

  });
```

Finally, you use code like this to obtain access tokens:

```
request.account = myMSALObj.getAccountByUsername(username);

return myMSALObj.acquireTokenSilent(request)
    .catch(error => {
        console.warn("silent token acquisition fails. acquiring token using popup");
        if (error instanceof msal.InteractionRequiredAuthError) {
            // fallback to interaction when silent call fails
            return myMSALObj.acquireTokenPopup(request)
                .then(tokenResponse => {
                    console.log(tokenResponse);
                    return tokenResponse;
                }).catch(error => {
                    console.error(error);
                });
        } else {
            console.warn(error);
        }

    });
```

Note For .NET, MSAL is implemented in `Microsoft.Identity.Client`.

Tip A more complete version of this sample is available at https://azsec.tech/jsx, and the source code and documentation for the JavaScript MSAL library can be found at https://azsec.tech/jsm. If you are new to MSAL, consider reading the article "Overview of the Microsoft Authentication Library (MSAL)" at https://azsec.tech/msal, as this provides a broad overview of its use.

Where is your application hosted?

This might seem obvious, but your application code—regardless of whether it is mobile, native, a web API, or something else—does not need to be hosted in Azure. For example, suppose you write an application in C# that runs on your users' desktops and accesses Cosmos DB in Azure. Under the hood, this application would perform all the appropriate authentication and authorization using MSAL and Azure AD.

OAuth2 roles

The OAuth2 "ceremony" involves various parties, or roles:

- **Resource owner**   This is often someone who grants a client application the ability to access data that belongs to them. For example, suppose Toby grants an email client read-only access to his email. In this case, the resource is email, and the resource owner is Toby.

- **Resource server**   This is a protected resource. Continuing with the example of Toby's email, an email server is the resource server, and it is accessible using REST APIs.

- **Client**   This is an application attempting to access resources on a resource server. The application could be a web browser used by a user, a VM using a Managed Identity, and so on.

- **Authorization server**   This authenticates the client and issues tokens for access to resource servers. In our Azure example, Azure AD is the authorization server. Authorization servers are often called *identity providers*.

Flows

OAuth2 defines various interactions among the roles defined in the preceding section, and these interactions are called *flows*. An example of a flow is the interaction between a client application and an authorization server. When using Azure AD, the result of these flows is a JWT that can be used to grant some level of access to a resource. Note that we say *a resource* and not *resources*. We will explain the distinction in the upcoming section on tokens.

> **Note** You will often see references to *grant flows*. The terms *flow* and *grant flow* are interchangeable.

There are various types of OAuth2 flows. Each flow has the same set of goals: to obtain a token that represents a set of permissions to act on behalf of a user, and to perform one or more tasks on the user's behalf. Obtaining a token involves two steps:

1. Getting the token from an identity provider such as Azure AD or Facebook

2. Using the token to perform a task on behalf of the user—for example, to read a user's email address or, in the case of Facebook, to post an image to the user's timeline

The various flows supported by OAuth2 vary only in the first step (getting the token). This is because different application types and deployment scenarios dictate which flows will work and which will not.

Three key OAuth2 flows are as follows:

- **Authorization code flow**   This is presently the most secure, and therefore the preferred, flow because it does not expose credentials to any other processes or services (except the OAuth2 identity provider—for example, Azure AD—which already has your password identifier and is trusted). You can learn more about it here: https://azsec.tech/acf.

Proof of Key for Code Exchange

Authorization code flows can be made even more secure through the use of an extension called Proof of Key for Code Exchange (PKCE), pronounced *pixie*. MSAL automatically uses PKCE whenever it can.

PKCE helps mitigate cross-site request forgery (CSRF) and other injection attacks, especially against public clients (explained in the upcoming section about client types). To do so, it uses an ephemeral client-generated secret called a *code verifier*. PKCE is defined in RFC 7363, located here: https://azsec.tech/pkce.

■ **Client credentials flow** This flow is often used when two services, such as two daemons, talk to each other. It permits the client web service to use its own credentials to authenticate when calling another web service. These clients are called *confidential clients* because they can store and protect credentials. For more information about this flow, see https://azsec.tech/ccf.

Warning Never publish client credentials flow credentials in your source code, embed them in web pages, or hard-code them in a client application that runs on user's devices or machines.

Tip You can also use an X.509 certificate and private key instead of a shared secret as a client application's credential. You should use X.509 certificates and private keys in production rather than shared secrets.

■ **On-behalf-of (OBO) flow** If you are familiar with Windows impersonation, the OBO flow is a close, but more secure, cousin. (We say more secure because in Windows, impersonation does not constrain access. So, for example, if Cheryl connects to a Windows service that impersonates her, the service can do anything that Cheryl can do on that machine.) OBO is used when an application calls a service or web API, which in turn needs to call another service or web API. The idea is to propagate the delegated user identity and permissions through the request chain. At the time of this writing, the OBO flow works only for user accounts, not for service principals. For more information about the OBO flow, see https://azsec.tech/obo.

Note OBO cannot be used with Azure AD B2C. For more information, see https://azsec.tech/s8z.

In addition to these flows, there are three flows that should *not* be used because they pose a security risk:

- **Implicit flow**   Invented more than a decade ago, the implicit flow is used with web browser clients. This flow has always been known to be weak, and in recent years, as web browser security technology has evolved, it has become obsolete and will soon be deprecated. The problem with the implicit flow is that when it is used, token information, which is sensitive data, is visible in the browser's address bar. You might not think this is a big deal until you consider that the data in the address bar will end up in the browser history, is potentially accessible to browser plug-ins, and could be synced to another browser on the user's phone or another computer. This means the company performing the synchronization has the data, too! You can learn more about the implicit flow here: https://azsec.tech/imp.

> **Note** With all this said, there is one scenario where implicit flow is OK. You can read about it here: https://azsec.tech/impok.

- **Resource owner password credentials flow (ROPC)**   Unlike, say, the application code flow, the ROPC flow exposes user credentials to potentially untrustworthy intermediate processes. This flow, which is supported only by the MSAL .NET library, carries risks that are not present in other flows and therefore requires a very high degree of trust. The ROPC flow also does not trigger Azure AD conditional access. In most scenarios, more secure alternatives are available and recommended. You can find out more about the ROPC flow here: https://azsec.tech/ropc.

> **Note** In general, we believe the ROPC flow should never be used. However, as with implicit flow, there is one scenario where ROPC is an option: for automated testing in nonproduction environments. For more information, see https://azsec.tech/ropcok.

- **Device code flow**   This flow is used to support clients that might not have rich input methods—for example, a smart TV. However, device code flow is subject to a new class of phishing attacks, described here: https://azsec.tech/6af. So, you should not use the device code flow unless there is a specific reason to do so and no other flow will work. For more on the device code flow, see https://azsec.tech/dcf.

> **Note** For more detailed information about all the flows discussed in this section, see https://azsec.tech/flows/.

Table 5-1 shows which flows apply to which application types. Note that this table does include the aforementioned flows that represent a security risk.

TABLE 5-1 Various application types and supported OAuth2 flows

Application Type	Supported OAuth2 Flow
Single-page application (SPA)	Authorization code with PKCE Implicit
Web app that signs in users	Authorization code
Web app that signs in users and accesses other web APIs	Authorization code
Desktop app that accesses other web APIs	Authorization code with PKCE Resource owner password
Browserless app	Device code
Mobile app	Authorization code with PKCE Resource owner password
Linux daemon or Windows service accessing other web APIs	Client credentials
API application acting on behalf of a client to access other APIs	On-behalf-of

Client types

OAuth2 divides clients into two categories:

- **Public**   These include web pages, such as single-page applications (SPAs), written using frameworks like Angular JavaScript, vanilla-JavaScript, or TypeScript. Mobile code is also a public client. Public clients cannot protect their secrets. If you refer to the list of supported flows and application types in Table 5-1, you will notice that the public clients use PKCE to provide more security.

- **Confidential**   These clients are usually server-based services, such as web server code. Because these services are not directly accessible by untrusted users, configuration data and process memory cannot be viewed. So, they can securely store secrets, including a secret treated as a credential.

Note Do not confuse the use of the term *confidential* in the context of OAuth2 with confidentiality computing (discussed in detail in Chapter 11, "Confidential computing"). They bear no resemblance to each other at all.

Tip For a full explanation of client types, see https://azsec.tech/conf.

Tokens

There are three common types of tokens, which you will hear about all the time:

- **ID tokens** OpenID Connect generates these after successful authentication.

- **Access tokens** OAuth2 generates these and gives them to the client so the client can use them to access resources on behalf of the resource owner. Access is often performed through APIs exposed by a resource server—for example, REST APIs used to access Key Vault. Access tokens are opaque to clients, but the resource server must verify the token and look inside it to determine access. An access token can access only a single resource type. For example, an access token used to access Key Vault cannot be used to access Azure Storage.

- **Refresh tokens** Also given to the client, these tokens are used to obtain new copies of ID tokens and access tokens once they are close to expiry. Refresh tokens can also be used to get multiple access tokens from a single authentication event. For example, you might get an access token for Key Vault and another for Azure SQL Database without having to log on multiple times.

As noted, access and refresh tokens are opaque to clients.

> **Note** We will cover tokens in more depth later in this chapter, in the section "Anatomy of a JWT."

Scopes, permissions, and consent

OAuth2 allows the use of scopes to achieve much more granular control of access rights. A *scope* is a permission or a set of permissions for accessing resources.

There are two main types of permissions for applications:

- **Delegated permissions** These enable a client application to act on behalf of a user. Note that with delegated permissions, the user's permission will also be used to determine whether the app can access the resource.

- **Application permissions** These allow an application to use its own identity—for example, a Managed Identity—rather than that of a signed-in user.

You can see these in the Azure Portal when you select an app's permission type.

Different resources have different permissions or scopes. Some of these are sensitive in nature, and using them requires administrative consent. For example, Microsoft Graph has many scopes, including scopes that pertain to the ability to read devices. These include the following:

- **Device.Read** This scope allows the app to read the current user's devices but does not require administrative consent because the user is using the app to read their own devices.

- **Device.Read.All**   With this scope, the app can read all devices of all users, which the user can read. This is clearly an elevated request, and as such, it requires administrative consent.

When a user uses an application for the first time, they are presented with a list of permissions and are prompted to grant or deny access requests. The list of permissions comes from the app itself. If you recall from the "Microsoft Authentication Library" section, the login scopes section of our sample application code was as follows:

```
const loginRequest = {
    scopes: ["User.Read"]
};
```

In this example, the consent screen would look like the one shown in Figure 5-2.

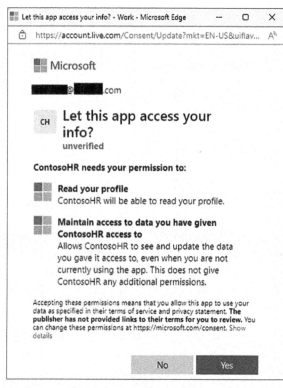

FIGURE 5-2 An example of a consent screen.

Although you can configure the desired permissions in the Azure Portal, what matters is whether the user consents or an administrator consents to a permission (or not). For example, in the screen shown in Figure 5-3, the application indicates its intention to request the Microsoft Graph permission User.ReadWrite.

Configured permissions

Applications are authorized to call APIs when they are granted permissions by users/admins as p
all the permissions the application needs. Learn more about permissions and consent

+ Add a permission   ✓ Grant admin consent for Michael Howard

API / Permissions name	Type	Description
∨ Microsoft Graph (1)		
User.ReadWrite	Delegated	Read and write access to user profile

FIGURE 5-3 Configuring permissions in the Azure Portal for an app registration.

However, our sample application makes the following request at runtime:

```
const loginRequest = {
    scopes: ["User.Read"]
};
```

So, the user has already consented to the User.Read scope as part of the login.

A little later in the sample application, the code wants to read your email. The code that forces the prompt is as follows:

```
return myMSALObj.acquireTokenSilent(request)
```

And the request is as follows:

```
const tokenRequest = {
    scopes: ["User.ReadWrite", "Mail.Read"],
};
```

At this point, the code prompts the display of another consent dialog box (see Figure 5-4), but only for the request the user has not yet consented to: Mail.Read. This is called *incremental consent*.

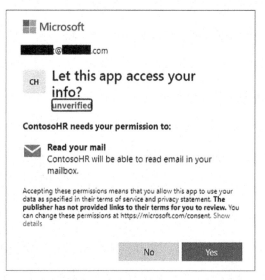

FIGURE 5-4 The Microsoft identity platform prompting the user to allow (or not) this application to read their email.

Some scopes are dangerous and often require administrative consent to use. The following scopes, or permissions, should be used with caution because they have serious security implications if misused. All of these are Microsoft Graph scopes, and the asterisks indicate all scopes—for example, read, write, and update.

- Mail.*
- Mail.Send
- MailboxSettings.*
- Contacts.*
- People.*
- Files.*
- Notes.*
- Directory.AccessAsUser.All
- Directory.ReadWrite.All
- Application.ReadWrite.All
- Domain.ReadWrite.All
- EduRoster.ReadWrite.All
- Group.ReadWrite.All
- Member.Read.Hidden
- RoleManagement.ReadWrite.Directory
- User.ReadWrite.All
- User.ManageCreds.All

Other scopes are not so dangerous, like these:

- User.Read
- openid
- email
- profile

 Note For a fuller explanation of permissions, scopes, and consent, see https://azsec.tech/perm.

Anatomy of a JWT

As mentioned, the Microsoft identity platform and Azure AD use JWTs. And, as mentioned, most of the time you need not bother with the contents of a JWT on the client side because JWTs are opaque. However, because developers are so inquisitive, we decided to add this section, just so you would know what is inside a JWT. Also, there are some scenarios where you might want to parse the token—for example to display the user's name. In this case, you can parse an `id_token` to get a display name claim.

A JWT is not a JSON file. Rather, it is a set of three JSON sections: the header, the payload, and the signature. The header describes the signature algorithm, a token type, and potentially a key ID (kid), which is used to create the signature. The payload contains individual items, called *claims*, and supporting data, and the signature is a digital signature.

Each section of the JWT is separated by a period. So, the format of a JWT is as follows:

```
Header . Payload . Signature
```

You can look inside a JWT by using sites like https://jwt.ms or https://jwt.io. To use one of these sites to spelunk a token (in this case, https://jwt.ms), perform the following steps:

1. Type https://azsec.tech/jwt in your web browser address bar. You will be redirected to https://login.microsoftonline.com/common/oauth2/v2.0/authorize with some OAuth2-specific parameters. (At this point in the chapter, you should understand what the parameters mean!)

2. Log in using an Azure AD account.

   The browser will display an error. This is fine—indeed, it is expected—because you do not currently have anything listening on the URI redirect, http://localhost/myapp. Also, the browser address bar will include a Base64-encoded implicit flow identity token. The entire contents of the address bar will look something like this:

   ```
   http://localhost/myapp/#id_token=eyJ0eXAiOiJKV1QiLCJhbGciOiJSUzI1NiIsImtpZCI6ImJXOFpjTWp
   CQ25KWlMtaWJYNVVRRE5TdHZ4NCJ9.
   eyJ2ZXIiOiIyLjAiLCJpc3MiOiJodHRwczovL2xvZ2luLm1pY3Jvc29mdG9ubGlu
   
   <snip>
   QXT1xRJRzUUIz472JMczIanGv81reUVG1UfTjAjvl4IMivwQuQMO4kyrGr2eIpn48KfL
   YZerApVeusj8j7zcvdGMPXqU7Y7FA2EUyeDER96obdjyznIelt8bnpN8nbcIMEwr6kGF8q-1wQ_
   J21vcw&state=12345
   ```

3. Select and copy the Base64-encoded token—in other words, everything after `#id_token=` on the first line shown previously and before `&state=` on the last line.

4. Direct your web browser to https://jwt.ms and paste in the Base64-encoded token you just copied. You should see output similar to what is shown in Figure 5-5.

> **Note** If you paste the same token into https://jwt.io, it will also verify the signature for you. If the signature is not valid, https://jwt.ms will display nothing, whereas https://jwt.io will display an Invalid Signature error.

Tip You can modify the full URL, so the `redirect_uri` parameter is https://jwt.ms. Try it at https://azsec.tech/fpd.

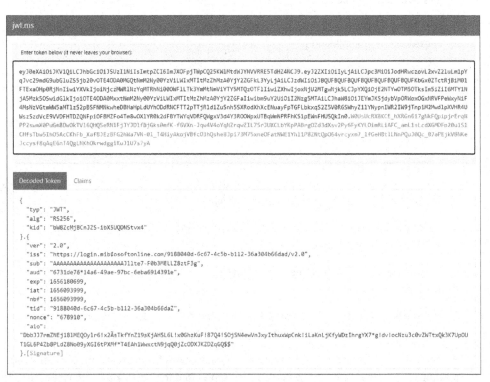

FIGURE 5-5 Viewing a JWT using https://jwt.ms.

5. Click the **Claims** tab to see a list and explanation of each claim in the token.

Tip For more information about each of the various claims, see https://azsec.tech/cla.

Validating tokens

If you are familiar with X.509 certificates, you know you need to validate them by verifying that their name, date range, signature, and other parameters are correct. The same holds true for JWTs—at least for servers. Remember, to most clients, JWTs are opaque, except for id_tokens. Apart from experimentation and learning, there is no need to do any of this work on a client. But you must perform JWT validation on any server that accepts JWTs.

For .NET 6.0 and later, the two namespaces to use for validation are as follows:

- **Microsoft.IdentityModel.Tokens**   This has the SecurityToken data type.

- **System.IdentityModel.Tokens.Jwt**   This contains all the validation functionality.

The JwtSecurityToken class contains many methods you can use to validate different parts of a token. These include the following:

- **ValidateToken**   This is a catchall that you can use to can set flags and values in one call. It uses a class named TokenValidationParameters that is populated with parameters you want to verify. For more about the ValidateToken method, see https://azsec.tech/val1. You can find additional information about the TokenValidationParameters class at https://azsec.tech/parm.

- **ValidateSignature**   This validates a symmetric signature (such as alg=="HS256", HMAC-SHA256) or asymmetric signature (such as alg=="RS256", RSA SHA-256). Read more about this method here: https://azsec.tech/val2.

- **ValidateLifetime**   This validates the not before and expires date/time claims. For more information, see https://azsec.tech/val3.

- **ValidateIssuer**   This validates the token issuer. You can find more details here: https://azsec.tech/val4.

- **ValidateAudience**   This validates the intended audience for the token. See https://azsec.tech/val5 to learn more.

You can use code like the following to pull individual claims from a JWT. This code pulls out the audience (aud) claim, which identifies who this JWT is intended for. The token is a Base64-encoded JWT.

```
var tokenHandler = new JwtSecurityTokenHandler();
var jwtToken = (JwtSecurityToken)tokenHandler.ReadToken(token);
string aud = jwtToken.Claims.First(claim => claim.Type == "aud").Value;
```

> **Note**   Web APIs must validate access tokens sent to them, and they must only accept tokens containing their aud (audience) claim, which is the audience for whom the token is intended.

Finding the certificate associated with the signing key

This is a little involved, and you do not really need to understand it, but it is always nice to know how things work. So, here goes.

Every JWT issued by Azure AD contains iss and kid claims. These are the issuer and key ID used to sign the token, respectively. They look like this:

```
iss: https://login.microsoftonline.com/9188040d-6c67-4c5b-b112-36a304b66dad/v2.0
kid: bW8ZcMjBCnJZS-ibX5UQDNStvx4
```

To find the certificate associated with the signing key, follow these steps:

1. Append the following code to the `iss` URL: `/.well-known/openid-configuration`. The URL should now read as follows:

   ```
   https://login.microsoftonline.com/9188040d-6c67-4c5b-b112-36a304b66dad/v2.0/.well-known/
   openid-configuration
   ```

2. Enter this URL in your web browser's address bar.

   This will direct you to a page containing the contents of a JSON file with useful information about the service's OpenID Connect configuration.

   One entry in the JSON file is `jwks_uri`, which is followed by the URI for a JSON file containing the public key information. It might look like this:

   ```
   https://login.microsoftonline.com/9188040d-6c67-4c5b-b112-36a304b66dad/discovery/v2.0/
   keys
   ```

3. Enter this URI into your web browser's address bar to fetch that JSON file.

   You will see a list of keys. One of these keys will have a `kid` that matches the `kid` at the start. In this example, the `kid` at the start is bW8ZcMjBCnJZS-ibX5UQDNStvx4. Notice here that this also appears in this list of keys:

   ```
   {
       "kty": "RSA",
       "use": "sig",
       "kid": "bW8ZcMjBCnJZS-ibX5UQDNStvx4",
       "x5t": "bW8ZcMjBCnJZS-ibX5UQDNStvx4",
       "n": "2a70SwgqIh8U-Shj1jM <snip> 5vK0mouQi8a8Q",
       "e": "AQAB",
       "x5c": [
   "MIIDYDCCAkigAwIBAgIJAN2X7t+ckntxMA0GCSqGSIb3DQEBCwUAMCkxJzAlBgNVBAMTHkxpdmUgSUQgU1RTIF
   NpZ25pbmcgUHVibGljIEtleTAeFw0yMTAzMjkyMzM4MzNaFw0yNjAzMjgyMzM4MzNaMCkxJzAlBgNVB

   <snip>

   FgXGPjYPLW0j10d0qzHHJ84saclVwvuOrpp75Y+0Du5Z2OrjNF1W4dEWZMJmmOe73e
   jAnoiWJI25kQpkd4ooNasw3HIZEJZ6cKctmPJLdvx0tJ8bde4DivtWOeFIw
   cAkokH2j1HmAOipNETw=="
       ],
       "issuer": "https://login.microsoftonline.com/9188040d-6c67-4c5b-b
   112-36a304b66dad/v2.0"
   }
   ```

   The x5c field is the X.509 certificate that contains the public key associated with the signing key used to sign this JWT. Your service should fetch these keys every 11 to 13 hours because the keys can change quickly.

For JWT verification, at a minimum, a server must validate the following:

- The **aud** (audience) claim must not be missing. Also, it must be your server **aud** and nothing else.

- The current date and time must be >= **nbf** (not before) and <= **exp** (expiry).

- The **alg** (signature algorithm) claim should be what you expect—in many cases, RS256. It must not be "None".

- The signature must be correct.

- The **iss** (issuer) claim must be valid.

Using OAuth2 in your Azure applications

Enemy #1 in the OWASP Top 10 2021 (https://owasp.org/Top10/)—discussed in more detail in Chapter 9, "Secure coding"—is broken access control. As explained in the OWASP documentation found at https://azsec.tech/kgp, this involves a lack of authentication and authorization to application endpoints.

As we will explain later, one way to authenticate and authorize access to an application endpoint such as a REST API is to use some secret string. This is common, and it is simple. But it is also insecure because the string must be secured somewhere.

A better solution to protect endpoints developed using ASP.NET, Node.js, Azure Functions, and so on, is to use OpenID Connect and OAuth2. This is precisely what the Azure REST APIs do. For example, when you create a Cosmos DB database and you use a C# class, a PowerShell cmdlet or the Azure CLI ultimately calls a REST API that accepts a POST method on https://{databaseaccount}.documents.azure.com/dbs. For this to happen, however, the user must first authenticate on Azure. Otherwise, the REST call fails, which looks something like this:

```
Invoke-WebRequest -Method POST https://foo.documents.azure.com/dbs
Invoke-WebRequest: {"code":"Unauthorized","message":"Required Header authorization is missing.
Ensure a valid Authorization token is passed.\r\nActivityId: c6412411-fbdc-4320-ab96-
b37f77172c32, Microsoft.Azure.Documents.Common/2.14.0"}
```

> **Note** How you protect your endpoint can vary by product because different products usually perform OpenID Connect and OAuth2 tasks using different libraries. Information about protecting ASP.NET applications can be found here: https://azsec.tech/xo7.

For the sake of example, let's add authentication and authorization to an Azure Function App. You can elect to use any of the following identity providers, but in this test, we will use GitHub:

- Microsoft

- Apple

- Facebook

- Google

- GitHub

- Twitter

- OpenID Connect

> **Note** The last one, OpenID Connect, essentially lets you use any OpenID Connect identity provider.

Each of these identity providers makes setting up an authenticated front end to your Azure Functions straightforward because the ability to federate both authentication and authorization within an identity provider is built into the Azure Function Apps portal experience. The quickest and easiest way to do this using an identity provider other than Azure AD is to use GitHub, because you probably already have a GitHub account.

Here's how this is configured. (Note that in this example, we are simply authenticating using GitHub, but there is no GitHub app.)

1. In the Azure Portal, open the Function App section, navigate to the **Authentication** page, and click **Add an Identity Provider**. (See Figure 5-6.)

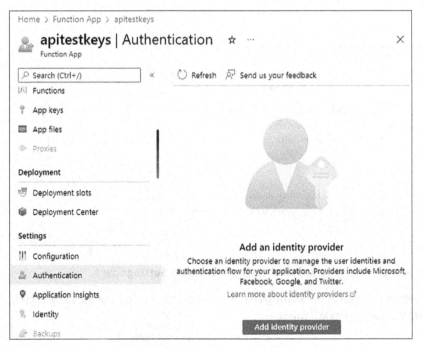

FIGURE 5-6 Adding an identity provider to an Azure Function app.

2. On the **Add an Identity Provider** page (see Figure 5-7), enter the following information:

- **Identify Provider**   Choose **GitHub**.

- **Client ID**   Leave this blank for now; you will fill it in in a moment.

- **Client Secret**   Leave this blank for now; you will fill it in in a moment.

- **Restrict Access**   Select the **Require Authentication** option button.

- **Unauthenticated Requests**   Select the **HTTP 302 Found Redirect: Recommended for Websites** option button.

- **Token Store**   Select this checkbox.

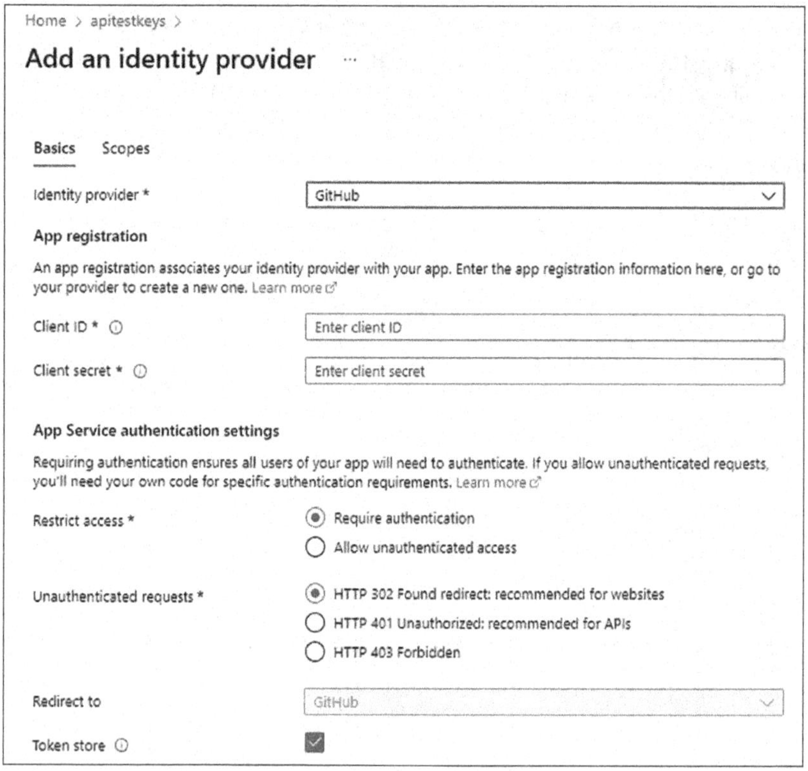

FIGURE 5-7 Configuring GitHub as an identity provider for your Function App.

3. Log in to GitHub.

4. Click your profile image in the top right and navigate to the **Settings** page.

5. In the **Developer** section of the **Settings** page (in the bottom-left part of the screen), click **New GitHub App**, and log in if prompted.

6. Add the necessary details about your application, such as its name and home page URL.

7. For this example, deselect the **Webhook Active** checkbox. Then click **Create GitHub App**.

> **Note** You can even add GitHub scopes, such as read-only or read-write access, to your repos, discussions, issues, projects, and even administrative rights.

8. In the **About** screen (see Figure 5-8), note the client ID listed, and write it down. Then click the **Generate a New Client Secret** button to generate a client secret. Write that down, too.

About

Owned by: @ ███████

App ID: 214383

Client ID: lv1.1df█████████3f9f8

Revoke all user tokens

GitHub Apps can use OAuth credentials to identify users. Learn more about identifying users by reading our integration developer documentation.

Client secrets   Generate a new client secret

🔑   *****a6a10057
Client secret   Added 12 minutes ago by ████████
                       Never used   Delete
                       You cannot delete the only client secret. Generate a new client secret first.

FIGURE 5-8 Setting up the GitHub app endpoint, including the client ID and client secrets.

9. Back in the **Add an Identity Provider** page of the Function App section of the Azure Portal (refer to Figure 5-7), enter the client ID and client secret in the **Client ID** and **Client Secret** boxes (respectively), and click **Add**.

10. In the pane on the left side of the Azure Portal, click **Functions**.

11. Click **Create** to create a simple HTTP trigger function with default scaffolding.

12. Select the **HTTP Trigger** template.

13. Give the function a name or just use the default, as this is only a test.

14. Leave **Authorization Level** set to **Function**.

15. Click **Create**.

16. Enter the Azure Function App's URL in your web browser. You will be prompted to log in with GitHub credentials, as shown in Figure 5-9.

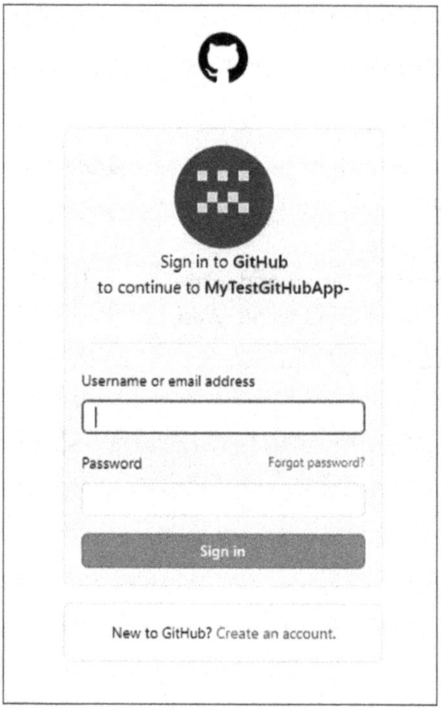

FIGURE 5-9 Accessing a Function App using your GitHub login.

> 💡 **Tip** To find out how to perform this same task but with other identity providers, like Facebook, Apple, and Google, see https://azsec.tech/ghu. You can also learn how to apply all that you have learned so far to Logic Apps at https://azsec.tech/ps0.

> 💡 **Tip** If you want to go further down the OAuth2 rabbit hole and read about current best practices, see the latest IETF draft on the topic at https://azsec.tech/sec.

Authentication

Authentication is the act of something or someone proving who or what they are to something else. There are a few important considerations related to this definition:

- Authentication occurs during some interaction with an external counterpart. Therefore, depending on where you set the line that defines what is "external" and what is "something else," you might not need to authenticate. This line is usually set as a trust boundary. (If you need a refresher on trust boundaries, refer to Chapter 4, "Threat modeling.")

- It is not enough to identify yourself to a server; you also need to prove who you are.

- As mentioned, you can prove your identity using one or more of three factors: something you know, something you have, and something you are.

Something you know

When you authenticate using something you know, it means you use information that only you know to prove your identity. This does not necessarily mean that you *provide* that information, simply that you can demonstrate that you have it.

The simplest way to perform authentication based on something you know is to supply a password. When your counterpart receives your name and password, it checks it against some stored information to determine if the password it received is indeed the right one.

This has a significant fallacy: it assumes that only a legitimate user knows the password. Of course, this is not always the case. A password could be intercepted when it is sent for authentication. It could also be stolen from the user's system or from the remote system that checks the password. And, of course, the password could simply be guessed if it contains words or numbers that are linked to the user, like their child's name. To address this fallacy, most organizations have introduced mechanisms to improve how passwords are stored in their systems or to steer users to select passwords that are more difficult to guess—sometimes in ways that border on unlawful. See https://azsec.tech/fvx for some examples of this.

Passwords have been the most-used approach to authentication since the dawn of computers. Over the years, however, they have demonstrated their weaknesses—so much that the current consensus is that they are not enough in most scenarios. In the following sections, you will read about a few ways to cope with this.

Zero-knowledge password proof

As mentioned, authentication using something you know typically means sending a password to a counterpart. When you do this, it puts the password at risk of being intercepted by a nefarious actor. Worse, each time you do it, the risk increases. For this reason, many organizations require their users to periodically change their passwords.

There are a couple of ways to avoid this, however. The most promising of these is zero-knowledge password proof (ZKPP). With ZKPP, you do not send the password; instead, you simply prove to the counterpart that you have it. So, the counterpart never receives the password in any form. Azure does not yet support ZKPP, but who knows, the next edition of this book might dedicate a few pages to it. In the meantime, you can learn more about it at https://azsec.tech/rv8.

Something you have

Authenticating with something you have typically requires you to have possession of some object, like a phone or a token.

This can be an effective form of authentication, but it is not without its risks. Using a phone as an example, it could be stolen or lost. But even if you do not lose the phone, if you use SMS for authentication purposes, an attacker could intercept it. One way they might do this is by launching a SIM swap attack. According to the FBI, SIM swapping involves "tricking the mobile carrier into switching the victim's mobile number to a SIM card in the criminal's possessio. Once the SIM is swapped, the victim's calls, texts, and other data are diverted to the criminal's device"—including SMS messages they receive for authentication purposes.

> **Note** A recent FBI alert warns that SIM swap attacks are increasing in frequency. You can read the alert here: https://azsec.tech/wao.

Microsoft recommends avoiding SMS-based authentication. Instead, consider adopting tools like Microsoft Authenticator or Google Authenticator or a hardware token like those based on FIDO2. Both these technologies are backed by cryptographic algorithms that guarantee their security. They also have mechanisms to mitigate their risk of being stolen and used by malicious actors. For example, Azure Temporary Access Pass (TAP), which is part of Microsoft Authenticator, allows you to define a mechanism to recover control over your identity if needed. For more information, see https://azsec.tech/sxz.

Passwordless authentication

The failure of password-based authentication has prompted the development of alternative approaches. One of those is called *passwordless authentication* and is based on the idea that we can ditch passwords altogether. Fast Identity Online (FIDO) 2 is one of the standards supporting passwordless authentication. It employs a combination of asymmetric keys and hardware-based protection to validate a user's identity. With FIDO2, you never exchange secrets with servers; your security key always remains on your device. So, it represents an example of zero-knowledge user authentication (see https://azsec.tech/gcu). This approach addresses some of the risks associated with password-based authentication and is therefore one of the most promising trends in authentication.

Something you are

When you authenticate with something you are, you use your physical characteristics for access. This mechanism is often used for authentication on devices, but rarely for authentication on external systems. As with passwords, using something you are for authentication is typically not adequately secure. Worse, while you can easily change a password, you cannot easily change your physical features—at least, not without expensive and painful surgery. Therefore, it is less commonly used.

The most attentive among you may be puzzled by the preceding sentence. After all, don't Windows and Azure support biometric authentication with Windows Hello for Business? Yes. But Windows Hello for Business does not use single-factor authentication. Rather, it uses multifactor authentication (MFA). To learn more about that, read on.

Multifactor authentication

Each example of something you know, something you have, and something you are is a form of single-factor authentication (SFA). SFA mechanisms have demonstrated their weaknesses over the years—so much so that nowadays, the most promising approach to authentication now involves using two or more of these mechanisms together.

This approach is called *multifactor authentication* (MFA). The idea behind MFA is that by combining the security characteristics of the different authentication mechanisms, you make it harder for an attacker to impersonate you. A classic example of MFA is using a username and password (something you know) with a number generated by an app (something you have).

As mentioned, Windows Hello for Business uses MFA, enabling you to authenticate users with a combination of something they have (a device on which to use Windows Hello for Business) and something they are (using fingerprint or facial recognition), which is stored on that device. It works like this:

1. You train your device to recognize you. When this happens, the information needed to recognize you in the future is stored on the device.

2. You use the device to access a Windows Hello for Business resource.

3. Windows employs the recognition information stored on the device to check your identity.

4. Assuming there is a match, Windows grants you access to cryptographic keys, which you use for authentication purposes to access the Windows Hello for Business resource.

The advantage of this approach is that it links your physical characteristics to a specific device. Therefore, it implicitly represents an example of MFA. That is, to authenticate, you must prove your identity using your physical characteristics (something you are) and a device that has already been onboarded with your parameters (something you have). Another person using that device would not be authenticated. Similarly, you will not be authenticated if you use a different device on which your parameters have not been onboarded.

When designing an MFA solution, you must take care to select the right authentication mechanisms. For example, we have worked with organizations that propose implementing MFA by requiring users to answer a predefined question in addition to entering their password. The problem with this approach is that both these mechanisms are based on something you know—meaning that an attacker who knows you well might be able to guess both your password and the predefined question. Therefore, this approach would not significantly increase security.

Who is authenticating whom?

So far, this chapter has been somewhat focused on user authentication. After all, this is what we normally deal with: users who need to access some resource in some capacity. However, this brings forth two questions:

- Who is really authenticating the user?

- Is it enough to authenticate the user?

In the early days of internet, every application was isolated, so the burden of authenticating users fell to the applications themselves. This approach had a lot of drawbacks, however; fortunately, it has been largely replaced by centralized authentication through identity providers (IdPs) like Azure AD.

For example, when you access a resource through the Azure Portal, it typically redirects you to Azure AD, which authenticates you. In other words, the Azure Portal does not perform the authentication; it delegates that responsibility to the Microsoft identity platform using Azure AD as the authority. This means two things:

- Azure Portal does not need to store credentials or other verification data.

- The Microsoft identity platform can enforce security policies like conditional access and MFA.

Once authentication succeeds, Azure AD creates a token. The Azure Portal then uses that token to allow access to the resource in question. However, the token received by the Azure Portal is not the authentication; it is a signed declaration of the user's identity. It does not contain credentials. Instead, it contains the user ID, claims that relate to what it can do, and other contextual information. Everything is signed by Azure AD; Azure Portal can then verify the signature to ensure that Azure AD did indeed issue the token. In other words, the Azure Portal Azure AD thus honors the token, assigning its bearer the attested rights.

This addresses the user's authentication, but is it enough? In any communication, there are at least two counterparts. In this case, they are the user (or client) and the resource, which is represented by an Azure service accessed through the Azure Portal. We have already explained how the resource can indirectly authenticate the user and obtain their identity and assigned rights by relying on Azure AD. But how can the user be sure they are interacting with the desired resource or that the instance of Azure AD is indeed a legitimate one? After all, it would not be that hard for some rogue nation-state to create a fake Azure AD given that it uses protocols based on public standards.

The answer is through authentication—in this case, using the Transport Layer Security (TLS) protocol. As explained in detail in Chapter 10, "Cryptography in Azure," TLS authenticates the server by performing a series of cryptographic operations as well as checking that the name in the certificate matches the name in the browser's address bar. This is called *server authentication*; essentially, the client authenticates the server.

Creating your own authentication solution

You might be considering creating some sort of authentication capability for your solution on your own. There are a few reasons to do this—namely, technical limitations or costs. For example, if you must handle millions of users from the internet, a pay-per-user commercial solution can generate significant expenses fast. But there are a lot more reasons *not* to do this. These include the following:

- Custom authentication solutions are typically created by developers and architects with limited (if any) experience with these types of tools. Moreover, these solutions are subject to limited tests because they are applied to a single scenario. Therefore, they most assuredly have significant security issues that are unknown and could be exploited.

- Monitoring and auditing tools for custom solutions are typically minimal or utterly neglected. So, you might not be able to detect attacks as they happen. In addition, your ability to learn from past mistakes may be hampered, as well as your ability to respond quickly to attacks and data breaches.

- You may not be able to manage the identities centrally. This means you would not be able to use security services that would enable you to identify potentially malicious behaviors. Because you would not be able to leverage an already existing identity provider solution, you would likely need to implement reporting capabilities and dashboards to highlight misuse, usage, and statistics.

- You could unknowingly violate regulations like GDPR by storing sensitive information and PII without protecting them adequately.

 Important   We strongly recommend against creating your own authentication solution.

The role of single sign-on

Authentication is a necessity. But let's be real: nobody likes to do it. Sometimes it becomes so cumbersome that people start taking shortcuts, like writing down passwords on sticky notes and sticking them to their screen or using the same weak password for every app. No wonder one of the most sought-after authentication features is single sign-on (SSO)!

> ### Real-world experience: SSO
>
> One of us has had direct experience building a SSO service. It happened more than 20 years ago on one of his first projects as a Microsoft consultant. Many organizations felt the need to simplify authentication for their employees and customers. The project was a huge success.

SSO essentially allows users to authenticate once and be recognized automatically by all the applications in their organization for a period of time without re-entering their credentials. How does this magic happen? It is performed by Azure AD.

SSO works like this: When you access an application, it forwards you to Azure AD. Azure AD then authenticates you and provides the application with information to allow it to assign you the required access rights. Depending on the application and its configuration, Azure AD might provide that information to the application in different ways:

- Using OpenID Connect and OAuth 2
- Using SAML
- Providing an application-specific username and password
- Using a header
- Using Integrated Windows Authentication (IWA)
- Using federation with a linked identity provider

These different approaches enable Azure AD to provide authentication information to the application in question in the manner the application expects to receive it. You specify what method to use in the application's configuration settings. You can also disable SSO in these settings if needed.

Integrating an application with Azure AD SSO is typically seamless for native cloud applications through the adoption of OpenID Connect. More traditional (that is, non–cloud native) applications might need to use Azure AD Application Proxy to ensure that Azure AD performs the authentication so it can provide to the application with the information required to grant access.

This does not explain how you can achieve SSO spanning multiple applications, eliminating the need to reinsert your credentials for days at a time. Again, this is achieved by Azure AD. The idea is that Azure AD stores locally on the device some information that allows it to recognize the user at a later stage. On Windows, this typically (but not necessarily) implies the creation of a type of token called a *primary refresh token* (PRT). This token is valid for 14 days and is automatically renewed every 4 hours by default. Valid PRTs are automatically sent to Azure AD every time you need to authenticate to ensure you do not need to reinsert your credentials.

> **Note** For more information on SSO, see https://azsec.tech/m4k.

Is SSO secure?

SSO somewhat weakens security because it stores locally on your system information that can be used to authenticate as you. In a blog post called "Digging Further into the Primary Refresh Token," Dirk-Jan Mollema describes how he and Benjamin Delpy were able to steal a PRT and reuse it on a different machine, even when it was in its most protected configuration, by leveraging a trusted platform module (TPM). You can read the post here: https://azsec.tech/j9s.

Given this, you might be tempted to disable SSO for all applications. This might not be the right thing to do, however. You might be surprised to know that many security experts consider SSO a mitigation for potential attacks because it reduces the psychological burden imposed by most security controls. More specifically, it reduces the need to reinsert credentials. So, it supports the selection of more secure passwords.

Ultimately, using SSO is recommended, and you should not disable it. But you do need to be aware of possible drawbacks. So, you should adopt tools like Microsoft Defender for Endpoint to detect when clients have been potentially compromised and then act promptly to remediate them—for example by forcing the user to reauthenticate and invalidating all PRTs.

Getting access without authenticating

Sometimes users need not authenticate to access a resource. Rather, they simply need to be granted access. If this sounds odd, here is an example to help explain. Suppose you have an application that requires users to upload a file. A typical example is an application that steps the user through the process of applying for an insurance policy; after the user provides their personal details, the application asks them to upload a scan of their ID card.

Now suppose that when the user uploads the scan of their ID card, you want it to be stored in an Azure Storage account. The easiest way to do this is to grant the user direct access to the Azure Storage account. The question is, do you need the user to authenticate when accessing the storage? Well, not really. It might be OK if the application simply generated a folder on the fly into which the user could upload their scan for a limited time. Only that folder would be accessible to the user, and that grant would be automatically revoked after a few minutes.

You can achieve this by using a shared access signature (SAS) token. Azure Storage supports three types of these tokens:

- **Service SAS tokens**   These are the most frequently used. They are associated with a specific service inside the Azure Storage account. This could be the Blob Storage service, the Queue Storage service, or the Azure Files service.

- **Account SAS tokens**   These grant access to multiple services belonging to the same Azure Storage account.

  Both service and account SAS tokens are generated using storage account keys, which are signing keys uniquely associated with the Azure Storage account.

- **User-delegation SAS tokens**   Unlike service and account SAS tokens, these tokens are not generated using storage account keys. Rather, they are generated by some user's credentials and provide user-delegated access to the bearer. Microsoft recommends this type of SAS token.

> **Note** For more information on SAS tokens, see https://azsec.tech/7np.

Note that you can associate SAS tokens with stored access policies (SAPs). It is recommended that you take this approach instead of using SAS tokens directly. By doing, so you can change the configuration of the SAS token even after it has been issued, and you can invalidate the SAS token more easily. See https://azsec.tech/ylu for more information about SAPs.

Speaking of invalidation, you can invalidate SAS tokens generated with storage account keys, but this implies that all SAS tokens generated with the same key will be invalidated at the same time. On a related note, Azure provides two storage account keys for each storage account to allow regeneration of the SAS tokens without downtime. For this reason, you should not use both storage account keys at the same time. In fact, we suggest you forget about storage account keys, using them only when there is no other option. You could even go one step further and disable the use of storage account keys altogether. Learn more here: https://azsec.tech/nosas.

Real-world experience: Misuse of storage account keys

We have seen a lot of situations where storage account keys have been misused, causing significant problems. For example, one of our customers decided to use one storage account key to generate SAS tokens and a second one for the connection string used by some service to connect with the storage account. This approach required an extra effort as soon as the customer needed to invalidate some SAS token.

Another frequent issue with storage account keys is that they can be used to access the storage account. This is unfortunately one of the more common ways of connecting with Azure Storage, but it is hardly something that we can recommend from a security perspective. Storage account keys are too powerful, and they do not allow you to determine who uses them. For this reason, it is far better to use a service principal or, even more preferred, a Managed Identity, because it allows you to assign rights granularly and to perform effective monitoring and auditing.

Authenticating applications

We have dedicated many pages to authentication concepts for users, but they are not the only subjects who need to authenticate. Applications also need to authenticate to access other resources. Typical examples are when an application needs to access a resource on Azure or on-prem. An application might also need to access external resources like third-party APIs exposed over the internet.

Authenticating for Azure resources

When you authenticate for resources on Azure, like Azure SQL, Cosmos DB, or Azure Storage, you have a couple options. In most cases, you can use a service principal, and for some services, you can use service-specific credentials. A service principal is an account that is assigned to an application. Each service principal has a name and a password, which the application code can use to access resources on Azure. You can assign roles to service principals, just as you would do with any other account. But as mentioned, because these accounts are not assigned to users, you cannot configure them to use MFA.

> **Note** Unlike users, service principals cannot use MFA because they do not own cell phones or FIDO keys and they do not have physical characteristics such as fingerprints.

Whereas service principals are defined in Azure AD, service-specific credentials, like SQL accounts, are handled directly by the service itself. Therefore, you cannot apply a centralized governance to them. For this reason, you should use service principals whenever possible. Even service principals have their limits, though. For instance, their passwords tend to be left unchanged for longer than they should, possibly even years. One approach to address this problem is to implement a process—preferably an automated one—to regularly change the password. Another approach is even better, though: using Managed Identities, which are provided by Azure AD.

A Managed Identity is a service principal whose credential is managed by Azure AD. Interestingly, with Managed Identities, you do not have to save the credentials anywhere! Consider the following code fragment, which shows how you can establish a connection to Azure Key Vault secrets using a Managed Identity on a virtual machine (VM) or Function App:

```
SecretClient client = new SecretClient(new Uri(uriKeyVault), new DefaultAzureCredential());
```

It uses `DefaultAzureCredential()` to refer to the Managed Identity. That's it! You need not specify anything else (except the address of the Key Vault instance, obviously).

The beauty of Managed Identities is that Azure automatically injects them at runtime. You do not even have access to the credentials in the memory space of your application! Having nothing to configure means that nothing can be stolen. The catch here is that not all services and resources support Managed Identities. Fortunately, though, many do, and you can access an updated list here: https://azsec.tech/hia.

> **Important** Managed Identities are the most recommended authentication mechanism on Azure, and you should use them whenever possible.

There are two types of Managed Identities: system-assigned and user-assigned. The only difference between them is that system-assigned Managed Identities are automatically assigned to services by the system, whereas user-assigned Managed Identities can be generated separately and assigned to multiple instances. This makes user-assigned Managed Identities an ideal choice for situations where you need redundancy or scalability.

Authenticating from Within a VM

It is common for some customers to authenticate for Azure services from a VM. A common example is having code running in a VM query Azure SQL DB. (This article explains how this is done: https://azsec.tech/6x3.) If you are using a Managed Identity on the VM, however, the process is a little different from what we have covered so far. At a high level, the steps are as follows:

1. Create a Managed Identity for the VM. In this example, we will call it *VMName*.

2. In Azure SQL DB, execute the following T-SQL commands:

    ```
    CREATE USER [VMName] FROM EXTERNAL PROVIDER
    ALTER ROLE db_datareader ADD MEMBER [VMName]
    ```

3. Using PowerShell code, pull the VM's access token from the Azure Instance Metadata Service listening on a private, nonroutable address—for example, 169.254.169.254. The code will look something like this:

    ```
    $response = Invoke-WebRequest -Uri 'http://169.254.169.254/metadata/identity/oauth2/
    token?api-version=2018-02-01&resource=https://database.windows.net/' -Method GET -Headers
    @{Metadata="true"}
    $content = $response.Content | ConvertFrom-Json
    $AccessToken = $content.access_token

    $SqlConnection = New-Object System.Data.SqlClient.SqlConnection
    ```

```
$SqlConnection.ConnectionString = "Data Source = <SQL-DB>; Initial Catalog = <DB>"
$SqlConnection.AccessToken = $AccessToken
$SqlConnection.Open()
```

> **Note** For more information about the Azure Instance Metadata Service, see https://azsec.tech/meta.

> **Note** If you receive an "Identity not found" error when you run this code, it means you have not set up a Managed Identity for the VM.

Notice the `resource=https://database.windows.net/");` at the end of the first line of the preceding code. The URL in this snippet will change depending on the resource for which you want a token. The following list indicates which URL applies for the various services:

- **Azure SQL DB**   https://database.windows.net

- **Key Vault**   https://vault.azure.net

- **Microsoft Graph**   https://graph.microsoft.com

- **Azure Storage**   https://storage.azure.com

- **Azure Management Plane**   https://management.azure.com

> **Note** For a full explanation of the process of accessing secured Azure resources from VMs, see https://azsec.tech/6x3.

Authorization

Azure authorization is based primarily on Azure AD and on roles. Some data storage services use alternate ways of authentication and subsequently have authentication tied to them. Services that do not use Azure AD authentication are being retrofitted with Azure AD so they can offer both the legacy approach to authentication and the modern Azure AD approach at the same time.

> **Important** Whenever possible, you should use Azure AD authentication and authorization with Azure roles.

Many Azure services—for example, Azure Key Vault, and Azure Storage—have separate permissions in two categories:

- **Control plane**   This is for managing the resource in Azure Resource Manager (ARM).

- **Data plane**   These control the data stored in the service.

In other words, roles are distinct for the control plane used by ARM functions and the data plane used during operations. These separate permissions enable the correct application of the least privilege principle and achieve separation of duties within an organization. Admittedly, the distinction is not always obvious, and we are using a simplified definition here. Basically, ARM is the gateway to the control plane, independent of the mechanism used—whether it is ARM templates, Bicep, Terraform, the Azure Portal, the Azure CLI, Azure PowerShell, or REST calls—and control plane operations are handled by the resource provider.

Azure AD roles and scopes

Azure AD provides modern authentication and support for authorization. Azure defines roles and permissions, which are assigned to Azure AD users, service principals, Managed Identities, and groups within a specific scope.

As mentioned, in the context of Azure, the word *scope* has a different meaning than it does in the context of OAuth2. With OAuth2, scope refers to a permission—for example, the Read scope grants users permission to access Microsoft Graph or to view another user's calendar. In contrast, Azure scopes are locations in the Azure hierarchy tree where actions take place. As shown in Figure 5-10, there are four scope levels in Azure:

- Management groups
- Subscriptions
- Resource groups
- Resources

> **Note** For more on scopes in Azure, see https://azsec.tech/t68.

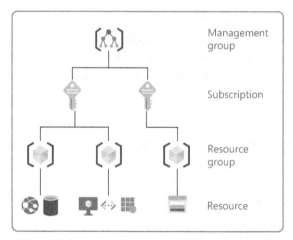

FIGURE 5-10 Azure scope hierarchy.

Here are a few important points about roles:

You can assign built-in roles or define custom roles to grant permissions at any scope. The roles you apply to one scope are inherited by all the scopes below it in the hierarchy.

Azure does not provide explicit deny permissions. Therefore, once permissions are granted, they cannot be directly revoked. Deny permissions are reserved for internal use by complex Azure services such as Azure Synapse. Blueprints and Azure Locks allow for an approximation of deny permissions, however. (For more, see the upcoming section titled "Denying assignments.")

Azure roles act like roles in any other role-based access control (RBAC) system. You grant a role based on the principle of least privilege to an individual user, an Azure AD group, a service principal, or a Managed Identity.

Azure control plane built-in RBAC roles

Azure control plane operations have four built-in roles, which adhere to the principle of least privilege. See Figure 5-11.

- **Reader** Those with this role can only read the resource configuration.

- **Contributor** Those with the Contributor role can read and update and, in some cases, create child resources. For example, a user assigned the Contributor role for a resource group can create, update, and own resources in that resource group. A user with the Contributor role in a management group can create, update, and own resources in that management group, plus create child management groups and include subscriptions in the management group.

- **User Access Administrator** This role grants rights to create roles and role assignments. In effect, this gives full control, because any roles not currently assigned can be assigned by someone with this role for the control plane or the data plane.

- **Owner** Those with the Owner role have all the rights of the Contributor and User Access Administrator roles.

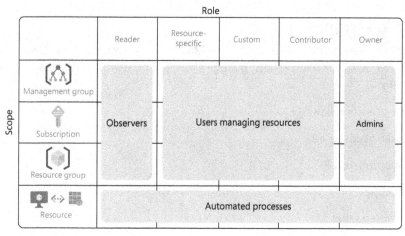

FIGURE 5-11 Azure roles and the least-privilege principle.

The Azure control plane does not grant rights directly on the data plane. Those with the Contributor and Owner roles can grant rights to data plane users, but those with the Reader role on the control plane can see only the control plane. As you will see later in this chapter, this can be useful for the segregation of duties and to adhere to the principle of least privilege. For example, creating, updating, deleting, managing, and shutting down VMs are control plane operations. However, VMs through Remote Desktop Protocol (RDP) is a data plane operation. Similarly, you create, update, and manage an Event Hub namespace through the control plane, whereas the data plane contains the operations needed to publish and consume events.

Azure data plane built-in RBAC roles

The Azure AD roles for data planes for various services can be found here, after the four control plane roles: https://azsec.tech/dav. Note that some specialized control plane operations are intermingled with the data plane roles. The classification of a role as a control plane role or a data plane role often does not matter.

Azure data plane operation permissions and roles depend on the authentication method and on the capabilities of the resource provider. Many resource providers support Azure AD for data plane operations. But while some resource providers started with Azure AD authorization, others relied or still rely on account keys, resource tokens, SAS tokens, and internal relational database authentication and authorization processes.

Managing role assignments

Role assignments grant a user, group, service principal, or Managed Identity the permissions defined in a built-in or custom role at a given Azure scope. To assign a role, you must provide values as shown in https://azsec.tech/x9g.

In general, the steps are as follows:

1. Determine who needs access.

2. Select the appropriate role.

3. Identify the scope.

4. Check your prerequisites.

5. Assign the role.

You can list role assignments in the Azure CLI, as shown here. If you specify -all, a list of all assignments at the current subscription or scope is returned.

```
az role assignment list --scope $scope --assignee $principalId
```

Custom role definitions

To explore the structure of a role definition, let's look at the built-in Contributor role. To retrieve the JSON definition of the role, use the following command:

```
az role definition list --name Contributor
```

The following structure is returned:

```json
[
  {
    "assignableScopes": [
      "/"
    ],
    "description": "Grants full access to manage all resources, but does not allow you to assign
roles in Azure RBAC, manage assignments in Azure Blueprints, or share image galleries.",
    "id": "/subscriptions/11111111-2222-3333-4444-555555555555/providers/Microsoft.
Authorization/roleDefinitions/b24988ac-6180-42a0-ab88-20f7382dd24c",
    "name": "b24988ac-6180-42a0-ab88-20f7382dd24c",
    "permissions": [
      {
        "actions": [
          "*"
        ],
        "dataActions": [],
        "notActions": [
          "Microsoft.Authorization/*/Delete",
          "Microsoft.Authorization/*/Write",
          "Microsoft.Authorization/elevateAccess/Action",
          "Microsoft.Blueprint/blueprintAssignments/write",
          "Microsoft.Blueprint/blueprintAssignments/delete",
          "Microsoft.Compute/galleries/share/action"
        ],
        "notDataActions": []
      }
    ],
    "roleName": "Contributor",
    "roleType": "BuiltInRole",
    "type": "Microsoft.Authorization/roleDefinitions"
  }
]
```

This definition contains the following elements:

- **assignableScopes** This can be any Azure scope, but it is usually a management group. In this case, it refers to the root tenant management group and anything below it. Note that you can provide more than one scope in a custom role definition.

- **description** This is a description of the role. Including the description is optional.

- **name** This is a unique name within the scope of the definition. It is always a GUID for built-in roles.

- **id** This is the fully qualified resource ID of the role definition. For built-ins, it is a concatenation of the current scope (a subscription here) and the name (GUID).

- **actions** This is a list of control plane actions allowed. An asterisk (*) denotes any.

- **dataActions** This is a list of data plane actions. If the brackets that follow are empty, it means there are none.

- **notActions** This is a list of excluded control plane actions—for example, create or delete role assignments.

- **notDataActions** This is a list of excluded data plane actions.

- **roleName** This is the role's display name to make it easier for users to understand.

You can view a list of built-in roles at https://azsec.tech/jvm. Alternatively, you can retrieve a list of these roles from the Azure CLI with the following command:

```
az role definition list
```

To define a custom role, you can simply modify the template for an existing role and deploy it using your favorite deployment technology. For example, when we need to define a custom role definition, we always copy and paste from a built-in role, and if this grants too many permissions, we remove actions and dataActions as needed. Here is an example in PowerShell, taken from https://azsec.tech/1ib:

```
$role = Get-AzRoleDefinition "Virtual Machine Contributor"
$role.Id = $null
$role.Name = "Virtual Machine Operator"
$role.Description = "Can monitor and restart virtual machines."

$role.Actions.Clear()
$role.Actions.AddRange(@(
        "Microsoft.Storage/*/read", "Microsoft.Network/*/read", "Microsoft.Compute/*/read",
        "Microsoft.Compute/virtualMachines/start/action", "Microsoft.Compute/virtualMachines/
restart/action",
        "Microsoft.Authorization/*/read", "Microsoft.ResourceHealth/availabilityStatuses/read",
        "Microsoft.Resources/subscriptions/resourceGroups/read",
        "Microsoft.Insights/alertRules/*", "Microsoft.Support/*"
    ))

$role.AssignableScopes.Clear()
$role.AssignableScopes.AddRange(@(
        "/subscriptions/00000000-0000-0000-0000-000000000000",
        "/subscriptions/11111111-1111-1111-1111-111111111111"
    ))

New-AzRoleDefinition -Role $role
```

> **Tip** You can find a list of all actions and dataActions to include in your custom role, divided by resource provider, here: https://azsec.tech/oc1. Each table starts with the actions as indicated in the header row. The dataActions start in the middle of the same table after a subheader row. (Press Ctrl+F to find this subheader row.)

Denying assignments

Only Azure services can create deny assignments to protect the services internals. For example, Azure Synapse does this to prevent users from modifying the included data warehouse and storage. In addition, Azure Blueprints Managed Locks are implemented through deny permissions. For more information, see https://azsec.tech/wl8.

> **Azure Blueprints**
>
> Because Azure Blueprints are in preview, we have omitted coverage of them in this book. However, we do believe that Blueprints should be used to deploy landing zones. That being said, Policy Assignments should not be deployed with Blueprints, because comingling Policy with infrastructure violates the separation of duty principle. For more on Azure Blueprints, see https://azsec.tech/mjj.

Role assignment best practices

Here are a few best practices to keep in mind when assigning roles:

- Always use Azure AD–based RBAC for the control plane and the data plane unless a special circumstance requires an alternative approach (for example, SAS tokens).

- Always assign users to Azure AD groups and grant roles to the groups. This enables management at scale and prevents you from exhausting the 2,000 role assignments limitation per subscription.

- We recommend avoiding custom roles to achieve "perfect" least privilege. It is likely that one of the built-in roles is close enough. There are good use cases for custom roles, however. For example, Azure Policy does not provide a built-in Policy Reader role, which you can create as shown here:

```
$role = [Microsoft.Azure.Commands.Resources.Models.Authorization.PSRoleDefinition]::new()
$role.Name = 'Policy Reader'
$role.Id = '2baa1a7c-6807-46af-8b16-5e9d03fba029'
$role.Description = 'Read access to Azure Policy.'
$role.IsCustom = $true
$perms = @(
    "Microsoft.Authorization/policyAssignments/read",
    "Microsoft.Authorization/policyDefinitions/read",
    "Microsoft.Authorization/policySetDefinitions/read"
)

$role.Actions = $perms
$role.NotActions = $()
$role.AssignableScopes = $pacEnvironment.rootScopeId
New-AzRoleDefinition -Role $role
```

- Users should not be granted write permissions in QA and PROD environments because all modifications should be handled through automation. In the rare case where users need direct access to such environments, use Azure AD Privileged Identity Management (PIM), discussed in the next section.

- Assign roles directly to service accounts. As with users, follow the least-privilege principle. For example, do not grant a process Publish privileges on an Event Hub if that processor is a consumer of events.

Azure AD Privileged Identity Management

For any privileged operation, be it read or write access, you should use Azure AD Privileged Identity Management (PIM). PIM temporarily allows access to privileged operations and data to authorized users. PIM assigns authorized users roles based on an approval, and these role assignments are limited to a short time frame (one hour by default). This mitigates the threat of stolen credentials being used for high-privilege operations and also mitigates user errors.

You can use PIM to:

- Provide just-in-time privileged access to Azure AD and Azure resources

- Assign time-bound access to resources using start and end dates

- Require approval to activate privileged roles

- Enforce MFA to activate any role

- Require that the user requesting a PIM role provide a justification (text)

- Get notifications when privileged roles are activated

- Conduct access reviews to ensure users still need roles

- Download an audit history for internal or external audit

- Prevent the removal of the last active Global Administrator and Privileged Role Administrator role assignments

> **Note** PIM requires an Azure AD P2 License. For more information about PIM, see https://azsec.tech/dil.

Azure attribute-based access control

As its name suggests, attribute-based access control (ABAC) is an authorization mechanism that defines access levels based on attributes associated with users, service principals, resources, requests, and the environment. ABAC builds on top of RBAC and is a data-plane control. With ABAC, you can grant access to resources based on a condition expressed as a predicate using these attributes.

Note At the time of this writing, ABAC is in preview and is available only for Azure Storage accounts. Over time, Azure will expand ABAC to other services.

Access conditions are added to specific data-plane roles, such as the following:

- Storage Blob Data Reader
- Storage Blob Data Contributor
- Storage Blob Data Owner
- Storage Queue Data Contributor
- Storage Queue Data Message Processor
- Storage Queue Data Message Sender
- Storage Queue Data Reader

One of the most useful uses for ABAC is to restrict access based on blob indexes. A blob index is a little like a resource tag. You can apply ABAC following these steps on an existing Blob Storage account:

1. In the Blob Storage account's page in the Azure Portal, click **Containers** in the left pane.

2. Click the container to which you want to apply ABAC.

3. In the left pane, click **Access Control (IAM)**.

4. Click **Role Assignments**.

5. Click **+Add** to add a new role assignment.

6. Select **Add Role Assignment**.

7. Select a data-plane role—for example, **Storage Blob Data Reader**. Then click **Next**.

8. Add a member to this role. This can be a user, a group, a service principal, or a Managed Identity. Then click **Next**.

9. Under **Conditions**, click Add **Condition**.

10. In the **Add Role Assignment Condition** page, enter the settings shown in Figure 5-12.

In this example, members assigned this role will have read access, but only if the blob index named Status is set to ReadyToEdit.

You can set ABAC policies using the visual interface just shown or using code. The code representation of this expression is as follows:

```
@Resource[Microsoft.Storage/storageAccounts/blobServices/containers/blobs/tags:Status<$key_case_
sensitive$>] StringEquals 'ReadyToEdit'
```

FIGURE 5-12 A sample condition added to a role assignment.

More ABAC resources

The following are some resources you can access to learn more about ABAC policies on storage accounts:

- "What Is Azure Attribute-Based Access Control (Azure ABAC)?" (https://azsec.tech/abac1)

- "Authorize Access to Blobs Using Azure Role Assignment Conditions" (https://azsec.tech/abac2)

- "Example Azure Role Assignment Conditions" (https://azsec.tech/abac3)

- "Actions and Attributes for Azure Role Assignment Conditions in Azure Storage" (https://azsec.tech/abac4)

- "New Attribute-Based Access Control for Blob" (https://azsec.tech/jsabac)

Summary

This was a complex chapter with many technical topics, but it covers a critical set of technologies. Identity, authentication, and authorization are at the heart of protecting anything you deploy on Azure. Because these topics are so important, a more-than-average knowledge of them is needed.

It is critically important that you understand the basics of OpenID Connect and OAuth2 because the technologies are so fundamental.

Authorization should always follow the principle of least privilege and utilize Azure AD RBAC for the control and data (where available) planes.

## CHAPTER 6

Monitoring and auditing

After completing this chapter, you will be able to:

- Describe the various types of logging.

- Identify the various components of the Azure monitoring platform and describe their role.

- Write basic queries in Kusto Query Language (KQL).

- Define a plan to monitor and audit your application.

- Implement custom events for your application.

Monitoring, auditing, logging, oh my!

"We are not a target. Therefore, we do not need to focus on security."

Customers often tell us their security level is OK because everyone loves their company. What this tells us, though, is not that they are not subject to attacks but that they do not know about them!

Everyone is subject to attacks. Just create a simple honeypot using HoneyPi or any other similar tool, and the first scans will come in a matter of seconds. Some of those scans are somewhat benign. For example, projects like Shodan, which is a search engine that specializes in identifying internet-connected devices on the internet, could identify potentially vulnerable systems to increase awareness and facilitate remediation. But most represent the first stage of an attack, known as *reconnaissance*, which is usually followed by attempts to compromise the resource. Automated reconnaissance is extremely common, but it is just one way to identify malicious counterparts.

> **Note** Read more about HoneyPi at https://azsec.tech/3pq. To learn more about Shodan, see https://shodan.io.

If you have any exposure at all, there is someone who has some interest in compromising you. Typical reasons are:

- To get money from you by causing some temporary damage and offering to remediate for a fee (ransomware).

- To obtain information from you, to use or sell it (industrial espionage).

- To cause damage because they see you as an enemy. This might happen if your business is controversial or located in some "enemy country."

- For the lulz—that is, the thrill of doing something forbidden for no particular reason.

Robert S. Mueller III, former director of the FBI, once said, "There are only two types of companies: those that have been hacked and those that will be hacked." This sentence has since been updated by John T. Chambers, former CEO for Cisco, to "There are only two types of companies: those that have been hacked and those that don't know they have been hacked." The question is, would you rather be oblivious of the hackers you already have inside your organization, or do you want to do something to identify and evict them?

If you want to get rid of them, you must invest in creating an effective monitoring and auditing strategy and in selecting the right tools. Here is the problem: there are a lot of tools, both within Azure and available from third parties. This can make it challenging to figure out what you need—how the features provided out of the box fit in and whether you need to do something else to cover for any missing capability. This chapter addresses this question.

Before delving into the answer, let's introduce some definitions:

- **Logging**   The activity of recording events or actions related to interactions of any type, including those internal to the system in scope.

- **Logging for auditing**   A form of logging in which the recorded information is stored for a significant time—usually in the order of months or years—to make it available later for legal, compliance, and root cause–analysis purposes.

- **Logging for development**   A form of logging used for troubleshooting. Development yields valuable information for understanding what is happening inside the solution to identify the causes of eventual misbehavior. It is characterized by limited retention needs—typically hours to a few days.

- **Monitoring**   A transient form of logging. Monitoring describes the current situation, highlighting eventual issues as they happen. It is characterized by very short retention requirements—typically from a few minutes to a few hours.

> **Note** Auditing, development, and monitoring are three different forms of logging. All three are usually required to ensure the security of your solution.

Leveraging the Azure platform

Azure provides a complete infrastructure for logging with Azure Monitor. Azure Monitor is a set of services and capabilities to store, ingest, visualize, analyze, and respond to events, including security events.

Diagnostic settings

Most Azure services are integrated with Azure Monitor and can generate predefined sets of events and metrics. Azure services collect a limited set of metrics by default, but they do not generate logs. You must enable logs expressly using the diagnostic settings for the service, as shown in Figure 6-1. You use the settings in this screen, which shows the diagnostic settings for a web application hosted on App Service, to enable specific categories of logs and metrics and where the logs should be stored.

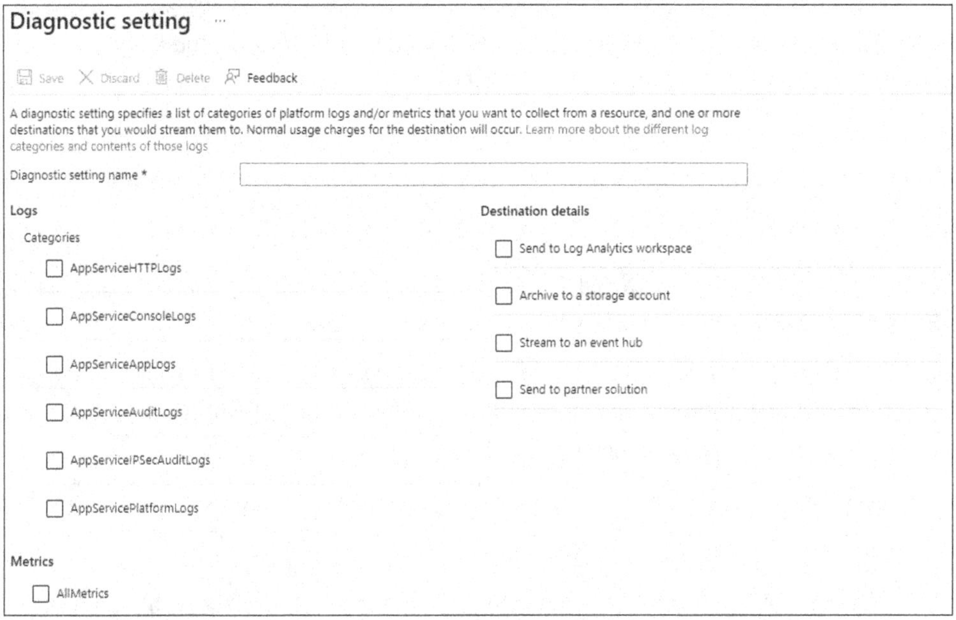

FIGURE 6-1 The diagnostic settings for a web application hosted on App Service.

The App Service supports the following log categories:

- **AppServiceHTTPLogs**   Logs in this category record incoming requests, including details such as the client's IP address, the URL, other request statistics, and the response code, but not the actual payload of the request or the response. This category corresponds to the web server logs.

- **AppServiceConsoleLogs**   This category includes standard console logs.

- **AppServiceAppLogs**   Logs in this category record traces generated by the application using tracers like AzureMonitorTraceListener, which is part of Microsoft.WindowsAzure.WebSites. Diagnostics.

- **AppServiceAuditLogs**   Logs in this category record publishing access. For example, it generates a trace every time someone logs on via FTP to upload new versions of the application files.

- **AppServiceIPSecAuditLogs**   This category includes logs that record information about IP access restriction rules. App Service allows you to define access restriction rules—for example, allowing access from only specific ranges of IP addresses. This configuration can prevent indiscriminate access to the application, but it could create undesired results, which you could detect and troubleshoot more easily using this category of events.

- **AppServicePlatformLogs**   These are logs used to show the output of the Docker commands used to manage the container.

This list is partial, specific to the chosen service, and subject to change. For instance, Azure Storage Account has a different list. It might also differ depending on what service tier you have. For example, if you have a Premium tier App Service, you will also see the AppServiceFileAuditLogs category, which highlights changes to site content.

> **Note**   When selecting the various log categories, you should enable only what is required, because many logs generate a lot of data, resulting in significant costs.

The Destination Details settings in the screen shown in Figure 6-1 enable you to specify where logs will be stored. Azure currently supports four different destinations:

- **Log Analytics workspace**   This destination target enables you to take full advantage of the Azure Monitor platform and related services like Azure Sentinel, which is Microsoft's security information and event management (SIEM) and security orchestration, automation, and response (SOAR) solution for Azure. This destination is typically useful for all logging purposes, particularly for monitoring and development logging.

- **Azure Storage**   This destination allows you to create logs as files to retain them for a longer duration, making it ideal for auditing. When you select Azure Storage, you can specify the data retention in days for each category. This setting allows for automatic data removal when the set retention time expires.

> **Note**   It is usually best to set the retention time to 0. If you change the retention time in the diagnostic settings, the new value applies only to new logs. This behavior is typically undesired because retention policies are usually retroactive. So, you must use a different mechanism, which is to leave the expiration time to 0. In this way, you disable retention control by the diagnostic settings and allow for the adoption of other mechanisms like Azure Storage Lifecycle Policy or a scheduled job to remove old log files.

- **Event Hub**   This is the premium mechanism to send events to other systems, like a supported third-party SIEM. You can apply this approach to all forms of logging.

- **Partner Solution**   At the time of writing, Azure supports Apache Kafka for Confluent Cloud, Datadog, Elastic, and Logz.io. For more information, see https://azsec.tech/4p2.

You might opt to configure multiple categories and destinations simultaneously. You might even create multiple diagnostic settings to configure different combinations to send specific categories to some destinations and not others. Still, it is rare to see a rule to cover more destinations, because they would need to receive different events.

Log categories and category groups

As mentioned in the preceding section, every resource type—and sometimes different SKUs within the same resource type—supports a different set of categories. This makes it difficult to use Azure Policy to manage diagnostics settings. To solve this problem, Azure introduced category groups. Currently, two groups are defined (see Figure 6-2):

- **allLogs** As the name implies, this is the equivalent of checking every checkbox in the portal. Every resource provider supports this category group.

- **audit** This category decides which subset of log checkboxes will be included. Not every resource provider supports this category group. When implementing diagnostics settings with Azure Policy, it is common to use the audit group for feeds to a SIEM/SOAR system, such as Azure Sentinel or a third-party SIEM.

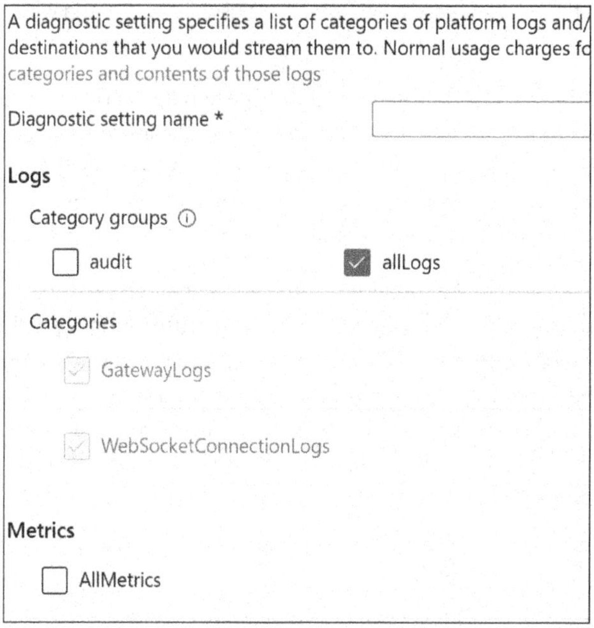

FIGURE 6-2 Category groups in the diagnostic settings for Azure API Management Gateway.

Policies for diagnostics settings

Heinrich has worked closely with the Azure Monitor team to define built-in policies and initiatives and has taken advantage of category groups to enable logging at scale. These DeployIfNotExists policies support Log Analytics, Event Hub, and Storage Account destinations.

Log Analytics

Log Analytics workspaces are the main destinations for logs and are where you, too, will most likely want to send yours. This is because Log Analytics workspaces allow you to use the Kusto Query Language (KQL) to perform queries to search for information and detect patterns.

> **Important** This does not mean you can just forget about the other destinations. Each has its uses. For example, Azure Storage retains logs for longer durations, and Event Hub can send logs to third-party systems like SIEMs. But in most situations, you will probably want to use Log Analytics workspaces because they enable a rich experience for operations.

Log Analytics also enables you to send information to other destinations more selectively. You already saw that the diagnostic settings allow you to specify different destinations, like Azure Storage or Event Hub, and how you can send some categories of logs to Log Analytics and others to Azure Storage. But while this capability is powerful, it might not be flexible enough in many situations. For example, you might want to send only specific types of logged events to an SIEM, like errors, rather than sending all your logs. This can significantly decrease costs, which are usually associated with the amount of data you send.

With Log Analytics, you can use KQL queries to define alerts, and then, when the alert is triggered, you can use an export rule to export only those logs you have identified as significant. You can also use this same approach to export events, alerts, and incidents detected by Azure's SIEM, which is Azure Sentinel, because Azure Sentinel uses Log Analytics to store its data. Moreover, you can use Logic Apps to selectively export events from Azure Analytics using KQL queries.

Using Logic Apps might be the best course in many situations. Later in this chapter, we discuss creating custom events to highlight attacks specifically targeting your solution. Because of their specificity, these types of attacks might go undetected by services like Azure Web Application Firewall (WAF). To manage these uncommon situations, you might want to design your solution to raise custom events and then use Azure Sentinel to raise alerts or create security incidents for them. Also, if you need to send these events to some external system, you will *have* to rely on Logic Apps, because diagnostic settings and Log Analytics export rules do not support custom logs.

Kusto queries

This book is not about Kusto, but it is still helpful to introduce its essential elements. Kusto is a data analytics platform that uses a rich query language called Kusto Query Language (KQL). Although Log Analytics does not leverage all KQL's capabilities, it capitalizes on enough of them to make a discussion of KQL, and of the specific KQL dialect used by Log Analytics, worthwhile.

In Log Analytics, the simplest KQL query contains just the name of a Log Analytics table. Each category discussed previously is mapped to a Log Analytics table. So, if you want to obtain the latest web server logs, you run `AppServiceHTTPLogs` as a query using the **Logs** page for the Log Analytics workspace in Azure Portal. (See Figure 6-3.) The Logs page also enables you to specify a time range.

This can be any date and time range, or even a custom one. The time range is 24 hours by default, but in the example shown in Figure 6-3, it is set to 7 days.

> **Tip** If you do not get the results you expect, check the **Time Range** setting.

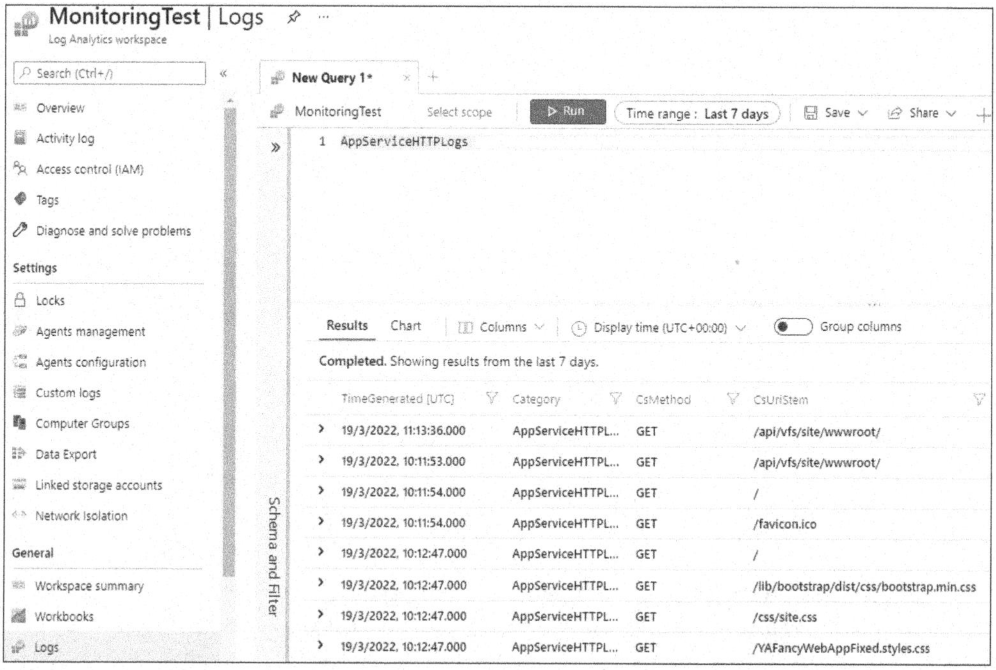

FIGURE 6-3 The simplest KQL query run in Log Analytics.

With KQL, you can concatenate commands using the pipe (|) character, like so:

```
AppServiceHTTPLogs
| take 10
```

By default, a KQL query returns up to 10,000 rows, but this query—called a *table query*—limits the returned items to the first 10 found.

In addition to table queries, you can use KQL to write search queries. The difference between search and table queries is that search queries enable you to search for specific content inside a table, while table queries return all the content inside a table. Also, search queries are typically slower than table queries.

The following search query searches the requested JavaScript files and returns the first 10 rows:

```
search in (AppServiceHTTPLogs) ".js"
| take 10
```

This search query searches all columns in the AppServiceHTTPLogs table. If you were to omit in (AppServiceHTTPLogs), the search would be global to all tables.

If you want to filter the content of a single column, you should use a table query like the one shown here, which returns only the first 10 requests completed with a 200 (OK) status code in the given period:

```
AppServiceHTTPLogs
| where ScStatus == 200
| take 10
```

You can use the where operator to apply more conditions. If you need to apply multiple conditions, you can also use the and operator, like so:

```
AppServiceHTTPLogs
| where ScStatus == 200 and TimeTaken > 100
| take 10
```

Alternatively, you can concatenate multiple where operators, as in the following code:

```
AppServiceHTTPLogs
| where ScStatus == 200
| where TimeTaken > 100
| take 10
```

KQL also supports the use of the or operator, like in this code:

```
AppServiceHTTPLogs
| where ScStatus <> 200 or TimeTaken > 100
| take 10
```

Usually, the result returned is sorted by time in ascending order. To sort the result by time in descending order by a different criterion altogether, you can use the sort operator:

```
AppServiceHTTPLogs
| sort by TimeGenerated desc
```

What if you want to return only the first 10 rows? One way to do this would be to write the following table query:

```
AppServiceHTTPLogs
| sort by TimeGenerated desc
| take 10
```

Alternatively, there is a shorter way to express the same command:

```
AppServiceHTTPLogs
| top 10 by TimeGenerated
```

In this case, descending is the default clause. Therefore, it can be omitted.

You have already seen how changing the Time Range setting in the Logs page in the Azure Portal affects the results you retrieve. But what if you want to control the range within the query itself? You can do so with a time filter, which is expressed between the parentheses. In the following example, we are applying a time filter to retrieve only the records that are older than 1 day.

```
AppServiceHTTPLogs
| where TimeGenerated > ago(1day)
```

You can also express specific dates. You do this using the `datetime` operator. For example, you could use the following query to get all traces between March 1, 2022, and today:

```
AppServiceHTTPLogs
| where TimeGenerated >= datetime(2022-03-01)
```

Sometimes you might not want to retrieve all the columns in a table, but just a subset of them. You can do this using the `project` operator:

```
AppServiceHTTPLogs
| project TimeGenerated, CsMethod, CsUriStem, CsUriQuery, ScStatus
```

You can also create calculated columns and change the names of the columns, like in the following example:

```
AppServiceHTTPLogs
| project TimeGenerated, CsMethod, CsUriStem, CsUriQuery, ScStatus, IsFast = TimeTaken < 100
```

If you want to maintain all the columns in the original table and add a calculated column, you can use the `extend` operator:

```
AppServiceHTTPLogs
| extend IsFast = TimeTaken < 100
```

KQL also allows you to aggregate rows, using the `summarize` operator. For example, the following query returns the maximum time spent on the requests by resource:

```
AppServiceHTTPLogs
| summarize max(TimeTaken) by CsUriStem
```

 Note There are other aggregation functions, too, like avg and count.

You can also perform aggregation on multiple columns, like in the following example:

```
AppServiceHTTPLogs
| summarize avg(TimeTaken) by CsUriStem, ScStatus
```

If you find yourself frequently using the same query over and over, you can save the query in the Logs page. For example, consider the following query. It returns requests resulting in an internal error in the web application, which has an HTTP status code of 500.

```
AppServiceHTTPLogs
| project TimeGenerated, CsMethod, CsUriStem, CsUriQuery, ScStatus
| where ScStatus == 500
```

Saving a query

If you find yourself using this query a lot and you want to save it, follow these steps:

1. Click the **Save** button along the top of the **Logs** page.

2. In the **Save as Query** panel, type a name for the query in the **Query Name** box.

3. Type a brief description of the query in the **Description** box.

4. Make sure the **Save as Legacy Query** checkbox is deselected. Otherwise, you will miss the ability to save to query packs.

5. Select the **Save to Default Query Pack** checkbox. This is the destination location for the query.

6. Use the **Resource Type**, **Category**, and **Label** drop-down lists to add tags to simplify research and retrieval.

In this example, let's call the query **Internal Server Errors** and accept all the defaults. (See Figure 6-4.)

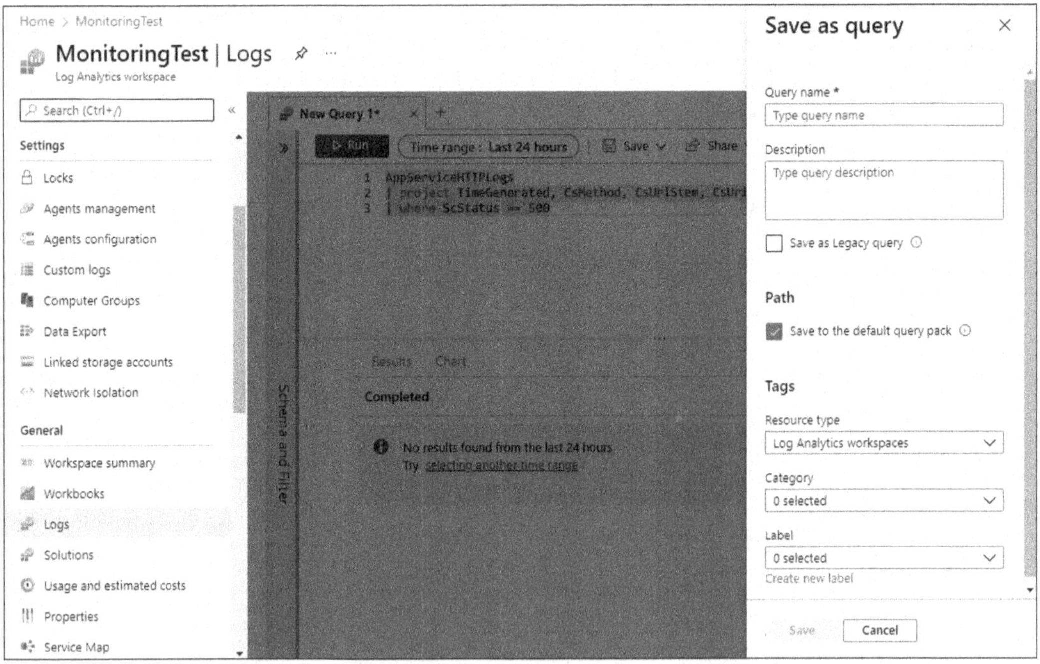

FIGURE 6-4 The Save a Query panel in the Logs page for the Log Analytics workspace in the Azure Portal.

Note We barely scratched the surface of KQL here. There is much more to it than this. Ideally, though, this is enough to serve as a jump start.

Raising alerts

After setting up log collection, you are ready to define the alerts you want to raise for the events you deem significant from a security perspective.

This section describes how you raise alerts from Azure Log Analytics. But the real question is, how do you identify what alerts you should raise? The best approach is to leverage threat modeling. Recall that Chapter 4, "Threat modeling," identified availability as a primary consideration. Fortunately, Log Analytics provides predefined events to determine if a solution is available. For example, you could use AppServiceHTTPLogs logs to check the execution time or the status of the response. If execution times are too long or you start getting too many internal server errors, then you have an availability problem.

You can raise alerts from Log Analytics using simple KQL queries. First, though, you need to create a rule to raise these alerts, which you do in the relevant Log Analytics workspace. For example, suppose you want to create an alert rule to raise an alert if your app experiences more than five internal server errors (500) within a 30-minute period. To do this, you would follow these steps:

1. Navigate to the **Alerts** page of the relevant Log Analytics workspace. Then click the **Create Alert Rule** button. (See Figure 6-5.)

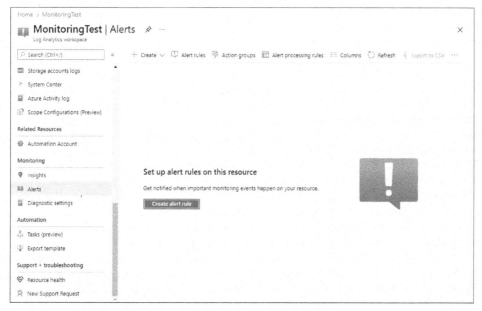

FIGURE 6-5 The Alerts page for the Log Analytics workspace.

The Create an Alert Rule tool starts with the Select a Signal page open. Here, you select the signal to be used as a condition for raising the alert. A signal is nothing more than a predefined KQL query; the target resource emits them. Azure provides many signals out of the box, and you can search them to see if there is something that fits your needs. For this example, however, you will select the Internal Server Errors KQL query you saved in the preceding section.

2. Click the **Custom Log Search** link in the Select a Signal page. (See Figure 6-6.)

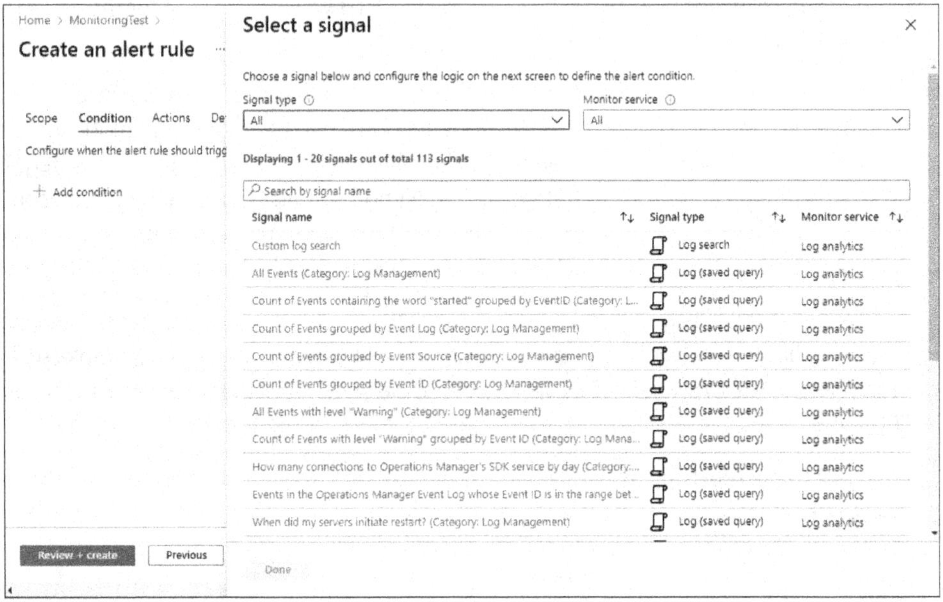

FIGURE 6-6 Creating an alert rule for a Log Analytics workspace.

The Azure Portal opens the familiar **Logs** page.

3. If necessary, open the **Schema and Filter** panel on the left side of the screen (see Figure 6-7). Then click the **Queries** tab.

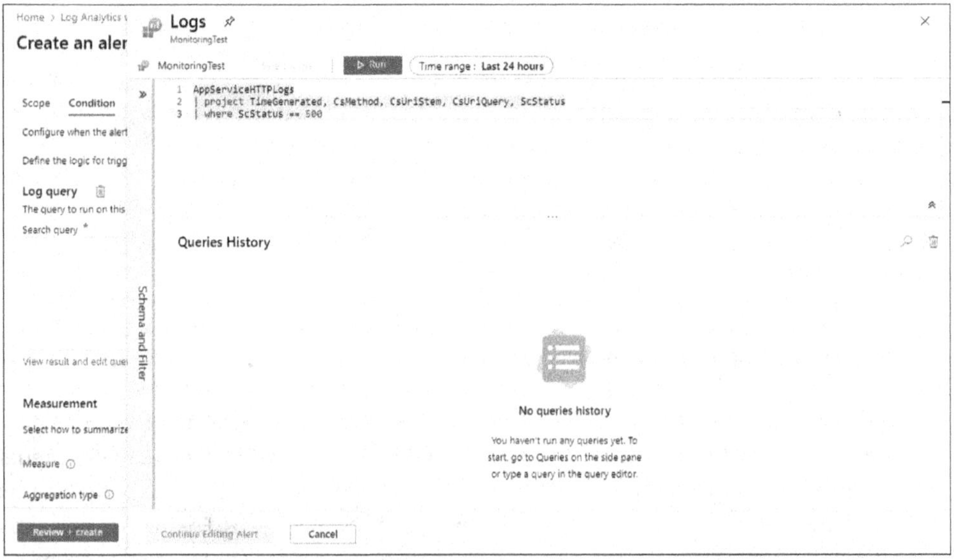

FIGURE 6-7 Specifying the query for the alert rule.

4. In the **Favorites** section of the **Queries** pane, under **Other**, select the **Internal Server Errors** checkbox.

> **Tip** You can filter the queries displayed in the Queries pane to easily locate the query you want.

5. Click the **Run** button to test the query.

6. When you are satisfied that the query works, click the **Continue Editing Alert** button.

7. In the **Create an Alert Rule** dialog (see Figure 6-8 and Figure 6-9), enter the following information:

   • **Measurement** These settings represent the rule to use to evaluate records returned by the query. For this example, leave **Measure** set to **Table Rows** to refer to the results of the query, change **Aggregation Type** to **Count** (to count the number of table rows), and change **Aggregation Granularity** to **30 Minutes** (to consider the last 30 minutes).

   • **Split by Dimensions** You need not split by dimensions in this case, so leave these settings as is.

> **Note** Splitting by dimensions would be helpful if you wanted to discriminate between the various nodes. To do this, you need to include the resource's identifier (_ResourceId).

   • **Alert Logic** In this section, change the **Operator** setting to **Greater Than**, change the **Threshold Value** setting to **5**, and change the **Frequency of Evaluation** setting to **30 Minutes**.

> **Note** You could have a higher frequency, but not one lower than the Granularity value, which is 30 minutes. Higher frequencies improve responsiveness but also increase the cost.

   • **Advanced Options** Click the down arrow to display these options. Then select **2** in the **Number of Violations** drop-down list, select **2** in the **Evaluation Period** drop-down list, and leave the **Override Query Time Range** setting as is. This will raise an alert if two violations occur in two hours. (See Figure 6-9.)

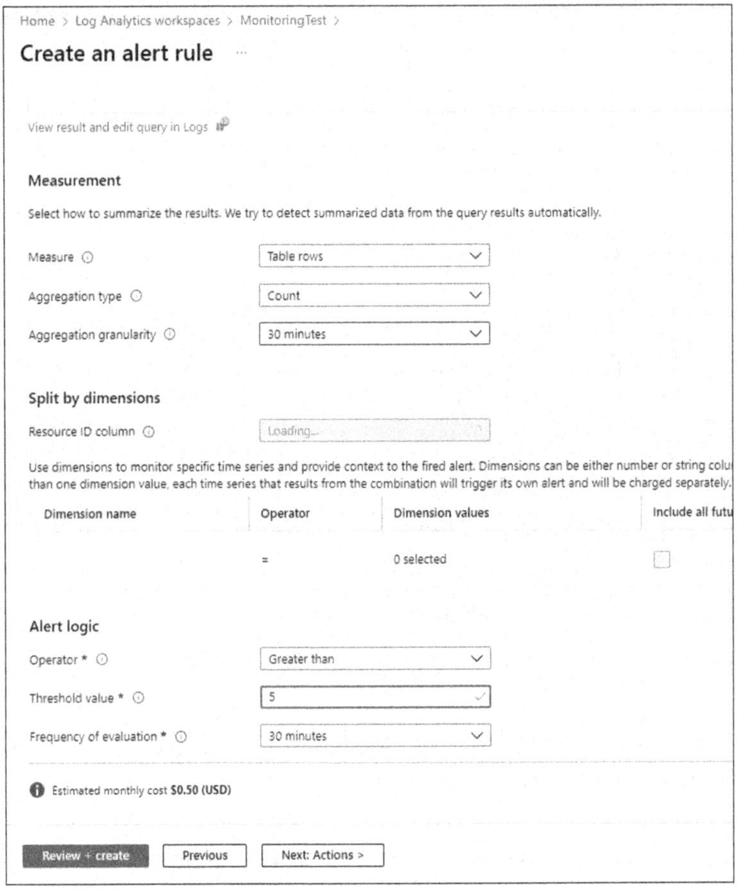

FIGURE 6-8 Configuration of the Measurement, Split by Dimensions, and Alert Logic settings for the new alert rule.

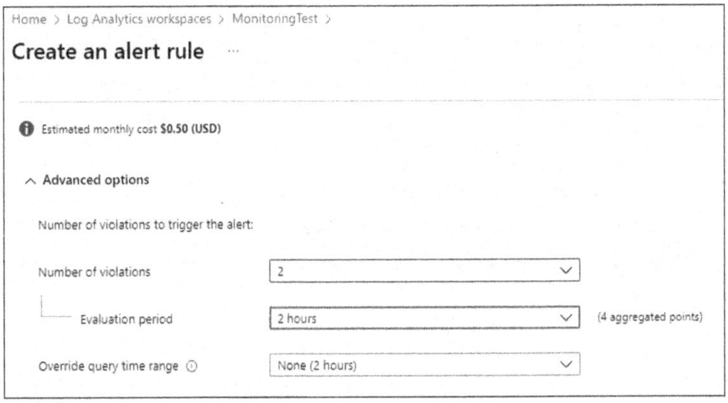

FIGURE 6-9 Configuration of the Advanced Options settings for the new alert rule.

Your next step is to create actions to be triggered automatically when the alert rule is triggered. To do this, you create an action group.

8. Click the **Add Action Groups** button in the **Actions** tab. This will open the interface shown in Figure 6-10. Enter now the necessary information, then click **Next**.

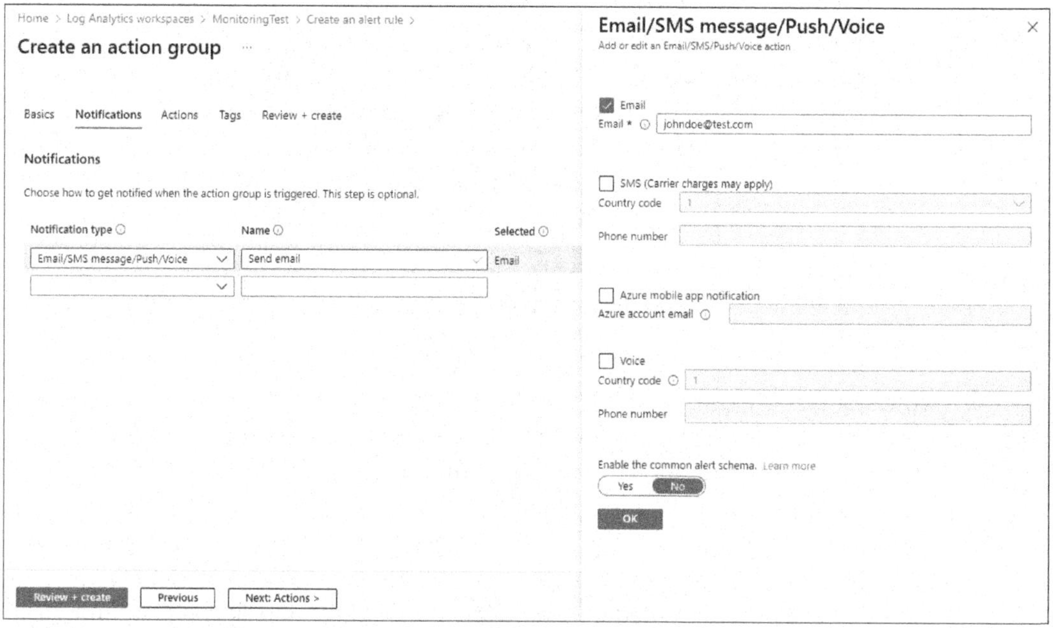

FIGURE 6-10 Configuration of an action group associated to the alert.

Action groups

An action group is a collection of actions triggered by an alert rule. You define an action rule by assigning a name and a display name and then choosing if the action group generates a notification (email, SMS, mobile app notification, or voice message) and/or one or more actions. Action groups currently allow you to include the following actions:

- Executing an automation runbook

- Triggering an Azure Function

- Sending the alert to the Event Hub

- Creating an ITSM ticket (provided an ITSM connection has already been established)

- Executing a Logic App

- Calling a secure webhook (a webhook authenticated with Azure AD)

- Calling a standard webhook (which does not require authentication)

9. Enter the following information in the **Details** tab and click **Review + Create**:

- **Alert Rule Details**   Open the **Severity** drop-down list and choose the severity level to be assigned to the generated alert, type a name for the alert rule in the **Alert Rule Name**, type a description of the alert in the **Alert Rule Description** box, and, optionally, open the **Region** drop-down list and select the region to which the rule should apply.

- **Advanced Options**   Select any of the following checkboxes, depending on your needs: **Enable Upon Creation** (to enable the alert rule right away), **Automatically Resolve Alerts** (when the issue disappears; this function is currently in preview), **Mute Actions** (to discontinue the execution of the actions associated with the alert rule even if the conditions have not yet been resolved), and **Check Workspace Linked Storage** (to tie the creation of the alert rule to the creation of a dedicated Azure Storage linked to the workspace).

After you create and enable the alert rule, it might take some time to become effective, but you will eventually see the alerts and configured actions running.

> **Note**   Many of the concepts discussed in this section also apply to Azure Sentinel, which, as mentioned, is Microsoft's SIEM and SOAR solution for Azure. Both Log Analytics and Sentinel allow you to create alerts and perform actions; this is a natural consequence of Sentinel being based on Azure Monitor. But this does not mean you can replace Azure Sentinel with Azure Monitor. Azure Sentinel focuses specifically on security and introduces specialized tools to manage security incidents, root-cause analysis, and forensic analysis; specialized rules; and integration with Microsoft's Threat Intelligence Platform. Azure Monitor does not offer these capabilities.

Protecting audit logs

Azure Monitor and its component services, including Log Analytics, are PaaS offerings, so a significant part of responsibility for their management and security falls to Microsoft. But users still bear part of the responsibility for protecting audit logs. This section discusses key practices for doing so.

Log Analytics uses Azure Storage to store its data, including the logs. This typically occurs under the hood, without your awareness. But sometimes, you might need to provision an Azure Storage instance managed directly by you—for example, to configure it with customer-managed keys (CMKs), also known as bring your own key (BYOK). When this happens, you assume the responsibility of managing the Azure Storage account.

With CMKs, you provide an encryption key that is stored in Azure Key Vault, preferably in the Premium SKU, which protects the private key in hardware. Storing encryption keys in hardware provides additional protection from Microsoft or someone else accessing the key without authorization. If you configure a CMK, you can virtually destroy all content in the Azure Storage by simply removing the key from the Azure Key Vault—a capability called *crypto-shredding*. For more details on configuring a CMK with Azure Monitor, see https://azsec.tech/w3r.

> **Important** Encrypting data with CMKs gives you more control—but more responsibilities, too. If you do not have a copy of the key or do not configure Key Vault with purge protection and limit who can manage it, it could be possible for malicious actors to remove the key from the system irremediably. This action would immediately render all the stored data inaccessible.

You can also configure Azure Monitor to restrict access to it by replacing its public endpoint with a private endpoint. This configuration allows you to control data-ingestion flows and queries separately. For example, you could decide to allow data to be sent to Log Analytics from systems located in authorized VNets on Azure or through ExpressRoute or a VPN connection and at the same time allow queries from authorized clients from the Internet as shown in Figure 6-11.

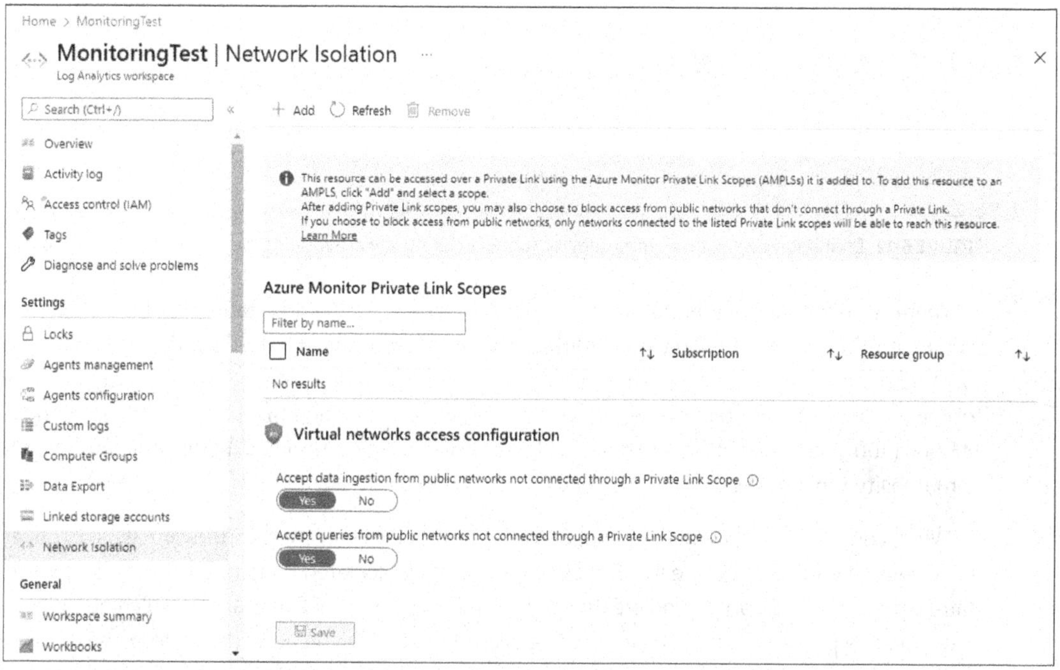

FIGURE 6-11 Configuring network isolation for a Log Analytics workspace.

The preceding points apply to Log Analytics. They also apply to another destination of events raised by the diagnostic settings, with a few minor tweaks: Azure Storage. On a related note, one of the most common use cases for Azure Storage as an event destination is as a long-term repository of audit log traces. In this scenario, you of course want to ensure that no one changes the logs. One way to control this is to assign the write rights sparingly. A more effective approach, however, is to make the Azure Storage immutable. You can apply immutability to the whole Azure Storage when you create it (see Figure 6-12), or you can apply an immutability policy at the container level at any time.

Create a storage account ···

✕

Basics   Advanced   Networking   **Data protection**   Encryption   Tags   Review + create

Tracking

Manage versions and keep track of changes made to your blob data.

☑ Enable versioning for blobs
  Use versioning to automatically maintain previous versions of your blobs for recovery and restoration. Learn more

☐ Enable blob change feed
  Keep track of create, modification, and delete changes to blobs in your account. Learn more

Access control

☑ Enable version-level immutability support
  Allows you to set time-based retention policy on the account-level that will apply to all blob versions. Enable this feature to set a
  default policy at the account level. Without enabling this, you can still set a default policy at the container level or set policies for
  specific blob versions. Versioning is required for this property to be enabled. Learn more

[Review + create]   [< Previous]   [Next : Encryption >]

FIGURE 6-12 Enabling version-level immutability support during the creation of the Azure Storage account.

There are two types of immutability policies. One type is legal hold retention policies. With these, files are protected until the legal hold is lifted. The other type, which is much more common in Azure for storing audit logs, is time-based retention policies. These policies enable you to apply immutability for the duration of the retention period. This is expressed in days and must be a value between 1 and 146,000 (400 years). After that, the data can be removed but not modified. In this way, you can apply immutability temporarily.

When you create a new policy, it applies to all relevant files you create afterward. It also applies to any relevant files that already exist. The expiration date is calculated dynamically based on the creation date of the blob. So, suppose you create a policy with a duration of five years. Any file you upload after you apply the policy will be protected for five years. But any file you uploaded before you applied the policy will be protected for a shorter period, based on when that file was created. For example, if you uploaded the file exactly one year ago, then Azure Storage would protect it for four years, instead of five.

Important If you configure a customer-managed instance of Azure Storage for Azure Log Analytics, do not configure it to be immutable, because this can lead to undesired results. Instead, consider this capability for Azure Storage instances that function as diagnostic settings destinations for various Azure resources or to receive extracts from Log Analytics.

Using policy to add logs

Configuring every resource in your subscriptions to raise the correct events to the proper destinations can be both cumbersome and error prone. For this reason, it might be best to use Azure Policy to define a logging baseline and apply it globally.

If you have never done it, creating appropriate Azure Policies for your logs can be complicated. To help, we talk more about it in Chapter 7, "Governance." In addition, here are two resources to get you started:

- Jim Britt's AzurePolicy repo on GitHub (https://azsec.tech/brt) is extremely helpful for creating Azure policies related to monitoring and logging. It collects various scripts required to generate policies and initiatives with DeployIfNotExists capabilities.

- The Enterprise-Azure-Policy-As-Code repo on GitHub (https://azsec.tech/iv8), which Heinrich maintains in collaboration with other experts, may also be of help. It contains a set of scripts dedicated to enterprise adoption of Azure policies. This repo does not focus just on monitoring and logging, but rather extends to all aspects of governance. It is a particularly good resource if you need a more comprehensive cloud-governance strategy.

Taming costs

The cloud provides seemingly unlimited resources, and you might be tempted to set services up and forget them. Although this might be acceptable in some situations, you must keep in mind that these services come with a cost, and logging services are no exception. Events are billed by the gigabyte, and you pay for the alerts you raise.

> **Tip** For more details on usage costs, see https://azsec.tech/9gp.

If you do not practice due diligence when selecting the events to be tracked, restricting the list only to what is necessary, you could incur unforeseen costs and, worse, spend money unnecessarily. For example, one customer of ours recently increased its Log Analytics costs by $100,000 in one week because of careless logging configuration. It is critical to first define a minimum set of infrastructure-related events to be gathered and then identify, application by application, additional needs.

> **Note** As you will see in the next section, it is not enough to focus on the infrastructural events because they do not consider the specifics of your solution.

Even if you need to generate and process many events, you can still do a lot to reduce your costs. For instance, instead of using a pay-as-you-go model, you can adopt the reserved-capacity model or attach Log Analytics to Sentinel. Both approaches guarantee significant savings. You can also monitor your logging costs and generate alerts when costs become too high. For more information, see https://azsec.tech/f5r and https://azsec.tech/oq1.

The need for intentional security monitoring and auditing

Many organizations adopt a DevOps-based development process—at least on paper. But few understand what DevOps really means. Microsoft defines DevOps as:

> "a compound of development (Dev) and operations (Ops), DevOps is the union of people, process, and technology to continually provide value to customers." Microsoft continues specifying that one of the goals of DevOps is to "[enable] formerly siloed roles—development, IT operations, quality engineering, and security—to coordinate and collaborate to produce better, more reliable products."

If you think about it, DevOps makes sense from a security perspective, because securing a system implies an intimate understanding of the characteristics of that system—how it works and how it could be abused. Having an intimate knowledge of your system is impossible for a centralized security operations center (SOC) team that manages security for all the solutions your organization owns. So, the SOC team must rely exclusively on standard tools and generic best practices to secure your various systems, and as a result, they miss all the specific threats.

This approach cannot provide an adequate level of security for all the systems in your organization. But if you link development, operations, and security, you can establish a communication channel that improves the effectiveness of all three. This collaboration enables your organization to implement the right strategy for monitoring and auditing each application.

The role of threat modeling

Chapter 4 talked about threat modeling. But what does it mean in practical terms?

To answer this, let's focus on your role and duties as a development team member for a solution—specifically, the web application built in Chapter 4 to book COVID vaccinations. You know that threat modeling is an effective approach for identifying ways malicious actors might attack your system, and conveniently, you have already built a threat model for this sample application. So, we will refer to it here.

Recall that during that analysis, we identified several significant vulnerabilities. These included the following:

- Authentication is weak, so an attacker could impersonate a citizen.

- The solution could become unavailable because it is not configured to support high availability.

- The API accesses all resources using credentials stored in a Key Vault, and it accesses the Key Vault using credentials stored in etcd. However, etcd is not secure.

- Vaccination centers access Azure Storage using an Azure Storage account key.

Chapter 4 focused mainly on the first vulnerability: weak authentication. So, let's continue focusing on it here.

If you recall, in Chapter 4, we identified two threats associated with weak authentication:

- The disclosure of sensitive information

- The ability of a malicious actor to change or delete bookings

For these, we considered a couple of possible mitigations:

- Adopting multifactor authentication (MFA)

- Including a registration procedure

Both those mitigations are preventive controls, meaning they attempt to reduce the attack's probability or impact. While these controls would block attackers lacking skill and/or resolve, they merely represent a delay for better attackers. So, what to do?

The defense-in-depth principle requires the adoption of multiple types of controls to increase security. Given that this chapter is about monitoring and auditing, this means that every time we identify a threat, because we have only preventive controls, we should ask ourselves two simple questions:

- How can we detect when this type of attack is actually happening?

- What information must we track to determine how this attack was executed?

The first question relates to identifying the required monitoring controls, while the second focuses on auditing.

Let's consider our specific threats. First, suppose an attacker authenticates as a citizen and, as a result, manages to access sensitive information or to change or delete bookings. Now ask yourself the first question: how can we detect when this type of attack is actually happening? Usually, when dealing with weak authentication, the attacker will make a few failed attempts before they finally succeed and breach the system. So, to detect when this type of attack is actually happening, you could raise an alert when you detect multiple failed access attempts within a set period. Then you could (and should) take certain actions—either manually or automatically—to control and limit the damage. Table 6-1 outlines just such a scenario, including events to monitor, alerts to issue, and actions to take.

TABLE 6-1 Events, alerts, and actions to detect when an unauthorized user is attempting to access your system

Event	Alert	Actions
Failed Authentication: This is when a user fails authentication. The event should contain the name of the account, the caller's IP address, and its user agent.	**Too Many Failed Authentications:** This should be raised when more than five Failed Authentication events occur in a span of 10 minutes.	Create a security incident if more than two Too Many Failed Authentication alerts are raised in 1 hour. Investigate and resolve the security incident. If more than 10 flagged events in the 10 minutes are related to the same IP address, disable it for 1 hour.

Event	Alert	Actions
Successful Authentication: This is when a user is successfully authenticated. The event should contain the name of the account, the caller's IP address, and its user agent.	None	None

> **Important** When selecting events, consider potential limitations imposed by relevant laws and regulations. For example, some privacy laws might not allow you to track IP addresses. Other fields could expose sensitive information, including the body of some messages. Also be aware that some laws, like the EU's General Data Protection Regulation (GDPR), might apply to your solution even if it is based in another country, because some users could reside in or be a citizen of the EU. Evaluate these situations carefully with the help of internal privacy experts or lawyers who specialize in privacy.

Not all events need to be monitored. For example, it probably is not necessary to monitor Successful Authentication events because in most cases these events do not pose a problem and tracking them would represent an additional burden and generate additional costs. This is why there are no alerts or actions listed for this event in Table 6-1. Still, you want to log Successful Authentication events in the Audit Log, because this could provide needed information during root-cause analysis in case of an incident.

In any case, it all starts with the two events: Successful Authentication and Failed Authentication. It does not matter if these events are raised by the Azure infrastructure or by the application itself, but they must be used somewhat, or they would be missed. In this example, both these events are raised by the application, because authentication is custom. It is then the responsibility of the operations team to define and generate related alerts when those events occur and perform the required actions.

To summarize, a possible approach to dealing with events, alerts, and actions is as follows:

1. Threat modeling is performed to identify which events you need and why you need them to detect a specific threat or threats and to describe how you would use those events.

2. Using input from the threat model and consulting with the security and operations teams, the development team designs the events to detect in the application.

   At the same time, consulting with the security team, the operations team designs alerts and related actions for each event (if needed).

3. The development team implements the events in the solution.

4. The operations team implements the alerts and actions in the solution.

Custom events

Everything discussed so far in this chapter is part of the Azure infrastructure or is a process you can implement within your organization. There is just one exception we have not yet discussed: creating custom events, like the Failed Authentication event mentioned earlier.

> **Note** The Successful Authentication event does not pose a problem. You can raise it as a standard console event. Alternatively, use something like AzureMonitorTraceListener, which is part of Microsoft.WindowsAzure.WebSites.Diagnostics, and then configure the diagnostic settings to send the event to Azure Storage.

Creating custom events in Log Analytics is based on the Log Analytics Data Collector API, which is currently in preview. Ideally, by the time you read this, it will have been made generally available. We believe that the best way to learn is by example, so we will introduce the API using a simple scenario involving a web application we created called YAFancyWebApp. You can find it here: https://azsec.tech/fq1. This application does not do much; it simply asks for your name and welcomes you. See Figure 6-13.

FIGURE 6-13 The YAFancyWebApp home page.

> **Note** This section focuses mainly on submitting custom events to Log Analysis. The repository provides a simple step-by-step guide for deploying this sample to your Azure subscription.

If you type **John Doe** in the **Please Specify Your Name** box and click the **Submit** button, the web app greets you with a friendly "Welcome John Doe!" message. Behind the scenes, the app's home page, Index.cshtml, performs a redirect to page Welcome.cshtml with a POST, sending the username in a field called Username. This is then recovered by the target page and shown as is, with no checks.

That would typically be OK, but the code in the example has been artfully crafted to be vulnerable to cross-site scripting (XSS). Chapter 9, "Secure coding," explains what XSS is in more detail. So, if you submit the text **John<script>alert('XSS!')</script>** in the app's home page, you get a message happily announcing **XSS!**. See Figure 6-14. This shows that, indeed, the site is vulnerable to XSS. So, an attacker would be able to execute a script of their choice.

FIGURE 6-14 The dreaded XSS! panel.

Important This site is based on ASP.NET MVC Razor from .NET 6. Such technology is typically enough to protect sites against common XSS attacks like this one. However, in this case it is not, because on the Welcome.cshtml page, we used `@Html.Raw(Model.Message)` instead of the more natural `Model.Message`. While this is OK for our example, such a choice would typically be a mistake because it introduces vulnerabilities.

How can we fix this behavior? Project YAFancyWebAppFixed shows you how. To begin, change the `OnPost()` method on the Welcome page as follows (see file Welcome.cshtml.cs):

```
public IActionResult OnPost()
{
    var username = Request.Form["Username"];
    if (Validate(username))
    {
        Message = "Welcome " + username + "!";
        return Page();
    }
    else
        {
            SecurityLogger.Instance.Log("xss", username);
            return RedirectToPage("./NiceTry");
        }

    }
```

The new code receives the username as a post field named `"Username"`, as the original code did. But, instead of directly applying it to the message, it first validates it using the `Validate()` method. If everything is correct, the message is updated, and the user sees the Welcome page. But if the validation fails, then a `SecurityLogger` is called to log the problem, and the browser is redirected to a NiceTry page.

Now, after deploying YAFancyWebAppFixed, try to call the site with `John<script>alert('XSS!')</script>`. You do not get the XSS message anymore, but a page using a strip from XKCD shows the consequences of not validating your inputs correctly.

This validation function is simple: it uses an essential regular expression accepting alphabetical characters and refusing anything else. Chapter 9 introduces much better ways to perform your validation, so we will refer to that chapter for the details. For now, the most important part of the example for our purposes is the `SecurityLogger` class. This class is based on `LogAnalytics.Client`, a NuGet package that wraps access to the LogAnalytics Data Collector API. This library is open source, and its repo is available at https://azsec.tech/vu0.

`SecurityLogger` is a singleton. You must initialize it before you use it by calling the `Initialize()` method. You can find this call at the start of Program.cs, which ensures it runs as early as possible. This method is asynchronous because it performs a few initialization activities that could require some time to complete:

1. It retrieves the URL of the Key Vault containing configuration information from the environment variable `"KeyVaultUri"`.

2. It creates a connection to the Key Vault, authenticating with the Managed Identity assigned to the App Service hosting the web application.

3. Using this connection to Key Vault, it retrieves the `WorkspaceId` and `WorkspaceKey` of the reference Log Analytics workspace.

4. It initializes with that information the `LogAnalyticsClient`, which is the client for the Data Collector API implemented by LogAnalytics.Client.

```
public class SecurityLogger
{
    private static readonly SecurityLogger _instance = new SecurityLogger();
    private LogAnalyticsClient? _client;

    private SecurityLogger()
    {
    }

    public static SecurityLogger Instance => _instance;

    public void Log(string category, string payload)
    {
        var encoder = HtmlEncoder.Create(allowedRanges : new[] { UnicodeRanges.BasicLatin
});
        _client?.SendLogEntry<PossibleAttackAttempt>(new PossibleAttackAttempt()
        {
            Category = category,
            Payload = encoder.Encode(payload)
        }, "Security");
    }

    public async Task Initialize()
    {
        var uri = Environment.GetEnvironmentVariable("KeyVaultUri");
        if (uri != null)
        {
            SecretClient client = new SecretClient(new Uri(uri), new
DefaultAzureCredential());
            var workspaceId = (await client.GetSecretAsync("WorkspaceId"))?.Value?.Value;
```

```
                   var workspaceKey = (await client.GetSecretAsync("WorkspaceKey"))?.Value?.
      Value;
                   if (!string.IsNullOrWhiteSpace(workspaceId) && !string.IsNullOrWhiteSpace
      (workspaceKey))
                   {
                       _client = new LogAnalyticsClient(
                               workspaceId: workspaceId,
                               sharedKey: workspaceKey);
                   }
              }
          }
      }
```

After initialization, it is possible to send an event to the Log Analytics Data Collector API with the
Log() method of SecurityLogger. This method takes two parameters: a category (for example, XSS
for detected cross-site scripting attacks) and the payload identified as potentially malicious.

The Log() method starts by defining an HTML encoder. Adopting this encoder is crucial because
it allows for the conversion of potentially malicious payloads to prevent them from causing additional
damage. For this reason, the code initializes the encoder to consider every character in the Basic Latin
Unicode character set as secure while encoding everything else.

After that, it calls the SendLogEntry() method of LogAnalyticsClient. This method is particularly important; therefore, it is necessary to spend some time on it. It is shown here:

```
_client?.SendLogEntry<PossibleAttackAttempt>(new PossibleAttackAttempt()
{
    Category = category,
    Payload = encoder.Encode(payload)
}, "Security");
```

SendLogEntry is a generic method taking a class as a parameter, an instance of said class as the
first argument, and a string as the second. The class, PossibleAttackAttempt, defines the event
fields you need in Log Analytics, as shown here:

```
public class PossibleAttackAttempt
{
    public string? Category;
    public string? Payload;
}
```

The PossibleAttackAttempt class represents the fields of the event as fields of the class. Not all
types are supported, however. Currently, only the following types are allowed:

- string

- bool

- double

- DateTime

- Guid

> **Note** As shown in the class declaration, these fields can be nullable.

In our case, we have just two fields as strings. The second one, `Payload`, is assigned the encoded value of the received payload, while the first is the category passed as the first argument of the `Log()` method.

The second parameter of the `Log()` method is the name of the custom log to be created—or to be exact, part of it. Azure Log Analytics appends the suffix _CL to the name passed as an argument to generate the custom log's name. If the second parameter has the value `"Security"`, the code generates a custom log named Security_CL.

The first time you send an event to Log Analytics, it takes a few minutes for that event to become visible, because Log Analytics must create the required tables from the received request. After this first request, though, the required time is much shorter.

Alerts from custom events on Azure Sentinel

Now that we have the first custom events in our system, you might wonder what you can do with them. You have already seen how to create alert rules in Log Analytics; this time, we want to show you something different: how to create alerts in Azure Sentinel. As mentioned, Azure Sentinel is Microsoft's SIEM for Azure. Since we have mentioned it a few times already in this chapter, you should have at least a vague idea about it. So, let's configure the alert on Sentinel.

First, you need to create an instance of Azure Sentinel and associate it with a Log Analytics workspace. To do so, you can create the instance of Azure Sentinel as you would create any other resource on Azure. The reference Log Analytics workspace is a required parameter for the creation of the Azure Sentinel instance. For our purposes, it is easiest to use the same workspace you have been using because it gives visibility over all the events stored there, including custom logs like Security_CL.

Next, you need to create an alert for when there are more than five events in 30 minutes. To do so, you create a scheduled query rule in the Azure Sentinel Analytics Rule Wizard from the Analytics configuration setting for Sentinel. See Figure 6-15. On the first tab of the wizard, called **General**, you specify the rule's name, description, classification by the MITRE ATT&CK (in the **Tactics and Techniques** field), and severity.

In the wizard's **Set Rule Logic** tab, you define a KQL query, which you can use to identify the events of interest. In our case, we could use the following query:

```
Security_CL
| where Category == 'XSS'
```

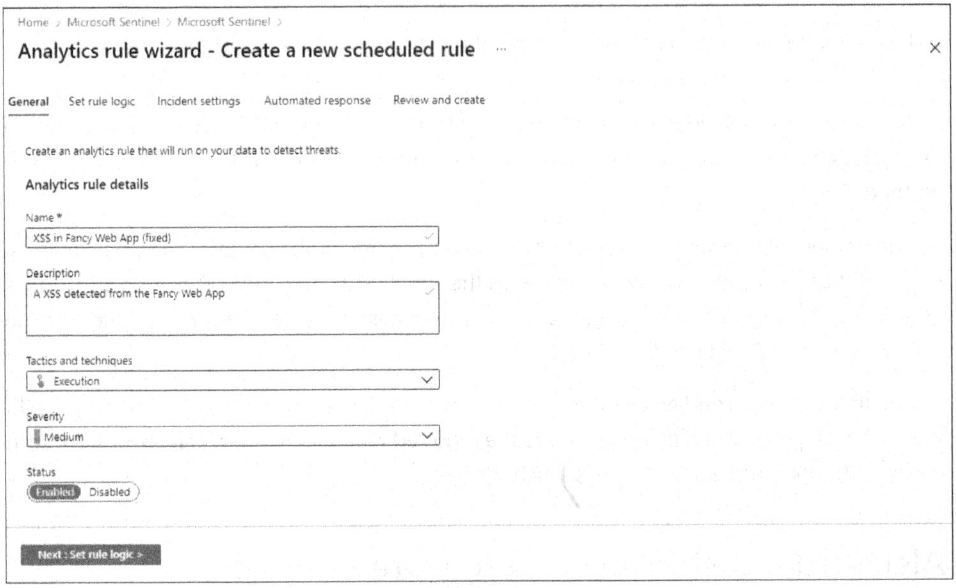

FIGURE 6-15 The General tab of the Analytics Rule Wizard.

On the same tab, in the **Alert Details** section, you can set some details for the alert to be generated, like the following:

- **Alert Name Format** This defines the format of the alert's name. In this case, specify that the parameters should appear between double curly brackets, like so: **"{{Category}} attempt"**.

- **Alert Description Format** This defines the format of the alert's description. This works like the Alert Name Format box. For example, you could use **"This is a {{Category}} attempt"**.

In the **Query Scheduling** section, you set the query's scheduling parameters:

- **Run Query Every** This defines the frequency of the query. Set this to **15 Minutes**.

- **Lookup Time** Per the alert's specifications, set this **30 Minutes**. This setting must be equal to or greater than the Run Frequency setting.

Finally, you should configure the additional parameters at the end of the **Set Rule Logic** tab:

- **Alert Threshold** Per the alert's specifications, select **Greater Than 5**.

- **Event Grouping** Group all events in a single alert to avoid too many alerts.

- **Suppression** Choose **4 Hours** to the query to expire four after Sentinel generates the alert. This reduces the number of generated alerts.

You can then enable the automatic generation of a security incident with the alert, accept all the other defaults, and create the rule. After a short while, try generating a few simulated attacks on the web application. After you execute the sixth attack in a few minutes, Sentinel generates an alert and a security incident. See Figure 6-16.

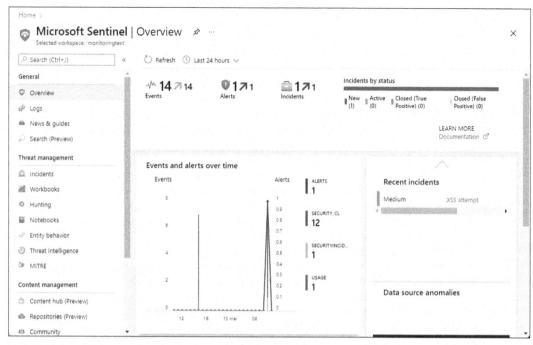

FIGURE 6-16 Alerts and incidents generated by the new rule.

Summary

Monitoring and auditing play essential roles in securing solutions. Too often, we consider them at the very end of the development process. While understandable, this approach can have devastating effects on the security of our solutions.

It is not enough to enable all the events raised by the infrastructure. This chapter covers the basic functionalities provided by Azure, and they are just the start. For example, with various Microsoft Defender services, Azure provides a full suite of tools to integrate and extend how you monitor the Azure infrastructure. But even if you enabled all of them, it would not be enough. This is because an effective monitoring and logging strategy is not based simply on the tools you use but, more importantly, on a clear understanding of the attacks you potentially face. This knowledge allows you to identify the events required to detect attacks in progress, raise alerts, and take actions to respond. A good response is possible only if monitoring is good, and good monitoring is possible only if it is based not just on the infrastructure that hosts your solutions, but on the specific characteristics of those solutions. This chapter introduced all those concepts, and it ideally helped you understand what first steps you can take to improve your monitoring and auditing strategy.

This chapter has briefly introduced the topic of governance; you will learn more about this crucial topic in Chapter 7.

Governance

After completing this chapter, you will be able to:

- Explain the purpose of governance.

- Understand the topics of governance and the impact of governance on your solution.

- Review your solution's compliance in the Azure Portal.

- Understand the increasingly stringent enforcement as your solution moves through the different environments toward production.

- Understand the role Microsoft Defender for Cloud plays in governance.

- Understand best practices about Microsoft Defender for Cloud Secure Score.

Governance and the developer

IT governance involves defining and aligning IT with corporate goals and strategies. A narrower definition, applied in this chapter, stems from the field of governance, risk, and compliance (GRC): IT governance deals with the creation of processes and policies, as well as with their enforcement through guardrails such as Azure Policy.

Every IT and cybersecurity organization uses governance to mitigate the risk of breaches. This same governance is also used to keep systems manageable. While much of this is hidden from solution developers, this chapter discusses governance and how it affects your projects.

General governance, such as allowed Azure locations, required tags, and allowed resource types, is often enforced with the same processes and technologies.

Areas of governance align closely with compliance frameworks such as CIS and NIST 800-53. Microsoft has codified this through the Azure Security Benchmark version 3 (https://docs.microsoft.com/en-us/security/benchmark/azure/overview).

Azure Security Benchmark version 3

The Azure Security Benchmark (ASB) provides prescriptive security best practices and recommendations to improve the security posture of your Azure workloads. When considering all things security, the ASB should be your primary reference, because many tools in Azure reference the ASB. You can get to the ASB here: https://azsec.tech/8ui. The ASB is structured as security control topics, which are discussed here.

Azure Security Baselines are the Azure service–specific implementation and enforcement guidelines of the ASB security control topics that follow the same structure and naming. The following list directs you to the security baselines for a few Azure services:

- **Cosmos DB** https://azsec.tech/09z

- **Azure Key Vault** https://azsec.tech/53x

- **Linux virtual machines (VMs)** https://azsec.tech/9xr

- **Logic Apps** https://azsec.tech/veb

> **Note** Many topics in ASB are global controls and do not require specific entries in the security baselines. In v1.x and v2.0, these global controls are sometimes repeated by the security baseline. Not all security controls are applicable to all Azure services.

Network security

This topic is the most visible one, as it directly drives the design and implementation of networks and requirements for solution architectures. Common patterns are as follows:

- Hub-and-spoke model for virtual networks (VNets), as defined in the Cloud Adoption Framework enterprise-scale landing zones (https://azsec.tech/54n).

- Perimeter defenses (for example, firewalls, network security groups, gateways, and so on) employed for network protection. This is the most mature form of security, as traditional defenses rely heavily on perimeter defenses.

- VM access, such as just in time (JIT) and Azure Bastion.

- PaaS services' network isolation with private endpoints, VNet integration, VNet injection, and Azure services–managed VNets. These are the most visible controls for software development because they restrict deployments and put additional demands on access, such as debugging.

- Distributed denial-of-service (DDoS) attack protection.

Identity management

If you use Azure Active Directory (AAD) as the identity system, IT will have a dedicated team tasked with designing, operating, and protecting identity systems.

The following points affect the solution architecture and security:

- Use modern authentication systems, such as AAD, for user and process authentication.
  - Use plain AAD, AAD B2B, or AAD B2C for end-user authentication.
  - Enforce MFA and other conditional access protections.
- Use Managed Identities for processes.
- Authenticate every consumed service endpoint with Transport Layer Security (TLS) or similar.
- For existing solutions with legacy identity management, identity management is important and must adhere to good practices. Consider upgrading to modern authentication and authorization, such as AAD.

Privileged access

Privileged access is likely handled by the identity team. Developers may notice the effects, such as multifactor authentication (MFA) requirements, JIT access rights, and approvals. Depending on the level of access, developers may also need to use a privileged access workstation (PAW).

Data protection

Data protection starts with knowing the value or sensitivity of data.

Real-world experience: Protecting trivial data with vigor

Heinrich dealt with an Azure integration solution to replace an existing solution that required approval by the infosec team. One of the issues was a storage account that had to be public for technical reasons and contained only trivial data with no discernable value to the company or any adversary. We could not convince the infosec team to grant us an exception, costing the company $30 million in licensing costs each month since the old system had to be maintained while the replacement systems deployment was blocked. To compound the problem, the security team insisted on a complex solution that made the real business data less secure while improving security for the worthless data.

Encrypting data at rest and in transit is considered a minimum bar for any system. For development teams, responsibilities arise around key management support, crypto agility, and not putting secrets into code. The responsibility for provisioning and rotating secrets, certificates, and keys is often handled by a small operations group with key management responsibilities. This ensures separation of duties and minimizes the number of people with access to such items. Chapter 10, "Cryptography in Azure," covers cryptography in Azure.

Azure supports customer-managed keys (CMKs) for many at-rest encryption services. Many professionals recommend avoiding CMK unless required otherwise by law or compliance. Manually handling secrets is a bigger risk than a cloud provider mishandling secrets. Instead, use Customer Lockbox for Microsoft Azure (https:// azsec.tech/o4z) to be included in the decision process when a Microsoft engineer needs access to your keys. However, CMK can be used to enable crypto-shredding. See Chapter 10 for more information.

Asset management

Asset management is an operational requirement and is essential for security. Ask yourself, how can I protect assets I don't know about? Cybersecurity personnel will be granted the Security Reader role at the tenant level to review the security posture and to investigate incidents. This is outside the responsibility of software development.

Logging and threat detection

Logging is often enabled via Azure Policy using the DeployIfNotExists effect, configured using the diagnostic settings (https://docs.microsoft.com/en-us/azure/governance/policy/concepts/effects#deployifnotexists).

Azure also provides advanced threat protection capabilities under the Defender brands. Defender is managed by the operations team, and any detection incidents are managed by security information and event management (SIEM) and security orchestration automation and response (SOAR) systems, such as Azure Sentinel. This is outside the responsibility of software development even in a DevOps organization.

Incident response

Incident response is the responsibility of cybersecurity operations. Solution teams will be asked to support incident investigations and recovery implementations.

Posture and vulnerability management

This topic contains several items of relevance:

- Secure configuration is achieved through IaC, where every deployment is the same. Reviewing the IaC will ensure that the repeatable deployment is secure.

- This is enforced with Azure Policy to audit and even deny deployments that do not meet security requirements.

- Core images are hardened.

- Updates for security vulnerabilities are rapid and automated. A common understanding among most security experts is that all updates to operating system (OS) and software components should be applied within hours of publishing or at most within days. The argument against this often relates to regression testing. In reality, IT organizations cannot fully regression-test a new OS release; therefore, the best approach is to apply the update but have strategies for breaking changes, such as blue/green deployment with gradual traffic redirection or ways to roll back updates. This approach does require a higher maturity level in the automated-deployment approach. At a minimum, every organization must define the process, timeframe, and audit trails for such updates, balanced with the security of the vulnerability.

- Perform red-team exercises to find vulnerabilities before your adversaries do.

Endpoint security

In this context, endpoint security refers to VM protection against threats such as viruses and others. This topic is not part of solution design or implementation.

Backup and recovery

While executing backups and recoveries is an operational responsibility, designing a system to enable backups and recoveries, and designing resiliency as well as disaster recoverability, is very much part of good system design.

DevOps security

This topic directly affects solution development and is covered throughout this book.

Governance and strategy

This area deals with enterprise strategy and how to define a governance architecture for the enterprise. It also encompasses the processes, controls definitions, enforcement, and auditing strategies around the other Azure Security Benchmark topics. This is handled by enterprise architects and cybersecurity architects.

Governance enforcement

Governance is enforced through processes (reviews and approvals), education/documentation (library of control objectives and controls), role-based access control (RBAC), and automated enforcement.

Enforcement through processes

The typical means for this kind of enforcement are architecture review boards (ARBs), pull request reviews/approvals, permission to operate (PTO), service ticket approvals, and continuous integration/continuous deployment (CI/CD) pipeline stage approvals.

Governance documentation and security education

Cybersecurity in cooperation will create a list of control objectives. Controls for the platform and individual Azure resource types are derived from these control objectives. For Azure, these items are codified in the ASB and Azure Security Baselines for the resource types with actionable recommendations. These documents must be available to all IT staff and solution developers in a library. Cybersecurity should provide training on how to read and use the control lists.

Role-based access control

Role-based access control (RBAC) is used to limit access to users and processes by following the least-privilege principle. For example, developers should not be granted modify access to production systems on a permanent basis, and any need for such must follow a stringed approval workflow. Service principals must also follow the principle of least privilege to prevent large-scale damage if the service is compromised.

Automated enforcement during deployment

Good governance requires automating anything that can be automated. In the cloud world, we use IaC to define every aspect of the infrastructure in every environment. IaC must be applied though CI/CD pipelines. Discipline like this keeps the environment stable, secure, compliant, and recoverable after a destructive attack (for example, by ransomware). It also enables advanced scenarios, such as CD at arbitrarily short time intervals and blue/green deployment scenarios.

Code must be checked with, at a minimum, static analysis security tools (SAST) and software component analysis (SCA) software to catch mistakes. This requirement applies equally to IaC.

Microsoft Defender for Cloud

Microsoft Defender for Cloud (DfC) plays an important role in your security posture generally and in governance specifically. In addition to service-specific defenders providing sophisticated detection, DfC also refers to security-related views in the Azure Portal, formerly known as Azure Security Center.

To stay on top of your Microsoft Defender for Cloud, keep the following URLs handy:

- **What's New in Microsoft Defender for Cloud** https://azsec.tech/cal

- **Important Upcoming Changes to Microsoft Defender for Cloud** https://azsec.tech/lnb

The second URL documents the dates on which you can expect updates to go live and affect your Secure Score (see the next section).

Secure Score

Secure Score does not represent an industry standard. It is defined by Microsoft and provides a point-in-time evaluation of a system. It cannot be used to compare systems. Furthermore, Secure Score does not consider business needs. For example, it will highlight Azure Storage accounts exposed over the internet, even if it is supposed to be like that and you have taken all precautions to protect it.

> **Note** Customers should not strive to reach a score of 100 percent. Every system will have exceptions. The point is to manage those exceptions in a structured way.

Secure Score is only one way to track your security posture over time and should be used as a baseline check. As with any metrics expressed as a percentage, do not strive for 100 percent. It is more important to track whether your score is going up or down. In general, it should not be going down, but it is a little more complicated than that. Secure Score is a point-in-time measurement, but measurement points vary because service checks occur at differing intervals. For example, some VM checks occur every 24 hours, and others every 8 hours. So, a change to the environment might not show up in your Secure Score for a day or so. It's also important to understand that Secure Score will go up and down over time. This is common and expected. It may go up as you apply recommendations or exempt noncompliant resources, and it may go down if new services are onboarded.

> **Important** If left alone, Secure Score will go down as new checks from Azure come online.

One final point: you should enable the Secure Score Over Time workbook. This will help you track your delta over time. It will also show you what has changed over the period of interest.

> **Real-world experience: Watching Secure Score**
>
> Someone in your organization must manage Secure Score to make sure it does not slide unexpectedly. That person will understand what is coming soon to Secure Score and help determine which checks to remediate or exempt.

Reviewing compliance state for solution

The Azure Portal has many ways of looking for noncompliant resources. Solution teams require Security Reader access to investigate noncompliant resources in development subscriptions.

Microsoft Defender for Cloud can show just the noncompliant resources, a security score, and a regulatory compliance view based on the control objectives in Azure Security Benchmark and other compliance frameworks. See Figure 7-1.

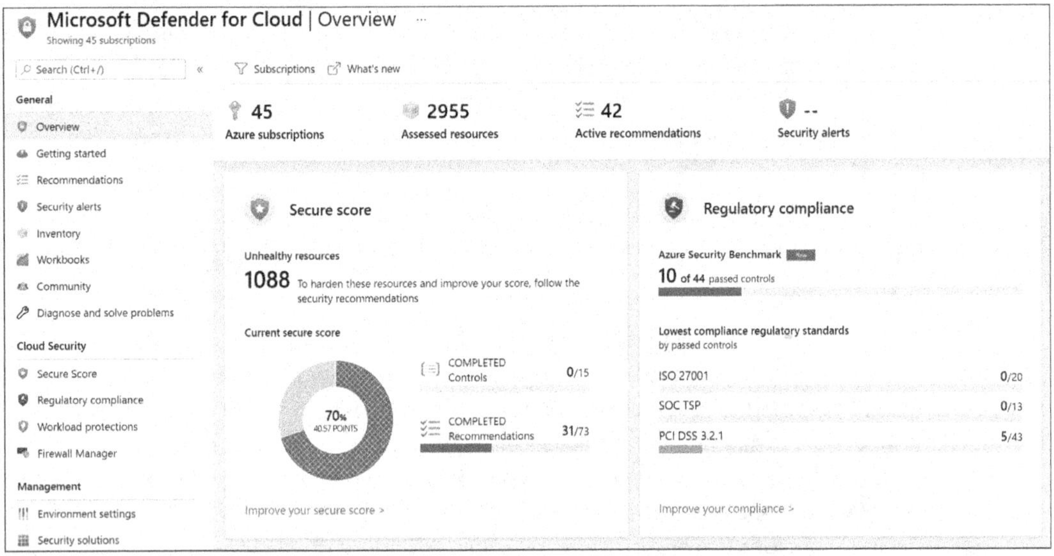

FIGURE 7-1   Microsoft Defender for Cloud Blade.

The Azure Portal's Policy blade shows definitions, assignments, compliance, and remediations. For development teams, compliance is the important blade. In addition to listing noncompliant resources, it is mapped back to compliance frameworks. See Figure 7-2. Compliance details are covered in Chapter 8, "Compliance and risk programs."

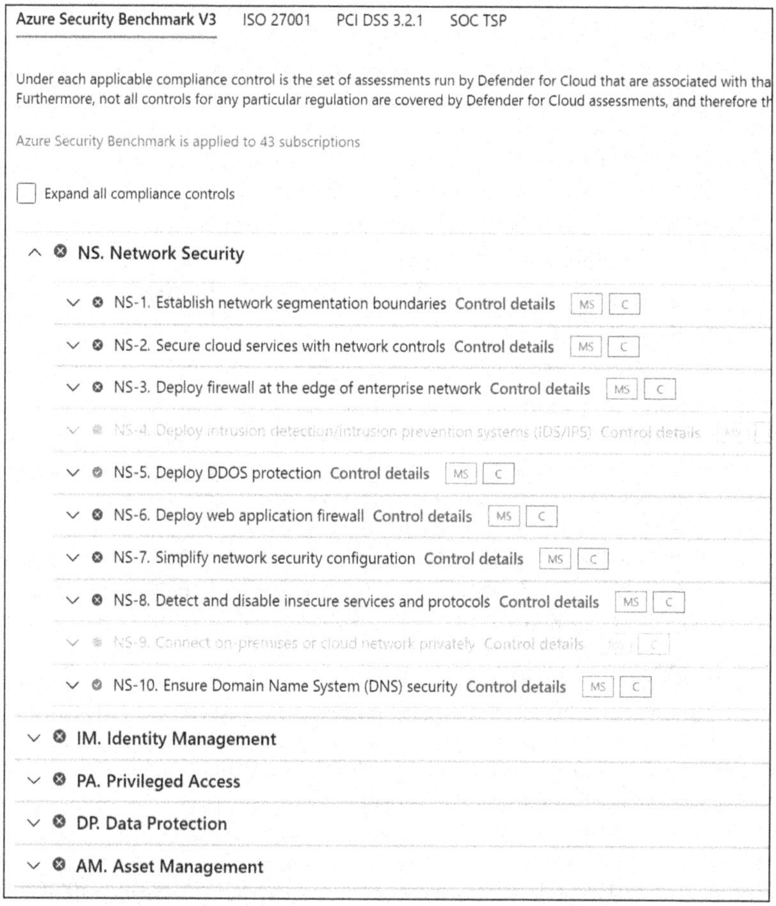

Azure Security Benchmark V3   ISO 27001   PCI DSS 3.2.1   SOC TSP

Under each applicable compliance control is the set of assessments run by Defender for Cloud that are associated with tha
Furthermore, not all controls for any particular regulation are covered by Defender for Cloud assessments, and therefore th

Azure Security Benchmark is applied to 43 subscriptions

☐ Expand all compliance controls

∧ ⊗ **NS. Network Security**

　∨ ⊗ NS-1. Establish network segmentation boundaries Control details [MS] [C]

　∨ ⊗ NS-2. Secure cloud services with network controls Control details [MS] [C]

　∨ ⊗ NS-3. Deploy firewall at the edge of enterprise network Control details [MS] [C]

　∨ ⊗ NS-4. Deploy intrusion detection/intrusion prevention systems (IDS/IPS) Control details [MS] [C]

　∨ ⊘ NS-5. Deploy DDOS protection Control details [MS] [C]

　∨ ⊗ NS-6. Deploy web application firewall Control details [MS] [C]

　∨ ⊗ NS-7. Simplify network security configuration Control details [MS] [C]

　∨ ⊗ NS-8. Detect and disable insecure services and protocols Control details [MS] [C]

　∨ ⊗ NS-9. Connect on-premises or cloud network privately Control details [MS] [C]

　∨ ⊘ NS-10. Ensure Domain Name System (DNS) security Control details [MS] [C]

∨ ⊗ **IM. Identity Management**

∨ ⊗ **PA. Privileged Access**

∨ ⊗ **DP. Data Protection**

∨ ⊗ **AM. Asset Management**

FIGURE 7-2 Compliance details tab for Azure Security Benchmark v3.

Azure Policy

Azure Policy (https://azsec.tech/t2s) is used to enforce governance for security and operational hygiene. Most ASB topics (discussed earlier in this chapter) have built-in Azure Policies to audit and/or enforce security-relevant settings. Most service baselines list the applicable service-specific policies for each topic.

> **Note** Azure Policy could fill an entire book; we are covering only the most pertinent topics here.

Azure Initiatives and compliance frameworks

Initiatives (originally called Policy Sets) bundle many policies into a single assignable entity. Most initiatives bundle the policies (controls) for a compliance framework.

The built-in Azure Security Benchmark Initiative bundles the relevant policies from ASB and the service-specific security baselines. Similar Initiatives for other frameworks exist (for example, NIST SP-800-53 r5, NIST SP-800-171, and so on). These Initiatives make policy assignments easier, bundling hundreds of policies together. Most important, they drive the display of compliance, Security Score, and many other views in DfC (discussed earlier in this chapter). This is done though a mapping called groupNames, in the JSON Initiative definition.

Azure Policy effects

Azure Policy uses the effect value (often passed as a parameter to the policy) to select which capability to use for a policy. For example:

- Audit resource settings for compliance with security controls through Audit or AuditIfNotExists (AINE) effects. Such a policy will flag a resource as noncompliant. This feature is available through Defender for Cloud and Azure Sentinel. If a resource in a solution is flagged, security operations will contact the owners.

- Reject the deployment and modification of noncompliant resources through the Deny effect.

- Remediate noncompliant resources during deployment or on-demand for existing resources through the DeployIfNotExists, Modify, or Append effects.

> **Note** When using IaC desired state management, such as Terraform, you must instruct the desired state system to ignore the direct properties that are remediated through a policy. This applies only to the Modify (often used for tags) and Append (rarely used) effects, not to the DeployIfNotExists effect (which creates dependent/child resources). If this is not done, Terraform will undo the changes made by the policy, and the policy will try to remediate the Terraform undo instructions *ad infinitum*.

Enforcement (effects) levels and RBAC by environment

The level of enforcement is often related to the environment type—for example, SANDBOX, DEV, DEVINT, QA, or PROD. In some cases, individual solutions might require even more stringent controls, such as PCI, HIPAA, and other compliance frameworks that address highly sensitive data. Except in SANDBOX and DEV environments, developers should not be allowed to modify environments directly. All deployments must be automated.

NONPROD environments may use different security enforcement levels to simplify development (not recommended) or to allow or even enforce the use of less-expensive SKUs—for example, HSM-based versus software-based keys in Key Vault, which call for the premium SKU, or a dedicated PaaS resource rather than a shared PaaS resource.

Table 7-1 indicates the appropriate enforcement settings, by environment.

TABLE 7-1 Azure Policy effect settings, RBAC settings by environment

Environment	Policy	Developer RBAC	Deployment Agent RBAC
SANDBOX	Disabled	Contributor or owner	Not applicable
DEV	Audit or Deny Disabled for policies that imply the use of expensive SKUs	Contributor	Contributor or lower
DEVINT	Deny Disabled for policies that imply the use of expensive SKUs	Reader	Contributor or lower
QA	Deny	Reader	Contributor or lower
PROD	Deny	None permanently or reader	Contributor or lower

Policy Assignments

Policy and Initiative definitions do nothing unless used in a Policy Assignment. A Policy Assignment should always be applied at the Management Group level. If you don't differentiate the enforcement levels by environment, the assignments should be done at the top-level Management Group, either root tenant or the single Management Groups just below root tenant (as recommended by the Cloud Adoption Framework). If you do differentiate, you should assign it to Management Groups defining the environment levels.

We recommend you have the following assignments:

- Security and Compliance

  - **Azure Security Benchmark Initiatives**   You should always apply these, because they drive the Secure Score. You must remove the automatic Policy Assignments at each subscription enrolled in DfC.

  - **Compliance Initiatives (for example, NIST SP-800-53)**   Apply these as required. If the same policy exists in multiple Initiatives, it is important to set it to Deny in only one of the Initiatives and set it to Audit in the other ones to avoid weird behaviors when granting exemptions.

  - **Org Security Benchmark Custom Initiative**   This is for bundling custom policy definitions and mapping them with groupNames to your compliance needs (mapping them in DfC the same way as built-in policies).

- Diagnostic settings deployment with DeployIfNotExists
  - Diagnostic settings Initiatives (see Chapter 6, "Monitoring and auditing")
  - Enroll subscriptions in DfC for all services supporting DfC
- Other governance
  - Required tags
  - Inherit tags
  - Allowed locations
  - Allowed resource types

Policy as code

Policy should be managed as code, like any other piece of infrastructure. Policy deployment is beyond the scope of this book. Heinrich recommends Enterprise Policy as Code (EPAC; https://azsec.tech/q6p); he is one of the maintainers of this open source solution.

Summary

Governance is the foundation of any systematic security approach. It deals with defining security controls, best practices, enforcement, and auditing. This chapter distilled the large volume of content related to governance to the salient points for developers. Governance must be considered in the implementation of compliance and risk programs, which are covered in the next chapter.

## CHAPTER 8

Compliance and risk programs

After completing this chapter, you will be able to:

- Understand the importance of compliance and risk programs.

- Find Azure compliance information, reports, and audits.

- Add core compliance and risk programs to your lexicon.

- Understand how compliance and risk programs might affect your security architecture.

- Understand the relationship between risk and compliance technical controls and threat modeling.

Something important to get out of way

Compliance is a complex topic, often with legal ramifications. There are people in organizations whose entire job is to handle compliance programs for the company. This chapter will *not* make you a compliance expert by any measure. It is a primer on the topic. The authors are not lawyers, nor are we compliance auditors, but we do have experience working with customer-compliance requirements and with the personnel involved with compliance programs. This chapter describes some compliance and risk programs we have encountered while working with customers deploying on Azure. If nothing else, this chapter should add important words to your professional lexicon.

What is compliance?

In the context of secure design and secure development, let's start with what compliance is *not*: compliance is not security! You can build secure solutions that might not be compliant with one or more compliance programs, and you can build compliant solutions that are not secure. The world is rife with compromised HIPAA-compliant healthcare organizations and compromised PCI-compliant organizations that handle credit cards.

This does not mean that compliance is worthless—far from it. Compliance is a critical part of any organization, and it cannot be ignored. There is a big overlap between many compliance programs and security, however, and compliance can be an integral part of a security program. In fact, compliance funding can help fund security programs. Over the last few years, every organization moving workloads to Azure that we have worked with had, or needed to comply with, one or more compliance programs.

So, what are compliance programs? There are many compliance programs that span various industries (healthcare, finance, government, and so on) and geographies at various levels (bloc, country, state, and city). Some are prescriptive—that is, you *must* do these things—while others are descriptive, providing guidance for best practices.

> **Note** Companies often derive their own internal compliance programs from external compliance programs like the ones discussed in this chapter.

A *compliance program* is a system of processes, policies, procedures, and controls that are developed to ensure compliance with all applicable rules, regulations, contracts, and policies governing the actions of an organization. At a higher level and in a broader context, compliance is one part of cybersecurity governance, risk, and compliance (GRC). GRC might be the purview of the chief information officer (CIO), the chief information security officer (CISO), the chief risk officer (CRO), or even the chief financial officer (CFO).

Many compliance programs require technical controls. Technical controls help mitigate risk, and many compliance programs are written in terms of risk. It is these technical controls that we, as engineering staff, have control over and should consider as part of our designs.

Most organizations have a compliance officer to manage the process and documentation requirements in support of various compliance program initiatives. These people liaise with compliance auditors and compliance bodies and might need supporting documents from the engineering team. This is where you come into the compliance picture. It's important that you provide whatever is needed by members of the compliance team so they can get their job done. Remember, your organization might not be able to release your solution if it is not deemed compliant.

There are many compliance programs, and there is not enough room in this book to cover even a small percentage of all that exist. Instead, we will spend a few moments discussing some of the most important and influential compliance, risk, and best-practice programs:

- HIPAA
- HITRUST
- GDPR
- PCI DSS
- FedRAMP
- NIST SP 800-53

- NIST Cybersecurity Framework

- FIPS 140

- SOC

- ISO/IEC 27001

- ISO/IEC 27034

- Center for Internet Security Benchmarks

- Azure Security Benchmark

- OWASP

- MITRE

> **Note** Don't worry, we will spell out all the acronyms as we progress!

You can find additional compliance information, reports, and independent audits about Microsoft Azure and Microsoft 365 at the Service Trust Portal, located here: https://servicetrust.microsoft.com/. This site should be your first stop when researching almost anything related to compliance and Azure. In addition, on a practical note, Azure has built-in Azure Policy initiatives to help you enforce various regulatory compliance programs within your subscriptions. For example, here's a link to more information about NIST SP 800-53: https://azsec.tech/u1y.

Now let's turn our focus to various common compliance programs. At the start of each section, we will itemize the high-level jurisdictions such as geography and industry vertical, if applicable.

HIPAA

Geography: US

Industry: Healthcare

Type: Regulation

The Health Insurance Portability and Accountability Act (HIPAA) of 1996 is a US federal law to protect sensitive patient healthcare data from disclosure without the patient's consent.

At a technical level, the most common item of concern to developers is the protection of sensitive healthcare data—often called *protected health information* (PHI)—at rest and in transit. The wording in HIPAA can be vague, however, and is often open to interpretation.

An example of a technical control in HIPAA is as follows:

> **§ 164.312 Technical safeguards. (iv)** Encryption and decryption (Addressable). Implement a mechanism to encrypt and decrypt electronic protected health information.

In 2009, the US government enacted the Health Information Technology for Economic and Clinical Health (HITECH) Act, which broadens portions of various HIPAA privacy and security laws and regulations and is more specific about encryption of data at rest and in transit.

HITRUST

Geography: Global

Industry: Originally healthcare, but now used in other verticals

Type: Risk framework

The Health Information Trust (HITRUST; https://hitrustalliance.net) is an organization governed by representatives from various industries. It is not a government agency. HITRUST created and maintains the Common Security Framework (CSF), a certifiable security and privacy controls framework to help healthcare organizations and their providers demonstrate security and compliance in a consistent manner.

The HITRUST CSF provides organizations with a comprehensive, flexible, and efficient approach to regulatory compliance and risk management. The HITRUST CSF cross-references more than 40 authoritative sources. The HITRUST CSF is regularly updated as mapped authoritative sources change and new authoritative sources are introduced. Because the HITRUST CSF is both risk- and compliance-based, organizations of varying risk profiles can customize the security and privacy control baselines using a variety of factors including organization type, size, systems, and regulatory requirements.

Although the HIRTUST CSF documentation is large—more than 500 pages—it is readable, specific, and structured. It is also a useful cross-reference for other compliance programs. For example, the HITRUST 9.6.0 documentation shows that HITRUST "Control Reference: 01.c Privilege Management" maps to the following and many others:

- FedRAMP AC-6

- NIST SP 800-53 R4 AC-21(2)[S]

- NIST Cybersecurity Framework v1.1 PR.AC-4

- PCI DSS v3.2.1 7.1

An example of a technical control in HITRUST is:

> **Control Reference: 01.a Access Control Policy:** An access control policy shall be established, documented, and reviewed based on business and security requirements for access.

GDPR

Geography: EU (also outside EU)

Industry: All

Type: Regulation

The General Data Protection Regulation (GDPR)—or more formally, Regulation (EU) 2016/679—is a privacy regulation in the European Union (EU) that "lays down rules relating to the protection of natural person with regard to the processing for personal data and rules relating to the free movement of personal data." In short, GDPR is a security and privacy regulation that has a major impact on how companies gather, store, and process personal data for EU citizens and residents.

The last point, "EU citizens and residents," is important; GDPR applies to any company handling this data, whether they are based in the EU or not—for example, a US company that provides services or goods to a person in Italy, or a company with a website based in Japan that uses cookies and logs the IP addresses of people visiting the site from the EU.

Article 32, "Security of Processing," has a large impact on software architects and developers. The following example is from Article 32:

1. Taking into account the state of the art, the costs of implementation and the nature, scope, context and purposes of processing as well as the risk of varying likelihood and severity for the rights and freedoms of natural persons, the controller and the processor shall implement appropriate technical and organizational measures to ensure a level of security appropriate to the risk, including inter alia as appropriate:

     a. the pseudonymization and encryption of personal data.

     b. the ability to ensure the ongoing confidentiality, integrity, availability and resilience of processing systems and services.

> **Note** Various jurisdictions outside the EU are now developing new regulations based on GDPR.

PCI DSS

Geography: Global

Industry: Finance (credit cards)

Type: Regulation

The Payment Card Industry Data Security Standard (PCI DSS) is a global information security standard that defines prescriptive control of credit card data. Compliance with PCI DSS is required for all organizations that store, process, or transmit payment or cardholder data.

The PCI DSS documentation not only describes requirements but includes testing procedures to determine whether issues exist or to verify that a procedure has not regressed when adding new functionality or fixing bugs.

PCI has also created the Payment Application Data Security Standard (PA DSS), which is designed to help software vendors develop security applications that manage payment data. PA DSS will be replaced by the PCI Software Security Framework (PCI SSF) by the end of 2022.

There are two standards under the PCI SSF umbrella:

- Secure Software Standard

- Secure Software Lifecycle Standard

Many of the items addressed in the lifecycle standard are outlined in Chapter 1, "Secure development lifecycle processes."

Variances and risk acceptance

PCI DSS is an example of a prescriptive compliance framework. Prescriptive frameworks do not typically include variances or risk acceptance processes unless they are expressly called out. In other words, you are either compliant or noncompliant, per the framework.

An example of a technical control in PCI DSS is as follows: calls the Windows CryptoAPI

2.4 Maintain an inventory of system components that are in scope for PCI DSS.

FedRAMP

Geography: US

Industry: Federal government

Type: Regulation

The Federal Risk and Authorization Management Program (FedRAMP), which dates to 2011, provides a standard approach to accelerate the adoption of secure cloud solutions by US federal agencies. It came into effect under the Federal Information Security Management Act (FISMA), which requires federal agencies to implement mandatory processes and controls designed to ensure security. In essence, FedRAMP allows cloud-based solutions to meet FISMA requirements.

FedRAMP derives its controls from National Institute of Standards and Technology (NIST) SP 800-53 (covered next) and uses differing controls based on the impact levels of the solution: Low, Medium, and High. The impact levels are described in NIST PUB 199. NIST PUB 199 defines the Low, Medium, and High categories based on the impact of confidentiality, integrity, and availability.

Note FedRAMP applies to cloud vendors.

Here's an example of technical control in FedRAMP High:

AU-09 Audit and Accountability: The information system implements cryptographic mechanisms to protect the integrity of audit information and audit tools.

Supplemental Guidance: Cryptographic mechanisms used for protecting the integrity of audit information include, for example, signed hash functions using asymmetric cryptography enabling distribution of the public key to verify the hash information while maintaining the confidentiality of the secret key used to generate the hash. Related controls: AU-10, SC-12, SC-13.

NIST SP 800-53

Geography: US

Industry: Federal government

Type: Risk framework

National Institute of Standards and Technology (NIST) is a nonregulatory agency within the US Department of Commerce that helps to develop and publish IT security standards.

NIST Special Publication (SP) 800-53, "Security and Privacy Controls for Information Systems and Organizations," is a catalog of security and privacy controls that applies to all federal information systems in the United States. It provides a process for selecting controls to protect organizations from cyberattacks and other threats. NIST SP 800-53 is just one of a series of other SP 800 documents, all of which relate to computer security. The current revision is revision 5, often abbreviated to r5 or R5.

Even though SP 800-53 applies to federal agencies, many nongovernment organizations use it, too, because it is exhaustive and well-documented. NIST SP 800-53 defines controls within a set of families:

- **AC** Access Control
- **AT** Awareness and Training
- **AU** Audit and Accountability
- **CA** Assessment, Authorization, and Monitoring
- **CM** Configuration Management
- **CP** Contingency Planning
- **IA** Identification and Authentication
- **IR** Incident Response
- **MA** Maintenance
- **MP** Media Protection
- **PE** Physical and Environmental Protection
- **PL** Planning
- **PM** Program Management

- **PS**   Personnel Security

- **PT**   PII Processing and Transparency

- **RA**   Risk Assessment

- **SA**   System and Services Acquisition

- **SC**   System and Communications Protection

- **SI**   System and Information Integrity

- **SR**   Supply Chain Risk Management

NIST SP 800-53 controls are often cited by other compliance and risk programs.

Here's an example of a NIST SP 800-53 technical control:

> ### AC-6 Least Privilege. (2) LEAST PRIVILEGE | NON-PRIVILEGED ACCESS FOR NONSECURITY FUNCTIONS
>
> Require that users of system accounts (or roles) with access to [Assignment: organization-defined security functions or security-relevant information] use non-privileged accounts or roles, when accessing non-security functions

NIST Cybersecurity Framework

Geography: US

Industry: Public and private sectors

Type: Risk framework

Released in 2014 under a presidential executive order, the NIST Cybersecurity Framework (NICT CSF), or, more formally, the Framework for Improving Critical Infrastructure Cybersecurity, has become an invaluable resource for private-sector enterprises and public agencies. A 2017 presidential executive order requires compliance with NIST CSF for federal government agencies and for entities in the federal government supply chain.

The NIST CSF core components are divided into five areas of cybersecurity:

- Identify

- Protect

- Detect

- Respond

- Recover

The NIST CSF is relatively high level but references documents like NIST 800-53 for more detail on how to implement specific controls and processes. The NIST CSF document is only approximately 40 pages long, while NIST SP 800-53 release 5 weighs in at a hefty 500 pages.

How do FedRAMP, NIST SP 800-53, and NIST CSF relate?

It's not as complex as it seems! Think of NIST SP 800-53 as a core set of technical controls used by other compliance programs. FedRAMP looks at the NIST SP 800-53 controls through the lens of federal agencies wanting to deploy solutions on a cloud platform. NIST CSF also uses NIST SP 800-53 controls, but looking through a high-level lens that applies not just to federal agencies but also to the private sector. Another document, NIST SP 800-171, "Protecting Controlled Unclassified Information in Nonfederal Systems and Organizations," also helps explain how to use NIST SP 800-53 controls. Ideally, that helps clear things up a little!

An example of a NIST CSF technical control is as follows:

> **PR.DS-7:** The development and testing environment(s) are separate from the production environment

Note that this control makes further references to NIST SP 800-53 CM-2, which starts with the following:

CM-2 BASELINE CONFIGURATION

> Control: a. Develop, document, and maintain under configuration control, a current baseline configuration of the system.

FIPS 140

Geography: US

Industry: Government (often used in the private sector)

Type: Regulation

As the name suggests, the Federal Information Processing Standard (FIPS) Publication 140, "Security Requirements for Cryptographic Modules," is a US government standard that specifies the security requirements satisfied by a cryptographic module. The FIPS 140 security requirements cover 11 areas related to the design and implementation of a cryptographic module. The standard provides four security levels, 1 through 4, with increasing levels of security. Most US government agencies require the use of FIPS 140–validated cryptographic modules, and maybe at specific security levels. Some commercial organizations require both.

Important Testing of cryptographic modules against FIPS 140-2 ended September 22, 2021, and is now replaced with FIPS 140-3.

There is a great deal of confusion about what FIPS 140 is, so let us clarify things. FIPS 140 is a standard by which the implementation of cryptographic modules is validated. A module could be a library that implements a cryptographic algorithm, or it might be a cryptographic device.

Here are two examples:

- FIPS 140

- SHA-2 in NET

FIPS 140 and SHA-2 in .NET

You might know there are three implementations of the various SHA-2 hash algorithms in .NET:

- System.Security.Cryptography.SHA256Cng

- System.Security.Cryptography.SHA256CryptoServiceProvider

- System.Security.Cryptography.SHA256Managed

There are also implementations of SHA384 and SHA512, but let's keep things simple and focus only on the 256-bit versions of SHA-2.

SHA-2 is defined in another FIPS standard: FIPS 180-4, "Secure Hash Standard." This document describes the code behind SHA-2 as well as test values to verify a correct implementation.

Other cryptographic algorithms are defined in other FIPS standards:

- AES is defined in FIPS 197.

- SHA-1 is defined in FIPS 180-1.

- 3DES is defined in FIPS 46-3.

Someone implementing a cryptographic algorithm can choose to have the implementation reviewed and validated using FIPS 140-3. The review is performed by an independent third party certified to perform the work.

Let's get back to the .NET SHA-2 implementations. SHA256Cng and SHA256CryptoServiceProvider call into the Windows SHA-2 implementations, which are both FIPS 140-2 (because it predates FIPS 140-3) validated implementations of SHA-2. If you look at the source code for these three implementations at the .NET source code site (https://referencesource.microsoft.com/), you can see that:

- SHA256Managed is a full implementation of the algorithm in C#.

- SHA256CryptoServiceProvider calls the Windows CryptoAPI `CapiHashAlgorithm()` function.

- SHA256Cng calls the Windows Cryptography Next Generation (CNG) `BCryptHashAlgorithm()` function.

Here's where things get interesting (and important): the Windows CNG and CryptoAPI implementations of SHA-2 are FIPS 140-2 validated, but SHA256Managed is not. All three are functionally the same, and all three are implementations of the FIPS 180-4 hash algorithm. What makes this important is your company or some of your customers may require the use of FIPS 140-validated implementations.

For compliance purposes, it is possible to put Windows into a FIPS 140 mode. Applications performing cryptographic operations can interrogate this setting to determine which algorithms to use. This setting should be used with caution, however, as it can cause some applications to fail in "mysterious ways" if they do not fail gracefully in the face of this setting. Also, setting this is not a guarantee that an application will use only FIPS 140–validated algorithms because the application might not read the setting, or it could simply ignore it.

You can set the FIPS policy from Group Policy. (See Figure 8-1.)

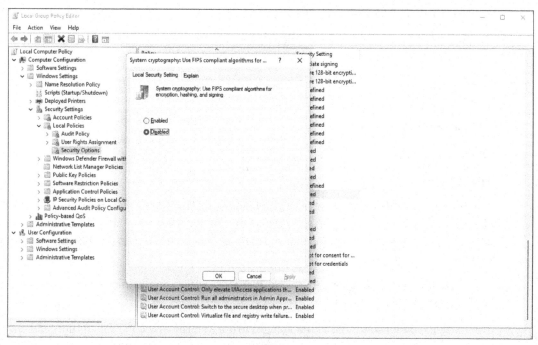

FIGURE 8-1 Using Windows Policy to require FIPS 140–validated algorithms.

You can also set the policy directly in the registry under HKEY_LOCAL_MACHINE\System\Current-ControlSet\Control\Lsa\FipsAlgorithmPolicy. Set Enabled to 1 or 0 to enable or disable FIPS policy, respectively.

FIPS 140 and Azure Key Vault and Managed HSM

Azure Key Vault is also a cryptographic module. Remember how we mentioned that FIPS 140-2 and FIPS 140-3 have increasing security levels from 1 to 4? The following list shows how the various members of the Azure Key Vault family map to various FIPS 140 levels:

- **Software-protected keys in vaults (Premium and Standard SKUs)**   FIPS 140-2 Level 1 validated

- **HSM-protected keys in vaults (Premium SKU)**   FIPS 140-2 Level 2 validated

- **HSM-protected keys in Managed HSM**   FIPS 140-2 Level 3 validated

> **Note** Managed HSM is discussed in more detail in Chapter 10, "Cryptography in Azure."

For Azure Key Vault, the FIPS 140 validation applies only to keys (RSA and elliptic curve), not to secrets or certificates. Managed HSM can store only keys.

You can read more about what the various levels mean in section 4, "Security Requirements," in the FIPS 140 documentation.

SOC

Geography: Global

Industry: All

Type: Regulation

System and Organization Controls (SOC, pronounced *sock*) are internal control reports created by the American Institute of Certified Public Accountants (AICPA). They are intended to examine services provided by a service organization so that end users can assess and address the risk associated with a service.

- SOC 1 is a financial auditing framework that analyzes the controls implemented to protect the integrity of financial data.

- SOC 2 is designed specifically for auditors to use when assessing the data security and privacy controls of service providers such as Azure.

- A SOC 3 report is a shorter version of a SOC 2 report intended to be used for public access.

To make things a little more complex, various SOC reports have two types:

- A Type 1 report evaluates controls at a point in time and whether their design is suitable to meet relevant trust principles.

- A Type 2 report details the operational effectiveness of the controls over a period, such as 6 or 12 months.

Various independent Azure audit reports, including SOC 2 Type 2, are available at the Service Trust Portal.

SOC 2 addresses five trust services principles (TSPs):

- Security

- Availability

- Processing integrity

- Confidentiality

- Privacy

An example SOC 2 Trust Service Criteria is as follows:

CC6.6 The entity implements logical access security measures to protect against threats from sources outside its system boundaries.

ISO/IEC 27001

Geography: Global

Industry: All

Type: Regulation

The International Organization for Standardization/International Electrotechnical Commission (ISO/IEC) 27000 family of standards outlines hundreds of controls and control mechanisms to help organizations secure their environments.

ISO/IEC 27001, "Information Security Management," is a security standard that mandates requirements that define how to implement, monitor, maintain, and continually improve security. It also outlines best practices, which include documentation requirements, divisions of responsibility, availability, access control, security, auditing, and corrective and preventive measures. The standard covers not only technical controls but also physical controls such as locks on doors and background checks, which are clearly outside the scope of software.

One of the benefits of ISO/IEC 27001 certification is it is internationally accepted, so it helps organizations comply with other regulatory and legal requirements that relate to the security of information.

In terms of size, it is similar to NIST 800-53:

- NIST 800-53 has 20 control families and hundreds of controls.

- ISO/IEC 27001 has 14 control categories and 114 controls.

An example of an ISO/IEC 27001 control is as follows:

A.9.4.1 Access to information and application system functions shall be restricted in accordance with the access control policy.

And another:

> **A.10.1.2** A policy on the use, protection and lifetime of cryptographic keys shall be developed and implemented through their whole lifecycle.

ISO/IEC 27034

Geography: Global

Industry: All

Type: Regulation

Another regulation under the ISO/IEC 27000 umbrella, ISO/IEC 27034, "Information technology — Security techniques — Application security — Part 1: Overview and concepts," focuses on secure software practices. It is not one document; rather, it is a set of six documents that help organizations to map their current software development practices to current security best practices.

Annex A of the first document, ISO/IEC 27034-1, presents a case study on how to map an existing software development process to some of the components of ISO/IEC 27034. That case study is the Microsoft Security Development Lifecycle that we explain in Chapter 1.

Center for Internet Security Benchmarks

Geography: Global

Industry: All

Type: Risk Framework

The Center for Internet Security (CIS) is an independent group of security professionals from academia, industry, and government who collaborate to build prescriptive security guidance for many products, including Azure, Microsoft Exchange, IIS, iOS, NGINX, and much more. The prescriptive guidance is delivered as extensive benchmarks. CIS also has hardened operating system images that embody the various benchmarks within the images. These OS images can be downloaded from within various cloud services, including Azure.

The CIS Benchmark is a comprehensive set of controls and is often cited in Microsoft documents, including the Azure Security Benchmark. The items in each benchmark map to one or more controls in the CIS controls (as well as PCI and SOC; more will be added over time). Each CIS practice is complete, with the rationale for the policy as well as steps to set the policy from the Azure Portal, the Azure CLI, PowerShell, and links to further resources. This is extremely beneficial.

Some example CIS controls for Azure include the following:

> **1.14** Ensure That 'Restrict access to Azure AD administration portal' is Set to "Yes" Database (maps to 6.8 'Define and Maintain Role-Based Access Controls' in CIS Controls v8.0)

2.8 Ensure that Microsoft Defender for Key Vault is set to 'On' Database (maps to 10.1 'Deploy and Maintain Anti-Malware Software' in CIS Controls v8.0)

3.10 Ensure Storage logging is Enabled for Blob Service for 'Read', 'Write', and 'Delete' requests Database (maps to 8.5 'Collect Detailed Audit Logs' in CIS Controls v8.0)

4.1.2 Ensure that 'Data encryption' is set to 'On' on a SQL Database (maps to 3.11 'Encrypt sensitive data at rest' in CIS Controls v8.0)

Azure Security Benchmark

Geography: Global

Industry: All

Type: Risk framework

The Azure Security Benchmark (ASB) is a set of security recommendations to help tenants secure their subscriptions. From the ASB, Azure products derive their own interpretation of each recommendation. These are called the Azure Security Baseline. Notice in Figure 8-2 how the ASB recommendations map to other compliance programs outlined in this chapter.

DP-2: Monitor anomalies and threats targeting sensitive data

CIS Controls v8 ID(s)	NIST SP 800-53 r4 ID(s)	PCI-DSS ID(s) v3.2.1
3.13	AC-4, SI-4	A3.2

FIGURE 8-2 Mapping an ASB recommendation to other compliance programs.

Here is an example of an ASB recommendation:

DP-3: Monitor for unauthorized transfer of sensitive data

Here is what the recommendation means when it maps to Cosmos DB:

Guidance: Cosmos DB supports Microsoft Defender for Cosmos DB, which provides an additional layer of security intelligence that detects unusual and potentially harmful attempts to access or exploit Azure Cosmos DB accounts. This layer of protection allows you to address threats, even without being a security expert, and integrate them with central security monitoring systems.

Here is what it means when it maps to Azure Media Services:

Guidance: Azure Media Services transmits sensitive data. But it doesn't support native monitoring of the unauthorized transfer of sensitive data. Organizations can configure events to be logged to Azure Monitor. Organizations can also set up custom Logic App automation flows to trigger on any anomalous activity.

Here is what it means when it maps to Azure Purview:

Guidance: Azure Purview offers lineage monitoring capability. Currently, Azure Purview supports the following extract, transform, and load (ETL) tools:

- Azure Data Factory

- Azure Data Share

- Power BI

Data lineage can display how data propagates from one system to another. This display helps eliminate duplication of sensitive data. It provides a graphical representation to increase data lineage visibility.

For your data sources that Azure Purview scans, monitor for the unauthorized transfer of data to locations outside of enterprise visibility and control. Use service-specific Microsoft Defender and log options to do the monitoring. This action typically involves monitoring for anomalous activities, such as large or unusual transfers. These activities might indicate unauthorized data exfiltration.

Tools like Microsoft Defender for Cloud offer, among other things, a direct mapping between an issue that might put an Azure tenant at risk and the appropriate ASB information. Figure 8-3 shows a partial view of the Regulator Compliance section of Microsoft Defender for Cloud. Note that SOC TSP is for SOC2 and SOC3.

FIGURE 8-3 The Regulatory Compliance section of Microsoft Defender for Cloud. In this example, PCI DSS 3.2.1 is selected.

OWASP

Geography: Global

Industry: All

Category: De facto best practices standard

The Open Web Application Security Project (OWASP) was started more than 20 years ago by Mark Curphey in response to the constant stream of security vulnerabilities in web-based applications. OWASP is most well-known for its OWASP Top 10 list, which is updated every few years and addresses the most pertinent vulnerability classes, impacts, and remedies. As of this writing, the latest version is OWASP Top 10 2021.

The OWASP Top 10 is absolutely not a regulation; it is a set of best practices. Every architect and developer should understand the OWASP Top 10 and have practices in place to prevent or mitigate each issue in the list. Having concrete practices in place to address the OWASP Top 10 is always a good idea because middle and upper management will often ask about them (even if they don't know what they are!).

Of course, there are vulnerabilities outside the Top 10. Tooling and processes should cover more than the Top 10, because the Top 10 is updated only every two years or so, and new issues are always found. As part of a good defensive posture, you should keep an eye on new and evolving threats. With all that said, addressing this list is always seen as a good, solid baseline.

> **Note** OWASP has other projects that extend beyond the Top 10, including security maturity, testing, and others.

MITRE

Geography: Global

Industry: All

Category: De facto standards and practices

No book on compliance, best practice, risk, and de facto standards is complete without a discussion of MITRE. MITRE is a US not-for-profit organization that works closely with industry, academia, and governments on, among other things, security research. While MITRE is based in the United States, it is well-respected around the world.

Over the years, MITRE has helped build and maintain some of the most important and influential security programs. The following list contains some of them:

- CVE
- CWE
- ATT&CK
- CAPEC

Let's dive into each.

CVE

Common Vulnerabilities and Exposures (CVE) has been the cornerstone for cataloging vulnerabilities. Every public vulnerability has its own unique value. Think of it as a primary key for all other references and research for a mitigation. CVE allows for precise communication among technical staff when referring to vulnerabilities. Here's a short list of some famous CVEs over the years:

- **CVE-2002-0649**   Memory-corruption bug in SQL Server that led to the Slammer worm

- **CVE-2014-0160**   Heartbleed vulnerability in OpenSSL

- **CVE-2008-1447**   DNS cache poisoning (the Kaminsky Bug)

- **CVE-2014-6271**   GNU Bash remote code execution (Shellshock)

- **CVE-2014-3566**   SSL 3.0 POODLE

- **CVE-2021-44228**   Log4J remote code execution

- **CVE-2002-0965**   Buffer overrun in Oracle 9i (one of a number found by David Litchfield to disprove Oracle's "Unbreakable" claim)

The beauty of CVE is that because it's a primary key, you can search using your favorite search engine and find information on the issue quickly.

Calculating the risk of a CVE using CVSS

The Common Vulnerability Scoring System (CVSS), defined by the Forum of Incident Response and Security Teams (FIRST), is a way to determine the severity of a vulnerability on a scale of 0 to 10, with 10 being the most severe. CVSS uses numerous conditions, such as whether a vulnerability is exposed locally only or over a network, what kinds of permissions or privileges are required, and more. To put things in perspective, CVE-2021-44228, the Log4J remote code execution vulnerability from December 2021, is rated a 10, which is the highest possible rating. This is why the world scrambled to get fixes out as soon as possible.

The CVE site is https://www.cve.org/. A CVSS calculator is available at https://nvd.nist.gov/vuln-metrics/cvss/v3-calculator and https://azsec.tech/3n0. First.org has a website dedicated to CVSS examples at https://azsec.tech/wt7 to help you learn how to score vulnerabilities.

National Vulnerability Database (NVD)

The NVD (https://nvd.nist.gov/) is a constantly updated list of publicly disclosed vulnerabilities managed by NIST. Each vulnerability is assigned a unique CVE and a severity rating using CVSS, and most are assigned one or more CWEs.

CWE

Common Weakness Enumeration (CWE) is a hierarchical list of software and hardware weaknesses. It is a common way to describe vulnerability classes. For example, the memory corruption in CVE-2002-0649 was a CWE-120 called "Buffer Copy without Checking Size of Input ('Classic Buffer Overflow')."

Other examples of CWEs include the following:

- **CWE-798**   Use of hard-coded credentials

- **CWE-89**   SQL injection

- **CWE-79**   Cross-site scripting (XSS)

- **CWE-20**   Improper input validation (parent to CWE-89 and CWE-9)

One output from CWE is the CWE Top 25, which is like the OWASP Top 10, but focuses on the top 25 weaknesses according to MITRE. The CWE-25 is more exhaustive than the OWASP Top 10. You should consider starting with the OWASP Top 10 and including CWE-25 over time because both have excellent documentation.

The CWE site is https://cwe.mitre.org/.

ATT&CK

ATT&CK is a knowledge base of attacker tradecraft. It maps common techniques used by attackers as they move from reconnaissance all the way to execution, persistence, evasion, command and control, and exfiltration.

ATT&CK is becoming a critical part of security tools. These include security information and event management (SIEM) systems such as Azure Sentinel, which allows analysts to better link attack chains. Microsoft has also mapped Azure security controls to ATT&CK. For more information about this, see https://azsec.tech/n2z.

The ATT&CK site is https://attack.mitre.org/.

CAPEC

Common Attack Pattern Enumeration and Classification (CAPEC) provides a catalog of common attack patterns that help software developers understand how attackers might exploit specific vulnerabilities. For example, CAPEC-66, "SQL Injection," explains how attackers can take advantage of SQL injection vulnerabilities in code. Other examples include the following:

- **CAPEC-34**   "How to Exploit HTTP Response Splitting"

- **CAPEC-63**   "How to Exploit XSS"

Each CAPEC entry also includes CWE references.

The CAPEC site is https://capec.mitre.org/.

Compliance synopsis

There are many more compliance and risk programs out there. These include the following:

- ISO 27002 code of practice for information security controls
- US Department of Defense Cybersecurity Maturity Model Certification (CMMC)
- Internet of Things (IoT) Cybersecurity Improvement Act of 2020
- Cloud Security Alliance Cloud Control Matric (CSA CCM)
- Criminal Justice Information Services (CJIS)
- International Traffic in Arms Regulations (ITAR)
- NIST SP 800-171, "Protecting Controlled Unclassified Information in Nonfederal Systems and Organizations"
- Gramm-Leach-Bliley Act (GLBA)
- UK Cyber Essentials Plus
- Sarbanes-Oxley Act (SOX)
- California Privacy Rights Act (CPRA)
- Children's Online Privacy Protection Rule (COPPA)
- New Zealand ISM Restricted

We could keep going! It is critically important that all engineering staff have a baseline level of knowledge about the most common compliance programs that might affect them as they design, develop, and test a solution.

 Important Compliance programs are an important way to manage security risk, but they do not guarantee a secure solution.

Real-world experience: How our customers use compliance and risk programs

All three of the authors of this book have worked with customers in almost every sector globally. In that time, we have seen various compliance and risk-management trends.

Almost every customer we have worked with refers to the OWASP Top 10 to guide their internal development practices. Many use CWE and a plurality use CVSS. Every public vulnerability has a CVE. Some customers use NIST SP 800-53 controls, many use NIST CSF (which uses NIST SP 800-53 controls), and others use ISO 27001 to guide their overall compliance strategy. SOC 2 is a common requirement.

Industries like healthcare and finance have their own programs they *must* comply with, like HIPAA and PCI. When it comes to cryptography, some customers have specific FIPS 140 needs, but it's not common. With that said, when customers do have specific FIPS 140 needs, they are cast in stone and are a must. Finally, because of the way compliance details are exposed in Microsoft Defender for Cloud, CIS and the ASB are commonly used on Azure, too.

One way to map the design of a system to the security controls required by compliance programs is to use threat models. This is covered next.

Using threat models to drive compliance artifacts

Compliance programs, such as those noted previously, have technical controls. Most compliance and risk programs also have nontechnical controls, such as locks on buildings, background checks on individuals, and so on. But it's the technical controls we care about in this instance. One key output of a threat model is a list of the technical controls that mitigate risk.

Let's take the example of Azure SQL Database storing sensitive data. The solution uses Always Encrypted, and the key encryption keys are stored in Azure Key Vault with an appropriate RBAC policy and audit policy in place.

Let's assume you must comply with PCI DSS and NIST SP 800-53. To make ongoing governance easier, your company will use ASB and track this in Microsoft Defender for Cloud. In fact, your company will use ASB and then map the appropriate ASB policies to PCI DSS and NIST SP 800-53. Looking at ASB, you can see that one item pertains to encryption of data at rest. (See Figure 8-4.)

DP-4: Enable data at rest encryption by default

CIS Controls v8 ID(s)	NIST SP 800-53 r4 ID(s)	PCI-DSS ID(s) v3.2.1
3.11	SC-28	3.4, 3.5

Security Principle: To complement access controls, data at rest should be protected against 'out of band' attacks (such as accessing underlying storage) using encryption. This helps ensure that attackers cannot easily read or modify the data.

Azure Guidance: Many Azure services have data at rest encryption enabled by default at the infrastructure layer using a service-managed key.

FIGURE 8-4 ASB DP-4 requiring of encryption of data at rest.

You can also see from Figure 8-4 that DP-4 maps to the following:

- **Center for Internet (CIS) controls** This reads "3.1.1 Encrypt Sensitive Data at Rest."

- **NIST SP 800-53** This reads "SC-28(1): Cryptographic Protection: Implement cryptographic mechanisms to prevent unauthorized disclosure and modification of the following information at rest."

- **PCI DSS** This reads "PCI DSS Requirement 3.4: Make PAN (Personal Account Number) unreadable wherever it is stored."

You can now do the same process for each mitigation in your threat model. Now you not only have a completed threat model, but you have a threat model that maps your mitigations to one or more compliance requirements. This is incredibly powerful. It helps the engineering staff bridge the gap between architecture, security, and compliance. Every compliance auditor we have spoken to loves this, as it provides a useful artifact that shows how the architecture uses specific mitigations and then how that maps to compliance. This reduces the friction of a compliance review because they can see the traceability. For example, the architecture indicates that data must be encrypted in SQL Server. The security control is Always Encrypted, and this maps to FedRAMP High SC-28(1).

> **Note** Think of this as a security Rosetta Stone, but instead of Greek, Demotic, and Hieroglyphics, a threat model with compliance information represents architecture, security, and compliance in one artifact.

The process of adding compliance data to a threat model is straightforward:

1. Determine your compliance needs ahead of time (HITRUST, PCI, SP 800-53, and so on).

2. Make sure the threat model is complete and accurate.

3. For each technical mitigation, determine what that mitigation satisfies in each of the compliance programs you care about.

4. Add that information to the threat model.

One of the beauties of Azure PaaS and SaaS solutions is that, because of the shared responsibility model, some mitigations are addressed by Azure and do not need to be addressed by the Azure customer. A great example is patching. Most compliance programs require patching, and for PaaS solutions, this is addressed by Azure.

Summary

Compliance programs are a critical baseline for most organizations moving workloads to the cloud. Compliance touches almost every Azure-based solution.

As someone designing or developing Azure solutions, you need to understand how compliance might affect the features you work on. At an absolute minimum, learn the OWASP Top 10 and the Azure Security Benchmark and how it relates to other programs like PCI DSS, NIST SP 800-53, and others.

As an exercise, look at the compliance section of Microsoft Defender for Cloud. Understand why some areas are flagged as noncompliant and then remedy them. Also understand why you missed them and how your designs will accommodate for them moving forward.

## PART II

Secure implementation

## CHAPTER 9

Secure coding

After completing this chapter, you will be able to:

- Understand the fundamental rules of writing secure code.

- Write defensive code that can withstand attack.

- Understand common insecure coding issues and how to fix them.

- Implement some effective security testing techniques.

Insecure code

Too much code written today is insecure. It's not because developers are lazy; it's often because developers simply don't know what constitutes secure code. But this is where it gets interesting. Most of the time, an insecure system works correctly and passes all functional tests. So why don't testers find security issues? There is a reason, and it lies in this statement:

"A secure system is a system that does what it is supposed to do, and nothing else."

Simply put, when the "nothing else" becomes "something else" is when security issues are found, because it's typically when a malicious actor takes advantage of a weakness.

Here's an example: a database system using SQL commands will probably pass all your functional tests, even if it has a SQL injection vulnerability. But an attacker can take advantage of this weakness and cause the system to do "something else," like view another table or delete data in a table or even the table itself. It's this "something else" that is a security concern!

Your goal as a developer is to avoid having "something else" conditions in your code. When developing systems, there are two high-level goals you need to keep in mind:

- Reduce the number of vulnerabilities in your code.

- Reduce the severity of the vulnerabilities you miss.

The first basically states, "Try to get everything right," and the second boils down to, "But assume you won't." It's a healthy tension to consider when writing code. Everything in this chapter revolves around these two guiding principles.

Rule #1: All input is evil

We have said this for over 20 years, and it is as valid today as it was at the turn of the century:

> *All input is evil.*

This statement transcends programming language, operating system, development process, deployment environment, and everything in between. It applies to Windows services written in C++, Linux drivers written in C, containerized applications written in Go on AWS, C# code running in Azure Functions, and a humble web app written in PHP running on nginx.

> **Important** The idea is simple: incoming data is at the root of numerous security vulnerabilities, so it is important that all data coming into your code be validated for correctness.

About 20 years ago, in the earliest days of trustworthy computing and the Microsoft Security Development Lifecycle (SDL), Michael was charged with educating new software engineering staff about secure design and development. New employees had to attend a four-hour class entitled "Basics of Secure Software Design, Development, and Test." The associated PowerPoint deck had about 100 slides of dense material. Slide 52, shown in Figure 9-1, was this somewhat tongue-in-cheek statement right before 50 slides of insecure code examples and remedies.

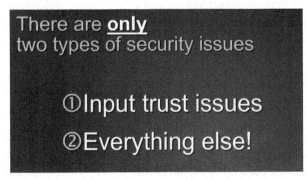

FIGURE 9-1 Slide 52 from a PowerPoint deck from the early 2000s at Microsoft.

Some of the most common and serious code-level security issues are simply the result of failing to verify that data coming from untrusted sources is correct. For example, the infamous Apache log4j (CVE-2021-44228) vulnerability of December 2021 was an invalid input issue. Examples of input trust issues include the following:

- Memory corruption (such as buffer overruns)
- Integer overflow and underflow
- Cross-site scripting (XSS)
- Directory traversal
- Open redirects

- Server-side request forgery (SSRF)

- Cross-site request forgery (CSRF)

- SQL injection

- XML injection

- Canonicalization

- OS command injection

We cover some of these vulnerabilities in this chapter, but not all of them, because each one can be remedied simply by verifying untrusted data as it enters your code. Our main focus here is on the core concept that underlies each of these issues: untrusted data.

> **Important** The core lesson is, if your code accepts input from a potentially untrusted source, it *must* validate that input for correctness.

Using threat models

You can use threat models to help determine whether incoming data is untrusted. Any data that crosses a trust boundary and is then read by some process must be validated for correctness.

Figure 9-2 shows a small portion of the COVID vaccination booking application threat model from Chapter 4, "Threat modeling." As you can see, data that comes in from the vaccination center is stored in an Azure Storage account and then read by an Azure Function. The box in this diagram represents a trust boundary. The vaccination center is outside the boundary, while everything else is inside. So, the code in the function *must* validate that the incoming data is correct because the vaccination data crosses a trust boundary. Each vaccination center might be one of our business and healthcare partners, but that does not mean we trust the data they provide to us!

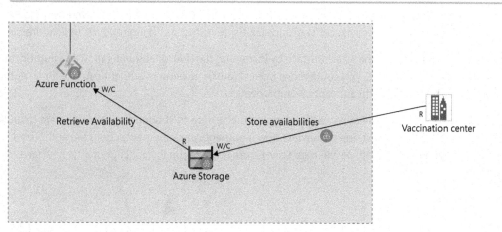

FIGURE 9-2 Data entering the environment from a vaccination center. The data crosses a trust boundary and must be validated for correctness.

Understanding who an attacker might be

Keeping in mind that "all input is evil," it's important to understand who an attacker might be and what an attacker can control. Let's look at each of these now.

With regard to who an attacker might be, let's use a simple example. Suppose you have two REST APIs:

- The first API is exposed to the internet, and it has no authentication.

- The second API is listening only on a small IP address range and requires modern authentication using your tenant Azure Active Directory as the identity provider.

Who is the potential attacker for the first API? Anyone on the planet! Potentially, billions of people—bored teenagers, nation-states, bots, and everything in between. In contrast, the potential attacker for the second API is anyone coming from the small IP address range who has an account in your tenant's Azure Active Directory. This might only be 100 or so users, depending on how many accounts you have.

Clearly, the first API is more "at risk." Data coming into that API could be from anyone—which means there is a high probability that the data will be malformed at best and malicious at worst. So, any code associated with this API must be rock-solid. The second API has a much lower probability of being a victim of malicious input because the population of potential attackers is so much smaller. This doesn't mean you can write any junk code in the second API; it just means you have a finite amount of time to work with, so you need to spend more time making sure the code for the first API is solid. (Remember, though, that insiders can pose a threat, too, as discussed in Chapter 3, "Security patterns.")

The level of exposure will help drive how you prioritize your time when it comes to code review and testing. We often refer to this exposure level as an application's *attack surface*. You should always try to reduce an application's attack surface. One way to do this is to reduce network exposure. In Azure, reducing network exposure means moving from public access to doing one of the following:

- Allowing subnet or VNet access only—for example, by using private endpoints

- Restricting access to a small set of IP addresses or CIDR range, often achieved by using PaaS firewalls and network security groups (NSGs) to restrict incoming requests to IP addresses

You can also reduce the attack surface by increasing the level of authentication and authorization. In the case of the first API, you could move from no authentication to authentication with no authorization or authentication with appropriate authorization.

When looking at data flows in a threat model that cross a trust boundary, it's important to understand how the lower-trust side of the data flow is authenticated and how actions are authorized, as well as the network accessibility of that data flow. Figure 9-3 sums up the concept of attack surface.

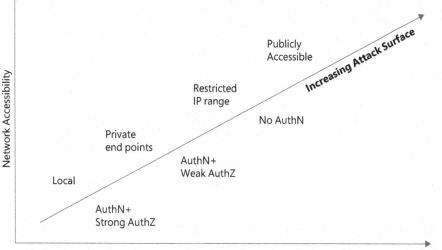

FIGURE 9-3 How network accessibility and authentication/authorization contribute to attack surface.

The effects of attack surface can be summed in one sentence: increased attack surface is bad; reducing attack surface is good. This is because an increased attack surface means more attackers and more potential vulnerabilities.

Understanding what an attacker controls

Imagine the following low-level C code:

```
char dst[4];
```

This simple code allocates 4 bytes (because a char is one byte) of memory for a variable named `dst` (for destination).

Now look at this code:

```
char dst[4];
dst[4] = 'X';
```

The second line *seems* to write `'X'` at the fourth element (offset) in the array. But in fact, it writes 'X' to the fifth element, because arrays in C (and any self-respecting programming language) start at 0, not 1. The element numbered 4 is in fact element 5: 0, 1, 2, 3, 4.

This is a classic memory corruption or a buffer overrun issue. But is it a security vulnerability? The answer is a resounding no! Because the attacker controls nothing. It is absolutely a code quality bug that should be fixed, however.

Now look at this variant:

```
if (recv(sock, (char*)data, sizeof(data), 0) >= 0) {
        dst[data.index] = data.value;
```

This code reads some data from a TCP socket and uses that data to write a value held in `data.value` into the array at offset `data.index`. If the socket has a high attack surface, it's accessible on the internet with no authentication. I think we can agree that this data cannot be trusted. But as this code stands, the code can write any data at any point in memory. For example, the following are all possible:

```
dst[12234] = 'a';
dst[-9872] = 'z';
```

In this scenario, the attacker has unfettered access to both the array offset and the data to write to that array offset. This is incredibly dangerous and is a serious security vulnerability. This must be fixed.

So, we just described two memory-corruption scenarios. One was a code-quality issue because the attacker controlled nothing, but the other was a bona-fide security vulnerability because the attacker controlled a great deal.

While our example is in C, this kind of issue applies to other languages, too. Imagine server code in Java that reads an untrusted index coming from a REST API and then uses that to index an array, like the following code snippet:

```
if (index < arr.length)
    arr[index] = n;
```

On the surface, the code looks fine—until you remember that Java does not have unsigned variables, so the index is signed. A value of –1 gets past the array length check and attempts to write n to a negative array offset, and the application crashes with a `java.lang.ArrayIndexOutOfBounds-Exception`. The same type of error would happen in C# if `index` were an int rather than a uint.

When you review code and you need to determine the likelihood of a code-quality bug being a security bug, be sure you understand what the attacker controls. The more they control, the higher the likelihood that the issue could be a serious security issue. Also be cognizant of idiosyncrasies like signed ints in Java.

Verify explicitly

President Ronald Reagan once said of the Soviet Union, "Trust, but verify." But in a world of zero trust we say, "Verify explicitly"—and that's exactly what we're going to discuss next.

There are three basic steps to constraining incoming and outgoing data:

1. Determine correctness.

2. Reject known bad.

3. Encode data.

Let's look at each in detail.

Determine correctness

Determining correctness means verifying data is well-formed. This is the opposite of determining incorrectness. Determining that data is incorrect is a good backup strategy, but it's not a replacement for validating that data is correct, because no one can know all the potential ways to malform incoming data.

> **Note** Testing for correctness and failing if the correct data is not found is an example of the fail secure principle, discussed in Chapter 2, "Secure design."

"Don't look for bad things." Doing so assumes you know all the bad things, and no one does. Instead, validate for correct and well-formed data. That way, your code always fails secure, sometimes called *failing closed*. Stop and think for a moment: if a user provides valid input but it's not seen as valid by your code, at worst you have a support ticket to deal with.

> **Important** If you know the data for a particular field should be an integer, why would you allow anything else? If a string should be no longer than 16 characters, why allow anything longer?

There are many strategies to constrain data to its correct form. Most programming languages offer library functions or methods that perform basic constraint checking. You can use regular expressions, too, but they should be reserved for more complex data formats or when alternate methods don't work correctly.

> **Important** All security-related data validation must be performed by the server. It's fine to validate at the client to prevent a round-trip to the server, but client-side logic does not provide any security benefit whatsoever.

Real-world experience: When input trust goes horribly wrong

In 2006, famed database researcher David Litchfield reported a nasty security bug in Oracle systems. You can read about the bug at https://azsec.tech/9md, but the short version is this: Oracle PLSQL Gateway is a tool that resides on a web server and allows users to execute SQL code in the database via the web server. In an attempt to tighten security, Oracle used an exclusion list that looked for "badness" and rejected any request that contained it.

One such construct is SYS. This account owns the database data dictionary as well as potentially sensitive tables. Because of this, the gateway code blocks any request that includes the string SYS. But as David found out, this can be bypassed by using a %0ASYS or S%FFS string.

%0A is a newline character, so a request containing the string %0ASYS bypasses the string check. For its part, %FF translates to a small letter y with a dieresis (ÿ). Obviously, SÿS is not the same as SYS, so SÿS gets passed to a string compare that looks for the "bad" SYS string. When the string is then passed on to underlying systems, the code sees an invalid ÿ and changes it to the closest ASCII character, which is a y. So now, the attacker has access to objects owned by the SYS account. Oops!

Let's return to the vaccination booking application as an example. Suppose the file uploaded by the vaccination center is a simple text comma-separated value (CSV) file with the following fields:

```
centerId, date and time, vaccination type, open spots, comment
```

It's simple. The formats for each data item are as follows:

- **centerID**   This is the vaccination center ID. It is a six-digit number. This field cannot be blank.

- **date and time**   For this, you use the ISO 8601 date and time format. This field cannot be blank.

- **vaccination type**   This is a string that represents the name of a valid vaccine manufacturer. This field cannot be blank.

- **open spots**   This is a number from 0 to 999. This field can be blank; when it is, it equates to zero.

- **comment**   This is a text field in which a representative from the vaccination center can enter a comment. This comment can be up to 200 characters long.

The CSV file will have one line for each vaccination center, date and time, and vaccine type. The file is uploaded to an Azure Storage account, and from there it is read by an Azure Function. With this in mind, you can build some code that checks that the data is correctly formed. There is more than one way of doing it, so we'll show a few examples.

When checking validity, you want to be as performant as possible. Regular expressions (regex) are a common way to validate data, but simple data formats do not require a regex, and other options are faster and good enough.

Before you validate each item in each line of the CSV file, you need to make sure each line contains the correct number of fields. This is simple. You just split the line based on the delimiter. If the file is JSON or XML, you could also make sure it's valid JSON or XML. You could also validate against a schema.

The following C# code checks that a line of the CSV file is five fields and only five fields. Anything other than five is incorrect data.

C#
```csharp
if (line.Split(",").Length == NUM_FIELDS) {
        // Correct number of fields
}
```

JavaScript

```javascript
if (line.split(",").length == NUM_FIELDS) {
        // Correct number of fields

}
```

C++ does not support a split() method. If you use the Boost C++ library (https://www.boost.org/), you could use boost::split. Failing that you must write your own method:

C++

```cpp
#include <vector>
#include <string>

using namespace std;

auto split(const string &str, const string &delim) {
        vector<string> vs;
        size_t pos = 0;

        for (size_t i = 0; (i = str.find(delim, pos)) != string::npos; pos = i + delim.size())
                vs.emplace_back(str.data() + pos, str.data() + i);

        vs.emplace_back(str.data() + pos, str.data() + str.size());
        return vs;
}

vector<string> v = split(line, ",");
if (v.size() == NUM_FIELDS) {
        // Correct # items

}
```

Using namespace std

Yes, we are aware of the argument for and against using the C++ "using namespace" construct, but we have chosen to use it.

Go

```go
import (
        "strings"
)
res := len(strings.Split(line, ","))
if res == NUM_FIELDS {
        // Correct # items

}
```

Python

```python
if len(line.split(",")) == NUM_FIELDS:
    # Correct # items
```

PowerShell

```powershell
if ($line.Split(",").Count -eq NUM_FIELDS) {
    # Correct # items
}
```

```Java
Java
if (line.split(",").length == NUM_FIELDS) {
        # Correct # items

}
```

Validating the vaccination center ID

This is a six-digit number that cannot be blank. In C#, you could use TryParse(). For example:

```
if (UInt32.TryParse(id, out val) == true) {
        // Is an unsigned int
        if (val >= 0 && val <= 999999) {
                // correct
    }

}
```

UInt32.TryParse() is fast, but imprecise, because a UInt32 can represent 0 .. 4294967295, but for detecting malicious input, this might be totally fine. You could use this code, and if it's successful, verify that the returning integer is between 0 and 999999. You could also use a regex for more precision, as shown in the following code:

```C#
C#
var re = new Regex(@"^\d{6}$");
if (re.IsMatch(id)) {
        // Is exactly six digits

}
```

This regex looks for input that is precisely six digits long; anything else is incorrect.

In JavaScript, you can't use isNaN() (is not a number) or parseInteger() because they are not precise enough. IsNaN() will flag -3.1415926536 as a number, but it's nothing like the data form we need. parseInteger() will return 42 if the incoming string is "42xyzzy123". The best solution is to use a regex.

```JavaScript
JavaScript
const re = /^\d{6}$/;
if (id.match(re) != null) {
        // Is exactly six digits

}
```

Java does not have unsigned integers, so extra validation is needed to make sure the result is within the defined range of 0–999999.

```Java
Java
try {
    int num = Integer.parseInt(id);
    if (num >= 0 && num <= 999999) {
        // valid
            } else {
                // Invalid
    }
} catch (java.lang.NumberFormatException ex) {
                // Invalid

}
```

Validating the date and time

Interestingly, this is more efficient and more correct than using a regex. The date format is in ISO 8601 format, so it has the following form:

```
2022-02-23T03:08:00-06:00
```
which is this syntax:

```
YYYY-MM-ddThh:mm:ss[+/-]hh:mm
```

The last part is the time offset from UTC or Zulu time. UTC is marked as +00:00 or having the string end in a Z for Zulu. Note that ISO 8601 date and time formats can have multiple arrangements, but this is the one we're choosing. Internet dates and times are defined in RFC 3339, which is a profile of ISO 8601, available at https://datatracker.ietf.org/doc/html/rfc3339.

The following C# performs this parsing for us correctly:

C#
```csharp
if (DateTime.TryParse(dt, out dt2) == true) {
    // Valid datetime
}
```

The following regex will match an ISO 8601 date and time, but not the time zone offset:

```
^(-?(?:[1-9][0-9]*)?[0-9]{4})-(1[0-2]|0[1-9])-(3[01]|0[1-9]|[12][0-9])T(2[0-3]|[01][0-9]):([0-5]
[0-9]):([0-5][0-9])(\.[0-9]+)?(Z|[+-](?:2[0-3]|[01][0-9]):[0-5][0-9])?$
```

Unfortunately, regexes get complex quickly and can be error prone and difficult to debug! There are websites that let you experiment with regexes and help parse apart the syntax so you can find errors. Examples include:

- https://www.regexpal.com/

- https://regexr.com/

- https://regex101.com/

Checking an ISO 8601 datetime in PowerShell is easy. If the format is incorrect, the following code will raise an exception:

PowerShell
```powershell
[datetime]::Parse($date)
```

Java has a class that can parse dates, including ISO 8601. There are many supported date formats; you just need to set the format in DateTimeFormatter.

Java
```java
try {
    DateTimeFormatter formatter = DateTimeFormatter.ISO_OFFSET_DATE_TIME;
    var odt = LocalDate.parse(dt, formatter);
} catch (java.time.format.DateTimeParseException ex) {
    // Not valid
}
```

Validating the vaccination type

This is simple. It's just a string compare against a list of vaccine types. The following C# example uses Language Integrated Query (LINQ) to search for the pharmaceutical company. It's not the only way to search a list, but it's short, concise, and obvious.

C#
```
string[] validPharam = { "PharmaA", "PharmaB", "PharmaC" };

bool valid = validPharam.Any(x => x.Contains(pharma, StringComparison.OrdinalIgnoreCase));
```

JavaScript
```
var validPharma = ["PharmaA","PharmaB","PharmaC"];
var valid = validPharma.find((str) => str === pharma);
if (valid != undefined) {
        // pharma is valid

}
```

The Contains() method in Go is specific to strings. Go 1.18 adds generics, but at the time of writing 1.18 was still in prerelease testing. Once generics are released, this code could be changed to support the most common data types.

Go
```
func Contains(s []string, e string) bool {
        for _, v := range s {
                if v == e {
                        return true
                }
        }
        return false
}

arrPharma := []string{"PharmaA", "PharmaB", "PharmaC"}
if Contains(arrPharma, pharma) == true {
        // pharma is valid
}
```

In these code examples, the list of drug providers is hard-coded, which is not a great idea. Instead, the list should be stored in a configuration file somewhere for the code to read at load time. But when you do this, you need to be aware of the authorization policy (RBAC, ACLs, permissions, etc.) on the file used to store the list of providers. From a threat-modeling perspective, we care about the tampering threat.

Validating open spots

This is a number from 0–999. It is highly unlikely there will ever be 999 spots open, but it gives you plenty of headroom. You can use code like this in C#, where min is 0 and max is 999.

C#
```
public bool IntegerRangeCheck(string input, out uint result, uint min, uint max) {
    return uint.TryParse(input, out result) && (result >= min && result <= max);
}
```

In Go, you'll use a regex. Note the use of backticks for the regex strings. This is so the string is treated literally, and you can use \ characters safely without having to resort to escaping special characters. This makes the string easier to read.

Go
```
re, _ := regexp.Compile(`^\d{1,3}$`)
if (len(re.FindString(dt)) > 0) {
        // 000-999
}
```

Python
```
val = int(line)
if val >=0 and val <= 999:
    # valid
```

For PowerShell, you could use the earlier PowerShell code that checks for 0–999999 but restricts the result to 0–999. You could also use the same Java code as before, which checks for 0–999999 but restricts the result to 0–999.

Validating the comment field, including international characters

This can be tricky, because a comment field is an area for text, but that text might include characters other than a–zA-Z0–9. For example, a comment might say, "This will be administered by Dr. Françoise d'Aubigné." Note the cedilla and acute accents under the c and over the e, respectively. Neither of these are in the range a–zA–Z, so you need to be mindful of this.

Because you don't trust the data, you need to make sure the data is well-formed. First, you need to define which subset of characters can go in the comment field. As noted, a–zA–Z does not represent all possible characters in other languages—for example, French, Spanish, Greek, and obviously many more. Thankfully, many modern regex's support international characters using a \p escape. The following is a sample testbed written in Rust:

```
use regex::Regex;
use lazy_static::lazy_static;

fn is_valid_comment(comment: &str) -> bool {
    if comment.len() > 200 {
        return false;
    }
    lazy_static! {
        static ref RE: Regex = Regex::new(r"^[\p{Letter}\p{Number}\p{Other_Punctuation}\s]+$").
unwrap();
    }
    RE.is_match(comment)
}
fn main() {
    let comments =
        vec!["تعلمت الكثير من هذا الكتاب.",              // Arabic
            "我从这本书中学到了很多东西。",                    // Chinese
            "Jeg lærte meget af denne bog.",            // Danish
            "He nui aku ako mai i tēnei pukapuka.",     // Māori
```

```
        "私はこの本から多くのことを学びました。",    // Japanese
        "I learned a lot from this book.",      // English
        "הזה רפסהמ הברה יתדמל .",                 // Hebrew
        "hჁՆ መጽሐፍ ብዙ ተምሬያለሁ ።",                // Amharic
        "This won't <script> work!"];

    for comment in comments.iter() {
        if is_valid_comment(comment) {
            println!("Valid: {}", comment);
        } else {
            println!("Invalid: {}", comment);
        }
    }
}
```

This code iterates through various languages and succeeds on each except the last because it includes characters that are not in the list of allowed characters.

> **Note** Remember, we're looking for "goodness" as our main defense against potentially malicious input, not "badness."

Breaking the regex down, you have the following:

- **^**   The start of the string.

- **[**   The start of a set of characters.

- **\p{Letter}**   Any Unicode letter, uppercase or lowercase—not just a–z or A–Z. Note that \p{L} is also valid.

- **\p{Number}**   Any Unicode number, not just 0–9. Note that \p{N} is also valid.

- **\p{Other_Punctuation}**   Various punctuation, including ¿ and ¡ in Spanish. Note that \p{Op} is also valid.

- **\s**   A space.

- **]**   The end of a set of characters.

- **+**   One or more.

- **$**   The end of the string.

In this example, you cannot use \p{Punctuation}, because it includes the < and > punctuation marks. These are used in HTML and can be employed in a cross-site scripting (XSS) attack. Also, the + in the regex could be replaced with other length constraints.

There's one important caveat: some languages don't natively include a regex library that can handle Unicode, and some languages don't support the long names for the character classes. For example, .NET supports \p{L} but not \p{Letter}.

For JavaScript, including Node.js, you need to use the u qualifier as part of the regex. The following short test code shows this in action. The first regex works, but the second returns null because it does not have a u qualifier.

```
let str = "Έμαθα πολλά από αυτό το βιβλίο.";
console.log(str.match(/\p{L}/gu) );

console.log(str.match(/\p{L}/g) );
```

> **Tip** For a good overview of Unicode strings in regular expressions, see https://azsec.tech/5tq.

Before we move on to the next section, we have to confess something: there is a bug in the code! We left it until now, mainly to show how easy it is to make simple mistakes. The problem is that the comment field is freeform with some restrictions. So, you can add commas to the comment field, but this would make the code that checks for fieldcount==5 wrong.

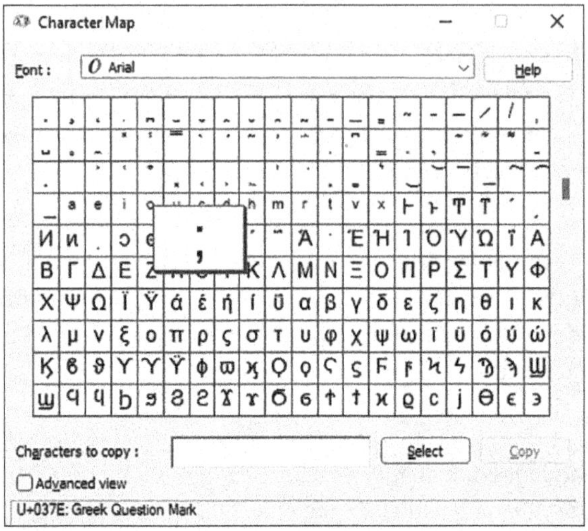

FIGURE 9-4 The Greek question mark in the Windows Character Map.

To fix this, you could always strip out commas from the comment field. But this is dangerous because it can lead to the "commas save lives" problem—that is, there is a big difference between "Let's eat, Grandma" and "Let's eat Grandma." Alternatively, you could escape all commas in the comment field with the HTML-escaped version, &#39. So, a sentence like, "Let's eat, Grandma" becomes "Let's eat' Grandma." It's ugly, but it's safe. Honestly, all this shows the fragility of CSV files. It might be better to use a JSON representation of the data.

Using high-level validation tools

This chapter has focused on using low-level, flexible server-side code for data validation. But some development platforms support built-in validation, too. For example:

- ASP.NET MVC (https://azsec.tech/76f)

- .NET Fluent Validator (https://azsec.tech/11b)

- Node.js using express (https://azsec.tech/1mc)

- JavaScript (server-side) Joi (https://joi.dev/)

- Python (https://azsec.tech/law)

- Go (https://azsec.tech/yyv)

What to do with errors

What should you do if you detect an error (malicious or accidental) in some incoming data? First, you don't want to tell the potential attacker too much, so keep the response short, terse, and devoid of anything they can use to change their plan of attack. For example, a simple 400 error might suffice. Also, be consistent. If you send a 400 error because an API argument is incorrect, then send a 400 error for other API errors, too.

Also, be sure to log the reason for the error so an admin can act. You could use a text file or a storage account for the data or custom logs for use in Azure Monitor. For more information about this, refer to Chapter 6, "Monitoring and auditing." You can also read more about it here: https://azsec.tech/js8.

Reject known bad data

Restricting to only known data is always the right strategy when verifying incoming data. However, some developers go one step further and add another defensive layer that checks for known illegal data. For example, let's say your code expects a filename in an argument, like in the following Python code:

```
import re
def is_filename_valid(filename):
    valid = re.match("^.+\.(?i)(jpg|png|gif|bmp|tiff)$",filename)
    return (valid != None)
```

This is a simple regex that also happens to be too loose and vulnerable. This will allow filenames like the following:

- diving-the-uss-vandenberg.jpg

- picsofdogs.bmp

- CatsBehavingBadly.png

This seems fine. However, the regex will also allow the following:

- ..\..\docs\taxreturn2022.jpg

- /home/blake/docs/mysecretinvention.doc

- c:\secretpics\nicoles-taxreturn2022.jpg

Oops!

One thing you could do is add another regex that looks for bad things to reject anything you might have missed in the first regex. For example:

```
def is_filename_valid(filename):
    valid = re.match("^.+\.(?i)(jpg|png|gif|bmp|tiff)$",filename)
    bad = re.match("[\:\\\/]+",filename)
    return (valid != None and bad == None)
```

This regex looks for bad things—most notably colon, slash, and backslash characters.

The real fix, though, is to create a more restrictive regex, like this one:

```
import re
def is_filename_valid(filename):
    valid = re.match("^(?i)[a-z0-9]{1,24}\.(?i)(jpg|png|gif|bmp|tiff)$").,filename)
    return (valid != None)
```

This regex is correct. However, there's no harm in taking a "the regex might not be right" view and adding a list of known bad characters in a filename—again, colon, slash, and backslash characters.

 Important Adding a check to look for bad things is fine, but not as a replacement for a check that looks for good things.

Regular expressions are a great way to validate data, but they have a dark side: adding them can make your code vulnerable! This is because some classes of regex are subject to a regex denial of service (ReDoS). For more information about ReDoS, read this write-up on the issue published by OWASP here: https://azsec.tech/z5y. Much of the earliest work on this topic was done by Bryan Sullivan at Microsoft.

Also, a regex can take up quite a bit of memory. It might look like a small string, but under the hood the regex code builds a state machine that can get complex and occupy large amounts of memory. This increased memory consumption is especially true for certain regex constructs. For example, the + (one-or-more) qualifier will create a smaller state machine than a {1,200} (between 1 and 200 characters inclusive) qualifier.

The following Rust code will fail ton run:

```
static ref RE: Regex = Regex::new(r"^[\p{Letter}\p{Number}\p{Other_Punctuation}\s]{1,200}}$").
unwrap();
```

The error is

```
thread 'main' panicked at 'called `Result::unwrap()` on an `Err` value:
CompiledTooBig(10485760)', src\main.rs:102:103
```

But the regex runs correctly if you switch out {1,200} with +. Why? As noted, the state machine for {1,200} is considerably more complex than a simple + and consumes more memory. By default, Rust will allow only a maximum 1 MB state machine, but this state machine weighs in at 22 MB!

In Rust, you can change the default memory limit by using code like this:

```
use regex::RegexBuilder;
let re = RegexBuilder::new(r"^[\p{Letter}\p{Number}}\p{Other_Punctuation}\s]{1,200}$")
        .size_limit(22 * 1024 * 1024)            // 22MB
        .build()
        .unwrap();
```

You can experiment with this code at the Rust Playground, located here: https://azsec.tech/y6i. Run the code, remove the .size_limit() method, and rerun.

> **Important** Different regex implementations have different memory implications, but it's worth understanding what the memory impact might be for your operating system, programming language, and library used.

The next issue is performance. To improve performance, don't put a regular expression definition in a loop or in a function that is heavily used. As mentioned, constructing the state machine takes time. That's why the sample Rust code uses a lazy static, so the regex is compiled on the first call and then referenced from then on. You could also create your regexes once using a class construction.

> **Tip** For .NET, you should read the following page for information about reusing regexes: https://azsec.tech/jfs.

One important final note about regular expressions: never use untrusted input as part of a regular expression string. In other words, the attacker should never control any part of the regex string.

> **Note** At the time of this writing, with .NET 7 RC 1 has been released, and it includes a Regex Source Generator. This dramatically improves the performance of regexes by precompiling the regex rather than building the regex at runtime. You can read more here: https://azsec.tech/leb.

Encode data

This is mostly for data that is echoed back to a user's browser. Even after encoding all the incoming data, it is beneficial and safer to clean up the data before it is sent back to a browser. This is mostly true of any data that comes from an untrusted source. The goal of this is to render potential HTML and scripting useless, primarily to mitigate XSS issues.

If you have any data that comes from a potentially untrusted source and is then echoed back in a browser, this data must be encoded before it is echoed back. The most well-known way to achieve this is to simply HTML-encode all output. Some frameworks—for example, ASP.NET MVC and Razor—do this automatically. For others, you might need to call a function that takes the data, encodes it, and then renders it in the browser.

The following C# code snippet demonstrates this:

```
using System.Text.Encodings.Web;
using System.Text.Unicode;
string bad = @"<script>alert(1);</script>";
var encoder = HtmlEncoder.Create(allowedRanges: new[] { UnicodeRanges.BasicLatin });
Console.WriteLine(encoder.Encode(bad));
```

Recall the comment field example from earlier in the chapter. Processing text entered in this field involves the following steps:

1. A user enters a comment.

2. The server accepts the input and runs it through a regex to make sure the comment is well-formed. If it is not correct, the comment is rejected. If the format is correct, the comment is written to a Cosmos DB database.

3. When another user scrolls through comments, each comment is read from Cosmos DB.

4. Each comment is passed through an HTML function.

5. The result of HTML encoding is rendered in the user's browser.

> **Tip** You can read more about encoding HTML by reading the OWASP XSS Prevention Cheat Sheet at https://azsec.tech/e33.

Common vulnerabilities

There are hundreds if not thousands of distinct vulnerability types, and there is no way we can cover every single one here. Because of this, we're going to focus on one of the industry's most well-known "go to" lists of vulnerabilities: the OWASP Top 10. This is discussed in a little more detail in Chapter 10, "Cryptography in Azure," and is available here: https://owasp.org/Top10. There is also an OWASP API Security Top 10 at https://azsec.tech/4tq.

If you want to learn as much as possible about each vulnerability class, we recommend taking the following steps:

1. Read about each of the 10 issues discussed in the following section.

2. For each issue on the OWASP website, read the issue and then look at the cross-reference of CWEs at the bottom of each page.

3. Click the link of any of the CWEs and learn about the issues in more depth.

Now let's look at each of the 10 issues through an Azure lens.

A01: Broken access control

Further information   https://azsec.tech/kgp

As we stress in Chapter 5, access control is critical. In Azure, this usually means using role-based access control (RBAC), although some services support attribute-based access control (ABAC). Some services in Azure, such as storage accounts, also support shared access signature (SAS) tokens, which are used to allow access to a process or user that has the token. A SAS token can include access requirements such as Read, Write, and Delete.

In Azure, implementing access control also means having a limited set of users with elevated roles, such as Owner and Contributor, but also extending to service-specific roles such as Storage Account Contributor. Accounts with these roles can often read and configure services but not change access policies.

> **Important** It is critical that all access policies be as restrictive as possible, allowing only principals the access they need to perform their tasks and nothing more.

A02: Cryptographic failures

Further information   https://azsec.tech/q8v

In part, this covers encryption of data at rest and in motion, or "on the wire." For data at rest, this means lack of cryptographic defenses or poor implementation, such as not encrypting a sensitive column in SQL Server. For data in motion, this usually means not using a secure protocol such as TLS 1.2.

Many of these can be enforced using Azure Policy, as discussed in Chapter 7, "Governance." For example, the sample found at https://azsec.tech/t0x enforces HTTPS (HTTP over TLS) for Azure Storage accounts. One level lower, this can include using insecure cipher suites in TLS (such as TLS_RSA_WITH_3DES_EDE_CBC_SHA) or insecure cryptographic algorithms (such as RC4, DES, 3DES, MD5).

Other examples of cryptographic failure include the following:

- Poor key generation, such as using a deterministic random number generator

- Poor key derivation, such as using a password directly as a cryptographic key

- Using "custom" cryptographic algorithms rather than industry-standard reviewed algorithms

- Encrypting data but not providing tamper-detection, too

- Reuse of initialization vectors (IVs)

> **Tip** If you use the Microsoft Crypto SDK, described in Chapter 10, many of the aforementioned points are addressed by the library.

A03: Injection

Further information https://azsec.tech/u90

Examples of injection include SQL injection (SQLi) and cross-site scripting. One way to resolve this collection of issues is by verifying input and encoding output. Another is to use technologies that have specific defenses to mitigate injection. For example, SQL has parameterized queries to neuter variables used as part of the query. The following C# code uses the SQLParameter class to build a dynamic SQL query safely:

```
SqlDataAdapter myCommand = new SqlDataAdapter(
"SELECT au_lname, au_fname FROM Authors WHERE au_id = @au_id", conn);
SQLParameter parm = myCommand.SelectCommand.Parameters.Add("@au_id",
                          SqlDbType.VarChar, 11);
Parm.Value = idAuthor;
```

> **Tip** SQLi is *not* a vulnerability in the back-end database. It's an issue in the way SQL statements are constructed by the client. This page has a good overview of SQLi: https://azsec.tech/30v.

Also, many application frameworks and constructs automatically create SQL statements from text. For example, in C# LINQ to SQL is designed to create secured SQL queries. You can learn more here: https://azsec.tech/5mh.

Azure Logic Apps are subject to SQLi, as explained here: https://azsec.tech/hzj. The same goes for Cosmos DB when using the SQL client, discussed here: https://azsec.tech/uwi. Microsoft Defender for SQL offers SQL Advanced Threat Protection to detect attempted SQLi attacks in near real time. You can learn more here: https://azsec.tech/p0g.

As mentioned, XSS is another example of injection. The core problem with XSS is accepting untrusted input—which could include HTML or scripts—and then using it as HTML output. The fix is simple: validate incoming data, and HTML encode outgoing data using methods like .NET's HttpUtility. HtmlEncode(). This combination of input and output logic is often called *filter input, escape output* (FIEO).

A04: Insecure design

Further information https://azsec.tech/4i6

This is mitigated with threat modeling. The whole point of threat modeling is to understand a solution's design and what defenses are used to protect that system. If security issues are found during the threat-modeling process, these issues can be resolved, which leads to a more secure design.

A05: Security misconfiguration

Further information https://azsec.tech/ng0

This is incredibly common. People deploy a secure configuration, but over time, small changes creep in, and services slowly drift away from the original secure defaults. This is why you use governance services in Azure such as Azure Policy: to restrict this drift and to prevent new services from deploying with insecure defaults.

One of the most common issues we have seen is virtual machines (VMs) with public IP addresses. VMs should be behind a load balancer or a bastion service such as Azure Bastion. But we've been in more than one conversation with customers whose VMs have an RDP or SSH port open directly to the internet. This is a bad idea.

> **Tip** Azure Resource Graph allows you to analyze settings on all services in use. For example, the query at https://azsec.tech/dwo displays all VMs with public IP addresses.

Misconfiguration often extends to how you configure various services. A classic and common error is failing to add security-related headers to HTTP servers. Any HTTP server should set the following headers, whether you're using an Apache server in a Linux VM or an App Service. These headers instruct the browser how to enforce specific security rules. The current list of common, security-related HTTP headers is as follows:

- `Content-Security-Policy`
- `Referrer-Policy`
- `Strict-Transport-Security`
- `X-Content-Type-Options`
- `X-Frame-Options`
- `X-XSS-Protection`
- `Access-Control-Allow-Origin` (cross-origin resource sharing [CORS])

This list is dynamic. Over the years, new headers have been added or updated. The Security Headers site (https://securityheaders.com/) has an excellent analysis of the various headers and what they should be set to, as does the Mozilla Developer Network (https://azsec.tech/ggb).

For Azure App services (for example, the service that runs https://azsecuritypodcast.net), you can update web.config. The following code is the web.config file used by the Azure Security Podcast:

```xml
<?xml version="1.0" encoding="utf-8" ?>
<configuration>
    <system.webServer>
        <httpProtocol>
            <customHeaders>
                <clear />
                <add name="Content-Security-Policy" value="default-src 'self' *.rss.com; script-src 'self' https://ajax.aspnetcdn.com "/>
                <add name="Referrer-Policy" value="strict-origin-when-cross-origin" />
                <add name="Strict-Transport-Security" value="max-age=63072000" />
                <add name="X-Content-Type-Options" value="nosniff" />
                <add name="X-Frame-Options" value="ALLOW-FROM https://player.rss.com" />
                <add name="X-XSS-Protection" value="1; mode=block" />
                <add name="Access-Control-Allow-Origin" value="https://player.rss.com https://apollo.rss.com" />
                <add name="Cache-Control" value="max-age=31536000" />
            </customHeaders>
        </httpProtocol>
    </system.webServer>
</configuration>
```

The Content-Security-Policy (CSP) header is complex and powerful, and having a good understanding of how it works is critical. Notice that the preceding sample contains references to *.rss.com. This is a media player implemented using HTML that allows a user to play an episode in the browser. If the various headers did not allow *.rss.com, the media player would not render, because the HTML is fetched from another site. Also, notice that script-src references ajax.aspnetcdn.com, which allows the browser to pull in jQuery from outside the core website. Again, without this, jQuery would not load when using CSP.

Finally—and this is important—these headers will often cause a site to incorrectly render, so you might need to change your site's code or tweak the headers. One good example is using inline code or styles to help you wrangle Content-Security-Policy. You should move inline code and styles to a separate file and reference it at the start of your HTML files.

Real-world experience: Inline script and inline styles

Inline script (that is, <script> blocks on the web page) and inline styles (for example, <img style=) are blocked by CSP. There are ways around this—for example, using hashes or nonces—but they are often difficult to use.

Do yourself a favor and move all scripts and styles to external files and reference them in your pages using constructs like <link rel="stylesheet" href="rss.css">. Trust us on this: it is easier to do this than to fight against CSP. This is what we had to do to get the embedded audio player from rss.com to work correctly on the Azure Security Podcast site.

You can use a tool like the one at https://report-uri.com/home/generate to help you build a policy string. For an Azure static website, you can add a new file in the root folder named staticwebapps. config.json like so:

```
{
    "globalHeaders": {
        "content-security-policy": "default-src 'self'",
        "Referrer-Policy":"no-referrer",
        "Strict-Transport-Security": "max-age=63072000",
        "X-Frame-Options": "SAMEORIGIN",
        "X-Permitted-Cross-Domain-Policies": "none",
        "X-Content-Type-Options": "nosniff"
    }
}
```

Other web servers and environments have their own header configuration files. For example, in Apache (running in a VM), you can edit httpd.conf to add this at the end of the file:

```
<IfModule mod_headers.c>
  Header always set X-Content-Type-Options "nosniff"
  Header always set Content-Security-Policy "default-src 'self'"
  Header always set Referrer-Policy "no-referrer"
  Header always set Strict-Transport-Security "max-age=31536000; includeSubDomains"
  Header always set X-Frame-Options "DENY"
  Header always set X-XSS-Protection "1; mode=block"
</IfModule>
```

> **Note** The industry is moving away from using X-Frame-Options to using Content-Security-Policy frame-ancestors instead because CSP is more encompassing.

There is one other new header: Permissions-Policy. It replaces Feature-Policy. You can learn more about it here: https://www.permissionspolicy.com/. To check if the browsers your applications support can handle the header, you can use the Can I Use site, located here: https://caniuse.com/?search=Permissions-Policy. The Azure Security Podcast site does not set this header on purpose. When it becomes more popular, we will enable it in the site.

Notice there is nothing to remove the Server: header, which announces the web server type and version number. Removing or replacing this header is of no real security value; it is just security theater, because a somewhat-knowledgeable attacker can easily "fingerprint" the server to determine its type and version.

On a related note, the Access-Control-Allow-Origin header, which is used to support cross-origin resource sharing, *does not* improve security. In fact, it reduces security somewhat by allowing a controlled weakening of the browser same-origin security policy. The reason CORS exists is to have a preferred way to send HTTP requests across websites without resorting to some disastrous work-arounds used in the past. CORS allows for some more secure OAuth2 flows. Some services in Azure support CORS—for example, Azure Functions, as shown in Figure 9-5.

FIGURE 9-5 An example CORS in an Azure Function.

Even though the screenshot shown in Figure 9-5 mentions using * as a wildcard, you should not allow all domains to access your Function App. Allow only required domains to interact with your Function app. Also, as shown in Figure 9-6, Microsoft Defender for Cloud warns against setting CORS to *.

> **Important** Don't set CORS to *.

Dashboard > Recommendations >

CORS should not allow every resource to access Function Apps

⊘ Exempt   ⚙ View policy definition   🔧 Open query

Severity	Freshness interval		Tactics and techniques
Low	🕐 30 Min		🖥 Initial Access

⌃ **Description**

Cross-Origin Resource Sharing (CORS) should not allow all domains to access your Function app. Allow only required domains to interact with your Function app.

⌃ **Remediation steps**

Quick fix:
Select the unhealthy resources and click "Fix" to launch "Quick fix" remediation. Learn more >
Note: After the process completes, it may take up to 30 min until your resources move to the 'healthy resources' tab.

Quick fix logic

Manual remediation:
To allow only required domains to interact with your web app, we recommend the following steps:
1. Go to the app service CORS page
2. Remove the "*" defined and instead specify explicit origins that should be allowed to make cross-origin calls
3. Click Save

FIGURE 9-6 The CORS recommendation in Defender for Cloud; note the manual remediation suggests removing *.

Contrary to popular belief, the HTTP Strict-Transport-Security (HSTS) heading does not force all HTTP connections to HTTPS. HSTS requires one validated HTTPS connection to the server (that is, with no certificate errors) before the browser will honor the HSTS header. The reason is because an attacker can manipulate an HTTP body, including headers, making the HSTS setting untrustworthy in an HTTP response. However, HSTS also maintains a preload database of known sites that require HTTPS. To add your site to the list, go to the HSTS Preload Submission site at https://hstspreload.org/.

Another header type, cookies, should set the following flags:

- HttpOnly
- Secure
- Expires
- SameSite

HttpOnly helps mitigate XSS attacks from stealing cookie content. While you should certainly set cookies to use this option, be aware that it has value only if the cookie is used for authentication purposes, and it's not a great defense against some forms of XSS. However, using cookies for session state and client configuration access is better than using HTML storage. You can read more on this here: https://azsec.tech/bpw. You should also mark cookies with the Secure flag so they are passed between the browser and server only when using HTTPS (HTTP over TLS).

Cookies should be set to expire using the Expires flag. The duration is up to you and depends on your business requirements because you need to balance security with usability. We have seen many developers set this flag to between one and six months.

SameSite provides some protection against client-side request forgery attacks by restricting when cookies are sent. If you set the SameSite=Strict flag on a cookie, then a browser sends cookies only for first-party context requests. These are requests originating from the site that set the cookie. If the request originated from a different URL than that of the current location, none of the cookies tagged with the Strict attribute is sent. You can read more about the flag at https://azsec.tech/bux to determine what cookie SameSite attribute works best for your sites. Here is an example cookie with these flags set:

```
Set-Cookie: sessionid=c92620e1; HttpOnly; Secure; SameSite=Strict; Expires=Fri, 1 Jul 2022
00:00:00 GMT
```

> **Important** HTTP security headers are a useful defense against some classes of attacks, but they should be considered an extra defensive layer only.

> **Real-life experience: Debugging security headers**
>
> As noted, these headers can cause your website to render incorrectly, and it is often difficult to understand why. Browsers like Edge (using the Chromium engine) and Chrome have superlative debugging tools. In the case of Edge, press **Ctrl+Shift+I** to bring up Developer Tools and then select **Console**. If you refresh the page, you can see the errors in red. Also, if you click **Network** and then a file used in the response—for example index.html—you can see the browser request and response headers.

A06: Vulnerable and outdated components

Further information   https://azsec.tech/it1

Many applications are built with other components such as libraries. These components might not be controlled by you, so if they contain vulnerabilities, you will need to update your solutions with new solutions.

It is incredibly important to maintain a software bill of materials (SBOM) that tracks all the components that comprise your applications. This includes the following:

- Component or package name

- Version number

- Vendor or source code repository

- Programming language

- Location of security information about that component

> **Note** A 2021 Executive Order in the United States called out the need to use an SBOM to improve cybersecurity. You can read the relevant document here: https://azsec.tech/kpi in §10.j.

GitHub has a tool called Dependabot to help you identify third-party packages you use that are out of date and have security issues. You can learn more here: https://azsec.tech/hud. This tool is just one part of GitHub's security supply chain initiative and is discussed in further detail at https://azsec.tech/m0q.

A07: Identification and authentication failures

Further information   https://azsec.tech/f3u

In the world of cloud-based solutions, identity is critical. Still, network boundaries are important—especially when it comes to the need for network segmentation in a zero-trust environment. A core part of identity is strong authentication. This is also a core element of your threat models. All processes must be authenticated, as well as devices and users.

Interestingly, the OWASP documentation calls out CWE-297, "Improper Validation of Certificate with Host Mismatch." We see this error often, but it extends beyond host name validation. If your code initiates a connection over TLS, it's important that the code performs all the relevant certificate checks. These include the following:

- The certificate's signature is valid. This verifies that it is not tampered with.

- The name in the certificate matches the name of the system or user you want to communicate with.

- The certificate chains up to a trusted root CA certificate. This is a critical step to prove the certificate is trusted.

- The extended key usage is correct—for example, server authentication.

- The date range is valid. That is, today is between the `NotBefore` and `NotAfter` fields.

- Whether the certificate is revoked. There are two common ways to check if a certificate is revoked. The first is to use a certificate revocation list (CRL). The location of the CRL is held in the certificate using a CRL distribution point (CDP), which is just a URL. The other way to check if a certificate is revoked is to use the Online Certificate Status Protocol (OCSP).

You will probably never write code to perform these steps. Instead, you should leave the validation to the libraries you use. For example, in .NET, the `SslStream()` class calls a delegate that can perform actions based on errors validating a certificate. Unfortunately, we see code like this quite often:

```
// This is invoked by the SslStream(..,..RemoteCertificateValidationDelegate, ..)
public static bool ValidateServerCertificate(
      object sender,
      X509Certificate certificate,
      X509Chain chain,
      SslPolicyErrors sslPolicyErrors) {
    // Ignore all certificate errors
    return true;
}
```

This code ignores certificate errors and is a serious security vulnerability.

On the topic of certificates, be careful with self-signed certificates. If you must use self-signed certificates, check the certificate's signature and thumbprint against a list of predetermined valid certificates. The list must have a strong access policy so it cannot be changed by untrusted entities.

Even then, be careful. Some people use self-signed certificates in test and use "real" CA-issued certificates in production. The problem with this is the test environment does not perform the same certificate tests as would be performed in production. The best way around this is to set up a certificate authority yourself—for example, using Active Directory Certificate Services (AD CS). You can install the root CA certificate from this CA on your development and test machines and test end-to-end certificate-based authentication including revocation. And because you control the certificates, you can create certificates that are invalid to see how your code reacts to, say, an expired server certificate or one where key usage is for client authentication when you expect server authentication.

> **Tip** Microsoft has a Learning Path on the topic of certificates here: https://azsec.tech/xkq. This site does suggest using self-signed certificates for testing, which we don't agree with, however.

Real-world experience: Revocation checking

Revocation checking has its downsides. The URL of the CRL CDP or the OCSP endpoint is in the certificate, so the code that checks to see if the certificate is revoked or not accesses that endpoint.

What if the endpoint cannot be accessed? Is it a firewall issue? Is the endpoint under attack? Figuring that out is the easy part! The hard part is figuring out what to do in your code if you cannot resolve the revocation endpoint.

The secure answer is to fail closed or fail secure and reject the connection. But the easy answer is, don't do revocation checking! The correct answer is somewhere in the middle. In our experience, it is best to make revocation an administrative policy or configuration and default to rejecting the certificate if a revocation endpoint is unresolvable. However, if your application downloads code, you should always verify the signature on the code and always check the revocation status, and if the revocation endpoint is not accessible, deny the code download.

A08: Software and data integrity failures

Further information   https://azsec.tech/0kv

The issue here is code or data being compromised and changed. If you download code that is not digitally signed or you do not verify an out-of-band hash, there's no way to know if the code or data is valid. In fact, looking at our vaccination booking example, the data really should be digitally signed by the vaccination center, so we know for certain it's from the correct one.

You can create a digital signature quite easily as long as you have a certificate that has key usage for digital signatures and the associated private key. In Windows, these certificates are often referred to as *Authenticode certificates*.

Not only does PowerShell support signing, but it can also be configured to only allow digitally signed PowerShell files to run—for example, using cmdlets such as `Set-AuthenticodeSignature` to sign PowerShell files. You can see the result in the following code. The signature size is relatively constant, so it seems large compared to one line of script, but for a large script, the signature would be about the same size as for one line of script.

```
"Hello, World!"

# SIG # Begin signature block
# MIIFkQYJKoZIhvcNAQcCoIIFgjCCBX4CAQExCzAJBgUrDgMCGgUAMGkGCisGAQQB
-- SNIP --
# 1vbbaAkl1AAg9aDVb6EXPY+AIKr5UYJli8WhCfVbWo+qV1EeWUXKlJEED0TTaH3K
# mvZISeSM+yS+yN+hz6hNPxdy3S6QuWhjrFleL5hj1p2+O08RAA==

# SIG # End signature block
```

Key Vault can perform signing operations within Key Vault, and the keys can be in hardware if you use an RSA-HSM or ECC-HSM key. The following simple C# test code demonstrates how to sign arbitrary data. This sample creates a signature by signing the SHA-512 hash using a P-521 elliptic curve.

```
using Azure.Identity;
using Azure.Security.KeyVault.Keys.Cryptography;
using System.Security.Cryptography;
using System.Text;

// You should pull the hash alg from a config file
string HASH_ALG = "SHA512";
SignatureAlgorithm SIG_ALG = SignatureAlgorithm.ES512; // P-521 Curve
var keyVaultUrl = "https://mykv.vault.azure.net/keys/key-name/version";

var creds = new DefaultAzureCredential(true);
var keyCryptoClient = new CryptographyClient(new Uri(keyVaultUrl), creds);

var msg = Encoding.UTF8.GetBytes("A message we want to sign");
var digest = HashAlgorithm.Create(HASH_ALG)?.ComputeHash(msg);

SignResult sig;
if (digest is not null) {
    sig = keyCryptoClient.Sign(SIG_ALG, digest);
    Console.WriteLine(Convert.ToBase64String(sig.Signature));
}
```

> **Note** You need to match the signature algorithm with the hash function correctly. For example, the previous code uses a P-521 curve with an SHA-512 hash.

This code emits a Base64-encoded signature block, which could travel with the text file or separately. For example, you could do something like this:

```
A message we want to sign
--SIG-
AALaNsWvS9atK8x14BqsqEdps0+IykG7bxwKXXZhyJ6zR/
rAKtYTTgpMvqqO1VyX6wEwFrwGTRb7S19kJeiPALmHAQ6BB6jeT/YnrRQHzBKqpoaMy9zRCWC/oDUW+ufAUnIOVsBM5WttcY
ZujOJcEAjraGwB6eQWoc9cK2301iM/DKNT
--ENDSIG--
```

You could then do the reverse operation: signature verification using CryptographyClient. Verify(). There is a twist, though: you probably won't pull the public key from Key Vault. Instead, you'll use the public key in a certificate so you can perform all the correct certificate checks mentioned earlier. This will not only verify the certificate, but it will also check that the data came from the name in the certificate. For example, if the certificate has a field CN=joe@contoso.com, then you know the data came from Joe. You could also use something like XMLDSig or JSON web signature to sign and verify data, so you don't need to do the low-level work.

Remember, this section is all about integrity and authenticity. There is no encryption. It is common to do both, however. Our vaccination file could append the signature to the CSV file. The data is not encrypted, but we still have integrity and authentication due to the digital signatures, as long as your code performs all the relevant certificate checks before verifying the signature.

> ## Real-world experience: Checking signatures
>
> Validating signatures is not as prevalent as it should be except for code that comes from various application stores such as those from Microsoft, Google, and Apple. These require signatures and verify the signatures explicitly. On boot, Windows 11 performs signature checks on critical binaries to make sure the system has not been tampered with through a rootkit.

If a service needs to verify data, it can also use a message authentication code (MAC), which uses a symmetric key rather than public/private key pair. This would require any services to have access to the MAC key. This is why systems that use a MAC are usually one-to-one rather than one-to-many: to keep the MAC key distribution as small as possible. For example, TLS uses a unique MAC key for client-to-server communication, and a different MAC key for server-to-client communication.

What about using a hash? You can use a hash so long as:

- The hash is not included with the data to be verified.

- The hash is available over an authenticated and protected channel—for example, using TLS.

The hash cannot travel with the data because the data could be tampered with and the hash recalculated.

> ## Real-world experience: Signing binaries
>
> If you have used a mobile phone, you may not realize that unless you put the phone into some form of developer mode, it will require all downloaded code to be digitally signed. For example, this page describes the process for Android developers: https://azsec.tech/2r1.
>
> You should consider digitally signing all your binaries and scripts (where supported), too. This will provide a degree of trust that the binaries have come from you and have not been tampered with. Humans should initiate the process after the appropriate checks have been made to make sure the executables are the correct ones and devoid of malware.

Signing binaries is a trusted process, and the reason we bring up the "require humans" directive is because of the attack against SolarWinds that started in 2020. The attackers infiltrated the company development pipeline and added malware to a DLL named SolarWindsOrion.Core.BusinessLayer.dll. The development pipeline automatically digitally signed any code that came from the pipeline, including, in this case, code that contained malware. A critically important asset used to sign binaries is the private key, which should be stored in a hardware security module (HSM) and accessed only by trusted personnel.

A09: Security logging and monitoring failures

Further information   https://azsec.tech/4oa

This topic is covered in detail in Chapter 6.

A10: Server-side request forgery (SSRF)

Further information   https://azsec.tech/3pn

Once again, this is an input trust issue. The core lesson here is to never allow an attacker to control a URL. If you must have a user control the URL, then have a list of valid URLs to validate against and only allow those URLs.

SSRF-based attacks are common against cloud-based solutions. It is believed the 2019 Capital One breach that yielded more than 100-million customer records was an SSRF attack against the company's AWS infrastructure. You can read about the Capital One attack here: https://ejj.io/blog/capital-one.

The problem is incredibly simple:

1. A vulnerable server accepts a URL from an untrusted source (an attacker).

2. The server does not verify the URL is valid and correctly formed.

3. The server accesses the data at that URL.

4. The server returns the object at that URL back to the attacker.

The problem is if the web server has access to internal resources and the URL (that came from the attacker) points to a resource on the internal network, the attacker can start reading resources on the internal network! An example of an internal resource that is common to cloud platforms is the Instance Metadata Service (https://azsec.tech/meta), which, on Azure, is accessible on a nonroutable IP address, 169.254.169.254.

> **Important** You must always verify any IP address or DNS name that could be provided by an attacker to make sure it is a valid address or name.

Another attack, cross-site request forgery (CSRF), sounds like SSRF, but the two are not the same. In fact, CSRF was on the OWASP Top 10 back in 2017, but it's not now, mainly because most web frameworks offer defenses, such as ASP.NET MVC. You can read more here: https://azsec.tech/0py. The remedy for CSRF is to include a random token in the session, but this is always best handled by the various web frameworks.

Comments about using C++

Some of the code samples earlier in this chapter were written in C++, and we want to explain ourselves. While we don't see much custom-written cloud-related code written in C++, we do see code in VMs running Linux and Windows, containerized code, embedded systems, and IoT solutions using C++.

We have three items of advice when it comes to writing C++ code:

- Don't write C++ as glorified C.

- Use all security-related compiler and linker defenses available to you.

- Use analysis tools.

Let's look at each.

Don't write glorified C

C is a low-level language designed as a replacement for assembly language. The lineage of many modern programming languages originates in C.

C is small, is efficient, and has unfettered access to process memory. It is this last point that also makes C a language that requires care. The documentation for the original commercial C compiler from Whitesmiths, Ltd., in 1982 said, "C is too expressive a language to be used without discipline." (A copy of this manual is available at https://azsec.tech/7c2; the quote is on page 22.)

C++ offers numerous quality, security, and robustness benefits over C. But you must use these features to obtain these benefits. You might have noticed that the sample C++ code we wrote, while simple, uses C++ idioms, has no direct pointer use, and passes large function arguments by reference. Honestly, it might have been easier in some examples to use low-level C, but using Modern C++ (https://azsec.tech/ko3) and the C++ Standard Library (STL; https://azsec.tech/odj) makes the code safer by far.

Use compiler and linker defenses

The two most popular C and C++ compilers are Microsoft Visual C++ and GNU gcc. Both provide extensive options to emit safer code that includes various defenses against memory corruption vulnerabilities.

For Visual C++, the following is a list of commonly used compiler and linker options and links to resources for more information. Some are enabled by default for C++ projects.

- **/SDL** This supports enhanced security checks, including enhanced stack-corruption detection (https://azsec.tech/azk).

- **/DYNAMICBASE** This uses address space layout randomization (ASLR) to randomly rebase the application at load time (https://azsec.tech/1s3).

- **/NXCOMPAT**   This indicates that the application supports No eXecute (NX), also known as Data Execution Prevention (DEP) (https://azsec.tech/3nt).

- **/SAFESEH**   This emits code that has a set of safe exception handlers (https://azsec.tech/18y).

- **/GUARD**   This enables Control Flow Guard (https://azsec.tech/c5y) and Exception Handler Continuation Metadata (https://azsec.tech/o1p).

- **/CETCOMPAT**   Opt in for hardware-enforced stack protection (https://azsec.tech/s1s and technical write-up at https://azsec.tech/i17).

- **/fsanitize=address**   This is a way to find security issues, mainly memory safety issues, at compile time, and to prevent security issues at runtime. It can be treated as a replacement for /RTC (runtime checks) and /analyze (static analysis) (https://azsec.tech/vom).

For gcc, the following is a commonly used set of options that should be employed:

- **_FORTIFY_SOURCE**   This a macro (for example, gcc -D_FORTIFY_SOURCE=2), not a compiler or linker flag, that performs checks for classes of buffer overflow (https://azsec.tech/fsp).

- **-Wformat-overflow**   This detects string format overflows (https://azsec.tech/3i8).

- **-Wstringop-overflow**   This detects overflows in memcpy and strcpy (https://azsec.tech/3i8).

- **-fstack-protector-strong**   This adds stack-based corruption detection (https://azsec.tech/qfg)

- **-fPIE**   This creates a Position Independent Executable (PIE) that uses ASLR (https://azsec.tech/opj).

- **/fsanitize=address**   This is the same technology used in VC++ (https://azsec.tech/m44).

> **Tip** The GitHub Gist at https://azsec.tech/y1r offers an up-to-date list of security-related gcc flags and options. Also, the following article about FORTIFY_SOURCE from Red Hat is a worthwhile read: https://azsec.tech/g4o.

All these options find or detect potential memory safety issues at compile time or runtime. You should use as many of these options as possible. Many of them will fail fast in the face of an issue, enabling you to debug and fix the issue quickly.

Use analysis tools

Both gcc and VC++ include baseline code analysis functionality. While you probably don't need to run the analysis on each build, you should perform it at least once per sprint so you can catch any issues quickly and fix them. Also, although these tools have a strong focus on security, they find other issues, too.

Visual C++ also has an /analyze option that performs various code quality and security checks on your code. There is an overlap between what /fsanitize=address can find and what /analyze can find. In our opinion, for native C and C++ code, you should use both until you determine that one performs better on your codebase. You can find information about /analyze here: https://azsec.tech/r7c.

In addition, Microsoft Research created the source-code annotation language (SAL) used in the Windows SDK and Microsoft Runtime headers. You should seriously consider using it in your custom C++ headers, too. You can read more about SAL here: https://azsec.tech/rxy.

Finally, the Visual C++ team wrote an excellent article about NULL-deference detection using the static analysis tools built into the compiler. You can read about it here: https://azsec.tech/bxv. For gcc, a compiler option was added to gcc v10 to provide lightweight static analysis. You can learn more here: https://azsec.tech/87z.

On the GitHub side, CodeQL is a tool that is free for research use and free when used with open source software. CodeQL (previously named Semmle) is a rich static analysis solution that offers advanced capabilities such as data flow and control flow analysis across various programming languages, including C, C#, C++, Go, Java, JavaScript, Python, Ruby, and TypeScript.

CodeQL builds a database of the code. Then, a developer can use SQL-like queries to search the code for specific conditions that indicate code quality bugs, including vulnerabilities. A nice feature is that the CodeQL query language is the same regardless of the underlying programming language. Also, because anyone can create CodeQL queries, CodeQL democratizes query creation.

If you are reviewing commercial analysis tools, consider using tools that support Static Analysis Results Interchange Format (SARIF). You can read more about it here: https://sarifweb.azurewebsites.

net/. SARIF allows the output of multiple analysis tools to feed into various reporting and all-up analysis tools. CodeQL supports SARIF, as discussed here: https://azsec.tech/7f2.

 Tip There are several other tools besides these. OWASP offers a list of analysis tools at https://azsec.tech/aww.

Security code review

Chapter 1, "Software development lifecycle processes," discusses security code review in the context of agile methods. This section covers it more generally.

Code review is critical to help secure your code. Over the years, we have devised a high-level approach to rapidly review code that leverages everything we have covered so far in this chapter. Remember, you have only a finite amount of time to review code, so we focus here on the code that is most at risk. Our code-review approach includes these steps:

1. Refer to the threat model to identify all the entry points into the code, especially those that cross trust boundaries. You should be able to match these entry points with some code construct such as a REST API, a WebSocket, a UDP socket, and others.

2. Order the entry points by attack surface, from high to low. This will be the order in which you review the code, from the top to the bottom.

3. From the entry point, determine the data that's coming in. This might be a JSON payload, arguments in an HTTP query string, or a buffer from a socket. This is the data you need to evaluate carefully. In analysis parlance, it is called the *source*.

4. Trace the data from step 3 through the code. At every line of code where the data is used, determine if the construct is safe. Data use is called a *sink*. Essentially, you want to track data from its source to all its sinks, making sure the data is correct and used appropriately. A correct pattern is, data enters a source, is correctly validated as early as possible, and is used safely by various sinks.

Let's take a simple example with the following parameters:

- A data source is a JSON payload that is part of a POST REST API call.

- One element of the JSON file is a number—let's say it's an unsigned 32-bit integer called 'count'—that indicates how many items to deal with.

- The code uses 'count' +1 to dynamically allocate some objects to store items. This is the sink. The +1 is added by the code as it can add another object.

- There is no checking to constrain the value of 'count'.

The last two points are unsafe for many reasons. For example:

- What if the count is not a number, but it's the letter *Q* instead?

- What if the number is 1,000,000? Do you really want the attacker to force your application to allocate 1 million objects?

- What if the number is 4,294,967,296? The code won't allocate 4 billion objects. It'll allocate zero! Why? Because $2^{32} + 1 = 0$. It's an integer overflow problem. So, your code allocates space for zero objects, it attempts to copy data into the memory, and it crashes.

Having code handle incorrect data gracefully is critically important to both the security and robustness of your code. Fortunately, there's a way to test your code against malformed data. That process is called *fuzz testing*, and it's discussed next.

Keeping developers honest with fuzz testing

At the start of the chapter, we pointed out how important it is to validate input. This is probably the most important defensive security skill a developer needs to understand. We also defined what the incoming data must look like to be deemed valid by the application.

Let's return to our vaccination booking application. To recap, the data coming from a vaccination center is a CSV file that comprises the following fields:

```
centerId, date and time, vaccination type, open spots, comment
```

The formats for each data item are as follows:

- **centerID**   This is the vaccination center ID. It is a six-digit number. This field cannot be blank.

- **date and time**   For this, you use the ISO 8601 date and time format. This field cannot be blank.

- **vaccination type**   This is a string that represents the name of a valid vaccine manufacturer. This field cannot be blank.

- **open spots**   This is a number from 0 to 999. This field can be blank; when it is, it equates to zero.

- **comment**   This is a text field in which a representative from the vaccination center can enter a comment. This comment can be up to 200 characters long.

The CSV file will have one line for each vaccination center, date/time, and vaccine type.

If we know what correct data is supposed to "look like," we should build tests that create data that is *purposefully* malformed and have the application—in this case, an Azure Function—consume the malformed data to see how the function reacts. If the programmers created robust code, the function should handle all incoming data whether it is well-formed or not.

> ### Understand the Azure rules of engagement
>
> If you want to test your application in Azure, please make sure you understand the rules of engagement. Failure to do so might have your attack code flagged as a real attack! Please read this for more information: https://azsec.tech/59p.

This kind of testing is just one form of nonfunctional security testing and is often called *fuzz testing*.

> **Important** You should add fuzzing to your application tests. Fuzz tests should be part of your normal set of regression or reliability tests. You can start small and add more coverage over time. But you should start today. Come up with a plan to add fuzz testing to your current development practices as soon as you possibly can.

Let's assume the function returns a 200 HTTP status on success and a 401 on any kind of failure. Now you need to build a test harness that creates malformed data and sends it to the Azure Function. You have two options:

- Use a preexisting fuzzing tool.

- Create your own custom test cases.

There are many open source and commercial fuzzing tools. For example:

- RESTler from Microsoft (https://github.com/microsoft/restler-fuzzer)

- OneFuzz from Microsoft (https://github.com/microsoft/onefuzz)

- Burp Suite (https://portswigger.net/burp)

- OWASP ZAP (https://www.zaproxy.org/)

- Google's OSS-Fuzz (https://github.com/google/oss-fuzz)

- Peach Fuzz (https://sourceforge.net/projects/peachfuzz/)

- American Fuzzy Lop (https://lcamtuf.coredump.cx/afl/)

- LLVM Compiler Infrastructure (https://llvm.org/docs/LibFuzzer.html)

It's worth spending some time reviewing all of these to see if they offer some value to you and your organization. If nothing else, these tools will help you understand how fuzzing works.

In our example, vaccination centers upload their CSV file to an Azure Storage account. From there, it is read by an Azure Function using a Blob Storage Account trigger. (Find out more here: https://azsec.tech/zu8.) It is this file we will fuzz.

Note If the Azure Function were called directly by the vaccination center by calling an API, we'd fuzz the API endpoint directly rather than upload a fuzzed file.

There are numerous ways to fuzz data. Here are a few:

- Generate totally random data.

- Mutate existing data.

- Intelligently manipulate data knowing its format.

Let's look at each of these methods through the lens of our sample CSV file. Fuzzing is an area of much research in academia and industry, but we'll keep things simple here.

 Important Don't fuzz using production data.

Generating totally random data

This is simple! Just create a random set of bytes. In our example, we'd probably create a series of lines of random data. The following PowerShell code does this:

```
Set-StrictMode -Version latest

function Get-RandomLine {
    param (
        [Parameter(Mandatory)] [int] $len
    )
    $charSet = 'abcdefghijklmnopqrstuvwxyzABCDEFGHIJKLMNOPQRSTUVWXYZ0123456789[]+-
[*=@:)}$^%;(_!&amp;#?>/|.'.ToCharArray()

    $rng = [System.Security.Cryptography.RandomNumberGenerator]::Create()
    $bytes = New-Object byte[]($len)
    $rng.GetBytes($bytes)

    $data = New-Object char[]($len)

    for ($i = 0 ; $i -lt $len ; $i++) {
        $data[$i] = $charSet[$bytes[$i] % $charSet.Length]
    }

    return -join $data
}

$fileName = "appointments.csv"
"" | out-file $filename

$numLines = Get-Random -Minimum 2 -Maximum 20
1..$numLines |% {
    $len = Get-Random -Minimum 10 -Maximum 256
    Get-RandomLine $len | out-file -Append $fileName
}
```

You could modify the $charSet variable to include other characters, of course, but this is a reasonable start. It creates a text file of random lines. This file could be uploaded to the storage account; the Azure Function then picks it up and parses it. The function code should utterly reject this file because it is syntactically incorrect, if for no other reason than the code cannot split the lines into the five discrete fields (unless, by luck, a random line includes four commas, which can happen, but it's unlikely).

Now let's make the fuzzing a little smarter. Rather than creating random data, let's create five fields of random data. This should get us past the code that checks the number of fields in each row. We can tweak the PowerShell code to this:

```
$fileName = "appointments.csv"

"" | out-file $filename

$numLines = Get-Random -Minimum 2 -Maximum 20
$numFields = 5

1..$numLines |% {
    $line = ""
    1..$numFields |% {
        $len = Get-Random -Minimum 0 -Maximum 64
        $field = Get-RandomLine $len
        $line += ($field + ",")
    }

    $line.TrimEnd(",") | out-file -Append $fileName
}
```

This produces a CSV file made up of a random number of lines, and each line comprises comma-separated random characters. This might get past the check for the number of fields, but some lines might fail because the comma is in the list of random characters, and we get more than four commas.

This will work in some cases, but not many. There's a fine line between data that's "corrupted a little bit" and data that's a complete mess. Most systems will detect incoming data that is completely random. Again, the CSV data is probably syntactically incorrect. We can do better!

Mutating existing data

This is a favorite among security researchers because it's effective. You take a corpus of valid data, tweak the data, and then send the data to the application and see how it reacts. For example, if this were a REST endpoint, you could tweak the JSON payload before it hits the wire, where it would then be consumed by the server.

For our example, we need to collect or generate a corpus of thousands of valid lines of data that go in the CSV file. But, to keep this simple, we're going to work with one line. Remember, the format is as follows:

```
centerId, date and time, vaccination type, open spots, comment
```

We will use this:

```
98722, 2022-03-16T15:50-06:00, PharmaA, 4, These are the last batches of PharmaA
```

Recall that we said you want to find the fine line between tweaking the data slightly and making it totally random. Here, we need to set a threshold, so we make tiny changes. Examples of these small changes might include the following:

- Inserting random characters

- Deleting random characters

- Setting or resetting the high bit of a character

- Byte swapping

- Truncating the data

- Adding data at the end or start of the data

- Inserting special characters (for example, file system special characters, like \, /, :, etc.) or character sequences (for example, HTML or SQL)

- Inserting interesting numbers, such as 2^n - 1, 2^n + 1, 0, MAX_INT, MAX_UINT

> **Tip** On the topic of interesting special characters, there's a "big-list-of-naughty-strings" at https://azsec.tech/oql worth looking at and using.

The following snippet of C# code takes a byte array (passed in the constructor, not part of this snippet) and fuzzes the array if a threshold is met. For example, we might only want to fuzz 5 percent of the incoming data. You need to find what this threshold is for your data. The code also performs multiple passes over the incoming data, so a string can have more than one mutation. Finally, you can set a random number seed to reproduce an error.

```csharp
public SimpleFuzz(int threshold=5, int? seed = null) {
        _rnd = seed is null ? new Random() : new Random((int)seed);
        _threshold = threshold;
    }
public byte[] Fuzz(byte[] input) {
    if (input.Length == 0) return Array.Empty<byte>();
    if (_rnd.Next(0, 100) > _threshold) return Array.Empty<byte>();

    var mutationCount = _rnd.Next(1, 5);
    for (int i = 0; i < mutationCount; i++) {

        if (input.Length == 0) break;

        var whichMutation = _rnd.Next(0, 7);

        int lo = _rnd.Next(0, input.Length);
        int range = _rnd.Next(1, 1+ input.Length / 10);
        if (lo + range >= input.Length) range = input.Length - lo;

        switch (whichMutation)
        {
```

```
            case 0: // set all upper bits to 1
                for (int j = lo; j < lo + range; j++)
                    input[j] |= 0x80;
                break;

            case 1: // set all upper bits to 0
                for (int j = lo; j < lo + range; j++)
                    input[j] &= 0x7F;
                break;

            case 2: // set one char to a random value
                input[lo] = (byte)_rnd.Next(0, 256);
                break;

            case 3: // insert interesting numbers
                byte[] interesting = new byte[] { 0, 1, 7, 16, 15, 63, 64, 127, 128, 255 };
                input[lo] = interesting[_rnd.Next(0,interesting.Length)];
                break;

            case 4: // swap bytes
                for (int j = lo; j < lo + range; j++) {
                    if (j + 1 < input.Length)
                        (input[j + 1], input[j]) = (input[j], input[j + 1]);
                }
                break;

            case 5: // remove sections of the data
                input = _rnd.Next(100) > 50 ? input[..lo] : input[(lo + range)..];
                break;

            case 6: // add interesting pathname/filename characters
                var fname = new string[] { "\\", "/", ":", ".."};

                int which = _rnd.Next(fname.Length);
                for (int j = 0; j < fname[which].Length; j++)
                    if (lo+j < input.Length)
                        input[lo+j] = (byte)fname[which][j];

                break;

            default:
                break;
        }
    }
    return input.ToArray();
}
```

Figure 9-7 shows part of the Locals window in Visual Studio, and you can see that the incoming string, named `data`, has been partially corrupted in the `res` variable. Part of the first field is removed, part of the second field looks like the upper bit is set, and some parts of the last field have been flipped.

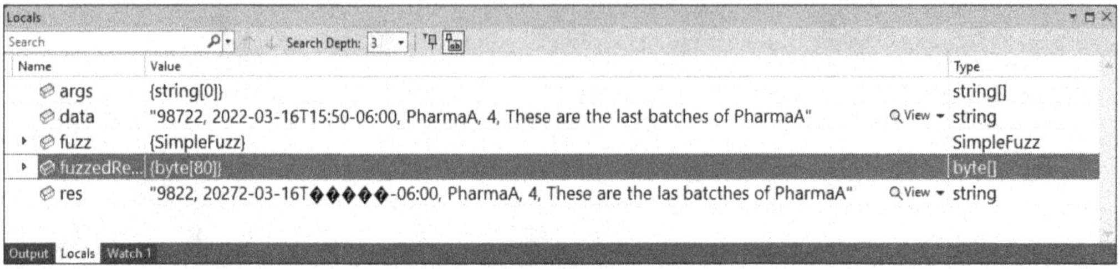

FIGURE 9-7 An example of a fuzzed row of the sample CSV file.

As you can see, the fuzzing is much subtler than the previous methods of using random data. The goal of more subtle fuzzing is to attempt to get greater code coverage, if possible.

> **Tip** This fuzzing code sample is available at the book's GitHub repository, at https://github.com/AzureDevSecurityBook.

Intelligently manipulating data knowing its format

The last type of fuzzing is when the fuzzing logic understands the data format—for example, if you have a custom-written graphic image parser that handles Portable Network Graphics (PNG) image files. Understanding the data format is important for some data types, because when the logic understands the format and structure of the file, it can make surgical changes to a file. A PNG file will have elements like X- and Y-dimensions, color depth, and more, that can be smartly fuzzed—for example, by the following:

- Setting X or Y to negative numbers

- Setting X or Y to alphabet characters

- Setting X or Y to massive values

- Setting the color depth to crazy values

Perhaps most importantly, PNG files also have checksums. If your code injects random data into the file, the file checksums will be incorrect, and the code you're trying to fuzz will reject the file quickly, before it gets further into the code. This means that after the file is fuzzed, the checksums will need to be recalculated.

Fuzzing APIs

We want to wrap this section up with one more important topic: fuzzing APIs. Today, exposed APIs are a common target of attack. These can relate to code-level vulnerabilities as well as design issues such as a lack of authentication or authorization and more. One website, APIsecurity.io (https://apisecurity.io/), is an excellent resource to learn more about real API vulnerabilities in the real world.

You should perform security testing of your APIs—for example, those exposed by Azure Functions, Azure App Service, or code written in Node.js running in a container. Fuzzing is one type of test; you can take the aforementioned practices and ideas and apply them to APIs, too. For example, if an API uses the HTTP GET method to read a resource, you can corrupt parameters on the query string. Or if you use a POST to create a resource, you can corrupt the JSON or XML payload in the HTTP body.

Suppose our vaccination booking application uses an HTTP POST API call with a JSON payload rather than uploading a file to Azure. A request might look something like this:

```
{
    "centerId" : "98722",
    "date_time" : "2022-03-16T15:50-06:00",
    "vaccination_type" : "PharmaA",
    "open_spots" : "4",
    "comment" : "These are the last batches of PharmaA"
}
```

Of course, the payload will probably have more than one item, but we want to keep things simple. Your fuzzing logic could apply the same tactics on this payload, but by manipulating the fields of the JSON file.

Be careful when fuzzing files like JSON and XML. You probably don't want to fuzz the structure of the file—for example, replacing the opening { with a random value—because corrupting the structure of the JSON file won't get beyond the JSON parser, let alone get to the code you really want to test!

The following code is an update to the preceding code that can handle a JSON file:

```
public byte[] Fuzz(JsonDocument doc) {
    byte[] fuzzResult = Array.Empty<byte>();
    using var stream = new MemoryStream();
    using (var writer = new Utf8JsonWriter(stream)) {
        writer.WriteStartObject();
        foreach (var elem in doc.RootElement.EnumerateObject()) {
            writer.WritePropertyName(elem.Name);
            byte[] fuzzed = Fuzz(elem.Value.ToString());
            writer.WriteStringValue(fuzzed.Length > 0
                        ? System.Text.Encoding.UTF8.GetString(fuzzed)
                        : elem.Value.GetRawText().Trim('"'));
        }
        writer.WriteEndObject();
        writer.Flush();

        fuzzResult = stream.GetBuffer();
    }
    return fuzzResult;
}
```

Figure 9-8 shows a run of about 15 generations of the preceding code. As you can see, every line has one or more subtle changes. Each line represents the same starting text, but the mutations are different each run. Ask yourself, do you think your API code could handle all these lines of JSON without crashing?

["centerId":"98722","date_time":"2022-03-16T15:50-06:00","vaccination_type":"PharmaA","open_spots":"\\","comment":"These are the last batches of PharmaA"]
["centerId":"98722","date_time":"2022-03-16T15:50-06:00","vaccination_type":"PharmaA","open_spots":"4","comment":"These are the last batches of PharmaA"]
["centerId":"98722","date_time":"2022\u002203-16T15:;0-06\u800100","vaccination_type":"PharmaA","open_spots":"4","comment":"These are the last batches of /\uFFFD\uFFFD\uFF
FDmaA"]
["centerId":"98722","date_time":"2022-03-16T15:50-06:00","vaccination_type":"PharmaA","open_spots":"4","comment":"These are the last batches of PharmaA"]
["centerId":"\u00102","date_time":"2022-03-16T15:50-06:00","vaccination_type":"PharmaA","open_spots":"4","comment":"These are the last batches of PharmaA"]
["centerId":"98722","date_time":"2022-03-16T15:50-06:00","vaccination_type":"PharmaA","open_spots":"4","comment":"These are the last b\u000Ftc\uFFFDes of PharmaA"]
["centerId":"\uFFFD\uFFFD282","date_time":"2022-03-16T15:50-\uFFFD\uFFFD.08","vaccination_type":"PharmaA","open_spots":"4","comment":"These are the last batc\uFFFDes of Pa
rmaA"]
["centerId":"98722","date_time":"2\u007F22-03-16T15:50:00","vaccination_type":"PharmaA","open_spots":"4","comment":"These are the last batches of PharmaA"]
["centerId":"98722","date_time":"2022-0\u000F-16T15:05-06\uFFFD6","vaccination_type":"PharmaA","open_spots":"4","comment":"These are the last batches of PharmaA"]
["centerId":"98722","date_time":"2022-03-16T15:50-06:00","vaccination_type":"PharmaA","open_spots":"4","comment":"These are the last batches of PharmaA"]
["centerId":"9/272","date_time":"2022-0\uFFFD-16T15:50%6-0\u00011","vaccination_type":"PharmaA","open_spots":"4","comment":"These are the last batches of PharmaA"]
["centerId":"98722","date_time":"2022-03-16\uFFFD15-06:00","vaccination_type":"PharmaA","open_spots":"\uFFFD","comment":"These are the last batches of PharmaA"]
["centerId":"98722","date_time":"2022-0..16T15:50-06:00","vaccination_type":"Pharm","open_spots":"4","comment":"These are the last batches of PharmaA"]
["centerId":"98\uFFFD22","date_time":"\uFFFD022-03-1\uFFFDT51:\u00010-06:00","vaccination_type":"Pha","open_spots":"4","comment":"These are the last batches of PharmaA"]
["centerId":"98\u007F7\\","date_time":"2022-03-16T15:50-06:00","vaccination_type":"Phars\uFFFDA","open_spots":"4","comment":"These are the \uFFFD\uFFFDst batches of Pharma
A"]
["centerId":"98722","date_time":"2022-03-16T15:50-06:00","vaccination_type":"   rma\uFFFD","open_spots":"4","comment":"ra\uFFFDA"]
["centerId":"98722","date_time":"2\u007F15-03T15:\b0-06:09","vaccination_type":"PharmaA","open_spots":"4","comment":"These are the \uFFFDast batches of7PharmaA"]
["centerId":"98722","date_time":"2022-03-16T15:50-06:00","vaccination_type":"PharmaA","open_spots":"4","comment":"These are the last batches of PharmaA"]
["centerId":"98\uFFFD22","date_time":"2022-03-16T15:50-06:00","vaccination_type":"PharmaA","open_spots":"4","comment":"These are the last batches of PharmaA"]
["centerId":"8722","date_time":"2022-03-16T15\uFFFD\uFFFD6-06:00","vaccination_type":"Ph\uFFFDrm\uFFFDA","open_spots":"4","comment":"These are the last batches of PharmaA"]
["centerId":"98722","date_time":"2022-03-16T15:50-06:00","vaccination_type":"Pha\uFFFDmaA","open_spots":"4","comment":"These are the last batches of PharmaA"]
["centerId":"98722","date_time":"2022-03-16T15:50-06:00","vaccination_type":"PharmaA","open_spots":"4","comment":"These are the last batches of PharmaA"]

FIGURE 9-8 The output of 15 runs of the JSON fuzzer.

One final note: you need to detect at the code level if the application fails to handle the incoming data. Historically, you would use a debugger and log the debug spew, but in Azure, you should use Application Insights to monitor the API or code as it responds to incoming nasty data.

Tip If you need general API guidance, see https://azsec.tech/l4m.

Important If applicable, you must test your IoT REST APIs, too. APIs are not just a "cloud-thing!"

Other ways to secure REST APIs

You should consider putting your APIs behind a firewall or web applications firewall (WAF) and some type of API management gateway. None of these can compensate for insecure code, but they can add extra defensive layers to stave off attacks. Of course, more defensive layers means more tools to manage, so you have to find that happy, secure middle ground!

Strong authentication and authorization are critical for securing REST APIs. The most common are OpenID Connect and OAuth 2.0, covered in Chapter 5, "Identity, authentication, and authorization." Some customers use API keys to restrict access to their REST endpoints, but this means API users must securely store the access keys. If you go this route, be sure your users understand how to protect the keys and that you have some way to revoke them or time them out. An example of a token used by Azure is the shared access signature (SAS) token, which has a built-in expiry. Sample code for SAS tokens is available here: https://azsec.tech/fbu.

If you ever need some structure around what should be tested when testing REST APIs, consider the POISED model. POISED is an acronym for the following:

- **Parameters**   The range of parameters passed to the API

- **Outputs**   Validating proper outputs for both good and bad parameters

- **Interoperability**   Ensuring consistency with other service APIs and other calls

- **Security**   Maintaining access and authorization for API calls

- **Errors**   Reporting errors clearly and accurately

- **Data**   Handling data structures and real data properly and with the appropriate timing

Applitools (https://azsec.tech/hf8) gives a good overview of the POISED model, as does this video delivered by Amber Race, who came up with the concept: https://azsec.tech/g6b.

Summary

We can't stress enough how important it is that your code validates all incoming data. As we say in zero trust, "verify explicitly." Most security vulnerabilities are input trust issues.

Be sure you review the OWASP Top 10 and stay on top of application security vulnerabilities in the industry. Review and learn from the OWASP Testing Guide at https://azsec.tech/fcr. Also, use static and dynamic analysis available in your development tools where possible.

Fuzz testing is a form of dynamic analysis. It is a useful technique for testing code that consumes files and code that exposes APIs. Even "light" fuzzing is a great test to make sure your code is resilient in the face of malformed input.

As discussed in more detail in Chapter 1, someone in your organization must stay up to date on new vulnerabilities, exploits, and defenses to make sure your code is built with the latest threats in mind. This is an important role!

## CHAPTER 10

Cryptography in Azure

After completing this chapter, you will be able to:

- Secure cryptographic keys

- Use Azure Key Vault securely

- Understand the differences between Azure Key Vault and Managed HSM

- Use cryptographic controls to securely protect data at rest

- Create code that is crypto-agile

- Use the Microsoft Data Encryption SDK

- Use cryptography in various Azure services

- Understand the basics of Always Encrypted in Azure SQL DB and Cosmos DB

- Use, enforce, and test TLS connections for compliance

Cryptography comes from the Greek words for "secret writing." It refers to a branch of information security that uses mathematical algorithms to provide security capabilities such as secrecy, integrity, and authentication.

This chapter is expansive, dense, and deeply technical. As such, it assumes you have a basic understanding of the various primitives used in cryptography. You don't need to know all these primitives in detail, but an understanding of the role they play in designing secure solutions is important. If you need a refresher, Appendix A, "Core cryptographic techniques," contains a brief overview of these primitives.

> **Note** When we say *crypto*, we mean *cryptography*, not digital currencies like Ethereum, Bitcoin, Litecoin, and Dogecoin.

You need not read the material in this chapter from start to finish; rather, because the chapter consists primarily of sections that stand on their own, it can be read by different people in differing roles in any order they need.

From a design perspective, the most important topic in this chapter is how to protect cryptographic keys. This includes having some knowledge of the nuances of Azure Key Vault—especially those readers whose area of expertise is architecture. Therefore, more than one-third of this chapter is dedicated to securing keys and using Key Vault correctly. The next section, "Cryptographic agility," is a must-read for developers, as it covers the Microsoft Data Encryption SDK. The section after that discusses how various Azure services use cryptography for data at rest. This section should be read by architects. Finally, we complete the chapter with in-depth coverage of Transport Layer Security (TLS) in Azure. This is important if you care about TLS protocol versions and ciphersuites. A *ciphersuite* is a combination of cryptographic algorithms used together to provide a combination of authentication, key exchange or key agreement, secrecy, and tamper detection.

A truth about security

You may have heard the phrase "Security is only as strong as the weakest link." This is not always true, however. Cryptographic controls are one example of a technical control that can compensate for weaknesses elsewhere in a solution. There is a reason many defenses are referred to as *compensating controls*.

> ### Real-world experience: Cryptography and complexity
>
> You can't just "throw cryptography" at a solution and hope it will work. Implementing cryptographic controls can be difficult and often adds a significant layer of complexity to a solution. In fact, some applications might not work when using cryptographic defenses. This is common with some types of "lift and shift" solutions; they simply don't work with encrypted data. An example of this might be a reporting solution that can't read encrypted data in a database.

Let's look at a scenario that demonstrates the value of cryptographic defenses. Imagine the following scenario, in which an attacker:

1. Finds an open port on your firewall.

2. Finds an open route through a network security group (NSG).

3. Gets into a virtual machine.

4. Smuggles an obfuscated payload into the VM.

5. Evades your anti-malware.

6. Compromises an elevated process.

7. Uses the payload to read files.

8. Bypasses file permissions because the compromised process is elevated.

9. Bypasses your data-loss prevention system and exfiltrates the files.

However, now imagine the exfiltrated files are appropriately encrypted. That is, they have secure key management; unique keys and/or initialization vectors (IV) per file; a modern, standards-based cryptographic algorithm; the correct block-cipher mode; and padding. So, the attacker got around half a dozen defenses, but the result was of no use to them. Cryptography compensated for all the other failed defenses. In a zero-trust world, this is a great example of using cryptography correctly to support an "assume-breach" mentality.

Of course, in this contrived scenario, the elevated process could have had access to the cryptographic keys. This is why you must always secure these keys. Securing cryptographic keys is covered next.

What are keys?

When we talk about keys in this chapter, we mean cryptographic keys. These are different from the keys used by some Azure services, which refer to values used for authentication and/or authorization. For example, some Azure Storage accounts use access keys; in this case, the term *access tokens* would probably be less ambiguous. With that said, many sections of this chapter that relate to keys will apply to secrets and certificates, too.

Securing keys

It's *always* about the keys! When reviewing a threat model in which some data is encrypted, you should always ask, "Where are the keys stored?" and follow that question up with, "And how are they protected?"

With Azure, the correct answer to "Where are the keys stored?" is Azure Key Vault. Key Vault is a fantastic service; it's inexpensive, is highly available, provides strong authorization policies, and provides auditing. Key Vault is also a means to centrally manage your keys, secrets, and certificates.

Securing keys is more complex than simply using Key Vault, however. This is because Key Vault turns a cryptographic problem into an authorization problem. One of the most common authorization mechanisms in Azure is role-based access control (RBAC), and it's imperative that you employ a strong RBAC policy on your Key Vault assets.

Almost half this chapter is dedicated to Azure Key Vault because of the critical role it plays in helping build secure solutions. A fundamental understanding of Key Vault is important, so please do not skip this section!

Note Using cryptographic primitives or cryptographic services is easy; it's key management that's hard.

Keys, secrets, and certificates

Key Vault can store keys, secrets, and certificates. Keys in Key Vault are asymmetric RSA or elliptic-curve keys. Secrets might be SQL Server connection strings or configuration data up to about 26 KB in length. Certificates are not just certificates; when you store a certificate, you store the certificate and its associated private key. This makes sense; certificates need not be stored securely because they contain no sensitive data. Moreover, certificates are digitally signed, so they cannot be tampered with. Although this chapter deals mostly with keys, much of the content also applies to certificates and secrets.

Keys in Key Vault

As mentioned, keys in Key Vault are RSA or elliptic-curve keys. But what about symmetric keys, like Advanced Encryption Standard (AES) keys? Key Vault can store AES keys as secrets, but Key Vault does not know they are AES keys. Key Vault can perform cryptographic operations (such as sign, decrypt, and unwrap) within Key Vault, but Key Vault cannot encrypt or decrypt using AES keys. However, another member of the Key Vault family, managed HSM, *can* store AES keys in hardware and can perform cryptographic operations on them, too. Managed HSM is discussed later in the chapter.

Real-world experience: Tags and keys

Many customers we have worked with tag assets in Key Vault, including keys, with owner information, so it's easy to discover which team owns a key and who the main contact is. You can learn more about tags here: https://azsec.tech/vib.

Access control and Azure Key Vault

We cannot stress this enough: applying the correct RBAC policy to Key Vault assets is critical and can be the difference between a system that is secure and one that is not.

The first step in the process of assigning an appropriate access policy is to choose an authorization mode. Key Vault has two authorization models:

- Vault access model

- Azure role-based access control

You can see both these options when setting up a Key Vault in the Azure Portal, under Permission Model. (See Figure 10-1.)

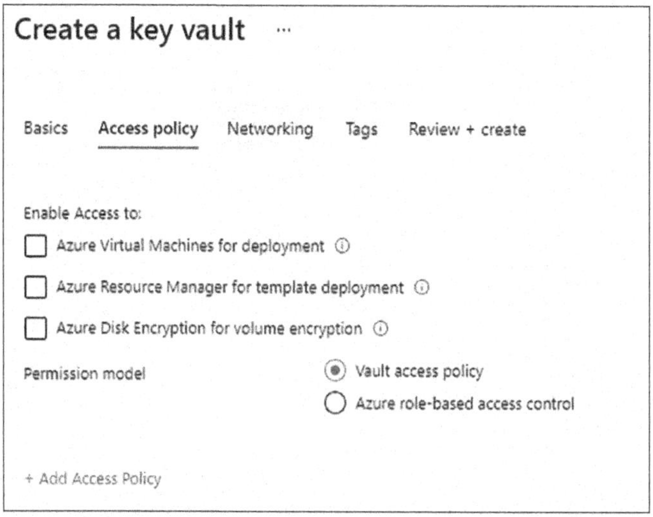

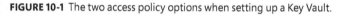

Create a key vault ...

Basics   **Access policy**   Networking   Tags   Review + create

Enable Access to:

☐ Azure Virtual Machines for deployment ⓘ

☐ Azure Resource Manager for template deployment ⓘ

☐ Azure Disk Encryption for volume encryption ⓘ

Permission model   ◉ Vault access policy

                                  ○ Azure role-based access control

+ Add Access Policy

FIGURE 10-1 The two access policy options when setting up a Key Vault.

Let's look at each permission model in detail.

Vault access model

The vault access model is the classic access model introduced when Key Vault was first released. It's a simple model. In a nutshell, with the vault access model, permissions are applied at the root key, secret, and certificate levels, and all keys, secrets and certificates under their roots take on the same access policy. This is easy to understand and easy to manage, but it does mean that you cannot enforce a different access policy between, say, two keys or two secrets.

When using the vault access model, you apply an access policy by choosing a principal (such as an Azure Active Directory user or group) or a managed identity and then selecting one or more permissions. To expedite the selection of appropriate permissions, you can choose from a predefined RBAC template. This isn't required, but it's often a useful starting point. You can also start with a template and add or remove permissions as needed. Figure 10-2 shows the selection of a specific principal—in this case, the managed identity of a process (such as an Azure function or a VM using a managed identity) named OnlineSalesApp—and six key permissions.

In this example, even though you cannot see them in Figure 10-2, the complete list of key permissions is as follows:

- Get

- List

- Sign

- Verify

- Encrypt

- Decrypt

- Wrap

- Unwrap

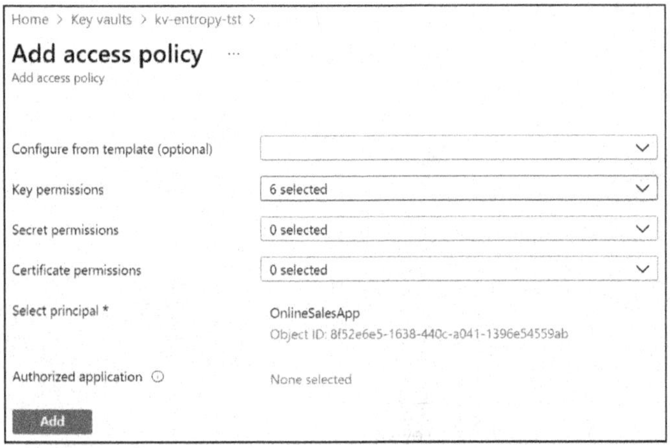

Home > Key vaults > kv-entropy-tst >

Add access policy   ···
Add access policy

Configure from template (optional)	⌄
Key permissions	6 selected ⌄
Secret permissions	0 selected ⌄
Certificate permissions	0 selected ⌄
Select principal *	OnlineSalesApp Object ID: 8f52e6e5-1638-440c-a041-1396e54559ab
Authorized application ⓘ	None selected

Add

FIGURE 10-2 Setting an access policy on a Key Vault.

This process identity (a managed identity), OnlineSalesApp, can read and list all keys, as well as perform four cryptographic operations on all keys (encrypt, decrypt, wrap, and unwrap). We want to stress the word *all* in this permission model; the level of access granularity is all keys or all secrets or all certificates.

Important: Vault access policy granularity

When using a vault access policy, you cannot set the access policy to an individual key, secret, or certificate. The access policy applies to all keys, secrets, and certificates. If a role has access to read a key, that role has read access to all keys.

In this example, if the process running under this identity attempts to perform any other operation, such as deleting a key, or any operation on secrets or certificates, the operation will fail.

Operations like decrypt, unwrap, and sign—which use the private key from the private/public key pair—are performed by Key Vault. If the keys are hardware keys (key types ending in -HSM), then the cryptographic operations are performed in hardware.

Encrypt, wrap, and verify operations

Because these operations use the public component of an asymmetric key pair, there is no secret involved. This means the operation does not need to be performed in Key Vault. For performance reasons, these can be performed in the client code. We wrote about this in the blog post "The Curious Case of the 'Un-Enforced' Azure Key Vault RBAC Policy," at https://azsec.tech/6la.

Get operations

Get operations on keys do not return the private key of the RSA or elliptic curve key pair. Get operations return only the public key and metadata about the key. The private key does not leave Key Vault, but it can be backed up, in which case it is encrypted using keys shared by Key Vaults in your subscription.

The following screenshot shows where to set the Vault access policy permission model in the Azure Portal.

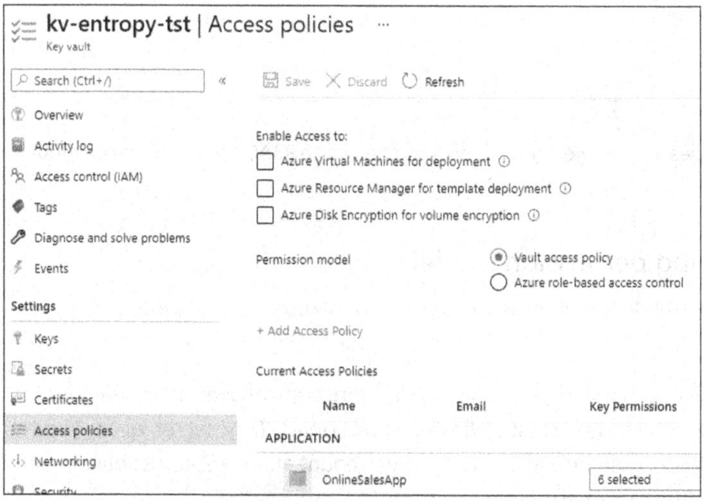

FIGURE 10-3 Setting access policies in Azure Key Vault when using the vault access policy permission model.

Azure role-based access control

This is the newer RBAC model and is sometimes referred to as the *data-plane* RBAC model. Rather than setting permissions solely at the root key, secret, and certificate levels, this model enables you to set permissions on individual keys, secrets, and certificates, thereby offering greater RBAC flexibility.

To set RBAC policies in the Azure Portal, you click the Access Control (IAM) option under Settings rather than the Access Policies option, which is selected when you use the vault access policy permission model. (See Figure 10-4.)

> **Note** If you are using the Azure RBAC model and you select Access Policies in the Azure Portal, you will be redirected to the use Access Control (IAM) screen.

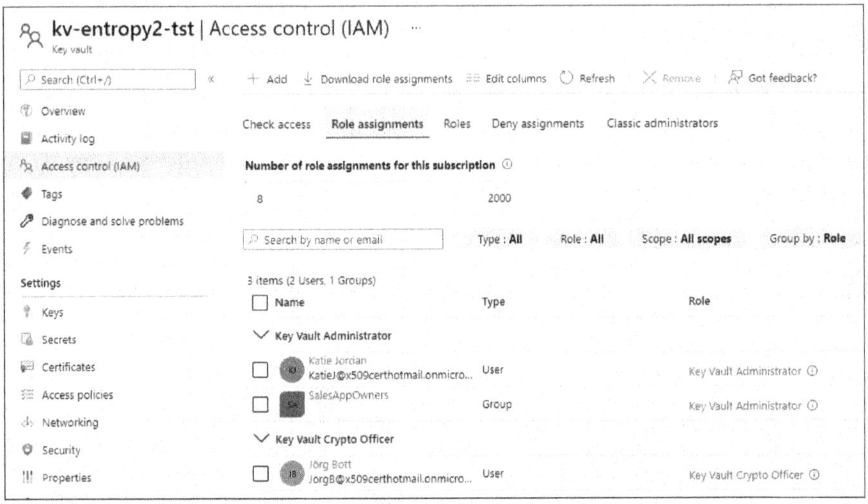

FIGURE 10-4 Setting access policies in Azure Key Vault when using the Azure RBAC policy permission model.

A note about switching permission models

You can switch between permission models whenever you want, but if you do, the existing permissions data is reset.

As mentioned, this newer permission model allows for more control over where the RBAC applies. This includes being able to set access policies on each object (key, secret, or certificate) if you want. For example, Key1 could be accessible by one account and Key2 accessible only by another account, all within the same Key Vault.

Figures 10-5, 10-6, and 10-7 show a sample RBAC policy using the RBAC permission model. Figure 10-5 shows the RBAC policy at the Key Vault level—in this case, one group (SalesAppOwners) and one user, a break-glass account, are Key Vault administrators. No other account has access.

FIGURE 10-5 Data-plane RBAC policy on a Key Vault.

Figures 10-6 and 10-7 show the RBAC policies on two keys. The first key, SalesEncrypt-1 (see Figure 10-6), inherits its permissions from the scopes above the key—one from the resource group and the other from the Key Vault. You can see where the permission is set in the Scope column. There is one other account with access to the SalesEncrypt-1 key: vm-sales-1, which is the managed identity for a VM with the same name, has the Key Vault crypto user role on this key. Figure 10-7 shows another key, SalesEncrypt-2. It, too, inherits two permissions from scopes above the key, but it has one extra permission that grants the Key Vault crypto user role to vm-sales-2.

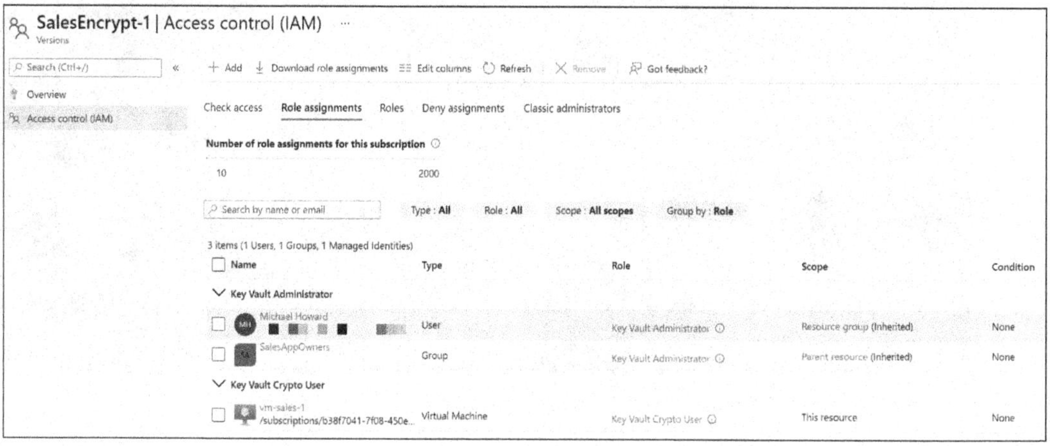

FIGURE 10-6 Vm-sales-1, the managed identity for a VM with access to one key, SalesEncrypt-1.

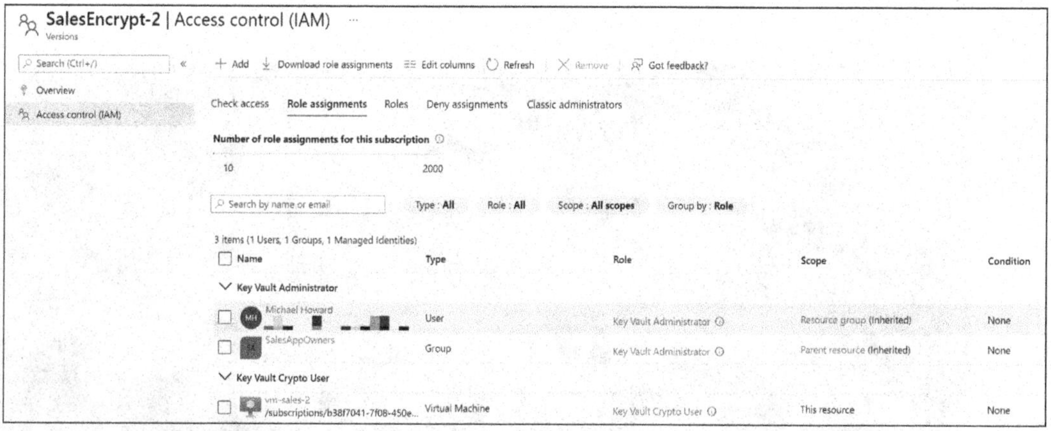

FIGURE 10-7 This is similar to Figure 10-6, but this time, the key SalesEncrypt-2 is accessible by vm-sales-2.

If a process in the VM named vm-sales-1 attempts to access the Sales-Encrypt-1 key, it will be denied access.

Figures 10-8 and 10-9 are from Ubuntu 20.04 LTS VMs running in Azure. After logging into the VMs using Secure Shell Server (SSH), we installed the Azure CLI tools. First, we connected from the console as the managed identity of the VM using the following command:

```
az login --identity
```

Then we entered the following command in the Azure CLI to read the `Sales-Encrypt-1` key:

```
az keyvault show -id "<url to vault and key>"
```

This works because the RBAC policy grants vm-sales-1 access. Figure 10-8 shows an abridged result.

FIGURE 10-8 Using the Azure CLI to get information about a cryptographic key.

Next, using the same VM, we attempted to read the metadata for the second key, SalesEncrypt-2. Here, the RBAC policy allows only vm-sales-2 to access the key, so we get an error message. (See Figure 10-9.)

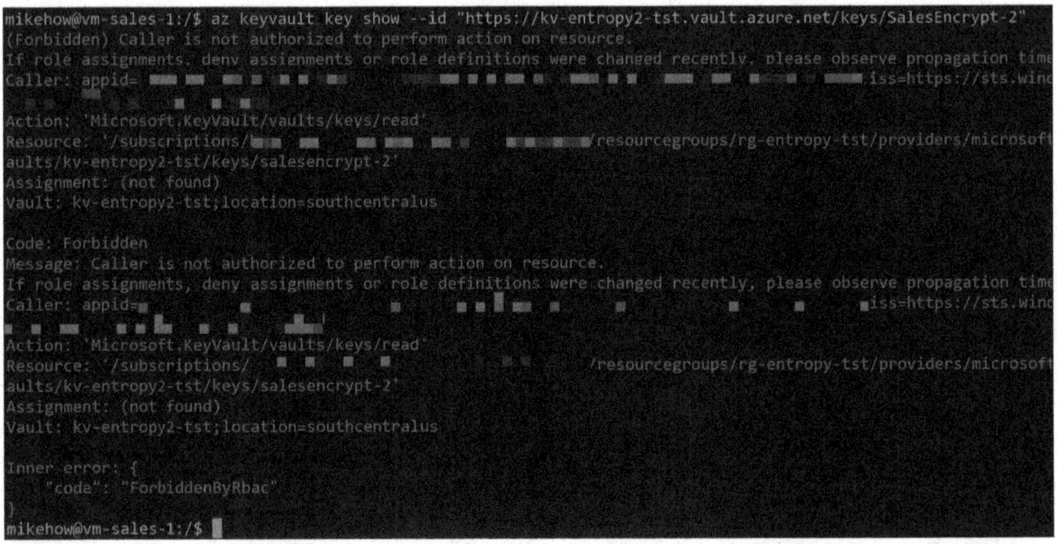

FIGURE 10-9 The VM vm-sales-1 does not have access to the SalesEncrypt-2 key, and this is the error you can expect if the VM attempts to access the key.

The `Inner error` text at the bottom of the output sums up the issue succinctly; Figure 10-10 offers a visual interpretation.

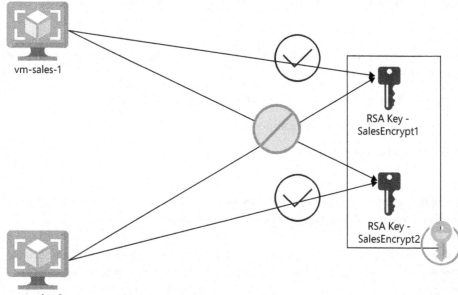

FIGURE 10-10 An access scenario using the Key Vault Azure RBAC permission model. Vm-sales-1 can access its own key, SalesEncrypt1, but not SalesEncrypt2. Vm-sales-2 can access its own key, SalesEncrypt2, but not SalesEncrypt1.

Which permission model should you use?

Now that you understand how permission models work, which one should you use? Most customers use the vault access model, but in a specific way, which is in line with current Microsoft guidance.

You use one Key Vault per:

- Application (for example, sales, HR, inventory, customer records, and so on)
- Geography (US, EU, Africa)
- Deployment environment (dev, test, pre-prod, prod)

> **Note** This is why standardized naming is so important! Microsoft's recommended naming conventions can be found here: https://azsec.tech/vdt.

This combination delivers a high level of isolation from other Key Vaults, but you still need to use appropriate RBAC policies. That's covered next.

What constitutes a good Key Vault RBAC policy?

In a perfect world, this would be easy to answer, but it's not. There is no single way to answer the question of what makes a good RBAC policy. But let's start with the following lemmas:

- We need to restrict access to keys as much as possible.

- It is as important to protect keys from write access (tampering in a threat model) as from read access (information disclosure).

- A resource is protected by a set of zero or more individual permissions.

- There must be a business need for all permissions.

- Access policies will evolve over time.

> **Note** The last point is critically important. Because a process, group, or user requires some level of access today does not necessarily mean it needs access tomorrow.

Most of this can be summed up as least privilege access. This is described in the Azure Security Baseline for Azure Key Vault in "PA-3: Review and Reconcile User Access Regularly" (available at https://azsec.tech/u7w) and "PA-7: Follow Just Enough Administration (Least Privilege Principle)" (available at https://azsec.tech/pdl).

With these in mind, there is a series of steps you can take to determine whether an RBAC policy on a resource is appropriate:

1. Get the permission policy for the Key Vault in question.

2. For each entry in the policy, ask this question: "What is the business requirement for this principal to have this level of access?"

3. For each entry in the policy, ask this question: "Can the access entry be removed or tightened?"

Get permissions on a Key Vault using the vault access policy

How you get the permissions on a Key Vault depends on whether the Key Vault is using the vault access policy or the Azure RBAC.

If you're using the vault access policy, you can obtain the permissions using PowerShell code like this:

```
$kva = Get-AzKeyVault -VaultName "<Key Vault Name>"
$kva.AccessPolicies |
    select DisplayName,
        PermissionsToCertificatesStr,
        PermissionsToKeysStr,
        PermissionsToSecretsStr | fl
```

The output looks something like this:

```
DisplayName                      : fn-dev-sales-tst (14651011-1845-43cc-b851-XXXXXXXXXXXX)
PermissionsToCertificatesStr :
PermissionsToKeysStr             : Get, List, Decrypt, Encrypt, UnwrapKey, WrapKey
PermissionsToSecretsStr          :


DisplayName                      : fn-dev-keyrotate-tst (4562b863-726a-4a7a-a3fc-XXXXXXXXXXXX)
PermissionsToCertificatesStr :
PermissionsToKeysStr             : Get, List, Update, Create, Import, Delete, Recover, Backup,
Restore, Decrypt, Encrypt, UnwrapKey, WrapKey, Verify, Sign
PermissionsToSecretsStr          : Get, List, Set, Delete


DisplayName                      : fn-dev-custlookup-tst (08132b25-d6dc-4ccf-a8f1-XXXXXXXXXXXX)
PermissionsToCertificatesStr :
PermissionsToKeysStr             :
PermissionsToSecretsStr          : Get, List, Set, Delete, Recover, Backup, Restore


DisplayName                      : Darrin Hanson (XXXXXXXXXXXX.onmicrosoft.com)
PermissionsToCertificatesStr : Get, List, Update, Create, Import, Delete, Recover, Backup,
Restore, ManageContacts, ManageIssuers, GetIssuers, ListIssuers, SetIssuers,
                                 DeleteIssuers
PermissionsToKeysStr             : Get, List, Update, Create, Import, Delete, Recover, Backup,
Restore, Rotate, GetRotationPolicy, SetRotationPolicy, Decrypt, Encrypt,
                                 UnwrapKey, WrapKey, Verify, Sign
PermissionsToSecretsStr          : Get, List, Set, Delete, Recover, Backup, Restore


DisplayName                      : fn-dev-signdoc-tst (1a4ed568-12bf-43d9-bfae-XXXXXXXXXXXX)
PermissionsToCertificatesStr :
PermissionsToKeysStr             : Get, List, WrapKey, UnwrapKey, Sign

PermissionsToSecretsStr          :
```

You can now ask the questions noted in the preceding section. For example, does the third entry, fn-dev-keyrotate-tst, really need all those permissions on keys and secrets? In contrast, the entry for Darrin Hanson looks like it's a "break-glass" administrative account that has access to everything. It is not common to assign permissions to a single user account, but in this case, it's probably OK. (With that said, who is Darrin Hanson, and should that person really have all that access?)

Important: Watch those contributor permissions

If a user has contributor permissions to a Key Vault control (management) plane, that user can grant themselves access to the data plane by setting a Key Vault access policy. You should tightly control who has contributor role access to your Key Vaults. Ensure that only authorized people can access and manage your Key Vaults, keys, secrets, and certificates.

Get permissions on a Key Vault using an Azure RBAC policy

If you're using the Azure RBAC model with Key Vault, you can obtain permissions using PowerShell code like this:

```
$rb = Get-AzRoleAssignment |
        where {$_.RoleDefinitionName -like '*key vault*'} |
        select DisplayName, RoleDefinitionName, Scope, ObjectType |
        fl | out-string

$rb -replace "/subscriptions/[a-f0-9'-]+/",""
```

This will produce output like this:

```
DisplayName        : Michael Howard
RoleDefinitionName : Key Vault Administrator
Scope              : resourceGroups/rg-entropy-tst
ObjectType         : User

DisplayName        : Michael Howard
RoleDefinitionName : Key Vault Administrator
Scope              : resourceGroups/rg-entropy-tst/providers/Microsoft.KeyVault/vaults/kv-
entropy-tst
ObjectType         : User

DisplayName        : mikehow-rng
RoleDefinitionName : Key Vault Secrets Officer
Scope              : resourceGroups/rg-entropy-tst/providers/Microsoft.KeyVault/vaults/kv-
entropy-tst
ObjectType         : ServicePrincipal

DisplayName        : SalesAppOwners
RoleDefinitionName : Key Vault Administrator
Scope              : resourceGroups/rg-entropy-tst/providers/Microsoft.KeyVault/vaults/kv-
entropy2-tst
ObjectType         : Group

DisplayName        : vm-sales-2
RoleDefinitionName : Key Vault Crypto User
Scope              : resourceGroups/rg-entropy-tst/providers/Microsoft.KeyVault/vaults/kv-
entropy2-tst/keys/SalesEncrypt-2
ObjectType         : ServicePrincipal
```

```
DisplayName        : rg-keyrotate-storagekey-rotation-fnapp
RoleDefinitionName : Key Vault Crypto User
Scope              : resourceGroups/rg-entropy-tst/providers/Microsoft.KeyVault/vaults/
kv-entropy2-tst/keys/testkey
ObjectType         : ServicePrincipal

DisplayName        : vm-sales-1
RoleDefinitionName : Key Vault Crypto User
Scope              : resourceGroups/rg-entropy-tst/providers/Microsoft.KeyVault/vaults/
kv-entropy2-tst/keys/SalesEncrypt-1
ObjectType         : ServicePrincipal
```

This code queries all role assignments in the subscription and filters the results to display those that have *key vault* in their name. Then, the `-replace` operator strips out some superfluous subscription information to keep the output relatively small.

You can also use the Azure CLI if you prefer. The command is as follows:

```
az role assignment list
```

As with the previous scenario, you can now look at this and determine whether the level of access is appropriate, and if not, remove the principal or reduce the access rights.

Compound identities, or application+user

If you peruse the Key Vault documentation, you might see references to a form of authentication and access control named *compound identities*. This uses an application's identity, such as a managed identity, plus the identity of the caller to allow access to the Key Vault. For example, Cheryl has no access unless she accesses the Key Vault via a specific Azure application—say, an Azure function named ManagementApp. The application must be designed and coded to use on-behalf-of (OBO) authentication flows. This access mode applies only at the control plane, not the data plane, and was designed for deployments by the Azure team on the Azure backplane. It also does not work with the newer Azure RBAC permission model. Because of these restrictions, it is generally not used by Azure subscribers.

Now let's look at other important aspects of securely using Azure Key Vault to protect keys (and other secret information).

Use Key Vault Premium in production

In production, you should use the Premium version of Key Vault to store your cryptographic keys. In the Premium version, keys are stored in hardware, and they never leave. Code can call REST APIs in Key Vault to perform cryptographic actions such as encrypting, unwrapping, and signing data, but the private keys never leave the hardware.

Keys can be backed up, however. When they are, they are encrypted by Key Vault and can be decrypted only by a Key Vault in the same geography (such as the United States, Europe, Asia Pacific, and others) and the same subscription.

You can use the Standard version of Key Vault in nonproduction environments, as this is a little cheaper to run than the Premium Key Vault version, and the APIs and management tools are the same. The big difference between the Standard and Premium versions is that the Premium version can store keys in hardware or software, while the Standard version stores keys in Key Vault system software. Figure 10-11 shows the Azure Portal with the two available versions displayed.

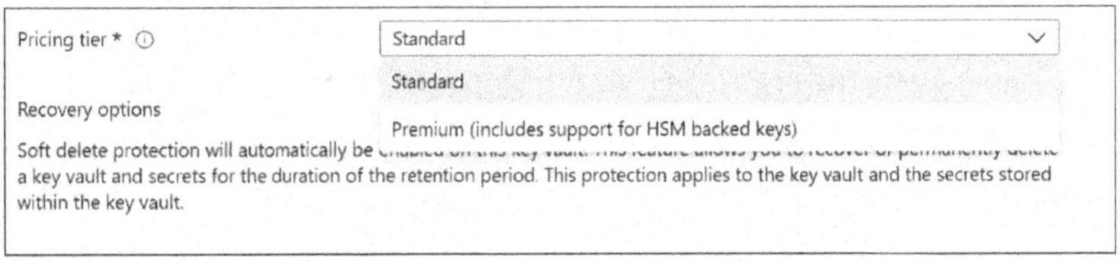

FIGURE 10-11 The two Key Vault pricing options. Premium provides hardware-backed RSA and elliptic-curve keys.

When you create an instance of a Premium version of Key Vault, you can opt to have an RSA or elliptic-curve key in hardware or software. A hardware key type ends with -HSM. You can see this aspect when you dump a key using the following command:

```
az keyvault key show --vault-name "akv-myvault-tst" --name "key-shopdb-tst"
```

Part of the output will look something like this:

```
"kid": "https://akv-myvault-tst.vault.azure.net/keys/key-shopdb-tst/3d39dab894ab46de9d487e5cab5dc7ef",
"kty": "EC-HSM"
```

Here, kty is the key type, and in this example, it's a hardware-based elliptic-curve key.

Note that with the Standard version of Key Vault, customer keys are encrypted using keys rooted in hardware managed by Azure. No one has direct access to the hardware keys used to encrypt and decrypt software keys managed by the Standard version of Key Vault. The encrypt/decrypt tasks are handled by Key Vault.

In addition to storing keys in hardware, the Premium version of Key Vault can store them in software, too. If you must always store keys in hardware—which you probably do because that's why you are using the Premium version—then you can set an Azure Policy that enforces the use of the Premium version of Key Vault and requires keys be stored in hardware.

Sample Azure Key Vault Policy templates are available here: https://azsec.tech/7t6. The Azure policy named "Keys Should Be Backed by a Hardware Security Module (HSM)" forces keys to be HSM-backed; this policy is available in your Azure Portal here: https://azsec.tech/6xu. The Azure policy called "Enforce Key Vault Premium SKU" forces use of the Premium version of Key Vault. This policy is here: https://azsec.tech/299.

Bring your own key

In cases where there are concerns or compliance requirements that constitute a "bring your own key" strategy, you will need to use Azure Key Vault Premium and import your keys rather than having Key Vault generate the keys. This is explained in detail here: https://azsec.tech/s9a.

Access control is important even when using hardware-backed keys

Even if keys are protected in hardware and can never leave the confines of that hardware, access policy is still important because cryptographic actions (encrypt, decrypt, sign, verify, wrap, and unwrap) can be performed on those keys. Hence, you need to restrict access to the appropriate principals who can perform those cryptographic actions.

While we're on the topic of production environments, as noted, we recommend you use one Key Vault per application per environment (development, test, preproduction, and production) per geography. This restricts sensitive data in Key Vaults across environments and regions and reduces the threat of disclosure in the case of a breach. Again, build systems with an assume-breach mentality.

Secrets and certificates are stored in software managed by Key Vault, regardless of the Key Vault version used. These are then backed by encryption keys managed by Key Vault.

RSA, elliptic-curve keys, and cryptographic operations

RSA can perform all cryptographic operations used by Key Vault: encrypt/decrypt, sign/verify, and wrap/unwrap. Elliptic-curve can only sign/verify. This is not an issue with Key Vault; rather, it has to do with the way the two algorithms work.

Enable logging and auditing

Logging and auditing at the control plane and data plane are critically important. At the control plane, you can see keys, secrets, and certificates that were successfully created, that failed to be created, that were deleted, and so on. At the data plane, you can see access to keys, secrets, and certificates.

Note This is called out in the Azure Security Baseline v3 for Azure Key Vault as "LT-4 Enable Logging in Azure Resources," available here: https://azsec.tech/1hs.

To enable auditing in the Azure Portal, follow these steps:

1. Navigate to the Key Vault in question.

2. Click **Diagnostic Settings**.

This is where you configure what to log and where to send the logging data.

3. Give the setting a name and, at a minimum, select an audit category.

4. Specify where you want the results to go.

A common destination is a Log Analytics account, so you can use Azure Monitor to view and analyze logs. If you have a SIEM, such as Azure Sentinel or Splunk, you can send the audit data directly to it or have it read from Log Analytics.

Figure 10-12 shows an audit policy that sends results to a Log Analytics workspace and to an Azure Storage account.

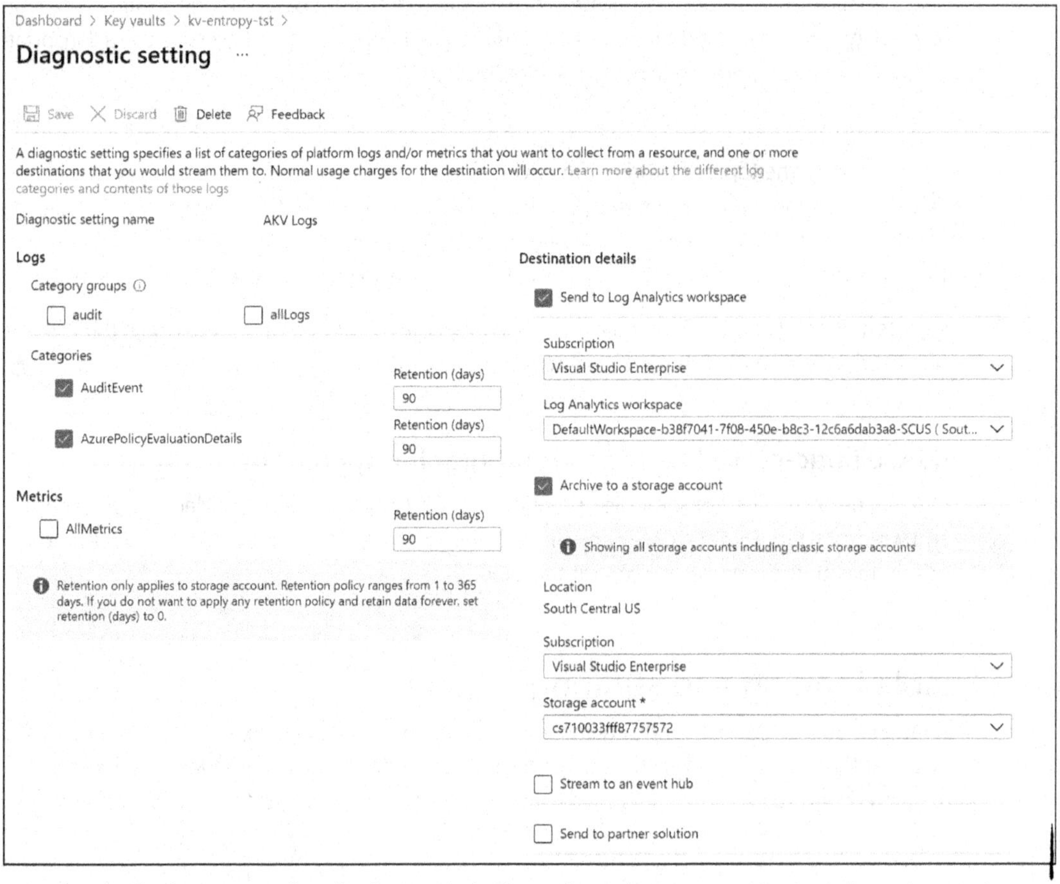

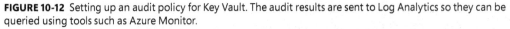

FIGURE 10-12 Setting up an audit policy for Key Vault. The audit results are sent to Log Analytics so they can be queried using tools such as Azure Monitor.

As with every operation in the Azure Portal, you can also use PowerShell, the Azure CLI, or low-level REST APIs to configure logging. For example, the following code uses PowerShell to set up logging of Key Vault data to an Azure Storage account:

```
$sa = Get-AzureRmStorageAccount -ResourceGroup rg-scratch-dev -name logs
$kv = Get-AzureRmKeyVault -VaultName kv-entropy-tst
```

```
Set-AzureRmDiagnosticSetting -StorageAccountId $sa.Id -ResourceId $kv.ResourceId -Enabled $true
-RetentionEnabled $true -RetentionInDays 60
```

> **Note** The logging-to-storage pattern shown in the preceding code applies to all Azure resources.

Figure 10-13 shows how to use Azure Monitor to query logging data in Log Analytics using the Kusto Query Language (KQL). This example shows various Key Vault operations in the logs. With Monitor, alerts can be raised on specific conditions or events if needed.

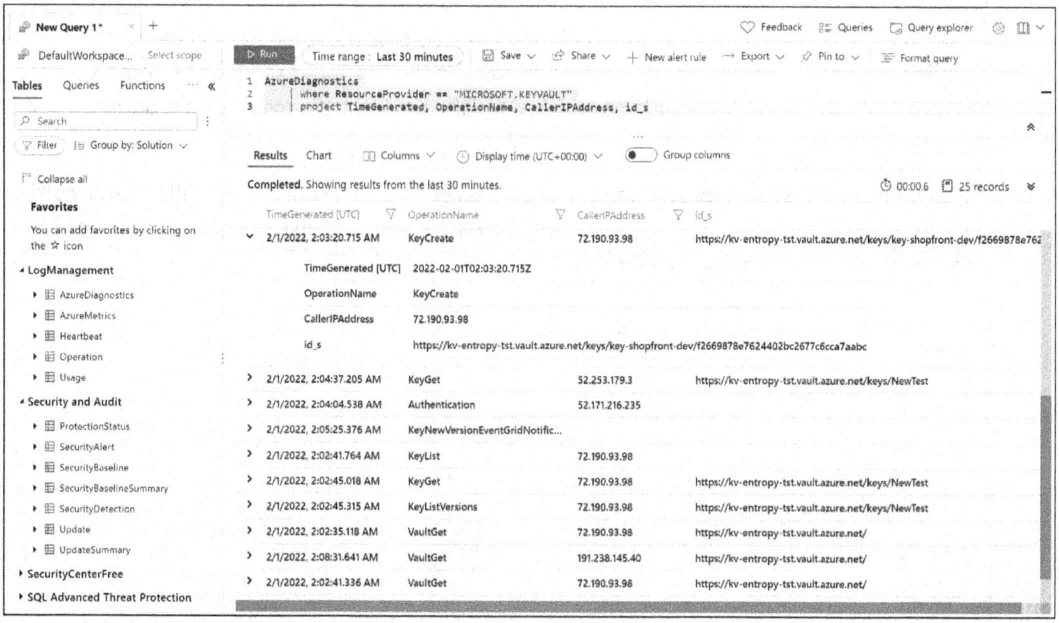

FIGURE 10-13 Using KQL to query Key Vault events sent to Log Analytics.

Honey keys

Some Key Vault administrators set up fake keys in their Key Vaults that should never be used but are there to detect potential reconnaissance attempts or attacks. You can create a key with a real-looking name, like key-salesdb-prod, and then use a custom query like the one that follows to send an alert to your SIEM if it is ever touched:

```
AzureDiagnostics
  | where id_s == 'https://kv-salesdb-prod02.vault.azure.net/keys/key-salesdb-prod'
  and OperationName == 'KeyGet'
```

You can learn more about alerts here: https://azsec.tech/epk. Microsoft Sentinel also includes deception techniques; you can read more about these here: https://azsec.tech/ci9.

Network isolation

You should never place a Key Vault directly on the internet. Even if you're just playing around to learn more about using it, you should at least use IP filtering to restrict access, but as a rule, it's better to use something more robust like private endpoints or service endpoints.

> **Note** This is addressed in "NS-3: Establish Private Network Access to Azure Services" in the Azure Security Baseline for Key Vault. You can read more information here: https://azsec.tech/1b0.

Like many Azure PaaS services, Key Vault has a simple firewall that allows you to restrict what IP addresses or CIDR ranges can access the Key Vault. In the previous example that showed a couple of VMs talking to Key Vault, we could restrict access to the Key Vaults to the private IP addresses of the two VMs.

Figure 10-14 shows that the Key Vault now only accepts network traffic from other services in the one virtual network (VNet). This is called using a *service endpoint*. You can read more about service endpoints here: https://azsec.tech/79d.

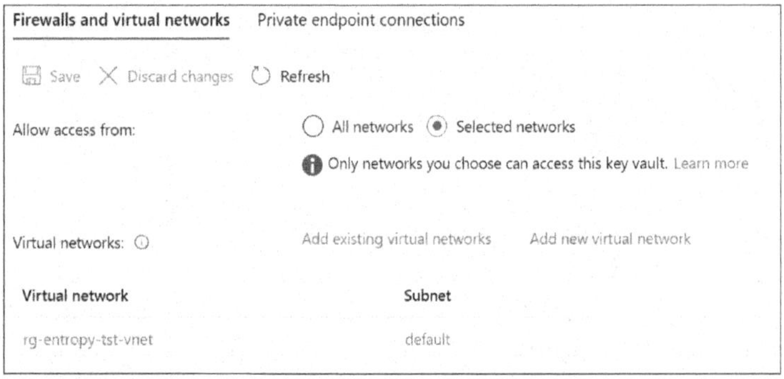

FIGURE 10-14 Access to a Key Vault is restricted to only those resources using the rg-entropy-tst-vnet VNet. The Key Vault will accept no other traffic, including the internet.

Our two Ubuntu Linux VMs, vm-sales-1 and vm-sales-2, are in the same VNet, and the Key Vault instance is configured to listen for traffic only from that VNet, so the VMs can access this instance of Key Vault. You can see this in Figure 10-15: this is vm-sales-1 enumerating keys in Key Vault.

However, as shown in Figure 10-16, running the same command in the author's laptop, using the same Azure account, fails because the call is across the internet and did not originate in the same VNet.

FIGURE 10-15 The vm-sales-1 VM is on the same VNet as the Key Vault, so code running in the VM can access Key Vault resources.

```
az keyvault key list --vault-name kv-entropy2-tst
Client address is not authorized and caller is not a trusted service.

Client address: 72.190.93.98
Caller: appid=04b07795-8ddb-461a-bbee-92f9e1bf7b46;oid=f074e14b-2a67-
41c2-b384-ea4b8bec54c4;iss=https://sts.windows.net/9eb23989-2aff-429c
-bd13-213d144372b8/
Vault: kv-entropy2-tst;location=southcentralus
```

FIGURE 10-16 Trying to access a Key Vault over the internet when the Key Vault is restricted to an Azure VNet.

> **Note** The preceding example uses service endpoints to restrict network access. However, the preferred mechanism is to use private endpoints. These are explained in more detail in Chapter 15, "Network security."

Important: Network isolation applies only at the data plane

Network isolation such as PaaS firewall techniques and other network rules apply only to the data plane. Control-plane operations (that is, administration of keys and so on) are not affected by firewalls and VNet rules. Key Vault is a PaaS service, so the various network isolation techniques apply only at the data plane, too. Further information can be found here: https://azsec.tech/u17.

Use Microsoft Defender for Key Vault

Microsoft Defender for Key Vault is one member of the Microsoft Defender family; others include Microsoft Defender for DNS, Microsoft Defender for Identity, and many more. Microsoft Defender for Key Vault detects unusual and potentially harmful attempts to access or exploit Key Vaults based on behavior analysis using machine learning in Azure.

> **Note** This topic is covered in the Key Vault Azure Security Baseline v3, "LT-1: Enable Threat detection for Azure Resources," at https://azsec.tech/9bz.

In production environments, Microsoft Defender for Key Vault is a must. In fact, if you have one or more Key Vaults, Microsoft Defender for Cloud will flag the omission of Microsoft Defender for Key Vault as a serious issue.

You can learn more about Microsoft Defender for Key Vault here: https://azsec.tech/m7s. Yuri Diogenes, principal PM manager on the Microsoft Defender team, has a great post explaining how to trigger alerts in Microsoft Defender for Key Vault to test your detection and response system, located here: https://azsec.tech/ulf.

Back up your Key Vault assets

One of the dangers of using customer-managed keys (discussed later in the chapter) in Key Vault is that if the keys are lost, they are lost—as in *gone*! In other words, Azure does not maintain a backup of your keys; that's your job. There's a reason they are called *customer-managed keys* after all! This is also a reason why keys have soft delete enabled by default. This allows you to recover an accidentally deleted Key Vault, key, or keys. (See Figure 10-17.)

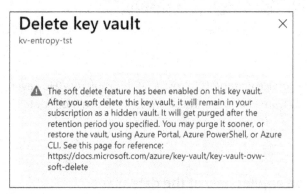

FIGURE 10-17 Attempting to delete a Key Vault will inform you that the Key Vault has soft delete enabled.

> **Note** This topic is covered in the Azure Security Baseline v3 for Key Vault, "BR-1: Ensure Regular Backups," at https://azsec.tech/o67.

Soft delete is sometimes confused with purge protection. However, they are different in these ways:

- Soft delete prevents the accidental deletion of Key Vaults, keys, secrets, and certificates. When you delete a Key Vault or a Key Vault object, it remains recoverable for between 7 and 90 days, defaulting to 90 days. Key Vaults in the soft-deleted state can be purged, which means they are permanently deleted.

- Purge protection prevents the potentially malicious deletion of Key Vaults, keys, secrets, and certificates. It is like soft delete, but with a time-based lock. You can recover items at any point during the configurable retention period, and you cannot permanently delete or purge a Key Vault or Key Vault object until the retention period elapses. When the retention period elapses, the Key Vault or Key Vault object will be purged automatically. Purge protection is designed such that a malicious administrator cannot override, disable, or circumvent purge protection. Once purge protection is enabled, it can never be disabled by anyone, including Microsoft. The ability to purge is also a permission for keys, secrets, and certificates.

 Note Learn more about Key Vault soft delete and purge protection here: https://azsec.tech/lgx.

When a key is backed up, all versions of the key are backed up, too—as many as 500 versions. You can back up a Key Vault object, such as a key, from the Azure Portal, the Azure CLI, or PowerShell, or by calling REST APIs. The following code sample shows how to use PowerShell to back up a key and all its versions into a single file, as well as the code to perform the restore:

```
Backup-AzureKeyVaultKey -VaultName kv-entropy-tst -name key-shopfront-dev -OutputFile kv-sales-01-key1.backup

Restore-AzureKeyVaultKey -VaultName kv-entropy-tst -InputFile OutputFile kv-sales-01-key1.backup -Verbose
```

This code sample shows the same thing using the Azure CLI:

```
az keyvault key backup -vault-name kv-entropy-tst -name key-shopfront-dev -file kv-sales-01-key1.backup

az keyvault key restore -vault-name kv-entropy-tst -file kv-sales-01-key1.backup
```

Note Learn more about Key Vault backup best practices here: https://azsec.tech/3s7.

Restoring key versions

Individual versions of a key cannot be restored. After performing a backup, you should always test that a restore works. Backups are important, but restoration more so! How and where a backup is stored is beyond the scope of this book, as it depends on your corporate policy. You should also back up the other Key Vault assets, too: secrets and certificates (plus the private key).

There's one final topic we want to discuss before we move on to low-level cryptographic code, and that is the difference between Managed HSM and Key Vault.

Managed HSM and Azure Key Vault

The Azure Key Vault family has a new member, named Managed HSM, where *HSM* is an abbreviation for "hardware security module." There are some big differences between Key Vault and Managed HSM, however, of which you should be aware:

- Generally, you use Key Vault to store and manage keys, secrets, and certificates.

- You use managed HSM when a customer requires a single-tenant device and FIPS 140-2 level 3 validated hardware.

> **Note** Key Vault uses FIPS 140-2 level 2 validated hardware, and Managed HSM uses FIPS 140-2 level 3 validated hardware. You can read more about the FIPS 140-2 (and -3) program in Chapter 8, "Compliance and risk programs."

Key Vault is multitenant, which means that multiple tenants share Key Vault hardware. Key Vault does have strong isolation guarantees to prevent one tenant from accessing secret data that belongs to another tenant. However, for certain workloads, some customers might require a single-tenant solution. This is where Managed HSM enters the picture. When you enable a Managed HSM for your tenant, you get your own hardware. The hardware is managed by Azure, but it's your hardware.

Real-world experience: Who uses Managed HSM?

Very few customers really need Managed HSM. We have hundreds of customers who use Key Vault, but only three customers require Managed HSM. But those that do need HSM *really* need it! Usually, this is due to a corporate policy that requires FIPS 140-2 level 3–validated hardware to meet a strict compliance requirement.

Table 10-1 summarizes the main differences between Key Vault and Managed HSM.

TABLE 10-1 Major differences between Key Vault and Managed HSM

	Key Vault Standard	**Key Vault Premium**	**Managed HSM**
Cost	$	$$	$$$$$
Tenancy	Multitenant	Multitenant	Single-tenant
Hardware Protected Keys	No	Yes	Yes
FIPS 140-2 validation (keys only)	Level 1	Level 2	Level 3
Manage Secrets	Yes	Yes	No

	Key Vault Standard	Key Vault Premium	Managed HSM
Manage Certificates	Yes	Yes	No
Manage Keys	Yes	Yes	Yes
RSA and ECC keys	Yes	Yes	Yes
AES keys	No	No	Yes
AKV REST APIs	Yes	Yes	Yes (small delta)
Management	Azure Portal REST APIs (PowerShell, Azure CLI, and so on)	Azure Portal REST APIs (PowerShell, Azure CLI, and so on)	REST APIs (PowerShell, Azure CLI, and so on)
Dedicated Capacity	No	No	Yes
Service health and failover	Microsoft	Microsoft	Shared
Root of Trust control	Microsoft	Microsoft	Customer

Dedicated HSM and Payment HSM

There are two other services in the Key Vault family that we have not covered in this chapter and won't cover in any real depth: Dedicated HSM and Payment HSM.

Dedicated HSM is a bare-metal HSM hosted by Azure for highly specific workloads—most notably, lift-and-shift from on-prem. It is not a general-purpose solution, nor is it a viable replacement for Key Vault.

Like Dedicated HSM, Payment HSM is a bare-metal service and is not a replacement for Key Vault. Payment HSM is geared toward payments using Thales payShield hardware. This hardware offers payment tokenization, transaction processing, card acceptance, and more, and is compliant with numerous financial services standards like ISO 9564, ANSI X3:92, and others. You can read more about Dedicated HSM at https://azsec.tech/gk8 and about Payment HSM at https://azsec.tech/q61.

Security domain

When setting up Managed HSM, the customer claims custody of and downloads a security domain, which they must keep secure. This security domain forms the core set of credentials needed to recover a Managed HSM in case of disaster.

In Key Vault, keys are asymmetric, RSA, or elliptic-curve. In contrast, Managed HSM also supports AES keys. These keys are of the key type oct-HSM. AES symmetric keys are referred to as *oct* (meaning *octet*) because that's the definition the JSON Web Key standard uses.

The following Azure CLI snippets show how to set up an AES key in Managed HSM and how to use the key to perform symmetric encryption using AES-GCM. This encrypt operation is all performed in the hardware of Managed HSM.

```
az keyvault key create --id 'https://zz.managedhsm.azure.net/keys/testaeskey' --kty oct-HSM
az keyvault key encrypt --id 'https://zz.managedhsm.azure.net/keys/testaeskey' --algorithm
A256GCM --value "Hello, world!" --data-type plaintext --aad "deadc0de"
```

These snippets produce output like this:

```
{
  "aad": "deadc0de",
  "algorithm": "A256GCM",
  "iv": "a4cf19e0e7b9dcec3e0d37d2",
  "kid": "https://zz.managedhsm.azure.net/keys/testaeskey/f20d80d0824d0f6e2b761a6362eb9475",
  "result": "W+1AWtO9Fo45w8QL4A==",
  "tag": "7f4c4677bcc68609ec9ee70869dedff2"
}
```

AES-GCM produces a tag, which is like a message authentication code (MAC); in other words, AES encrypts and produces an authenticated integrity check. It's not like a hash; it's closer to a MAC, because the result uses the symmetric key as well as the content to create the tag. If an attacker changes the ciphertext of a message, the tag will be invalid.

Notice there is an --aad argument. The AES-GCM algorithm supports authenticated encryption with associated data (AEAD), which provides both authenticated encryption (confidentiality and authentication) and the ability to check the integrity and authentication of additional authenticated data (AAD) sent in the clear. For Managed HSM, the AAD data must be an even (as in, not odd) series of hex values. We discuss AEAD in more detail in Chapter 13, "Database security," when we discuss Always Encrypted in SQL Server and Cosmos DB.

Encrypt with Key Vault

You can encrypt data with Key Vault. However, Key Vault supports the use of RSA only to encrypt and decrypt. The problem with using RSA is that it's incredibly slow compared to AES, and you are restricted to encrypting and decrypting a single block of plaintext. Because of this, RSA is usually used to encrypt a symmetric key, and the symmetric key is then used to perform bulk encryption.

The following simplified code shows how to encrypt and decrypt with RSA and Key Vault:

```
using Azure.Identity;
using Azure.Security.KeyVault.Keys;
using Azure.Security.KeyVault.Keys.Cryptography;

var creds = new DefaultAzureCredential(true);
var client = new KeyClient(new Uri(keyVaultUrl), creds);
var key = client.GetKey(keyName);
var cryptoClient = new CryptographyClient(key.Id, creds);
var alg = EncryptionAlgorithm.RsaOaep;
```

```
var plaintext = Encoding.UTF8.GetBytes("Just one block of plaintext!");
var encryptResult = cryptoClient.Encrypt(alg, plaintext);
var ciphertext = Convert.ToBase64String(encryptResult.Ciphertext);

var decryptResult = cryptoClient.Decrypt(alg, encryptResult.Ciphertext);
var plaintext = Encoding.Default.GetString(decryptResult.Plaintext);
```

RSA can encrypt, at most, a block of data, unlike symmetric ciphers that can deal with arbitrary lengths of data. The block size is equal to the number of bytes of the RSA modulus, less space for the padding, which is typically optimal asymmetric encryption protocol (OAEP) in Azure. OAEP is defined in RFC 3447 at https://azsec.tech/c5i.

When you dump an RSA key's metadata with the following code:

```
az keyvault key show --id 'https://kv-shopdb-tst.vault.azure.net/keys/shopkey'
```

the modulus is the n parameter:

```
    "kid": "https://kv-shop-tst.vault.azure.net/keys/shopkey/a7095ca1796744dd89dea0964a305091",
    "kty": "RSA",

    "n":
"1xrNCg8tIEVumWNIOSLLlnOyjIPaQJzuh4upYvfSIR1iEkdOYIPQ6h+sgN+bSpXcxSSuLrk1ZnImiSP3XrRDepB8INg/
dNJXomTOPTmGHUQ+uW7KKSedD1HxJgwmOPLO8Yro8mIOeN+K/4DONbEdowoV6a76wMAlrUPY7SrO8wOsxhTkf/
wg6nSWMjY9SG/UDMKh9io/in422JeeughXkh764jfKOhj5+Oxae7qN7cE2bsoKQR581l/
vC+AEzsyrQ7ZFligbmCu5kd1ytjhXW4/A2np4IWZ25IVaIqUhkFdzO2OSLSsNbYYuzuFiOMIiendN/gpxUwyf/
ecjQHWzeQ==",
    "p": null,
    "q": null,
```

The following list is a summary:

- **RSA-2048** Modulus n is 256 bytes long, so the block size is approximately 245 bytes.

- **RSA-3072** Modulus n is 384 bytes long, so the block size is approximately 370 bytes.

- **RSA-4096** Modulus n is 512 bytes long, so the block size is approximately 500 bytes.

An AES-256 key is only 32 bytes long, which fits well within any of the block sizes noted in the list.

You can also use Key Vault to perform other cryptographic operations. You can learn more by reading the Azure Key Vault Developer's Guide at https://azsec.tech/g6q and by reviewing code samples in various languages, such as the following:

- .NET (https://azsec.tech/y1w)

- Java (https://azsec.tech/nc5)

- Python (https://azsec.tech/5fy)

- TypeScript (https://azsec.tech/qas)

- JavaScript (https://azsec.tech/wuf)

Secure keys with Key Vault summary

Almost 30 pages later, we're done with the topic of securing keys using Key Vault. We realize that this is a chapter about cryptography, but no Azure solution that uses cryptographic controls is complete without Key Vault, and architects and developers must understand the nuances of this important service. Key Vault is probably the most critical and pivotal service in Azure when it comes to securing Azure solutions.

In the next section, we'll move on to cryptography, starting with a design pattern that can future-proof your solutions against ongoing cryptologic research: cryptographic agility.

Cryptographic agility

For better or worse, most companies have some custom-written cryptographic code, and in our experience, most of it has many weaknesses. Because of this, you should always use the cryptographic capabilities built into the platform or environment. For example, you should use Azure Storage Encryption rather than your own code.

 Note We'll cover storage encryption strategies later in the chapter.

For those of you determined to write your own crypto code, let's start with a pop quiz. What's wrong with this Node.js code?

```
let crypto = require('crypto'),
    algorithm = 'aes-256-ecb',
    password = 'ssshhh!!';

function encrypt(plaintext) {
    let cipher = crypto.createCipher(algorithm,password);
    let ciphertext = cipher.update(plaintext,'utf8','base64');
    ciphertext += cipher.final('base64');

    return ciphertext;
}

function decrypt(ciphertext) {
    let cipher = crypto.createDecipher(algorithm,password);
    let plaintext = cipher.update(ciphertext,'base64','utf8');
    plaintext += cipher.final('utf8');

    return plaintext;
}
```

There are plenty of errors!

■ There's a hard-coded password in the code. You should *never* hard-code a password, key, secret, or anything else sensitive. But you already know that, right?

- The password is low randomness or entropy, which makes it easy to guess if an attacker can't read it from the source code. Applying Shannon Entropy (https://azsec.tech/rqp), this password has a value of about 1.6. Normal English text has an entropy value of about 3.5, a good-quality key has a value of 7.5, and the highest possible value is 8.0. So, 1.6 is bad.

- The code uses the Electronic Code Book (ECB) block-cipher mode. This should never be used because it has serious weaknesses.

> **Note** Some of you might notice that the code does not generate an Vector (IV). Because the code uses ECB, there's no need for an IV, because it's not used.

There's one other issue in the code that might not seem obvious: the JavaScript code has a hard-coded cryptographic algorithm. This is bad, and it is a common mistake developers make.

Important: Don't do this!

Ideally, we are all beyond code that is not secure, in which some ciphertext is simply XORed with an embedded "secret" to yield plaintext, like this Python code:

```
def decrypt(ciphertext):
    key =
[0xf,0x8,0x0,0x19,0x15,0x40,0x59,0x62,0x41,0x3,0xd,0x41,0xf,0x52,0x4,0x4e,0x5,0x4c,0x26,
0x62,0x42,0x4,0xb,0xa,0x4e,0x10,0x57,0x2,0x1b,0x17,0x44]
    plaintext = ""
    index = 0
    for k in key:
        v = chr(ord(ciphertext[index]) ^ k)
        plaintext += v
        index += 1
    return plaintext
```

That's all we want to say on the topic!

Using CredScan

Your build pipeline should use tools like CredScan to find secrets, keys, passwords, and credentials in your code. You can find more information about CredScan here: https://azsec.tech/pgr. GitHub also scans for credentials in public repos. See this site for more details: https://azsec.tech/dn9.

Imagine if some JavaScript code lived for 10 years, and over that time, 170 TB of data was encrypted. Then, one day, a researcher finds a weakness in the algorithm configuration used. Now what? You can't just change your code to use a new algorithm, because if you do, you will no longer be able to read the 170 TB. Even worse is if the vulnerability is bad, putting that 170 TB at risk of disclosure. Then what?

This is why crypto agility is so important. It allows you to easily change to a more secure set of cryptographic algorithms and parameters over time as cryptographic weaknesses are found, requiring relatively small changes in your code and design while also maintaining backward compatibility.

You will often hear about crypto agility in the context of post-quantum cryptography (PQC). With PQC, the rules of cryptography come crashing down, making the strong asymmetric algorithms we use today significantly easier to crack. If you want to learn more about PQC, start at this NIST site: https://azsec.tech/nb8.

One of the earliest documented descriptions of crypto agility is from Bryan Sullivan at Microsoft in his 2009 article "Security Briefs—Cryptographic Agility," available at https://azsec.tech/yt9. RFC 7696, "Guidelines for Cryptographic Algorithm Agility and Selecting Mandatory-to-Implement Algorithms," also has some useful guidance; it can be found here: https://azsec.tech/08d.

How to achieve crypto agility

While there is some documentation on the topic, we want to focus on the *practical* aspects of crypto agility. Attaining crypto agility isn't difficult, but there are some steps you must follow to make it a reality. Here are the steps:

1. Decide you want to make code crypto-agile.

2. Inventory the applications that use custom cryptographic code.

3. Document the strategies within your company to address crypto agility.

4. Do it!

Step 1: Decide you want to make code crypto-agile

The first step is to simply make crypto agility a priority. Honestly, that's all there is to it. Someone in senior development management needs to decide that crypto agility is as important as scalability or internationalization. Once that decision is made, the company needs to work out how to do crypto agility.

> **Real-world experience: Old code or new code?**
>
> Once you decide you want to make code crypto-agile, you need to determine whether you want to retrofit old code and make it agile or to apply crypto agility only to new code. Most customers we have worked with don't bother updating their old code, as it can lead to regressions. Instead, they adopt crypto agility only for new code and new systems. This is certainly better than doing nothing, but if a vulnerability is found in a cryptographic algorithm you use, you need a plan to update it. So, keep that in mind.

Step 2: Inventory the applications that use custom cryptographic code

If you decide to retrofit existing code, you need to know where crypto code is used. There are tools that can help you find where you use cryptographic algorithms.

Step 3: Document the strategies within your company to address crypto agility

There are two basic ways to achieve crypto agility, and there are pros and cons to each. We will explain what they are shortly. For now, your organization must define how to achieve agility in the various programming languages you support. At a high level, the same strategies apply to any programming language, but the low-level mechanics will vary in Java, C#, Rust, Python, JavaScript, Go, C++, and any other programming language.

> **Tip** You will probably need to create some training so everyone understands why crypto agility is important and how to do it.

Step 4: Do it!

This means having your developers write code that performs cryptographic operations in a crypto-agile manner, and implementing test plans to test the code to make sure it can successfully read and write data in an agile manner.

Now let's look at the strategies to implement crypto agility.

Implement crypto agility

There are two main ways to implement crypto agility:

- Add cryptographic metadata to the resulting ciphertext.

- Add a version number at the start of the resulting ciphertext.

Over the years, Microsoft has added crypto agility to various products. Three of these products lead the way in support for crypto agility: Microsoft Office, SQL Server, and Cosmos DB.

Use cryptographic metadata

All Microsoft Office documents add cryptographic metadata to the start of the document XML file (DOCX, XLSX, PPTX, and so on). You can read about the cryptographic metadata in the "Office Document Cryptography Structure" specification, found here: https://azsec.tech/a7u. Figure 10-18 shows the part of the specification that explains the XML cryptographic data stored with each document.

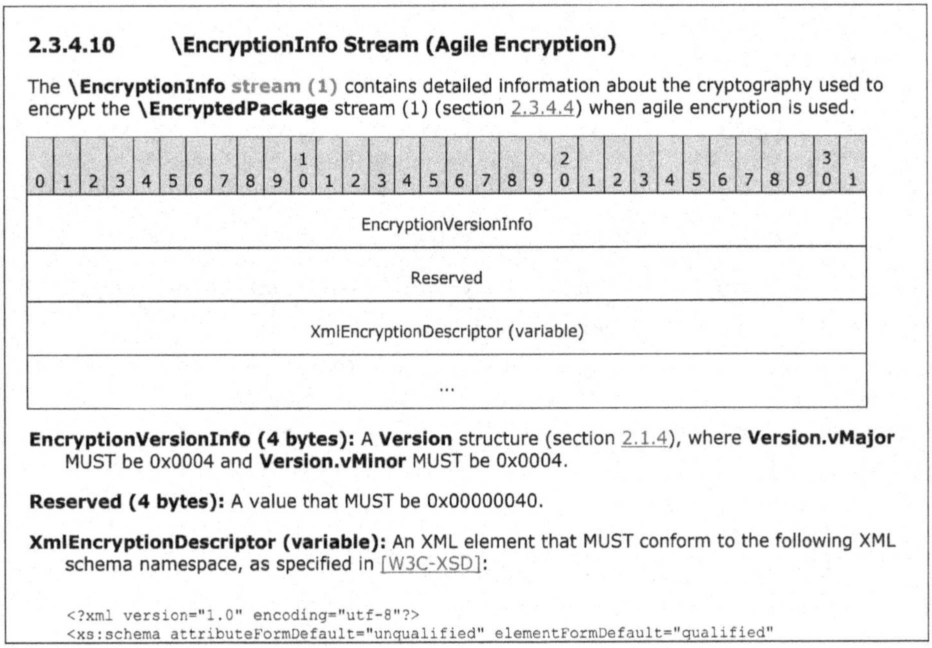

2.3.4.10   \EncryptionInfo Stream (Agile Encryption)

The **\EncryptionInfo** stream (1) contains detailed information about the cryptography used to encrypt the **\EncryptedPackage** stream (1) (section 2.3.4.4) when agile encryption is used.

0	1	2	3	4	5	6	7	8	9	1 0	1	2	3	4	5	6	7	8	9	2 0	1	2	3	4	5	6	7	8	9	3 0	1

EncryptionVersionInfo
Reserved
XmlEncryptionDescriptor (variable)
...

EncryptionVersionInfo (4 bytes): A **Version** structure (section 2.1.4), where **Version.vMajor** MUST be 0x0004 and **Version.vMinor** MUST be 0x0004.

Reserved (4 bytes): A value that MUST be 0x00000040.

XmlEncryptionDescriptor (variable): An XML element that MUST conform to the following XML schema namespace, as specified in [W3C-XSD]:

```
<?xml version="1.0" encoding="utf-8"?>
<xs:schema attributeFormDefault="unqualified" elementFormDefault="qualified"
```

FIGURE 10-18 Part of the "Office Document Cryptography Structure" specification.

The metadata is stored in an XmlEncryptionDescriptor structure and includes the following:

- Cipher
- Cipher mode
- Cipher block size
- Key size
- Hash algorithm
- Hash size
- Salt size
- Spin count

When an Office application, such as Microsoft Word, opens a document, the application reads the metadata and uses it to dynamically create the appropriate cryptographic algorithms. It then reads the ciphertext and decrypts it. So, rather than hard-coding the cryptographic algorithms into the Office code, the code creates the appropriate cryptographic classes using class factories.

Many developers write code like this C# code, where every aspect of the symmetric cryptography is hard-coded:

```
var cipher = new AesManaged();
cipher.Mode = CipherMode.CBC;
cipher.Padding = PaddingMode.Zeros;
cipher.KeySize = 128;
```

In contrast, Office follows this kind of pattern:

```
var cryptoConfig = ReadCryptoConfig();
var cipher = SymmetricAlgorithm.Create(cryptoConfig.algName);
cipher.Mode = cryptoConfig.cipherMode;
cipher.Padding = cryptoConfig.paddingMode;
cipher.KeySize = cryptoConfig.keySize;
```

Using this pattern, the code reads cryptographic configuration data, which includes all the information needed to dynamically build the required algorithms at runtime. This configuration data comes from two sources:

- A configuration file
- Metadata associated with the protected data

Source 1: Configuration file   When data must be encrypted and then written to storage, the code needs to know what settings to use. These settings come from a configuration file. When the data is read and decrypted, the configuration data comes from the metadata stored with the protected data. This is the important part: our code can read and decrypt any data, regardless of how it was encrypted. But when the code encrypts and writes the data out, it will use whatever setting is in the cryptographic configuration.

At any time, we can tweak the configuration file to accommodate new cryptographic settings, and the code will adopt those settings when it writes out encrypted data. For example, suppose your company has some old files that are encrypted with 112-bit Triple-DES, ECB mode, and all-zeros padding. (Clearly, this would be considered subpar today, but it was probably fine 20 years ago.) Recently, the company decided to change the corporate cryptographic policy to require 128-bit AES, cipher block chaining (CBC) mode, and ISO10126 padding. You can update the crypto-configuration file with the newer standard; the code will read old Triple-DES files and then write using the newer AES settings.

In short:

- You read and decrypt using the crypto settings described in the metadata of the protected file.

- You encrypt and write using the crypto settings in the crypto-configuration file.

It's simple, really!

How you represent the metadata is totally up to you. You could use XML, JSON, or even something as simple as cryptographic parameters separated by a delimiter before the protected data. The latter is easy to create, but it might cause issues if you use an algorithm that requires different cryptographic parameters in the future, in which case JSON or XML might be more appropriate.

You may have noticed that we used the word *protected* rather than *encrypted* earlier. There's a good reason for this. Office not only encrypts files, but it also adds a Message Authentication Code (MAC) to the document. That's why you'll notice the reference to hash details. You can read about how this is done in section 2.3.14.4 of the "Office Document Cryptography Structure" specification.

You will often see the word SpinCount. This is used when deriving encryption keys and adding a MAC to the document. Most password-based key derivation functions (PBKDFs) refer to *spin count* as *iteration count*. Iteration count is important because passwords are low-entropy, and a PBKDF function can turn a poor password into a high-entropy key.

Think of the iteration count as a sort of Moore's law compensator; as machines become faster, the iteration count can be increased to slow an attacker down if they try to perform offline brute-force attacks against the password. For example, the following Go code employs the same sample key that appeared earlier in the Node.js code but now uses a PBKDF function to "salt and stretch" the password. The spin, or iteration, count is 75,000, which means the loop keeps building up the key 75,000 times.

```
package main

import (
        "crypto/rand"
        "crypto/sha256"
        "encoding/base64"
        "fmt"
        "pbkdf2"
)

func main() {
        salt := make([]byte, 32)
        rand.Read(salt)
        dk := pbkdf2.Key([]byte("ssshhh!!"), salt, 75000, 32, sha256.New)
```

```
    fmt.Println(base64.StdEncoding.EncodeToString(dk))
}
```

The output from this is a Base64-encoded string that looks like this:

j/HB3/IMQasOS7mUr/fCInE4uR8IYVNlMfWbhTCLO1Y=

This has significantly more entropy than "ssshhh!!"

Back to cryptographic agility. All this cryptographic metadata is part of every encrypted Office document. All a user needs to do is open the file and enter the password, and the underlying cryptographic machinery spins up dynamically to ensure the document is not tampered with. If this machinery determines no tampering has occurred, the document is decrypted and rendered in the application.

You can look at this metadata for any encrypted Office file by changing its file type to ZIP, unzipping it, extracting the EncryptionInfo file, and viewing the file in an XML viewer. All the data needed to verify and then decrypt the data is in this XML file (except, of course, the decryption key, which is provided by the user). Figure 10-19 shows the EncryptionInfo XML data in an encrypted Word DOCX file.

```xml
<encryption
    xmlns="http://schemas.microsoft.com/office/2006/encryption"
    xmlns:p="http://schemas.microsoft.com/office/2006/keyEncryptor
      /password"
    xmlns:c="http://schemas.microsoft.com/office/2006/keyEncryptor
      /certificate">
    <keyData saltSize="16" blockSize="16" keyBits="256" hashSize
      ="64" cipherAlgorithm="AES" cipherChaining="ChainingModeCBC"
      hashAlgorithm="SHA512" saltValue="teP64rBFHZpqMRZXYEpzQA=="
      />
    <dataIntegrity encryptedHmacKey="d835G8E2hznZ1Q/RiSFlCrje
      +QLvfGjxRYiMwU1EoeTMk+GgDSEp6Jyqz5QWzUuX06pMy
      +rFFdblI8eijl1XmA==" encryptedHmacValue="o5
      +wgxB44hUMRmchXtp6rpz6MD6tD4oWojfX9+15Crej8RJ
      +sCrXQCBC1SJHMSg6UPqdYPt7ojWyb4tmsCiynQ=="/>
    <keyEncryptors>
        <keyEncryptor uri="http://schemas.microsoft.com/office/2006
          /keyEncryptor/password">
            <p:encryptedKey
                spinCount="100000"
                saltSize="16"
                blockSize="16"
                keyBits="256"
                hashSize="64"
                cipherAlgorithm="AES"
                cipherChaining="ChainingModeCBC"
                hashAlgorithm="SHA512"
                saltValue="7TusAYkzuAqLQAlr9Y5e/w=="
                encryptedVerifierHashInput="D8fxjmEWW+zQoyxN6DB=="
                encryptedVerifierHashValue
                  ="Cd8ZcsV3ZUnwCZW7PmdGBx1JX0MpzaArFX1rgYF2rgZYxE
                  BI2xgMkwZOx8ze3zt7idgSP0oCkZtedcJ9h2kzzw=="
                encryptedKeyValue="5fHAsKaUW0KBdDBtlt+JwEIgDGWRrFQK
                  +aIt8mMK+ks="/>
        </keyEncryptor>
    </keyEncryptors>
</encryption>
```

FIGURE 10-19 Part of an encrypted Office document's XML encryption data.

Adding metadata in this fashion is useful when the resulting document is relatively large (because the metadata size is acceptable in larger documents). This is an incredibly flexible way to support cryptographic agility.

Use a version number

The other way to support cryptographic agility is to assign a version number to a set of cryptographic settings. This is what SQL Server, Azure SQL Database, and Cosmos DB do when they use Always Encrypted: the version number is prepended to the resulting protected data. (We explain Always Encrypted in Chapter 13.)

If you dump Always Encrypted data from SQL Server or Cosmos DB, the version details are plainly obvious, as shown in the first byte of each row in the SSN column in Figure 10-20.

```
SQLQuery_1 - sql-cr...ft.com)  ●

▷ Run  ☐ Cancel  ⋇ Disconnect  ⟳ Change Connection   Cust          ⌄    │   ⣿ Explain  ⧉ Enable SQLCMD  ↦
    1   SELECT TOP (6)[Surname]
    2         ,[Firstname]
    3         ,[State]
    4         ,[Zip]
    5         ,[SSN]
    6    FROM [dbo].[Customers]
```

	Surname	⌄	Firstname	⌄	State	⌄	Zip	⌄	SSN	⌄
1	HARMETZ	...	Adam	...	AZ		85303		0x0100001FA8A58F8AF9153713F2...	
2	HAY	...	Jeff	...	MD		21401		0x0100003126801FCFEE0E94D339...	
3	HERP	...	Jesper	...	KY		40245		0x01000044D3B6496978D099D65B...	
4	RAILSON	...	Stuart	...	OK		73069		0x0100006B0A64194AF9ED2CD638...	
5	ILYINA	...	Julia	...	FL		33954		0x010000762720002794E4C09A5B...	
6	REID	...	Miles	...	DC		20011		0x0100009C26D5D631BB3A4A003E...	

FIGURE 10-20 Viewing data encrypted using SQL Server Always Encrypted.

The first byte is 0x01; this is the version number of the cryptographic configuration currently used by SQL Server and Azure SQL Database. When SQL Server sees the 0x01 version number, it knows precisely what crypto to use.

For version 1, the algorithm suite name is as follows:

AEAD_AES_256_CBC_HMAC_SHA_256

Let's parse that:

- **AEAD** this stands for *authenticated encryption with associated data*. This means that some data is not encrypted, but that a message authentication code (MAC) is added that includes the unencrypted data to protect it from tampering.

- **AES_256_CBC**   This is the bulk encryption algorithm: 256-bit AES using CBC.

- **HMAC_SHA_256**   This is the authenticated integrity check added to the data to make sure it's not tampered with.

> **Note**   You can read the draft IETF standard on AEAD_AES_256_CBC_HMAC_SHA_256 here: https://azsec.tech/su4.

If at some point in the future the SQL Server team were to add a new algorithm, they could make it version 2 and set the first byte to 0x02. Then, the SQL Server client code could still read version 1, but any new or updated data could use version 2.

> **Note**   The C# source code for the SqlClient class with support for Always Encrypted is on GitHub at https://azsec.tech/t7u. In the code, you can see how the encrypted result is defined, including the version number.

Put version number crypto agility in action

How you put version number crypto agility into action depends on the programming language used. At its core, you'll probably use an abstract class to represent a concrete implementation of the symmetric algorithm. (This is certainly the case for .NET.) For example, a partial C# crypto-agile class might look like this:

```
private SymmetricAlgorithm   _symCrypto;
private HMAC                 _hMac;
private DeriveBytes          _keyDerivation;
private int                  _iterationCount;
private Version              _ver;

private byte[]               _salt;
```

SymmetricAlgorithm, HMAC, and DeriveBytes are all abstract classes.

When the version number is read from the protected blob, the following switch statement determines the concrete classes and settings:

```
switch (_ver) {
    case Version.Version1:
        _symCrypto = SymmetricAlgorithm.Create("TripleDes");
        _symCrypto.Padding = PaddingMode.PKCS7;
        _symCrypto.Mode = CipherMode.ECB;
        _hMac = HMAC.Create("HMACSHA1");
        _iterationCount = 1000;
        _keyDerivation = new Rfc2898DeriveBytes(_keyMaterial, _salt, _iterationCount);
        break;
```

```
case Version.Version2:
    _symCrypto = SymmetricAlgorithm.Create("AesManaged");
    _symCrypto.Padding = PaddingMode.ISO10126;
    _symCrypto.KeySize = 128;
    _symCrypto.Mode = CipherMode.CBC;
    _hMac = HMAC.Create("HMACSHA256");
    _iterationCount = 20000;
    _keyDerivation = new Rfc2898DeriveBytes(_keyMaterial, _salt, _iterationCount);
break;

default:

    throw new ArgumentException("Invalid crypto version.");
```

The core cryptographic operations are then performed using _symCrypto and _hMac.

> **Note** Sample C# code, along with other resources for this book, is available on GitHub at https://github.com/AzureDevSecurityBook/.

Java extensions (javax) use strings to reference cryptographic settings, which drastically helps support agility. For example:

```
import javax.crypto.Cipher;
import javax.crypto.Mac;
Cipher cipher = Cipher.getInstance(cipherName);
Mac mac = Mac.getInstance(macName);
```

In Java, Cipher and Mac are both abstract classes. In this code snippet, the strings for Cipher and Mac could be AES/CBC/PKCS5Padding and HmacSHA256, respectively.

Real-world experience: Crypto agility in the real world

One hundred percent of customers we have worked with have some custom cryptographic code. However, 100 percent of this code was not crypto agile. Worse, 100 percent of customers did not even know about crypto agility. But ultimately, 100 percent of customers thought it was a great idea!

What you should include in the ciphertext output

You need to write more than just a version number and the ciphertext output. You must also include enough information to create concrete classes. This includes the following:

- Version number

- Initialization vector

- Salt value (if you derive keys from passwords)

The salt value and initialization vector do not need to be encrypted. In fact, if you think about it, they *can't* be encrypted, because they are needed to perform the decryption! Also, a salt value and IV don't have to be random, but they do need to be unique.

"But we can't implement crypto agility just yet!"

If you can't implement a full crypto agility design today, at least add a version number and potentially a delimiter at the start of your ciphertext for projects currently in development. Your code can ignore the first one or two bytes to get to the ciphertext until you implement crypto agility; then, when you do move to a fuller process, you can make it version 2 and add more data to the resulting protected blob. If you don't at least add the starting version number, you will not know if that first byte is a version number of the first part of valid ciphertext. This is simple and paves the way to a more complete crypto agility process.

Use of delimiters

You don't need to use a delimiter if you know each field length. You could place the variable-length data at the end of the output stream.

Here is some sample code that is available in the book's GitHub repo. The following line of code:

```
string ctext = new AgileCrypto(AgileCrypto.Version.Version4).Protect(pwd, plaintext);
```

produces a result like this:

```
4|GIhGYvZqSSK+2Mrsebmo4Q==|YgGkQpL6fF8ztaCaWMoe/A==|LQHB6iKjOjCe1Svqqs4BCg==|
tMDXkWHcvOgbfBDPQvgXc1lXwTF7JtrvT9iwOoOXQUk=
```

And the format of the output is as follows:

```
Version | Base64(IV) | Base64(Salt) | Base64(Ciphertext) | Base64(HMAC)
```

As noted, this output could be JSON, XML, or whatever works for you.

Another option is to not require a password but rather to generate a random symmetric key. You could then wrap that key with the public portion of an asymmetric key—for example, RSA—along with the fingerprint of the certificate that contains the public key, and use the private RSA key to unwrap the symmetric key and then decrypt the ciphertext. You would need appropriate access controls on the private key, however.

Crypto agility summary

With a little forethought and design, adding crypto agility to new applications that include custom cryptographic code is not difficult. When you do, the benefits are immense, as new vulnerabilities are found by security researchers. Of course, as noted at the outset of this section, writing your own cryptographic code should be a last resort—done only if the underlying platform does not solve your specific needs.

Crypto agility is an important mitigation adopting zero trust's assume-breach principle. If an algorithm is broken and practical attacks exist, your code can nimbly move onto another algorithm. But what if you must create a solution that includes code-level cryptography? For cases like this, Microsoft offers the Microsoft Data Encryption SDK, which is the subject of the next section.

A fun fact about GUIDs and version numbers

Create a GUID (also called a UUID), any GUID, and then create some more. Here are two I created using an extension in Visual Studio Code:

- b45ef00f-e4ff-4ba5-aada-e6404a66d430

- 3c785987-1163-4c18-96f4-a7ebdbc5e4ff

If you look at the third block, you'll see it always starts with a 4. That's the GUID version number as defined in RFC 4122 (https://azsec.tech/m4p). The RFC defines five types of GUIDs, and type 4 is totally random. Now you know. You're welcome.

The Microsoft Data Encryption SDK

At the time of this writing, the Microsoft Data Encryption software development kit (SDK) is in public preview. The downloadable packages presently support only .NET, but it's worthwhile to familiarize yourself with the SDK for when it is released.

Real-world experience: The Microsoft Data Encryption SDK and customers

Even though the SDK is in public preview, the authors have used the SDK with customers in production workloads.

One of the main features of the SDK is its simplicity. It provides few options and errs on the side of being boring. In the world of cryptography, boring is good! The SDK offers a single secure ciphersuite. This is a good, because it removes the potential for errors. The SDK also supports crypto agility by way of a version number.

Here are the steps to get started and kick the tires on the SDK:

1. Open a command prompt. (Ideally, by now, you are using Windows Terminal.)

2. Make a folder named cryptotest.

3. Type the following command to switch to the cryptotest folder:

    ```
    cd cryptotest
    ```

4. Type the following command:

```
dotnet new console
```

5. Type the following command:

```
dotnet add package Microsoft.Data.Encryption.Cryptography --prerelease
```

6. Replace the contents of program.cs file with the following C# code:

> **Note** This code uses C# 10 and .NET 6, which allows for top-level statements and implicit using statements (https://azsec.tech/q7r).

```csharp
using Microsoft.Data.Encryption.Cryptography;

string plaintextString = "Hello, World!!";

var encryptionKey = new PlaintextDataEncryptionKey("MyKey");

var ciphertext = plaintextString.Encrypt(encryptionKey);
Console.WriteLine("Ciphertext");
var asHex = String.Join("",ciphertext.Select(c => ((int)c).ToString("x2")));
Console.WriteLine($"   B64: {ciphertext.ToBase64String()}");
Console.WriteLine($"   Hex: {asHex}");

var decrypted = ciphertext.Decrypt<string>(encryptionKey);
Console.WriteLine($"Plaintext: {decrypted}");
```

7. Type the following command:

```
dotnet run
```

You should see output that looks like this:

```
Ciphertext

  B64: AVCUKr2X00DNVjyD5foLXd87 <snip> GEzQqNKkUPiWN/dstIBT
  Hex: 0150942abd973b40cd563c83e5fa0 <snip> 89637f76cb48053

Plaintext: Hello, World!!
```

The code is simple because all the cryptographic mechanics are removed from the developer. The most important lines of code are as follows:

```csharp
var encryptionKey = new PlaintextDataEncryptionKey("MyKey");
var ciphertext = plaintextString.Encrypt(encryptionKey);
string decrypted = ciphertext.Decrypt<string>(encryptionKey);
```

The first line generates a new AES symmetric key named MyKey. The second line encrypts the plaintext string using the key information previously defined. Finally, the code decrypts the ciphertext using the same encryption key.

To be honest, this is not production code. The AES key is ephemeral and works only as long as the application is running. It might be fine for protecting a long-running but nonpersistent secret in memory, but not much more than a quick demo.

8. Run the code again and take note of the first hex byte of the ciphertext. Run it again. Then again.

I ran the code four more times and got the following hex output:

```
Hex: 01581d4e2ef88a81bf24b7fe02b0386977bf6acd6822da131bffe <snip>
Hex: 0132cf1297f1430ad8b00c4a00598aa57cd01e8582cdac179d8d7 <snip>
Hex: 017953fe0f7a491df4f1ec47ffd289c27367fc3425c870f6b6635 <snip>
Hex: 01c87dbc79741a9a7b21b15aaf797e5d16d64580b5dd75cbd2dd3 <snip>
```

Can you see a pattern? The first byte is always 0x01. This is the version number to help support crypto agility. Also, the output is quite large relative to the plaintext size because it's not just ciphertext; it's a complete crypto-agile-protected result. The output is as follows:

```
version + HMAC + IV + ciphertext
```

The version 1 ciphersuite used by the SDK is AEAD_AES_256_CBC_HMAC_SHA_256. Sound familiar? It's the same set of algorithms used by Azure SQL Database, SQL Server, and Cosmos DB when using Always Encrypted. This is a simple and conservative cryptographic ciphersuite that provides both confidentiality and an integrity check. From a STRIDE perspective (explained in Chapter 4, "Threat modeling"), it mitigates the Information Disclosure (I) and Tampering (T) threats.

Now build on the sample to add more features. You can persist a secret outside of the application and then build an AES key using code like this:

```
// Build a symmetric key, Base64-encoded source (secret) is from outside this code
var key = System.Convert.FromBase64String(secret);
var encryptionKey = new PlaintextDataEncryptionKey(secretName, key);
```

The data encryption key (DEK) is derived from the secret password or passphrase. The secret could be stored as a secret in Key Vault. For example, if this code were used in a larger solution that runs in a VM, you could use a VM managed identity to restrict access to the secret.

Optional parameters

There are some optional parameters that you can set:

```
// Crypto options and parameters
var encryptionSettings = new EncryptionSettings<string>(
    dataEncryptionKey: encryptionKey,
    encryptionType: EncryptionType.Deterministic,
    serializer: StandardSerializerFactory.Default.GetDefaultSerializer<string>()
);
string plaintextString = "Hello, World!";

var ciph = plaintextString.Encrypt(encryptionSettings);
```

Encryption type

There are two encryptionType options:

- **EncryptionType.Deterministic** This uses the plaintext as the IV. Two sets of plaintext encrypted with the same key using deterministic encryption will always yield the same ciphertext.

- **EncryptionType.Randomized** This uses a random and unique IV. Two sets of plaintext encrypted with the same key using randomized encryption will always yield differing ciphertext because each encryption operation uses a unique IV. You will need to store the IV in plaintext with the encrypted data.

Deterministic encryption exists to support Always Encrypted, which allows for some types of SQL queries over ciphertext without decrypting the ciphertext. Chapter 15 explains this in more detail. Most developers will not need to use the deterministic option if they are using the library as a stand-alone library to encrypt custom data.

Serializer

Another option you can set is the serializer. Generally, the default set of serializers is enough for most developers. Serializers become critical when interfacing with database engines using Always Encrypted. For example, SQL Server does not store a DateTime type as YYYY-MM-DD mm:ss. Instead, it uses a much more concise and efficient 3-byte representation that is the number of seconds since January 1, 0001. So, 2^{24} is approximately 46,000 years in one-second increments. The SqlDateSerializer class converts a C# DateTime to this 3-byte representation and vice versa.

The default serializer can map many common .NET types, including the following:

bool	byte and byte[]	char
DateTime	DateTimeOffset	decimal
double	float	Guid
Int	long	sbyte
short	string	TimeSpan
Uint	ulong	ushort

The default serializer will also handle nullable versions of the data types such as int? and string?.

When encrypting data, you will usually use the default serializer. If you have two fields you want to encrypt and one is a DateTime and one is a TimeSpan, you can use two EncryptionSettings each with its own serializer. You can also use differing keys held in Key Vault.

Managing SDK keys in Key Vault

The SDK also has native support for using Key Vault to manage keys. This uses a classic key-wrapping model. Key Vault does not store the DEK directly; rather, it wraps the DEK in an RSA key, called a *key encryption key* (KEK). The RSA key is stored in Key Vault. The resulting protected key blob can be stored somewhere accessible by the application—for example, with the ciphertext.

A strong RBAC policy on the KEK is critical. Whoever has decrypt permission (which means access to the private key) on the KEK can decrypt any DEK encrypted with that KEK. While it's not uncommon to protect the wrapped DEK with good access policy, too, it's not as critical as protecting the KEK, because getting the DEK would require an exhaustive key search attack against RSA. This key-wrapping process is a common key-protection model used by many cryptographic systems.

In this final example, you'll use Key Vault to store the KEK used to wrap the DEK, which is then used by the sample code. Before you do this, you'll need to add a couple of modules first. To do so, run the following commands in the same folder as the sample code:

```
dotnet add package Azure.Identity
dotnet add package Microsoft.Data.Encryption.AzureKeyVaultProvider --prerelease
```

Then change program.cs to use this C# code:

```
using Azure.Identity;
using Microsoft.Data.Encryption.AzureKeyVaultProvider;
using Microsoft.Data.Encryption.Cryptography;

var AzureKeyVaultKeyPath = "https://<your key vault>/keys/<key name>/<key version guid>";
var TokenCredential = new DefaultAzureCredential();
var azureKeyProvider = new AzureKeyVaultKeyStoreProvider(TokenCredential);
var keyEncryptionKey = new KeyEncryptionKey("KEK", AzureKeyVaultKeyPath, azureKeyProvider);
var dataEncryptionKey = new ProtectedDataEncryptionKey("DEK", keyEncryptionKey);

var original = DateTime.Now;
Console.WriteLine ("PT: " + original);

var encryptedBytes = original.Encrypt(dataEncryptionKey);
var encryptedHex = encryptedBytes.ToHexString();
Console.WriteLine ("CT:" + encryptedHex);

var bytesToDecrypt = encryptedHex.FromHexString();
var decryptedBytes = bytesToDecrypt.Decrypt<DateTime>(dataEncryptionKey);
Console.WriteLine ("PT: " + decryptedBytes);
```

A couple important points:

- The key must be an RSA or RSA-HSM key. ECC will not work.

- The account accessing the Key Vault must have appropriate cryptographic rights to get, sign/verify, and wrap/unwrap keys.

Finally, the wrapped DEK could be persisted using code like this:

```
using System.Text.Json;
...
var jsonWrappedDEK = JsonSerializer.Serialize(dataEncryptionKey);
File.WriteAllText("wrappedDEK.json", jsonWrappedDEK);
```

A note about DefaultAzureCredential()

The preceding sample code includes DefaultAzureCredential(), which calls a series of credential APIs until one works or they all fail. For example, if this code were called from within a VM in Azure that used a managed identity, then DefaultAzureCredential() would attempt to create a ManagedIdentityCredential object. You can read more here: https://azsec.tech/xt1.

This contains all the information needed to access the KEK in Key Vault, as long as the account has access, of course. As an experiment, you should add this code and look at the resulting JSON. If you turn on auditing for the Key Vault as described earlier in the chapter, you can see your code hitting Key Vault and audit events getting raised.

You can read more about the Microsoft Data Encryption SDK on GitHub at https://azsec.tech/xdv. You will find sample code here, too. Also, Travis Nielson, a Cloud Solutions Architect at Microsoft, has sample code and documentation at his GitHub repo, located here: https://azsec.tech/c69.

Now let's turn our attention to some of the services in Azure and the cryptographic services they natively offer.

Azure services and cryptography

This section briefly covers the native cryptographic services provided by various Azure services for data at rest. It discusses the following products:

- Azure Storage
- Azure VMs
- Azure SQL Database
- Cosmos DB

Most Azure services that support encryption of data at rest provide one or more of the following models:

- Server-side encryption with platform-managed keys
- Server-side encryption with customer-managed keys
- Client-side encryption

> **Note** Most Azure services use KEKs to wrap DEKs. Wrapping uses a public key from an asymmetric key pair, such as from RSA, to wrap (encrypt) the DEK, which is usually a random AES key. Unwrapping the key uses the private part of the RSA key pair to unwrap (decrypt) the AES key.

Server-side encryption with platform-managed keys

Platform-managed keys (PMKs) are common for many Azure services, such as Azure SQL Database transparent data encryption (TDE) and Azure Storage account service-level encryption. In fact, it's the default option for many of these services.

With this approach, the volume on which data resides is encrypted using a DEK that is wrapped by a KEK managed by Azure. The key lifecycle—which includes provisioning, rotation, management, backup, auditing, and deprovisioning—is all handled by Azure. This helps mitigate damage that could be caused from an offline attack, if a hard disk is stolen, or if a failed hard drive is not destroyed correctly. From an Azure viewpoint, these risks are diminishingly small, however.

Server-side encryption with customer-managed keys

Most Azure services also offer server-side encryption with keys managed by the customer. These are called *customer-managed keys* (CMKs).

In most cases, the keys—or more accurately, the KEKs—are stored in Key Vault. This mitigates the same risks as noted in the preceding section, but with one major change: the root KEK is not managed by Azure. Rather, the key lifecycle is managed by the customer.

This has important implications. If the key is lost, Azure does not have a copy. You can't call support and get the key back. This is why, as noted in the "Back up your Key Vault assets" section earlier in this chapter, Key Vault has soft delete enabled by default. Still, if the key is gone, it is *gone*—and that means your data is gone, too, unless you have a backup. Essentially, if this happens, you effectively ransomware yourself, only nobody can pay the ransom!

Some customers want to manage their own keys. If a key needs to be rotated, the customer can do it, and if a key expires, it can be disabled by the customer. The customer has complete control. For some customers, this also gives them the ability to disable a key in case of a catastrophic attack. In other words, if the key is disabled, the attacker cannot get anything but the ciphertext. Once the customer cuts off the attack, they can re-enable the key. Of course, disabling the key means *no one* can access the data—including valid users! This is obviously a "break-glass" scenario, but some customers want this level of control.

> **Note** Azure SQL Database can use customer-managed keys for TDE, as can Azure Storage accounts and many other services.

> **Important: What threat does volume encryption mitigate?**
>
> Volume encryption is designed to mitigate a stolen storage device or a failed device that is not destroyed correctly. It should be used in conjunction with other controls such as strong authentication, authorization, and audits.

> **CMKs are not for everyone**
>
> CMKs require a level of security maturity to do well. If you must use CMKs to protect data at rest, please do so only if you have expertise, processes, and tooling in place to manage the keys. CMKs are managed by you, not by Azure. If you lose them, they're gone, and so is your data.

Client-side encryption

In this scenario, keys are not stored in, nor are they accessible by, the service in question. Two good examples are Azure SQL Database Always Encrypted and Azure Blob client-side encryption. If correctly designed, the keys are accessible only to the valid users of the resource.

From an attacker's perspective, as long as the keys are protected with good authentication, RBAC, and network isolation policies, they will only be able to access ciphertext—even if they have unfettered access to the database or storage account. This is a great example of applying an assume-breach mentality from zero trust. In the event of a catastrophic attack, the attacker gets nothing of use.

Azure Storage cryptography

Azure Storage is composed of four major storage types:

- Blobs
- Files
- Queues
- Tables

When you create an Azure Storage account, you can opt to use volume-level encryption with PMKs or CMKs. You can also choose to apply cryptographic controls to the following:

- Blobs and files only
- All services (blobs, files, tables, and queues)

This option cannot be changed after this Azure Storage account is created. You can read more about Azure Storage encryption here: https://azsec.tech/9jd.

> **Note** Azure Storage accounts support automatic KEK rotation. This is explained later in this chapter in the section titled "Key rotation."

Encryption scopes

Blob storage (except Azure Data Lake Storage Gen2) supports encryption scopes. These enable you to use a different DEK and KEK per scope on a single blob store. A common usage pattern for scopes is to have a blob store with two containers, with each container encrypted with its own KEK and DEK. This is a way to provide cryptographic isolation between customers.

To set up an encryption scope when configuring a blob store in the Azure Portal, follow these steps:

1. On the Storage account page, select **Encryption** from the menu on the left.

2. Click **Encryption Scopes** and then click **Add**.

3. On the **Create Encryption Scope** page (see Figure 10-21), enter the following information, and click **Create**:

-   **Encryption Type**   For each scope, choose **Microsoft-Managed Keys** or **Customer-Managed Keys**.

-   **Encryption Key**   If you selected Customer-Managed Keys, you'll see two Encryption Key settings: **Select from Key Vault** and **Enter Key URI**. Here, **Select from Key Vault** is selected.

-   **Subscription**   Choose the subscription with the Key Vault you want to use.

-   **Key Vault**   Select the Key Vault you want to use.

-   **Key**   Select the KEK you want to use.

-   **Infrastructure Encryption**   Select **Disabled** (as shown here) or **Enabled**.

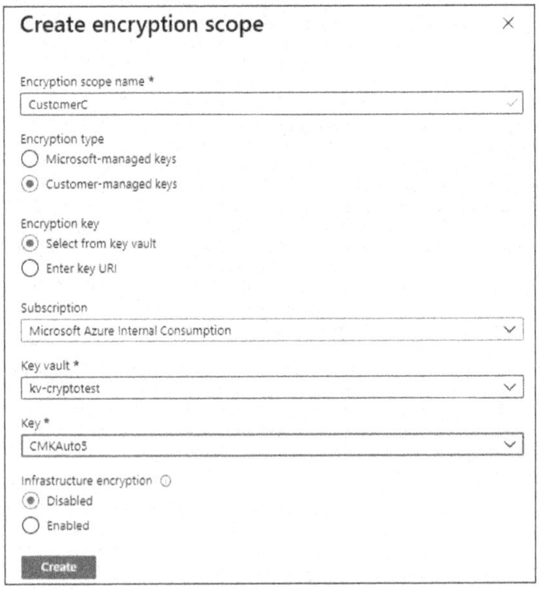

FIGURE 10-21 Creating a new blob store encryption scope.

This will automatically generate a DEK and use it to encrypt the contents of the data within that scope when it is applied to an Azure Storage account container.

You are returned to the **Encryption** page, where you can see all the encryption scopes created so far. (See Figure 10-22.)

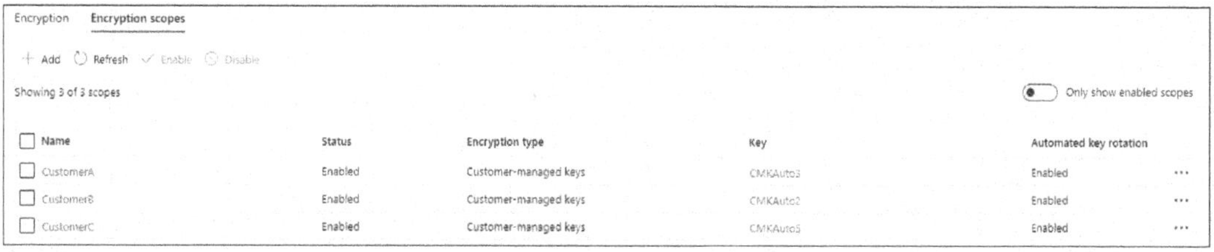

Name	Status	Encryption type	Key	Automated key rotation	
CustomerA	Enabled	Customer-managed keys	CMKAuto2	Enabled	...
CustomerB	Enabled	Customer-managed keys	CMKAuto2	Enabled	...
CustomerC	Enabled	Customer-managed keys	CMKAuto3	Enabled	...

FIGURE 10-22 Viewing current encryption scopes.

Next, you need to apply an encryption scope to a container.

4. Open the menu and click **Containers**.

5. Click **+Container** to add a new container.

6. On the **New Container** page, enter the following information:

   • **Name**   Type a name for the new container.

   • **Public Access Level**   Choose the level of access you want to allow, Public or Private.

> **Note** If you have an Azure Policy (see Chapter 7, "Governance") restricting public access, this option is grayed out, and Private is the only option.

7. Expand the **Advanced** section, and enter the following information:

   • **Encryption Scope**   Select the encryption scope you want to apply.

   • **Use This Encryption Scope for All Blobs in the Container**   Select this checkbox.

8. Select the Azure Storage account container and associate it with the encryption scope. Then click **Create**. (See Figure 10-23.)

> **Note** You can do this with as many containers as you want. You can also use different Key Vaults, not just different KEKs, for each scope.

FIGURE 10-23 Assigning an encryption scope to an Azure Storage account blob container.

Client-side Azure Storage account encryption

The Azure SDK includes classes that provide client-side encryption for all Azure Storage account types. It is recommended that you use v12.12 or later of the SDK, as it provides more flexibility than previous versions.

The following C# 10 and .NET 6 code shows the basics of how to use the blob upload-to-encrypt and download-to-decrypt functionality. This code interfaces with Key Vault.

```
using System;
using Azure.Identity;
using Azure.Security.KeyVault.Keys.Cryptography;
using Azure.Storage;
using Azure.Storage.Blobs;
using Azure.Storage.Blobs.Specialized;

var kvUri = "https://kv-entropy-tst.vault.azure.net/keys/BlobKey";
// might need to add the complete access token, too, to the URL
// it depends on how you secure access to the blobs
var storageConnStr = "BlobEndpoint=https://xyzzy.blob.core.windows.net/crypto?sp=<snip>";
var containerName = "crypto";
var encryptBlob = "encrypt.txt";
var localblobPath = @"C:\tempfiles\123.txt";
var localblobPath2 = @"C:\tempfiles\123-decrypt.txt";

var creds = new DefaultAzureCredential();
var cryptoClient = new CryptographyClient(new Uri(kvUri), creds);
var keyResolver = new KeyResolver(creds);

var encryptionOptions = new ClientSideEncryptionOptions(ClientSideEncryptionVersion.V2_0)
{
```

```
        KeyEncryptionKey = cryptoClient,
        KeyResolver = keyResolver,
        KeyWrapAlgorithm = "RSA-OAEP"
};

var options = new SpecializedBlobClientOptions()
{
    ClientSideEncryption = encryptionOptions
};

var blobContainerClient =
    new BlobServiceClient(storageConnStr, options).GetBlobContainerClient(containerName);
var blobClient = blobContainerClient.GetBlobClient(encryptBlob);

blobClient.Upload(localblobPath, true); // Encrypt on upload

blobClient.DownloadTo(localblobPath2);  // Decrypt on download
```

The SDK uses an RSA KEK in Key Vault to wrap a random symmetric AES 256-bit DEK, which is then used in conjunction with a unique IV to encrypt the blob. The IV, the wrapped symmetric key, and other data is added to a blob's metadata. This means every blob gets its own DEK and IV when the blob is uploaded.

Note You can read more about this here: https://azsec.tech/ci5. This page includes details about using .NET, Java, and Python.

Azure VM cryptography

VMs in Azure support three kinds of at-rest encryption:

- Server-side encryption

- Azure disk encryption

- Encryption at host

For the most part, these all mitigate the same threat—an offline attack against the VM or perhaps a failed hard drive that is not destroyed correctly. Both of these are highly unlikely, but most compliance programs still call for disk encryption of some kind. The following sections examine each of these at-rest encryption options in more detail.

Note Chapter 11, "Confidential computing," covers other aspects of VM cryptography.

Server-side encryption

VMs reside on managed disks. Managed disks use Azure Storage accounts. Azure Storage accounts use server-side encryption (SSE). Both operating system (OS) and data disks use managed disks, so both can use SSE. Temporary disks are not managed disks and are not encrypted by SSE unless you enable encryption at the host (covered later).

You don't directly set SSE on a VM's managed disk. Rather, you set the encryption policy on disk encryption sets. This is because you also use a managed identity on the disk encryption set and then grant the managed identity access to Key Vault. Using a disk encryption set simplifies key management because you can associate several VMs—let's say 100—to one disk encryption set and then one disk encryption set to a Key Vault. This is easier to manage than assigning 100 managed identities of different VMs to one Key Vault or managing 100 encryption policies. Also, when you bring a new VM online, you can associate it with a disk encryption set and thereby avoid having to worry about cryptographic policies.

Disk encryption sets use a managed identity to provide access to Key Vault keys. Again, granting disk encryption sets access rather than individual VMs is much more manageable! You can also use disk encryption sets with VM scale sets (VMSSs).

Here are a few more important points regarding SSE:

- SSE can use both PMKs managed by Azure or CMKs managed by you.

- SSE supports automatic KEK rotation. (This is explained a little later in this chapter.)

- SSE does not use the VM's virtual CPU (vCPU) to perform cryptographic operations.

Azure Disk Encryption

Azure Disk Encryption is not SSE. SSE applies to the Azure Storage account on which the VM's managed disk resides, while Azure Disk Encryption is applied through either BitLocker on Windows VMs or DM-Crypt on Linux VMs. Essentially, Azure Disk Encryption is part of the OS within the VM.

Azure Disk Encryption uses an agent that runs in the guest operating system to manage the underlying technology—BitLocker or DM-Crypt—as well as the key management of keys in Key Vault. One downside of Azure Disk Encryption is that the VM uses its vCPU to perform the cryptographic operations, so there is a small performance hit.

> **Note** Azure Disk Encryption and SSE with a CMK are mutually exclusive.

Encryption at host

Encryption at host (E@H) is the newest member of the VM encryption family. E@H is a VM feature that works with SSE so that the encryption keys used for SSE are used locally on the compute host (which is where the VM resides when it executes) to protect caches, local temporary disks, and the data before it is sent from the compute environment to storage. It effectively extends the protection from the Azure Storage account to all the other data related to the VM's disks. This means all disk data is protected at rest and while flowing between compute and storage. In short, E@H offers the benefits of Azure Disk Encryption and SSE *and* is the future of VM encryption on Azure.

> **Note** To be honest, *encryption at host* does not describe the technology very well. Encryption at host implies the defense is at the host VM, which is not accurate. A more apt term might be *end-to-end encryption*.

At the time of this writing, E@H is not enabled by default. However, you can use the following PowerShell command to enable it:

```
Register-AzProviderFeature -FeatureName "EncryptionAtHost" -ProviderNamespace "Microsoft.
Compute"
```

Not all types of VMs support E@H. To obtain a list of supported VMs, use the following PowerShell code, which looks for EncryptionAtHostSupported and ensures it is set to `true`:

```
$vmSizes=Get-AzComputeResourceSku |
        where{$_.ResourceType -eq 'virtualMachines' -and $_.Locations.Contains('southcentralus')}

foreach($vmSize in $vmSizes) {
    foreach($capability in $vmSize.capabilities) {
        if($capability.Name -eq 'EncryptionAtHostSupported' -and $capability.Value -eq 'true') {
            $vmSize
        }
    }
}
```

> **Note** You can read more about E@H here: https://azsec.tech/5be.

Azure SQL Database and Cosmos DB cryptography

These are both covered in detail in Chapter 13. Suffice it to say, both products provide robust volume encryption, as well as column encryption in SQL Server and property encryption in Cosmos DB.

Key rotation

Key rotation is one part of a key lifecycle. This lifecycle includes tasks like the following:

- Secure generation

- Onboarding

- Access control

- Storage

- Usage

- Monitoring and audit

- Rotation

- Secure destruction

Rotation means switching out one key for another. Many compliance programs require regular key rotation. For example, PCI DSS 4.0 requires the following:

> **3.7.4** Key management policies and procedures are implemented for cryptographic key changes for keys that have reached the end of their cryptoperiod, as defined by the associated application vendor or key owner, and based on industry best practices and guidelines, including the following: A defined cryptoperiod for each key type in use, and a process for key changes at the end of the defined cryptoperiod.

The words *key* and *rotation* belie a complex topic. First, what is meant by *key*, and how often should we rotate?

The keys you choose to rotate determine how often to rotate them. In many cases, key rotation involves KEKs, but there are other keys that could be rotated. Let's look at some:

- **KEKs** Rotating KEKs is easy. The process usually involves decrypting a relatively small DEK and then re-encrypting with a new key. It's quick and has low potential for failure.

- **DEKs** Rotating DEKs is complex if the target service has no built-in support for DEK rotation—and few products do. Rotating DEKs involves decrypting all the data at rest, which could be terabytes or perabytes in size, and then re-encrypting with a new DEK. This can take a significant amount of time and is costly. Also, it is risky if the rotation fails, not to mention it can lock data so it cannot be read or written to, thereby impeding the business. As noted in Chapter 13, "Database security," Azure SQL Database and SQL Server, when using Always Encrypted, support DEK rotation on live data.

- **Signing keys** These are usually coupled with a certificate that contains the public key associated with the private key used to perform signing operations. The public key is used to verify a signature; as long as the public key is available, it can do so. However, if the certificate is expired or revoked, the signature check is invalid. With all this said, rotating signing keys is low-risk and easy.

- **Authentication keys #1** This involves using private keys associated with X.509 certificates for authentication—for example, when using TLS to authenticate a server. Like signature keys, these are usually coupled with a certificate that includes expiry dates, so you know how to rotate the private keys or simply issue a new certificate. This is an easy process and is low-risk as long as you stay on top of the certificate lifecycle.

- **Authentication keys #2** This is another authentication scenario, but the keys are not cryptographic keys. Rather, they are access tokens, such as Shared Access Signatures (SAS) or Cosmos DB primary and secondary keys. Rotating these tokens is easy; you just need to make sure valid users have access to the rotated token. The main risk is if you rotate a key and it's not shared with the appropriate users, barring them access.

Azure Key Vault key rotation

Azure Key Vault has a feature to automatically rotate asymmetric RSA and ECC keys. You can set a policy on when to rotate them, and Key Vault does the rest. In the past, this required an Azure function listening for key expiration events raised by Key Vault through Event Grid and then the function writing an updated key to Key Vault. Because the rotated keys are asymmetric, they are usually KEKs, which for many corporate compliance programs is adequate.

> **Note** When a key is rotated, Key Vault raises an auditable event so you can verify the rotation.

Configuring the rotation policy requires the calling principal to have one of the following:

- Get Rotation Policy and Set Rotation Policy permission when using the vault access policy.

- Microsoft.KeyVault/vaults/keyrotationpolicies/* action when using the Azure RBAC model. Roles such as Key Vault administrator and Key Vault crypto officer can perform rotation operations.

Figure 10-24 shows the Rotation policy options in the Azure Portal.

> **Note** New permissions have been added to support rotation.

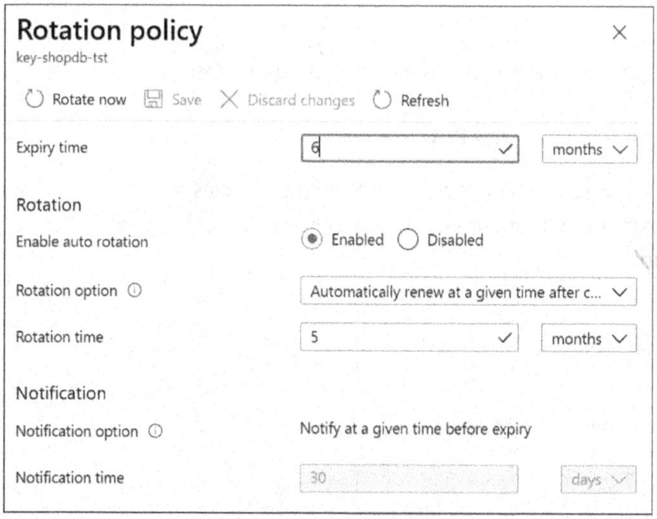

FIGURE 10-24 Azure Key Vault Automated Key Rotation in the Azure Portal.

You can test rotation by creating a key version in Key Vault and then using that key to encrypt an Azure Storage account (see Figure 10-25).

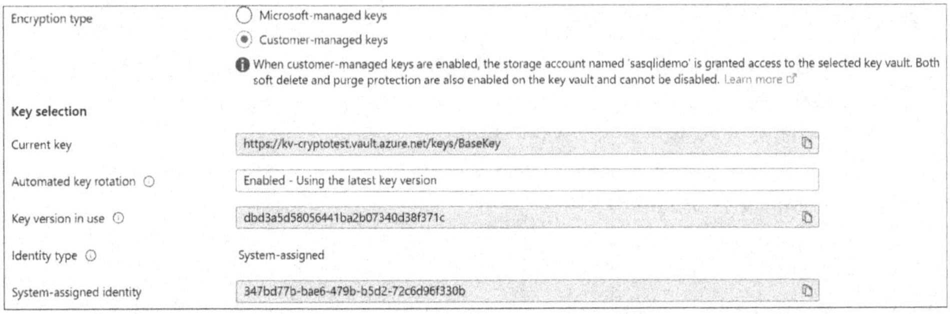

FIGURE 10-25 Storage account set to use automated key rotation. Notice that the key version number is the same as in Figure 10-26.

To create a new key version, follow these steps:

1. Click **Keys** in the left menu.

2. Select an existing key. This opens a screen like the one shown in Figure 10-26.

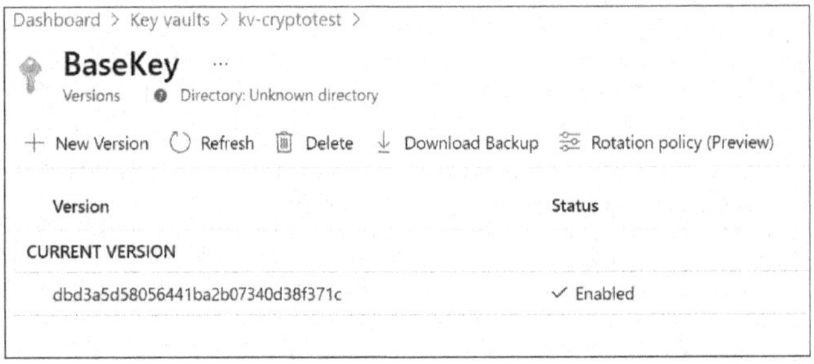

FIGURE 10-26 Creating a new key in Key Vault. Make a mental note of the version number.

3. Click the **Rotation Policy** button. Then click **Rotate Now**.

   As shown in Figure 10-27, a new key version is created. Note that it takes about 15–20 minutes for the Azure Storage account to poll for any key changes and swap out the current KEK for the newly rotated KEK. (See Figure 10-28.)

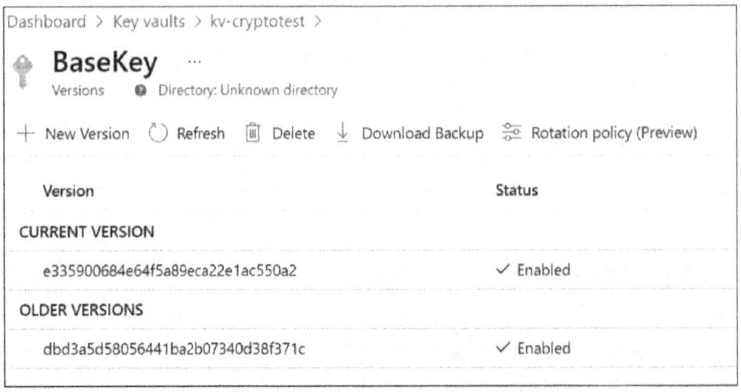

FIGURE 10-27 A new key version is created when you rotate the key.

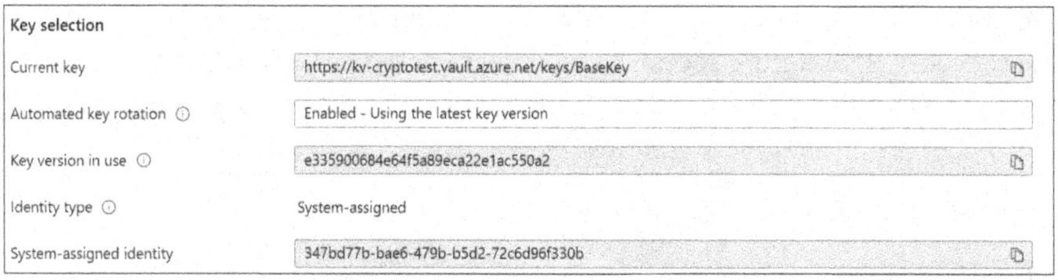

Key selection	
Current key	https://kv-cryptotest.vault.azure.net/keys/BaseKey
Automated key rotation ⓘ	Enabled - Using the latest key version
Key version in use ⓘ	e335900684e64f5a89eca22e1ac550a2
Identity type ⓘ	System-assigned
System-assigned identity	347bd77b-bae6-479b-b5d2-72c6d96f330b

FIGURE 10-28 The Azure Storage account has rotated its KEK; note the version number is the same as the current version number in Figure 10-27.

When you set a rotation policy, the rotation time is defined using ISO 8601 format durations, which always start with a P (for *period*). For example:

- P6M means rotate after 6 months.

- P90D means rotate after 90 days.

- P1Y means rotate after 1 year.

> **Note** You can read more about rotation here: https://azsec.tech/vw7.

Real-world experience: Using hashes in code

Sometimes developers want to use a hash function for noncryptographic purposes—for example, hash-bucket lookups and insertions. The problem with this is that many developers use older algorithms such as MD4 or MD5 because they are quick. However, their use will alert your security team because they are unsecure, and their use is often forbidden. For situations like this and to avoid drawing the ire of your security engineers, use something like CRC-64 instead—for example, the System.IO.Hashing package for .NET.

This ends the coverage on cryptography of data at rest. Let's now turn our attention to protecting data in transit.

Protecting data in transit

When we talk of data in transit, we mean network data, although some developers include interprocess communication (IPC) mechanisms, too, such as RPCs and pipes, even on the same host.

When looking at data flows in a threat model, these flows represent data in transit. You must pay close attention to data flows that cross trust boundaries, because these are the flows that are most at risk of an attack. For example, the data flow that goes from a web browser to a web server over the internet is clearly at risk. Because these cross-trust boundary data flows are at high risk, they need to include commensurate defenses.

Protections on data flows are cryptographic controls, and the most common protocol, by far, is Transport Layer Security (TLS). Secure Sockets Layer (SSL), invented by Netscape, is the precursor to TLS. You can think of TLS as the IETF-ratified version of SSL that has evolved over the years to be more flexible and secure.

The various versions of SSL and TLS over the years are as follows:

- SSL 2 (1995)

- SSL 3 (1996)

- TLS 1.0 (1999)

- TLS 1.1 (2006)

- TLS 1.2 (2008)

- TLS 1.3 (2018)

In 1995, Microsoft created a version of SSL named Private Communication Technology (PCT) that addressed serious security issues with SSL 2. Think of PCT as SSL 2.5. PCT worked only with Microsoft products. (For completeness, SSL 1 never saw public release.)

Real-world experience: SSL and TLS naming

Even though TLS is the name of the protocol we use today, it's not uncommon to still see references to SSL or SSL/TLS, even in Azure.

Important: Which versions of TLS to use

The only versions of TLS anyone should use today are TLS 1.2 and TLS 1.3. TLS 1.2 should be used with a reduced set of ciphersuites, however. More on this later.

When people think of TLS, they think of preventing eavesdropping on the network connection. However, TLS offers more than this, including the following features:

- **Server authentication**   TLS uses X.509 certificates to provide server authentication. Server authentication is critically important, because private communication means nothing if you don't know who you are talking to.

- **Channel encryption**   This is typically what we think of when considering TLS. With channel encryption, keys are exchanged or agreed upon by the client and the server, and they are used to encrypt the channel. A different key is used in each direction: client to server and server to client.

- **Channel tamper detection**   Like Always Encrypted, TLS provides tamper detection by using an HMAC. Note that TLS merely provides tamper *detection*; it does not prevent tampering.

- **Client authentication**   This is at the end of the list because it is optional. TLS client authentication is not often used because there are other viable options that perform the same function, such as OpenID Connect. A common authentication form factor for TLS client authentication is smart cards, where the private key resides in hardware.

The use of TLS varies across Azure services. Some require TLS 1.2 or higher; others allow you to select from TLS 1.0, TLS 1.1, or TLS 1.2. A few have the option of not using TLS. However, there is now a move across all services to allow only TLS 1.2 and above.

TLS and crypto agility

TLS is a great example of crypto agility. It allows a client and a server to negotiate to a mutually agreed-upon secure set of algorithms (called a *ciphersuite*, as you've learned). If the two parties cannot agree, then there is no communication. It is the server that determines which ciphersuite to use, but again, it must be a ciphersuite that the client supports.

Ciphersuites at the client and server should always be in preferred order, with the most-preferred ciphersuite at the top and least preferable at the bottom. For example, if the client has A, B, C, D, and E ciphersuites, and the server has B, D, F, G, and H, the server will select B because it is shared by both parties and is the highest in the list at the server.

Ciphersuites

Earlier you learned that if you want to use TLS 1.2, you should employ a smaller set of ciphersuites with no known security issues. So, here's a whirlwind tour of ciphersuites.

A *ciphersuite* is made up of a set of algorithms. The format of ciphersuites changed with TLS 1.3, so we'll go over TLS 1.2 ciphersuites first and then explain what changed. A TLS 1.2 ciphersuite has four parts:

- **Key exchange or agreement**   Examples include RSA, Diffie-Hellman, elliptic-curve Diffie Hellman, and pre-shared key.

- **Authentication**   Examples include RSA, DSA, and elliptic-curve DSA.

- **Symmetric cipher**   Examples include AES, 3DES, RC4, IDEA, DES, and ChaCha20. These also include cipher modes such as CBC and GCM.

- **Message integrity**   Examples include HMAC-SHA1, and HMAC-SHA2-256.

Here is an example of a TLS 1.2 ciphersuite:

```
TLS_ECDHE_ECDSA_WITH_AES_256_GCM_SHA384
```

This means:

- **TLS**   We hope this is obvious!

- **ECDHE**   Key agreement algorithm, elliptic-curve Diffie-Hellman Ephemeral.

- **ECDSA**   Signature used for authentication: elliptic-curve Digital Signature Algorithm.

- **AES_256_GCM**   Bulk encryption cipher: 256-bit AES in Galois/Counter Mode (GCM).

- **SHA384**   HMAC algorithm using SHA2-384.

Some ciphersuites are more secure than others. For example, the following is weak in several ways:

TLS_RSA_WITH_RC4_128_MD5

Here's why this ciphersuite is weak:

- RC4 is no longer allowed in TLS owing to real vulnerabilities. This is documented in RFC 7465.

- MD5 has known issues, too, such as practical collisions.

- RSA does not support perfect forward secrecy (PFS).

As you can imagine, no host should use this ciphersuite.

Key agreement vs. key exchange

You might have noticed references to *key agreement* and *key exchange*. Some ciphers perform key exchange and others key agreement, and they are not the same. In a key exchange, one side generates a key and sends it to the other. In a key agreement, the two sides arrive at a shared key that wasn't chosen by one of them. The end effect is often the same, but the words have clearly defined meanings, and the distinction is important when designing protocols that use these constructions. Cryptographers are finicky and care about this kind of subtle wording.

Perfect forward secrecy (PFS)

Perfect forward secrecy (PFS) can protect your data against a *future* (hence the word *forward*) compromise of the encryption key. For example, suppose you use TLS with RSA key exchange. An attacker could record all ciphertext packets on the wire and then next month compromise the server to extract the RSA private key. The attacker can then decrypt the key exchange key and recover all the plaintext of the session recorded a month ago. PFS protects you against this. TLS ciphersuites that use ECDHE for key agreement support PFS. The *perfect* part of this is that the server discards the local private key quickly.

A more formal description can be found in NIST SP 800-77 Revision 1, "Guide to IPsec VPNs: Perfect Forward Secrecy (PFS)":

"IPsec endpoints create session keys that are changed frequently, typically once an hour. Afterwards, the endpoints wipe the old session keys from volatile memory, and no entities are left with a copy of these private decryption keys. Since expired keys are not saved, any encrypted traffic monitored and stored cannot be decrypted at a later time by compromising an IPsec endpoint and obtaining the encryption/decryption keys belonging to past IPsec sessions.

"Normally, new keys are generated based on the generated shared secret of the original key exchange using a key derivation function (KDF). To guarantee that new key material has no relationship to the old key exchange, fresh session keys can, optionally, be generated by performing a new Diffie-Hellman (DH) key exchange instead of reusing the old key exchange's generated shared secret to generate new session keys. This method of using a fresh key exchange provides perfect forward secrecy (PFS)."

TLS 1.3 ciphersuites

TLS 1.3 does away with the key exchange/agreement and authentication components of the ciphersuite and just lists the algorithms used for symmetric encryption and the integrity/authentication algorithm. For example:

TLS_AES_256_GCM_SHA384

When using TLS 1.3, DHE and ECDHE are the most common key-exchange algorithms, but TLS 1.3 also supports pre-shared keys (PSK), too.

At the time we write this, TLS 1.3 is preferred over TLS 1.2, and all current TLS 1.3 ciphersuites are deemed secure. If you must use TLS 1.2, it's important to use a small set of secure ciphersuites.

TLS in Azure PaaS

As noted, TLS 1.3 support in Azure should be available by the end of 2022. Most PaaS services in Azure will allow you to choose a minimum TLS version, but some, like Azure Storage accounts, support only up to TLS 1.2. (See Figure 10-29.)

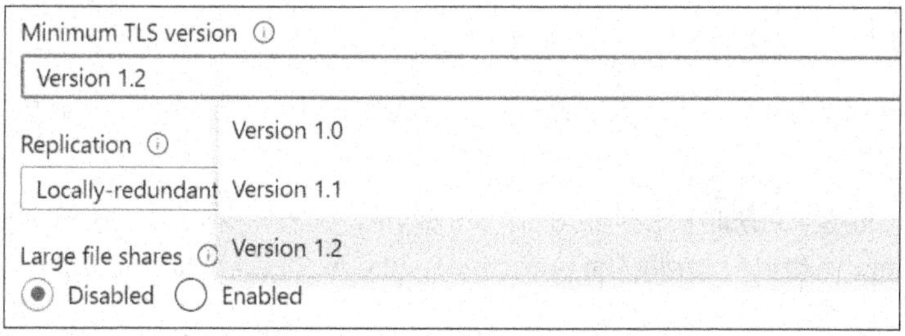

FIGURE 10-29 Setting the minimum TLS version on an Azure Storage account.

Many services allow you to use Azure Policy to enforce TLS 1.2. Again, here's an example for Azure Storage:

```
{
  "policyRule": {
    "if": {
      "allOf": [
        {
          "field": "type",
          "equals": "Microsoft.Storage/storageAccounts"
        },
        {
          "not": {
            "field": "Microsoft.Storage/storageAccounts/minimumTlsVersion",
            "equals": "TLS1_2"
          }
        }
      ]
    },
    "then": {
      "effect": "deny"
    }
  }
}
```

You can also use an Azure Resource Graph query to determine the minimum TLS version. Here's an example for Azure Storage accounts:

```
resources
| where type =~ 'Microsoft.Storage/storageAccounts'
| extend minTlsVersion = parse_json(properties).minimumTlsVersion
| project resourceGroup, name, minTlsVersion
```

Setting ciphersuites

Some services that front-end other PaaS services allow you to select not just the TLS protocol version, but also the ciphersuites. The following are the two most used services:

- **Azure Application Gateway**   A layer 7 cloud-native load balancer

- **Azure API Management**   A service that allows you to control and secure APIs such as function apps

Figure 10-30 shows the Create SSL Profile page for Azure Application Gateway, where you can set a TLS policy (referred to as *SSL* in the Azure Portal). The policy is a minimum TLS version and a configurable set of ciphersuites.

Azure API Management also supports the configuration of TLS protocol versions and ciphersuites, as shown in Figures 10-31 and 10-32.

FIGURE 10-30 Defining an SSL/TLS policy in Azure Application Gateway.

FIGURE 10-31 Configuring SSL/TLS protocol versions in Azure API Management.

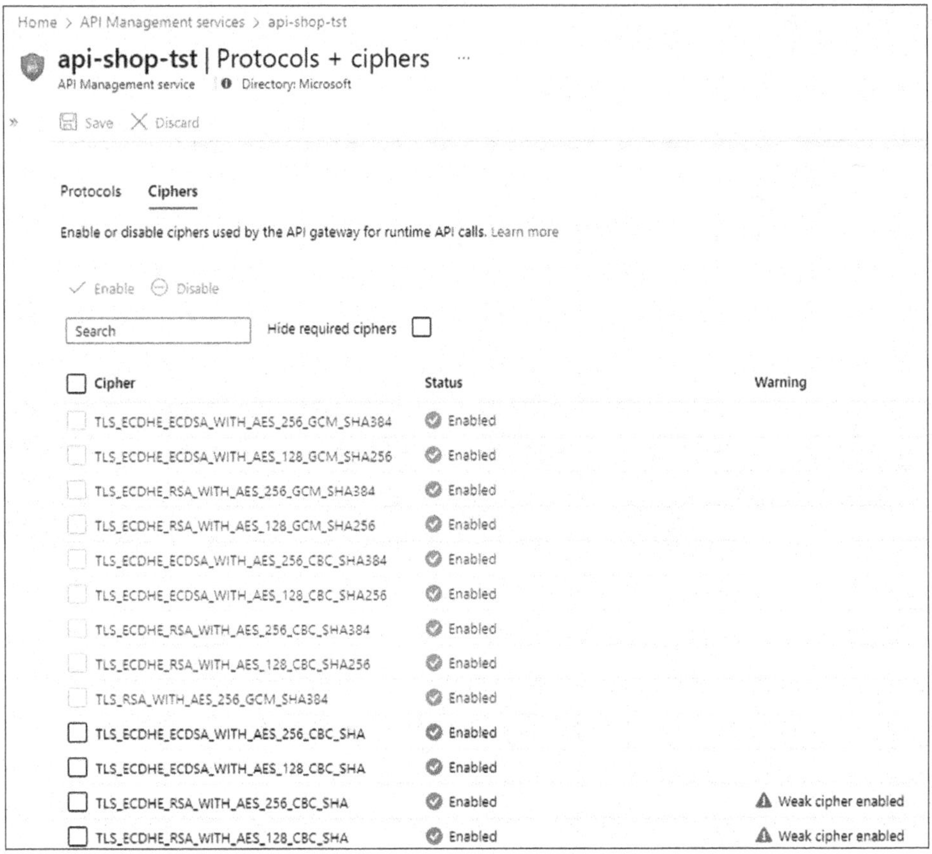

api-shop-tst | Protocols + ciphers ···
API Management service   ❶ Directory: Microsoft

»   🖫 Save ✕ Discard

Protocols   **Ciphers**

Enable or disable ciphers used by the API gateway for runtime API calls. Learn more

✓ Enable ⊖ Disable

| Search | | Hide required ciphers ☐ |

☐ Cipher	Status	Warning
☐ TLS_ECDHE_ECDSA_WITH_AES_256_GCM_SHA384	✅ Enabled	
☐ TLS_ECDHE_ECDSA_WITH_AES_128_GCM_SHA256	✅ Enabled	
☐ TLS_ECDHE_RSA_WITH_AES_256_GCM_SHA384	✅ Enabled	
☐ TLS_ECDHE_RSA_WITH_AES_128_GCM_SHA256	✅ Enabled	
☐ TLS_ECDHE_ECDSA_WITH_AES_256_CBC_SHA384	✅ Enabled	
☐ TLS_ECDHE_ECDSA_WITH_AES_128_CBC_SHA256	✅ Enabled	
☐ TLS_ECDHE_RSA_WITH_AES_256_CBC_SHA384	✅ Enabled	
☐ TLS_ECDHE_RSA_WITH_AES_128_CBC_SHA256	✅ Enabled	
☐ TLS_RSA_WITH_AES_256_GCM_SHA384	✅ Enabled	
☐ TLS_ECDHE_ECDSA_WITH_AES_256_CBC_SHA	✅ Enabled	
☐ TLS_ECDHE_ECDSA_WITH_AES_128_CBC_SHA	✅ Enabled	
☐ TLS_ECDHE_RSA_WITH_AES_256_CBC_SHA	✅ Enabled	⚠ Weak cipher enabled
☐ TLS_ECDHE_RSA_WITH_AES_128_CBC_SHA	✅ Enabled	⚠ Weak cipher enabled

FIGURE 10-32 Configuring TLS ciphersuites in Azure API Management Service.

Note that in Figures 10-31 and 10-32, the ciphersuites are in preferred order, with the most preferable at the top and the least preferable at the bottom. If you don't want to support a ciphersuite, do not include it in the list.

Azure Front Door presently supports the selection of only TLS 1.0, 1.1, or 1.2. If you select TLS 1.2, Azure Front Door supports only the following ciphersuites:

- TLS_ECDHE_RSA_WITH_AES_256_GCM_SHA384

- TLS_ECDHE_RSA_WITH_AES_128_GCM_SHA256

- TLS_DHE_RSA_WITH_AES_256_GCM_SHA384

- TLS_DHE_RSA_WITH_AES_128_GCM_SHA256

NIST SP 800-52r2 guidelines

NIST SP 800-52r2, "Guidelines for the Selection, Configuration, and Use of Transport Layer Security (TLS) Implementations" (https://azsec.tech/kmq), describes, among other things, TLS 1.2–preferred ciphersuites. Section 3.3.1.1, "Cipher Suites for TLS 1.2 and Earlier Versions," states the following preferences when selecting ciphersuites:

> "Prefer ephemeral keys over static keys (i.e., prefer DHE over DH, and prefer ECDHE over ECDH). Ephemeral keys provide perfect forward secrecy.

> "Prefer GCM or CCM modes over CBC mode. The use of an authenticated encryption mode prevents several attacks (see Section 3.3.2 for more information). Note that these are not available in versions prior to TLS 1.2.

> "Prefer CCM over CCM_8. The latter contains a shorter authentication tag, which provides a lower authentication strength."

This means that for most VMs, the following set of ciphersuites is an aggressive set of strong ciphersuites:

- TLS_ECDHE_ECDSA_WITH_AES_256_GCM_SHA384

- TLS_ECDHE_ECDSA_WITH_AES_128_GCM_SHA256

- TLS_ECDHE_RSA_WITH_AES_256_GCM_SHA384

- TLS_ECDHE_RSA_WITH_AES_128_GCM_SHA256

This list is secure, but it might cause compatibility issues, so be careful!

Real-world experience: Ciphersuites

Be careful when you reduce your set of ciphersuites on your server platform. Being overly aggressive in the name of security might cause connection errors. If that happens, be prepared to roll back to a less secure set of ciphersuites until you work out what the issue is.

Real-world experience: Corporate policy

You will need to determine what constitutes an appropriate set of ciphersuites for your business. It should be a secure subset that does not overly affect application compatibility. https://ciphersuite.info/ is a great resource to understand the characteristics of the various ciphersuites available today.

TLS in Azure IaaS

VMs running Linux and Windows can have services that support TLS. Because they are complete operating systems, you have total control over the TLS policy.

TLS in Linux VMs

Many applications in Linux use OpenSSL or a derivative to provide TLS support, and most will have their own TLS configuration. For example, nginx sets the configuration in /etc/nginx/nginx.conf or the /etc/nginx/vhosts.h/*site-name*, where *site-name* is the name of the virtual host. The file looks like this:

```
server {
    listen 443 ssl http2;
    ssl_protocols TLSv1.2 TLSv1.3
    ssl_ciphers ECDHE-ECDSA-AES128-GCM-SHA256:ECDHE-RSA-AES128-GCM-SHA256:ECDHE-ECDSA-AES256-
GCM-SHA384:ECDHE-RSA-AES256-GCM-SHA384:ECDHE-ECDSA-CHACHA20-POLY1305:ECDHE-RSA-CHACHA20-
POLY1305:DHE-RSA-AES128-GCM-SHA256;
    ## More config ##
}
```

Another example is Apache, which uses the configuration in httpd.conf, which looks like this:

```
SSLProtocol -all +TLSv1.2 +TLSv1.3

SSLCipherSuite EECDH+AESGCM:EDH+AESGCM:AES256+EECDH:ECDHE-RSA-AES128-SHA:DHE-RSA-AES128-GCM-
SHA256:AES256+EDH:ECDHE-RSA-AES256-GCM-SHA384:ECDHE-RSA-AES128-GCM-SHA256:DHE-RSA-AES256-GCM-
SHA384:ECDHE-RSA-AES256-SHA384:ECDHE-RSA-AES128-SHA256:ECDHE-RSA-AES256-SHA:DHE-RSA-AES256-
SHA256:DHE-RSA-AES128-SHA256:DHE-RSA-AES256-SHA:DHE-RSA-AES128-SHA:ECDHE-RSA-DES-CBC3-SHA:EDH-
RSA-DES-CBC3-SHA:AES256-GCM-SHA384:AES128-GCM-SHA256:AES256-SHA256:AES128-SHA256:AES256-SH-
A:AES128-SHA:DES-CBC3-SHA:HIGH:!aNULL:!eNULL:!EXPORT:!DES:!MD5:!PSK:!RC4
```

Notice the use of ! at the end. This ensures there are no ciphersuites using NULL, DES, MD5, and so on. EXPORT was a set of ciphersuites during the "old days" when the United States would not allow export of strong cryptography, which was in part defined as any symmetric cipher with a key size over 40 bits. By today's standards, 40-bit keys are pathetic in strength, and brute-force attacks against 40-bit keys, where you guess every key value from zero to 2^40, can be done rapidly. Remember, every time you add a bit to a symmetric key length, you double the overall key space. By the way, 2^40 is 1,099,511,627,776, which is just over one trillion. Like we said, that's pathetic, especially when you consider a 128-bit symmetric key is 2^128, which equals 340,282,366,920,938,463,463,374,607,431,768, 211,456, or 340 undecillion, 282 decillion, 366 nonillion, 920 octillion, 938 septillion, 463 sextillion, 463 quintillion, 374 quadrillion, 607 trillion, 431 billion, 768 million, 211 thousand, and 456.

Cost of breaking keys and passwords

Brute-force attacks against keys and complex passwords cost a lot of money. You need incredible amounts of expensive massively parallel compute power to attack a key or password as quickly as possible. But over the last decade, the economics have changed dramatically. There is no longer a need to spend millions of dollars on such hardware because now you can rent it. How? It's called the cloud!

At the time of this writing, you can spin up an NC4as T4 v3 series VM (https://azsec.tech/8o8) in Azure, which has four NVIDIA T4 GPUs, each with 2,560 CUDA-capable cores. You can then write (or download) C++ key-cracking code that uses CUDA or OpenMP to run the code on all 10,240 GPU hardware threads. The cost? About $230 a month, if you reserve one year in the East US. The prices change often, so please verify the price in your region of choice.

Finally, when using Node.js (this applies to Windows, too), you can use the `-tls-cipher-list` argument when starting node. Then, once in node, you can dump the default ciphersuites with the following command:

```
node -p crypto.constants.defaultCoreCipherList
```

This outputs something like this:

```
TLS_AES_256_GCM_SHA384:TLS_CHACHA20_POLY1305_SHA256:TLS_AES_128_GCM_SHA256:ECDHE-RSA-AES128-
GCM-SHA256:ECDHE-ECDSA-AES128-GCM-SHA256:ECDHE-RSA-AES256-GCM-SHA384:ECDHE-ECDSA-AES256-GCM-
SHA384:DHE-RSA-AES128-GCM-SHA256:ECDHE-RSA-AES128-SHA256:DHE-RSA-AES128-SHA256:ECDHE-RSA-AES256-
SHA384:DHE-RSA-AES256-SHA384:ECDHE-RSA-AES256-SHA256:DHE-RSA-AES256-SHA256: HIGH:!aNULL:!eNULL:!
EXPORT:!DES:!RC4:!MD5:!PSK:!SRP:!CAMELLIA
```

Mozilla offers an excellent web-based tool to help you configure the TLS settings for various tools such as Tomcat, Redis Cache, MySQL, and more. The tool is the Mozilla SSL Configuration Generator (see Figure 10-33) and can be found here: https://ssl-config.mozilla.org/.

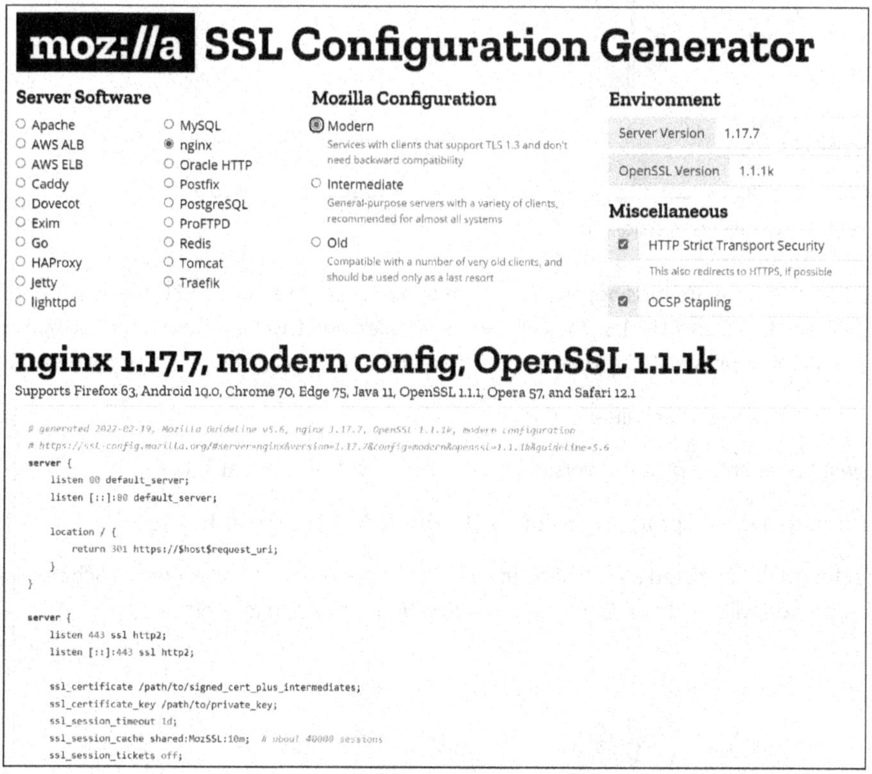

FIGURE 10-33 Using the Mozilla SSL Configuration tool to create an HTTPS configuration file for nginx.

TLS in Windows VMs

Versions of Windows since Windows 10 and Windows Server 2019 support TLS 1.3. Windows takes a different approach from Linux, however; rather than leaving the TLS configuration to each application, it applies a systemwide policy that every application inherits. The Security Channel (Schannel) security package provides TLS support to the operating system; as shown in Figure 10-34, you can set the TLS configuration in the registry at HKEY_LOCAL_MACHINE\SYSTEM\CurrentControlSet\Control\Security-Providers\SCHANNEL.

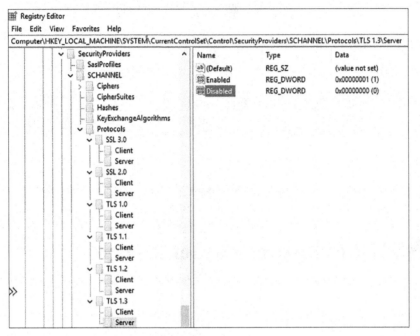

FIGURE 10-34 Setting TLS protocol versions in Windows.

By default, these settings are missing, and you need to add them. We have a REG file at our book GitHub that enables TLS 1.2 and TLS 1.3. You can set the Enabled and Disabled option for each protocol version and whether it applies to TLS servers (web servers) or TLS clients (browsers). Follow these rules:

- Make the client and server values the same.

- If you want to enable a protocol version, set Enabled to 1 and Disabled to 0.

- If you want to disable a protocol version, set Enabled to 0 and Disabled to 1.

You must set both the Enabled and Disabled values because of the way the internal Schannel APIs work. Additionally, you will need to reboot the Windows VM for these to take effect.

After you have done this, you can set the ciphersuites. There are two ways to do this in Windows:

- **The registry**   This has the drawback of requiring a reboot if you make a small change.

- **PowerShell cmdlets**   These can be run, and they do *not* require a reboot to take effect.

Before you go any further, be sure to delete this registry setting, if it's there:

```
HKEY_LOCAL_MACHINE\SOFTWARE\Policies\Microsoft\Cryptography\Configuration\SSL\00010002
```

You can then obtain a list of ciphersuites by typing the following command:

```
Get-TlsCiphersuite
```

This dumps all the currently enabled ciphersuites. The list by default is long, so let's prune it by using `Disable-TlsCiphersuite`. The following code will do the work for you:

```
Set-strictmode -Version latest

$cs = Get-TlsCipherSuite
$csOk = 'TLS_AES_256_GCM_SHA384',
        'TLS_AES_128_GCM_SHA256',
        'TLS_ECDHE_ECDSA_WITH_AES_256_GCM_SHA384',
        'TLS_ECDHE_ECDSA_WITH_AES_128_GCM_SHA256',
        'TLS_ECDHE_RSA_WITH_AES_256_GCM_SHA384',
        'TLS_ECDHE_RSA_WITH_AES_128_GCM_SHA256'

foreach ($c in $cs) {

    if ($csOk.Contains($c.Name)) {
        $c.Name + ' Valid - Enable'
        Enable-TlsCiphersuite -Name $c.Name
    } else {
        $c.Name + ' Disable'
        try {
            Disable-TlsCiphersuite -Name $c.Name
        } catch {
            $PSItem.Exception.Message
        }
    }
}
```

As noted, this is an aggressive list, so you might need to add some ciphersuites back in. For a more extensive blog post on this topic written by one of the authors of this book, see https://azsec.tech/9o6.

A note about RSA and ECDSA

You might notice that the preceding list has ciphersuites that include _RSA_ or _ECDSA_. This is the algorithm used when verifying the authenticity of the host you connect to. The algorithm used to sign the host's certificate must be acceptable in your list of ciphersuites. For example, if you remove all the _RSA_ ciphersuites and the signature used to sign the host's certificate is ECDSA, then the communication will fail.

A common TLS mistake in .NET code

We see this a lot: developers forcing a TLS version in the code. The problem with this is that developers often set it to TLS 1.2, which means your code cannot use TLS 1.3. So, rather than using code like this that enforces TLS 1.1 or TLS 1.2 only:

```
ServicePointManager.SecurityProtocol = SecurityProtocolType.Tls11 | SecurityProtocolType.Tls12;
```

use this:

```
ServicePointManager.SecurityProtocol = SecurityProtocolType.SystemDefault;
```

This offloads the TLS protocol selection to the operating system. In this way, you can change the policy without changing your code.

Testing TLS

At some point, you need to verify that the TLS configuration is correct rather than merely hoping it is. One way to do this is to use OpenSSL as a client. First, you need to have a service running on the host, such as IIS for Windows, Apache, or nginx, or an Azure front end like API Management. Next, you can run OpenSSL against the IP address or DNS name and the TLS port, such as 443 for HTTPS.

The following example tests whether TLS 1.2 and TLS 1.3 are supported:

```
Openssl s_client -connect <ip>:443 -tls1_2
openssl s_client -connect <ip>:443 -tls1_3
```

This example tests TLS 1.2 and TLS 1.3 with various ciphersuites:

```
Openssl s_client -connect <ip>:443 -ciphersuites 'TLS_AES_256_GCM_SHA384' -tls1_3
openssl s_client -connect <ip>:443 -ciphersuites 'TLS_AES_128_GCM_SHA256' -tls1_3
openssl s_client -connect <ip>:443 -ciphersuites 'TLS_ECDHE_ECDSA_WITH_AES_256_GCM_SHA384'
-tls1_2
openssl s_client -connect <ip>:443 -ciphersuites 'TLS_ECDHE_ECDSA_WITH_AES_128_GCM_SHA256'
-tls1_2
```

The following examples should all fail because they attempt to use TLS 1.0 or TLS 1.1, or TLS 1.2 with weak ciphersuites, depending on your configuration:

```
Openssl s_client -connect <ip>:443 -tls1_0
openssl s_client -connect <ip>:443 -tls1_1
openssl s_client -connect <ip>:443 -ciphersuites 'TLS_RSA_WITH_AES_256_CBC_SHA' -tls1_2
openssl s_client -connect <ip>:443 -ciphersuites 'TLS_RSA_WITH_AES_128_GCM_SHA256' -tls1_2
openssl s_client -connect <ip>:443 -ciphersuites 'TLS_RSA_WITH_3DES_EDE_CBC_SHA' -tls1_2
```

Finally, you can display OpenSSL's supported ciphersuite list by using the following command:

```
openssl ciphers -v
```

Debugging TLS errors

Sometimes failures happen, and you might need to understand why a TLS connection has failed. On Windows, you can use Schannel logging to find out why a connection failed. The article at https://

azsec.tech/4vv explains how to set Schannel logging and where to find the log data. Set the EventLogging value to 7 to obtain a list of all failures and successes.

Using Wireshark

If all else fails, you can use a network sniffing tool like Wireshark. We don't want to give a Wireshark tutorial, but Figure 10-35 shows what a successful connection looks like. Packet 47 shows the server completing the TLS handshake with the Server Hello, Certificate, Server Key Exchange, and Server Hello Done messages. Further down the packet, you can see the server agreeing to a cipher-suite. This is a success.

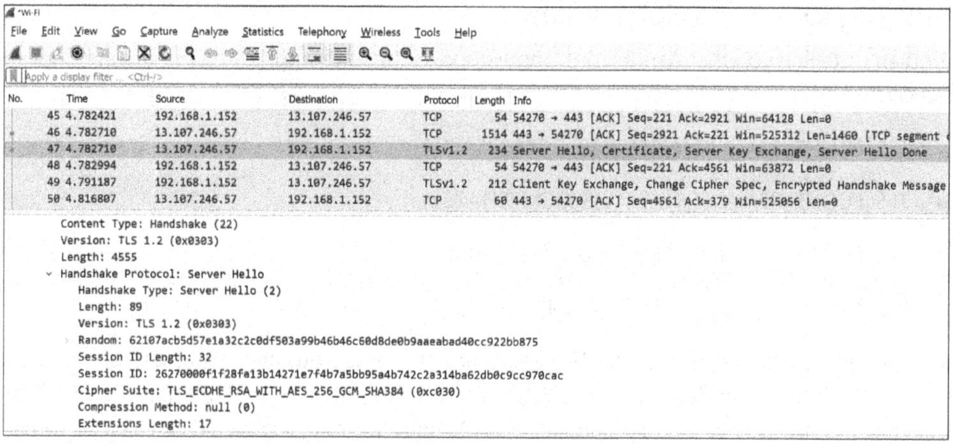

FIGURE 10-35 Using Wireshark to view a successful TLS 1.2 connection.

Figure 10-36 shows a failure. The client has attempted to connect with TLS 1.2, which is supported by the server, but the client tried to use a ciphersuite the server does not support. You can see the client making the initial TLS connection in packet 15—the Client Hello—and its attempt to use TLS_AES_128_CCM_SHA256, which is unsupported by the server (in this case an Azure Front Door instance). The server rejects the connection, and there are no other TLS-related packets.

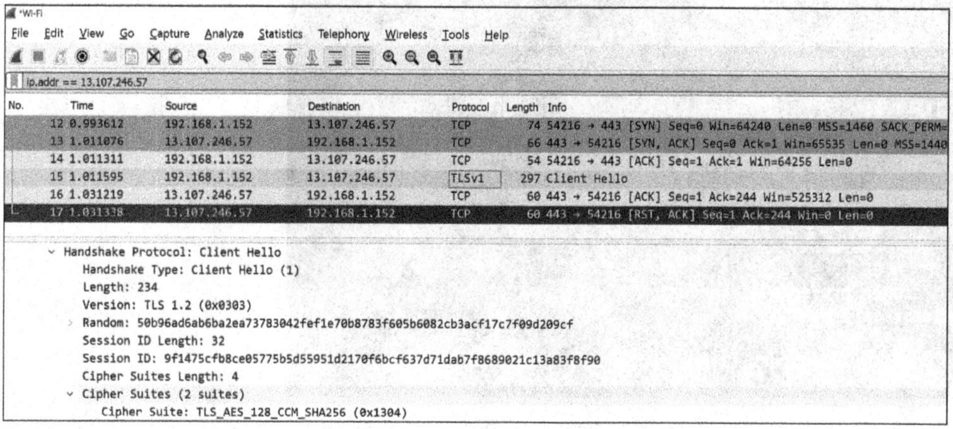

FIGURE 10-36 An attempted TLS connection from a client. You can see the Client Hello, but the server does not support the ciphersuite.

The following is the command sent to the server that caused the Wireshark output in Figure 10-36:

```
Openssl s_client -connect shopapp.z01.azurefd.net:443 -tls1_3 -ciphersuites TLS_AES_128_CCM_
SHA256
```

> **Note** If you want to learn more about using OpenSSL to troubleshoot TLS connections, Feisty Duck has the OpenSSL Cookbook (https://azsec.tech/bme), which is well worth the read.

Identifying supported ciphersuites

Other than us telling you that Azure Front Door supports the following TLS 1.2 ciphersuites, how do you *really* know?

- TLS_ECDHE_RSA_WITH_AES_256_GCM_SHA384

- TLS_ECDHE_RSA_WITH_AES_128_GCM_SHA256

- TLS_DHE_RSA_WITH_AES_256_GCM_SHA384

- TLS_DHE_RSA_WITH_AES_128_GCM_SHA256

If the server in question has a public IP address or DNS name, you can use the SSL Server Test page from Qualys at https://www.ssllabs.com/ssltest/. You can also use nmap for public and private IP addresses. nmap started life as a port scanner and an OS fingerprinting tool, but it can also do some TLS analysis, too. For example, try using the following command:

```
nmap -script ssl-enum-ciphers -p 443 <ip>
```

Figure 10-37 shows the output you can expect.

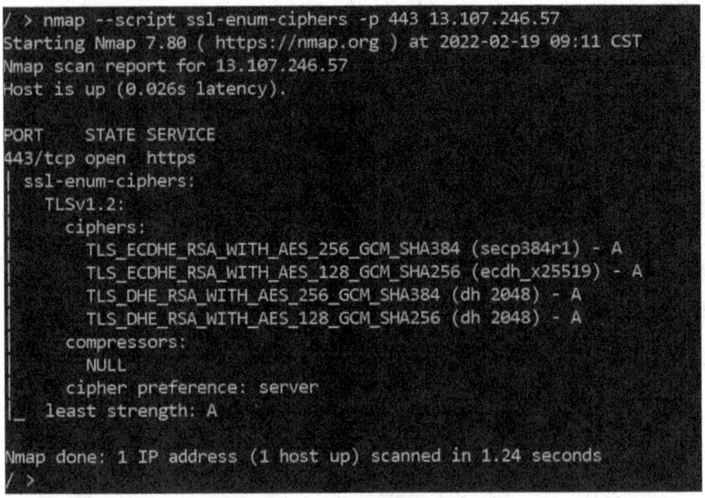

FIGURE 10-37 Using nmap to determine a server's supported ciphersuites.

Unsecure use of SSH

SSH is in some ways similar to TLS, in that it provides server authentication as well as channel protections. The client connects to the server using SSH and then enters its credentials, which is usually a username and password or a key. One of the issues with SSH, however, is the initial server authentication step. More specifically, initial server authentication is weak because it relies on the user accepting a public key or a public key thumbprint to authenticate the server. There is no way to know if the ECDSA key fingerprint shown here is valid or not; most people just type yes, and the server is trusted.

```
ssh azureuser@40.xxx.xxx.xxx
The authenticity of host '40.xxx.xxx.xxx (40.xxx.xxx.xxx)' can't be established.
ECDSA key fingerprint is SHA256:XKQ9gwKCfF2dJxfTmen1eTEg7lmxeZlr5BvsrhAOAoo.
Are you sure you want to continue connecting (yes/no/[fingerprint])?
```

NIST covers this issue (among other things) at the end of section 3.3 in NIST IR 7966, "Security of Interactive and Automated Access Management Using Secure Shell (SSH)." This document is available here: https://azsec.tech/y7u.

Summary

Correctly designed cryptographic solutions offer unrivaled last-line-of-defense compensating controls, but key management and secure, audited access to cryptographic keys are critical. Key Vault is at the heart of any secure Azure solution, and an understanding of how to use the service securely is paramount. Cryptography is also an important tool in the zero-trust, assume-breach toolkit.

You should not write your own crypto code, but if you must, make it crypto-agile so you can move on to new algorithms as weaknesses are found.

Use TLS 1.3 where possible, but TLS 1.2 with a restricted set of ciphersuites is also valid to secure your network traffic.

## CHAPTER 11

Confidential computing

After completing this chapter, you will be able to:

- Grasp the goals of confidential computing.

- Understand the core elements of confidential computing.

- Identify the various Azure services that embrace confidential computing.

What is confidential computing?

Confidential computing is critically important to Azure. It enables highly secure workloads that protect against rogue administrators and even rogue cloud operators. Confidential computing supports highly protected trust boundaries, making it a cornerstone of many zero-trust designs. But what is confidential computing? The Confidential Computing Consortium defines it as "the protection of data in use by performing computation in a hardware-based trusted execution environment."

Confidential computing requires support from specialized hardware, most notably processors that support strong isolation and other protections. Note that we purposefully use the term *processors* rather than CPUs because confidential computing can extend to other devices, such as GPUs and network cards.

At the lowest level, Azure offers virtual machines (VMs) and other products that support specialized processors from AMD, Arm, and Intel. These provide isolation all the way down the processor. Above the processors are IaaS VMs that expose the capabilities of the processors below them.

Azure offers many PaaS services that execute within the confines of VMs that run processors that support confidential computing. Examples include Azure SQL Database, Azure Kubernetes Service, Azure Confidential Ledger, and more. All these take advantage of specialized capabilities in the Intel and AMD processors. Azure Container Instance and Azure Kubernetes Service also support confidential containers.

The topic of confidential computing can quickly become incredibly complex—so much so that this topic could easily fill a book. Indeed, the solutions now enabled by confidential computing were unimaginable a decade ago! However, this chapter merely provides an overview of the topic, so you will have some idea of what confidential computing services are available in Azure and how you might use them in your secure designs. Before we get started, here are some relevant terms you will need to understand:

- **Hardware root of trust**   This ensures data is protected using silicon. Trust is rooted to the hardware manufacturer; not even Microsoft operators can modify the hardware configuration.

- **Remote attestation** This allows customers to directly verify workloads are running on approved hardware and software and ensures they follow the security policy before accessing data or performing work.

- **Trusted launch** This guarantees that VMs boot with customer-verifiable and authorized software. It uses Secure Boot and Virtual Trusted Platform Module (vTPM) technology to defend against rootkits, bootkits, and malicious firmware.

- **Memory isolation and encryption** This certifies that data is protected while processing using hardware-based cryptography. Azure uses CPUs that offer memory isolation by VM, container, and application.

- **Secure key management** This ensures keys stay encrypted during their lifetime and are released only as authorized code in wrapped form.

New to confidential computing?

If you are completely new to confidential computing, here are a few resources to get you grounded:

- **Azure Confidential Computing** In this short video—it is less than two minutes long—Microsoft CEO Satya Nadella explains the overarching goals of confidential computing. You can watch it here: https://azsec.tech/cco. We strongly urge you to watch this before you read the rest of this chapter.

- **Common Terminology for Confidential Computing** This page on the Confidential Computing Consortium website provides clear definitions of key terms. This is helpful, as some of the wording can be subtle. It is available here: https://azsec.tech/term. For more general information about the Confidential Computing Consortium, see https://confidentialcomputing.io.

- **Confidential Computing: Hardware-Based Trusted Execution for Applications and Data** This is a whitepaper published by the Confidential Computing Consortium, of which Microsoft is a founding member. You can read it at https://azsec.tech/ccc, **and it will give you a better understanding of the technology and the problems it solves.**

Real-world experience: Adopting confidential computing

Not every solution deployed on Azure requires confidential computing, but some do, such as those in regulated industries such as healthcare, finance, military, and energy. We have found that many leading-edge customers in these sectors support a small group of senior architects and developers who focus on Azure confidential computing services to see where each one might fit in their environment and to make recommendations about which services to use in which situations. This is a disciplined approach that makes better use of people's skills and is more time- and cost-effective than leaving it up to individual development teams.

Confidential computing processors

At the root of confidential computing are processors that have extra instructions and functionality to support confidential computing. The three currently supported CPUs in Azure are as follows:

- Intel processors that support Software Guard Extensions (SGX)

- AMD processors that support Secure Encrypted Virtualization-Secure Nested Paging (SEV-SNP)

- Arm processors that support TrustZone

Let's take a quick look at each in a little more detail.

Intel Software Guard Extensions

Azure VMs in the DC-series support Intel's Software Guard Extensions (SGX). SGX is a security technology that creates one or more trusted execution environments (TEEs), which Intel calls *enclaves*. Enclaves are isolated and encrypted protected memory whose isolation control, cryptographic keys, and security boundary are managed by the CPU. This is important, because you want security defenses like these as low as possible in the stack, and for the root of trust to be immutable such that these defenses cannot be compromised by malware or even a bad actor who works at a cloud service provider (CSP).

From the outset, SGX was designed for purpose-built applications that can be refactored or built from the ground up to run in this restricted environment. However, there are now library OS (LibOS) solutions that run the most sensitive parts of their workloads in an SGX enclave and require little or no code changes to do so.

Learn more about SGX

For more information about SGX, check out these resources:

- **Enhanced Security Features for Confidential Computing**   This Intel product brief provides a technical overview of how SGX enclaves work. It is available here: https://azsec.tech/x4q.

- **Azure Confidential Computing Partner Webinar Series**   This page, located at https://azsec.tech/wme, contains links to webinars from Intel SGX partners and demos of third-party solutions.

- **Azure – Protect Your Data with Azure Confidential Computing**   This article offers a gentle introduction to Open Enclave C development. You can find it here: https://azsec.tech/w1c.

Simply deploying a DC-series VM (series 2 and 3) offers no security benefit until you load some trusted code into the TEE. This requires that you either write some code or use some code that comes as part of a product. For example, under the hood, Azure SQL Database uses these VM types when the Always Encrypted with Secure Enclaves setting is applied. (This is covered in Chapter 13, "Database security.") Azure SQL Database loads part of the query engine into the TEE, where the query engine decrypts and analyzes data. The only time data is in plaintext is in the TEE; outside the TEE—both on disk and when the query results are sent to a client for client-side decryption—only ciphertext is used.

There are two confidential computing models that use a TEE. The first is a per-process TEE, which is how Azure SQL Database works when using Always Encrypted with Secure Enclaves. The second is an app-level TEE, which is used by tools like Enarx and Occlum.

> **Tip** For more information on these two confidential computing models, see https://azsec.tech/uwz. In addition, you can read more about Enarx and Occlum here: https://azsec.tech/tai.

The Signal Messenger app is a great example of effective use of SGX using the first model. To quote Signal's website (https://signal.org/):

"State-of-the-art end-to-end encryption (powered by the open source Signal Protocol) keeps your conversations secure. We can't read your messages or listen to your calls, and no one else can either. Privacy isn't an optional mode—it's just the way that Signal works. Every message, every call, every time."

The Signal server runs on Azure and parts of its internal system run on VMs that support SGX. So, when Signal says, "We can't read your messages or listen to your calls," this is how they do it. It is a great example of plausible deniability. You can read a case study on Microsoft's website about Signal's use of SGX here: https://azsec.tech/sig.

TEE code is frequently written in C and C++. This is because the runtime dependencies tend to be smaller for C and C++, and you always want to run the smallest amount of code possible in secured environments. These small, highly secure environments are often referred to as *trusted computing bases* (TCBs). Use of the Rust programming language (https://www.rust-lang.org/) is growing in popularity, however, because of its correctness and safety guarantees.

If you want to write your own code that executes in a TEE, you can use an SDK. The recommended approach is to use the Open Enclave SDK because it is hardware agnostic. You can learn more at https://openenclave.io/sdk/.

Malware in TEEs

Just because code runs in a TEE does not mean it is defect-free, nor does it mean it is invulnerable to malware. If you are creating your own code, you must perform all the appropriate due diligence to make sure the binary is secure and not infected with malware.

AMD Secure Encrypted Virtualization-Secure Nested Paging

AMD Secure Encrypted Virtualization-Secure Nested Paging (SEV-SNP) feature bears no resemblance to Intel's SGX. Although they both exist under the banner of Azure confidential computing, they solve hardware-isolation problems differently.

When you use AMD SEV-SNP, the entire VM image is protected. So, everything in the VM is encrypted and isolated down to the CPU level. This is different from SGX because you need not create custom code or modify existing code to take advantage of the hardware-enforced security boundary. This makes it easier to lift and shift workloads that run on-prem or other VMs and move them to a considerably more secure and isolated environment.

At the time of this writing, AMD SEV-SNP VMs are available in preview using the following VM types:

- **DCasv5**   A confidential VM with remote storage and no local temporary disk

- **DCadsv5**   A confidential VM with a local temporary disk

- **ECasv5**   A memory-optimized confidential VM with remote storage and no local temporary disk

- **ECadsv5**   A memory-optimized confidential VM with a local temporary disk

Be aware that if an Azure VM using AMD SEV-SNP requires support, Microsoft employees cannot access it, even if authorized by the customer. This renders certain recovery and support scenarios unavailable for confidential VMs. This is by design.

> **Tip** For a great technical overview from AMD of how SEV-SNP works, see https://azsec.tech/amd.

Arm TrustZone

Arm TrustZone takes a different approach to isolation. With the previously discussed architectures, the normal OS can address enclave memory, but encryption prevents it from accessing the enclave memory. In contrast, with TrustZone, the normal OS cannot even address the enclave memory. For example, consider a 32-bit processor. With this type of processor, addresses use a 33-bit address space (re-read that if you missed it: 33-bit, not 32-bit), where the extra bit is secure versus normal. So, a 32-bit register can express an address only within its own 32-bit space. Although Azure IoT Edge uses Arm TrustZones, you cannot currently create a VM image that supports Arm processors. You can learn more at https://azsec.tech/arm/.

DCsv3-series VMs, SGX, Intel Total Memory Encryption, and Intel Total Memory Encryption Multi-Key

SGX requires the use of DCv2 VMs. However, the newer DCsv3 VMs (https://azsec.tech/6qc) support Intel SGX and Intel Total Memory Encryption Multi-Key (TME-MK). On the surface, TME-MK is similar in principle to the VM encryption provided by AMD, but it is not. If you define confidential computing the way the CCC does, Intel TME/TME-MK is not confidential computing. To be more precise, TME/TME-MK is closer to another AMD technology, called Secure Memory Encryption (SME), than to SEV-SNP.

Figure 11-1 compares TME/TME-MK, SEV-SNP, and SGX. Note the trust boundaries and that the Intel TME/TME-MK attack surface is larger than that of SEV-SNP and SGX. Also notice that SEV-SNP trusts the guest VM, but on the Azure host, SGX does not trust the guest VM.

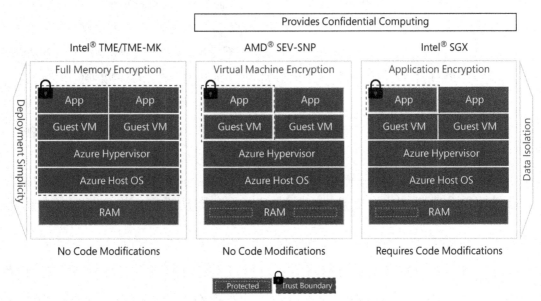

FIGURE 11-1 Comparing TME-MK, SEV-SNP, and SGX. The dotted line denotes trust boundaries; everything inside these boundaries is trusted, and everything outside these boundaries is untrusted.

Keys

As noted in Chapter 10, "Cryptography in Azure," protecting cryptographic keys is paramount.

SGX has many keys, all in a complex key hierarchy. Memory encryption keys are stored in the CPU and are changed randomly on each power cycle or when the VM restarts.

Recall that the SEV part of SEV-SNP means Secure Encrypted VM. So, with AMD, each VM is encrypted with a unique key held in the CPU.

Note To clarify, by *encryption*, we mean encrypted memory while the VM or Enclave is executing.

Attestation

Attestation is a process that verifies that software binaries are correct and properly instantiated on a trusted platform, such as SGX or an SEV-SNP VM. The Confidential Computing Consortium defines attestation as follows:

Attestation is the process by which one party, called a "Verifier," assesses the trustworthiness of a potentially untrusted peer, i.e., the "Attester." (These terms are consistent with the Internet Engineering Task Force's "Remote Attestation Procedures Architecture.") The goal of attestation is to allow the Verifier to gain confidence in the trustworthiness of the Attester by obtaining an authentic, accurate, and timely report about the software and data state of the Attester.

> **Note** Microsoft Azure Attestation Service (https://azsec.tech/opn) performs this validation.

Attestation uses policies to validate that some code is valid and meets your security requirements. A sample policy follows:

```
version= 1.0;
authorizationrules
{
    [type=="x-ms-sgx-is-debuggable", value==false]
    && [type=="x-ms-sgx-product-id", value==4639]
    && [type=="x-ms-sgx-svn", value >= 0]
    && [type=="x-ms-sgx-mrsigner", value=="e31c9e505f3 <snip> c450b6e33e5"]
  => permit();
};
```

Here is what some of these claims mean:

- **x-ms-sgx-is-debuggable**   This can be set to `true` or `false`. If it is set to `false`, the enclave cannot be debugged.

- **x-ms-sgx-product-id**   This is an integer that identifies the code in the enclave. It allows for the segmentation of enclave code signed by the same entity. In the preceding example, 4639 is the ID for the Azure SQL Database Always Encrypted enclave.

- **x-ms-sgx-svn**   This is the security version number of the code that runs in the enclave. This is important when fixing vulnerabilities in the code. If v1 has a vulnerability and you fix it, you can make the fixed version v2 and can set the attestation to load only v2. If someone tries to load the insecure v1, the operation will fail.

- **x-ms-sgx-mrsigner**   This is a hex-encoded hash of the signer's public key associated with the private key used to sign the binary that runs in the enclave.

Notice the `=> permit()` line at the end. This essentially means, if all these claims are correct, then permit the code to execute in the enclave.

You can also deny the attestation based on specific claims. For example, the following code is part of a policy that is applied when loading Azure VMs configured for Trusted Boot (covered later):

```
[type=="secureboot", value==false] => deny();
```

This code indicates that if the VM is not configured for Secure Boot, the load operation should be denied.

> **Tip** We highly recommend that you digitally sign attestation policies so the policy is authenticated and not tampered with.

> **Tip** There are many more claims you can add to policy files. The brave of heart can learn more at https://azsec.tech/jzh. Also, you can view other sample policies at https://azsec.tech/sem.

When using a feature that uses attestation, you must reference the attestation endpoint using HTTPS. For example, when using Azure SQL Database with secure enclaves, you can set the URL in tools like SSMS and Azure Data Explorer, as shown in Figure 11-2.

SECURITY	
Always Encrypted	Enabled ⌄
Attestation Protocol	Azure Attestation ⌄
Enclave Attestation URL	https://sql-clinic-tst.attest.wus.attest.azure.net
Encrypt	True ⌄
Persist security info	True ⌄
Trust server certificate	False ⌄

FIGURE 11-2 Setting the attestation URL for an Azure SQL Database using Always Encrypted and Secure Enclaves.

At some point, if you are dealing with anything related to confidential computing, you will probably need to use an attestation service. The Microsoft Azure Attestation Service is a general-purpose service that will probably meet your needs.

Trusted launch for Azure VMs

Some years ago, Microsoft added Secure Boot and Trusted Boot technology to Windows in response to increasingly sophisticated malware targeting the boot sequence using kernel malware, bootkits, and rootkits. (You can read more about Secure Boot and Trusted Boot here: https://azsec.tech/9is.) Trusted launch is a similar technology, but for Generation 2 Azure VMs.

Trusted launch is a simple option you can set during deployment or in an ARM template:

```
"securityProfile": {
    "uefiSettings": {
        "secureBootEnabled": true,
        "vTpmEnabled": true
    },
    "securityType": "TrustedLaunch"
},
```

And it is no cost!

The goal of Azure trusted launch is to provide confidence in the entire boot chain's integrity and to serve as a major defense against sophisticated attackers. You should use this feature for your VMs if possible. (Note, however, that at the time of this writing, this feature does not support Ultra disks.)

Certain layered technologies are used to enable Azure trusted launch. One of these is Virtual Trusted Platform Module (vTPM), a virtualized TPM, like those found in Windows 11 laptops; it is also TPM 2.0 compliant. Trusted launch provides your VM with its own dedicated TPM that is not directly accessible by code running in any VM and that can provide Microsoft Defender for Cloud telemetry and alerts about the security health of your VMs.

> **Tip** Learn more about trusted launch here: https://azsec.tech/trb.

Table 11-1 compares mitigations provided by trusted launch VMs, hardware-confidential VMs with AMD SEV-SNP, and hardware enclaves with Intel SGX.

TABLE 11-1 A comparison of trusted launch VMs, hardware-confidential VMs with AMD SEV-SNP, and hardware enclaves with Intel SGX

	Trusted Launch	AMD SEV-SNP	Intel SGX
Defends against Bootkits	Yes	Yes	Yes
Defends against Datacenter admins	No	Yes	Yes
Defends against VM admins	No	Yes	Yes
Defends against other Azure services	No	Yes	Yes
Defends against Hypervisor and Azure OS	No	Yes	Yes
Defends against malicious code in the VM	No	No	Yes

Here is another way to look at the protections provided by the three capabilities:

- **Trusted launch VMs** Only known, trusted code runs on the VM.

- **AMD SEV-SNP VMs** Microsoft cannot touch the code or data in a VM.

- **Intel SGX VMs** Users can trust only their application and the processor.

Azure Services that use confidential computing

This section covers services that form part of the Azure confidential computing family. It does not contain all the services, and there are more to come. One thing these services share is they abstract away the intricacies of confidential computing from the developer, administrator, and users.

SQL Server Always Encrypted

Various aspects of Always Encrypted are covered elsewhere in the book. For example, Chapter 10 explains which cryptographic primitives are used, and Chapter 13 explains the database-specific aspects of using Always Encrypted, such as how to configure Always Encrypted for SQL Server, Azure SQL Database, and Cosmos DB. The SQL Database products can use enclaves (with a small caveat we discuss in a moment), but Cosmos DB does not.

There is an important difference between the current implementation of Always Encrypted using secure enclaves in Azure SQL Database and SQL Server running in a Windows VM or on-premises. Azure SQL Database loads the query engine into an SGX enclave. SQL Server uses a different approach: it loads the query engine into another kind of isolation technology called *virtualization-based security* (VBS). VBS is similar in principle to SGX, but the implementation is different. The isolated region of memory used by VBS is controlled entirely by the Windows hypervisor. Essentially, the hypervisor creates a logical separation between the "untrusted world" and the "secure world," designated by virtual trust levels (VTLs)—VTL0 and VT1, respectively. You can learn more about VBS technical details at https://azsec.tech/vbs.

Another difference is the way attestation works in SQL Server. Specifically, rather than using Microsoft Azure Attestation, SQL Server uses Host Guardian Service (HGS). (For more information, see https://azsec.tech/8gh.)

Azure Confidential ledger

Chapter 13 discusses Azure SQL Database ledger. In its coverage of this topic, the chapter mentions that you can store hashes created by Azure SQL Database ledger in Azure Confidential ledger (ACL—not to be confused with access control lists!). These services might share the same word (*ledger*), but they are different products that solve different problems.

Azure Confidential ledger is a managed PaaS offering of the Confidential Consortium Framework (CCF). CCF is a Microsoft Research–developed open source framework for building secure, highly available, and high-performing applications that focus on consortium-based (that is, multiparty) solutions. CCF has a similar goal to blockchain, but Azure Confidential ledger users and developers are not expected to have blockchain knowledge. For more information about the CCF, see https://microsoft.github.io/CCF/.

> **Important** The CCF is different from the Confidential Computing Consortium (CCC). The word *consortium* in CCF means building applications that support multiparty (consortium) solutions, while the word *consortium* in CCC means a community of companies and nonprofits that provide guidance to build confidential computing solutions.

The Azure Confidential ledger managed service hides the internal complexity of the CCF. It provides Azure customers and developers with a REST API endpoint that can be used to store and retrieve key-value pairs to and from an immutable, tamper-proof ledger, and to verify the integrity of that ledger.

Azure Confidential ledgers can be private (encryption and integrity) or public (integrity only) and require Azure Active Directory (AD) or certificates to authenticate for both control-plane and data-plane operations. There is no anonymous access.

The code behind Azure Confidential ledgers runs in SGX enclaves. When client code sends data to an Azure Confidential ledger over a protected TLS channel, the data enters an SGX enclave. There, cryptographic operations are performed over the ledger plaintext. The cryptographic keys never leave the enclave in an unprotected form.

> **Note** When referring to data sent to a Confidential ledger over a protected TLS channel, we mean the Confidential ledger endpoint is authenticated, that the channel between the client and the Azure Confidential ledger service is encrypted, and that the channel uses hashed message authenticate codes (HMAC) to protect against tampering.

Confidential ledgers are created as blocks in blob storage containers in an Azure Storage account. Transaction data can be stored either encrypted or in plaintext. But remember, the core rationale for Azure Confidential ledgers and Azure SQL Database ledgers is to mitigate tampering threats. It is a strong nonrepudiation defense.

You will need to know some settings for your ACL instance, such as the identity service URI (for example, https://identity.confidential-ledger.core.azure.com). You can get the core metadata by using the following Azure CLI command:

```
az confidentialledger show --name "<ledgername>" --resource-group "<rg>"
```

The name is just the name, not the complete URI. For example, the name for https://ledger-clinic-tst. confidential-ledger.azure.com is `ledger-clinic-tst`.

Learn more about Confidential ledgers

To learn more about Confidential ledgers, see these resources:

- **Cryptography** This page, located at https://azsec.tech/gap, covers the cryptographic algorithms and designs used by Azure Confidential ledger and dictated by the CCF.

- **Choose an Azure Multiparty Computing Service** This page compares multiparty computing options in Azure, including the two ledger products. You can find it here: https://azsec.tech/mhm.

- You can start learning to develop code that takes advantage of Azure Confidential ledger at https://azsec.tech/rk4. For .NET code, the NuGet package is named Azure.Security. ConfidentialLedger.

Confidential containers

Confidential containers, used in AKS and ACI, enable you to wrap a container inside an SGX enclave with little work and little SGX knowledge. You can learn about the process here: https://azsec.tech/gub.

When considering deploying any container-based workload, you must think about it from an application-development standpoint as well as a DevOps standpoint, and the same holds true for confidential containers.

Confidential container–related tasks for developers are as follows:

- Developing applications following security practices

- Running security and validation tests

- Containerizing the application

- Wrapping the container in an SGX runtime

- Rerunning all tests to make sure there are no regressions

- Storing the image in a container registry

For the DevOps teams, these are the tasks:

- Adding SGX-enabled nodes to the node pool

- Adding the confidential computing AKS add-on

- Deploying SGX-enabled containers

Confidential container resources

Here are additional resources about confidential containers:

- **The helloworld Sample**   The Azure confidential computing team has created a sample that loads an Open Enclave SDK (helloworld) application into a confidential container. It is available here: https://azsec.tech/4k0.

- **SGX wrappers**   Occlum and Gramine offer sample open source SGX wrappers. You can find them here: https://occlum.io/ and https://gramineproject.io/.

- **Quickstart: Deploy an AKS cluster with confidential computing Intel SGX agent nodes by using the Azure CLI**. This article, located at https://azsec.tech/cry, gives step-by-step instructions for creating an AKS cluster that uses SGX agent nodes. The AKS confidential computing plug-in documentation is available here: https://azsec.tech/vj4.

- **Cloud Native Computing Foundation Confidential Containers**   This project, available at https://github.com/confidential-containers, contains documentation and tools for using confidential containers. Microsoft is actively involved in this project.

Microsoft also provides two references regarding confidential container architectures: a Confidential Healthcare Platform demo, at https://azsec.tech/00n, and an article on big data analytics on confidential computing with Apache Spark on Kubernetes, at https://azsec.tech/gmr. Finally, Chapter 12, "Container security," includes additional container-related security considerations.

Summary

Azure confidential computing opens a new world of possibilities for highly secure workloads in Azure. If you are deploying highly sensitive workloads that handle confidential data, then you should consider using some aspects of confidential computing, such as isolated and encrypted VMs that use AMD CPUs to enforce strong security boundaries that deny access even to malicious admins and cloud operators. Alternatively, you could use specific features, such as Always Encrypted or Confidential ledger, to secure specific data-oriented solutions. Finally, you can orchestrate confidential containers using AKS.

The confidential computing technology and services currently available in Azure today are only the start. There is more to come. To stay up to date, read the Azure confidential computing team's blog at https://aka.ms/ACCblog.

## CHAPTER 12

Container security

After completing this chapter, you will be able to:

■ Choose among IaaS and various Azure container-related services to find the best approach for you.

■ Understand and cope with current problems with container technologies.

■ Secure your containerized solutions by adopting sound principles and best practices.

What are containers?

The last three or four years have seen increased interest in containers and the proliferation of competing container technologies. But what are containers, and why are they so important?

Containers are small, independent units that package an application or an execution environment with all its dependencies. They address a very real problem: how can you run multiple applications with different dependencies on the same hardware and avoid the typical incompatibilities that occur when you must share the same host? Containers decouple the application and its dependencies from the execution runtime. This separation simplifies the whole development process, accelerating the development, testing, and deployment of containerized applications.

These are not the only advantages of containers. Sometimes applications are so big and complex that you must dedicate an entire server to them. However, this approach often leads to wasted resources. The introduction of virtual machines (VMs) addressed this problem, but VMs are far from lightweight, and they do not support interesting scenarios like microservices-based applications. These applications require a leaner approach, with a simpler and more efficient virtualization layer. This is another place where containers excel.

With containers, you can host multiple applications on the same machine, each stored in a bubble with all its dependencies, even at the OS level. Of course, said operating systems are very thin; typically, they are bare-bones Linux distributions or Windows Nano Servers.

If you have ever heard of containers, chances are you associate them somewhat with Docker and Kubernetes (K8s). These are very different objects, however. Docker is a tool that allows you to create, share, and run containers. It supports multiple platforms and has extensive backing from many organizations and tools. In contrast, K8s is a tool to automate the deployment, scaling, and management of containerized applications. So, a containerized application needs Docker (or similar) technology to execute its container(s), but K8s is necessary only if you need to execute complex distributed applications based on containers. K8s does not run containers; rather, it is an infrastructure to execute and manage them.

Using Docker is not the only way to create and run containers. There are many alternatives, including containerd, LXC, Podman, rkt, runC, crun, and Kata. K8s can use many of these runtimes; specifically, it supports all runtimes compliant with Container Runtime Interface (CRI). These include containerd, the Docker Engine (cri-dockerd), and Mirantis Container Runtime (or MCR) through their CRI plugins. Other engines like Kata and runC can be used through CRI-O, an open source implementation of CRI that allows the use of the Open Container Interface (OCI), another standard interface for container runtimes. The difference between OCI and CRI is that CRI focuses on the essential actions related to containers, like starting and stopping them, while OCI extends these capabilities with container registry integration and provides support for metrics and logs.

Do you need a container runtime to execute containers? Yes, sure. Do you need K8s to execute containers? No, you don't. K8s does not execute containers. What it does is use container runtimes to execute containers. K8s provides tools to automate some usage scenarios for complex applications and mechanisms to control how the containers interact.

If this sounds confusing, that's because it is. Containers are handy and powerful, but they are also fragmented and continuously evolving. For this reason, it may be best to avoid using them as a go-to solution to cover all possible payloads and instead rely on them only when necessary. On a related note, because of their complexity, it might be best to avoid using solutions like K8s if you have high-security requirements. As you saw in Chapter 2, "Secure design," the economy of mechanism principle demands simple architectures because complexity is the enemy of security.

You do not need containers for that!

Once you embrace containers, you typically want to use them everywhere. After all, it is always simpler to adopt the same paradigm for every need than to adopt specific solutions. While this is understandable, it does not represent the best choice from a security perspective—and most of the time, from an efficiency perspective either.

The many web applications we work on as security experts are clear examples of this. Most of these applications consist of static content (received and processed on the client side) and dynamic content (handled on the server side). Many development teams implement these web applications as containerized applications hosted on K8s, meaning their static content and their dynamic content are hosted in containers. Hosting static content in a container in K8s is inefficient, because K8s and the container execution engine represent additional infrastructure, which implies additional costs and execution time. It is also less secure than it should be because the container runtime and K8s unnecessarily extend the attack surface, potentially introducing additional attack vectors. The right move here is to use the most lightweight approach for the static content, like Azure Storage Static Website Hosting or Azure Static Web Apps, and then adopt containers and K8s only for the APIs.

> **Tip** See https://azsec.tech/043 for more information about Azure Storage Static Website Hosting. For information about Azure Static Web Apps, see https://azsec.tech/b0d.

How to proceed from here

This chapter is not a primer on containers or K8s, nor is it meant to provide an in-depth introduction to container security. Rather, it is intended to teach you some fundamental concepts so you will understand what essential aspects to consider when securing solutions based on containers and K8s. If you want to go deeper, here are two books you might try:

- *Container Security: Fundamental Technology Concepts That Protect Containerized Applications* by Liz Rice (O'Reilly Media, 2020)

- *Learn Kubernetes Security: Securely Orchestrate, Scale, and Manage Your Microservices in Kubernetes Deployments* by Kaizhe Huang and Pranjal Jumde (Packt Publishing Ltd., 2020)

> **Note** Container technologies are evolving extremely quickly. At the time of this writing, these books are almost three years old. Although most of their value is unaffected, things have already changed substantially, and many covered concepts and tools no longer apply!

Container-related services on Azure

Azure supports many container technologies, and the list is continuously expanding. At the moment, you can choose among Azure App Services Web App for Containers, Azure Functions, Azure Container Instances (ACI), Azure Kubernetes Services (AKS), Managed OpenShift, and Azure confidential containers. More recently, a new service called Azure Container Apps has been added to the list. All these are PaaS offerings.

Microsoft manages all these services, but they offer varying levels of flexibility. Typically, the most flexible approaches are the most complex and are thus harder to secure. Microsoft mitigates most typical risks for every option, but you should not assume this is enough to secure your solutions. If you recall the cloud shared responsibility model discussed in Chapter 2 and shown here in Figure 12-1, you know some of the responsibility for securing your application is still on you, whatever model you choose. And even among offerings of a particular type, like PaaS offerings, each one might require a different security approach.

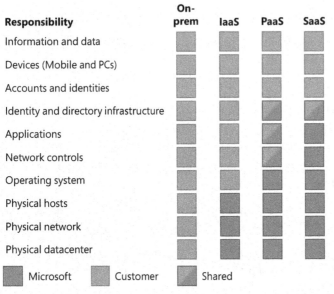

Responsibility	On-prem	IaaS	PaaS	SaaS
Information and data				
Devices (Mobile and PCs)				
Accounts and identities				
Identity and directory infrastructure				
Applications				
Network controls				
Operating system				
Physical hosts				
Physical network				
Physical datacenter				

Microsoft   Customer   Shared

FIGURE 12-1 The cloud shared responsibility model. Source: https://azsec.tech/o6w.

Using containers on IaaS offerings

When working with containers, you are not limited to PaaS offerings. You can also use IaaS offerings to install and configure a K8s cluster. This approach offers you almost complete control over the cluster and facilitates your movement from Azure to other clouds or even to an on-premises configuration if you decide this is necessary sometime in the future. In contrast, PaaS offerings have the disadvantage of causing various degrees of vendor lock-in, depending on the chosen approach. Therefore, you might face problems if you decide to move away from Azure later.

Adopting an IaaS offering does, however, pose a risk from a security perspective—and even more so for containers, due to their complexity. With a PaaS offering, the cloud service provider (CSP) assumes a significant part of the responsibility of securing the system, so PaaS implementations are already hardened and therefore represent a safer bet if you do not have a better-than-average security team to support your development.

> **Note** It is not easy to include IaaS solutions in this analysis because there are too many possible combinations. For this reason, we are restricting it to the PaaS services.

Comparing Azure container services

This section explores current container-related PaaS offerings from Azure, from the simplest to the most complex, to help you determine the best approach for your next project.

Azure App Services Web App Containers

Azure App Services Web App Containers are probably the simplest way to go if you intend to deploy a containerized web application. They fully abstract all the various characteristics of the execution environment so you can focus on creating the container.

The advantage of this approach is that it provides the very same experience in various environments due to the containerization of the web application. So, testing and troubleshooting is a straightforward experience. Moreover, most developers find the approach to be a natural extension of the traditional web application development process. The disadvantage of this approach is that it focuses on a specific goal: publishing a web application. Everything else requires significant work or might not be supported.

Azure Functions Containers

Azure Functions Containers are another straightforward approach for deploying applications. Azure Functions are serverless applications that you can use to write logic triggered by various events, such as incoming web requests or the uploading of a file to some Azure Storage. They provide considerable flexibility, including the ability to adopt third-party runtimes like Go. As a result, they are sometimes the preferred way to implement stateless web applications. The advantages and disadvantages of using Azure Functions Containers are the same as those for Azure App Services Web App Containers.

Azure Container Instances

Azure Container Instances (ACI) is a Docker container hosting environment that allows for the deployment of single containers. It does not provide features typically required for distributed applications or microservices, like scaling and load balancing. If you want these features, you must build them yourself—for example, by adopting Azure Load Balancer and creating multiple instances of containers.

ACI supports the creation of container groups, which you can use to group multiple containers together. All the containers in a container group must be hosted on the same physical machine. This provides some configuration-related benefits—for example, you can assign the same Managed Identity to all containers hosted in the same group. It also helps with resource management because the assigned quotas apply to all containers in the group, which saves some resources.

> **Note** Like Azure App Services Web Containers and Azure Function Containers, ACI is a simple mechanism. But it does involve more concepts typical of containerized applications than the other two services.

Microsoft manages ACI, so it offers good security out of the box. Per the Microsoft documentation, "Azure Container Instances guarantees your application is as isolated in a container as it would be in a VM." This is significant because you cannot achieve this isolation with most other container technologies. Of course, this does not mean the container is fully isolated. An attacker could still jump out of their container to get into your container by leveraging some zero-day vulnerability. Still, this is a sporadic occurrence, and you can be sure that Microsoft will patch it much more quickly than you can.

One disadvantage of ACI is that it is a basic solution. It's more flexible than App Services Web Containers and Azure Function Containers, but it still requires considerable development to support more complex scenarios.

> **Tip** For more information on ACI, see https://azsec.tech/5yk.

Azure Container Apps

Azure Container Apps is a new service that fills the gaps associated with more straightforward container approaches and complete infrastructures like those based on K8s. It can be used to develop event-driven applications and microservices architectures.

Azure Container Apps is the simplest service to support the implementation of both containerized and distributed applications. Azure Container Apps is a fully managed K8s infrastructure, but it prevents access to the underlying infrastructure. The advantage of this is that Azure Container Apps is more flexible than, say, ACI, without the complexity of a whole AKS cluster.

Azure Container Apps is fully managed, so it offers better security than other services like AKS, Managed OpenShift, and Azure Spring Cloud. Being fully managed, while also hiding K8s, offers a more stable experience than the alternatives. K8s changes so often that using a managed offering like AKS means updating the execution environment every few months. With Azure Container Apps, most changes should be transparent for you. One disadvantage of this service, however, is that you forfeit some of the control you have with less-managed alternatives.

Azure Kubernetes Services

Azure Kubernetes Services (AKS) is the main container infrastructure managed by Microsoft based on K8s. Microsoft manages all K8s components on the control plane, but it is your responsibility to manage the nodes (the virtual servers that host the containers) and the containers themselves.

The most fundamental services of the K8s control plane are as follows (see Figure 12-2):

- **API Server** The main K8s logic is exposed here. It is used by various tools, including the K8s dashboard, to access the functionality of the K8s cluster.

- **Scheduler** This controls the nodes and determines when to start them.

- **Controller Manager** This manages the controllers. K8s has a modular structure, and controllers represent the logic to perform actions like restarting a node that has gone down and executing jobs to initialize resources and namespaces.

- **etcd** A distributed configuration database is also present on each cluster node and provides a key-value pairings configuration.

> **Note** If you are a Windows developer, you might wonder what's behind the name etcd. The *etc* portion of the name comes from the /etc folder, which contains system configuration files on UNIX systems, and the *d* indicates a distributed configuration.

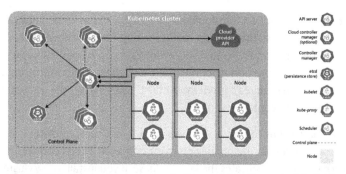

FIGURE 12-2 Kubernetes components. Source: https://azsec.tech/eek. The Kubernetes authors have created the image. It is licensed under CC BY 4.0 (https://azsec.tech/3um).

Even though the nodes are the customer's responsibility, AKS still manages them, because it deploys images that are already hardened and updates them regularly. In this case, your responsibility as a customer is limited to restarting the nodes when a fix applies to the kernel, which happens just a few times per year.

Your responsibility is to secure the pods and the containers. A pod is the minimal unit managed by K8s and is composed of one or more containers plus some configuration. The pod's configuration determines what the logic inside the containers can do.

AKS recently introduced an integration layer with Azure Policy called Azure Policy for Kubernetes, which is currently in Preview. Azure Policy for Kubernetes relies on Open Policy Agent and Gatekeeper to define, enforce, and audit policies. For example, these policies could be used to restrict the capabilities of a pod. For more information about Azure Policy for Kubernetes, see https://azsec.tech/yra.

The extensibility of K8s offers significant benefits. For example, it makes it possible to adopt service meshes, like Istio, Linkerd, and Consul Connect. These are extensions that transparently introduce capabilities like the following:

- **Cryptographic protection (encryption and integrity)** This applies to all cluster-related traffic between pods, and possibly even to and from external systems. This capability is typically linked to mutual authentication of the pods using certificates.

- **Routing support for canary and phased rollouts** With a canary rollout, updates are deployed to a small percentage of users for validation before being extended to the whole population. Phased rollouts are similar to canary rollouts, but they deploy new versions in waves. This is typically achieved by installing more than one version simultaneously and redirecting requests to the version assigned to the caller. The advantage of both these approaches is they allow you to gradually move traffic from an old version of the application to a new version. They also allow you to safely gather information about the new version's behavior without fully committing to it.

- **Traffic management to support testing**   Service meshes allows you to mirror live traffic to a development environment—for example, to troubleshoot or to inject faults to verify the behavior of the solution.

- **Observability**   Service meshes provide observability of the solution by introducing metrics and logs for ingress and egress.

We have barely scratched the surface of AKS. Still, it should be clear that with the service's extreme flexibility comes much complexity—so much so that it could represent a problem for developers designing solutions based on this infrastructure. This complexity is not a peculiarity of AKS, however; it applies to all K8s-based solutions except Azure Container Apps. Because all these K8s infrastructures have so many moving parts, securing them requires considerable effort. You'll learn more about this later in this chapter, in the section "Securing container services."

K8s is a very dynamic environment. The K8s community releases new minor versions of K8s roughly every three months. Although these releases are minor, they often introduce breaking changes. AKS supports the last *N-2* minor versions, where *N* indicates the latest release. If you install a new cluster with the latest supported version, you will have at most nine months before your version is deprecated, after which you will receive support for only 30 more days. So, if you adopt AKS, you must implement a process to regularly update the K8s version as part of your project.

Azure confidential containers

Chapter 11, "Confidential computing," introduced confidential containers, which enable you to execute containers in a hardware-based isolated environment. Azure confidential containers are not a replacement for other services like Azure confidential instances or AKS. Instead, they provide an infrastructure to host containers in a secure and highly isolated way. You can then integrate these containers into an existing AKS cluster by creating Intel SGX-based computing nodes and using the Confidential Computing add-on for AKS.

As an example, you might use this approach to apply a confidential computing model to existing, unmodified containerized examples simply by deploying them in a confidential enclave on one of these Intel SGX-based nodes. It is also possible to deploy enclave-aware applications. This can provide tighter control of the application flow, allowing discrimination between trusted and untrusted portions of the application.

The advantage of using Azure confidential containers is that they improve a solution's security by providing support for confidential computing. The disadvantage is that it adds yet more complexity to the solution, beyond the already complicated AKS.

> **Tip** For more information about Azure confidential containers, see https://azsec.tech/gub.

Managed OpenShift

Managed OpenShift is a managed configuration of Red Hat OpenShift. OpenShift is an extended K8s infrastructure that provides additional capabilities beyond the regular installation. Using Managed Open simplifies the migration of your applications from a CSP like Azure to another CSP—for example, AWS.

If you want to move a solution deployed on AKS to AWS or Google Cloud Platform, you might need to plan additional work to cope with the differences. Managed OpenShift can reduce this extra effort, at the expense of being more limited in integrating with Azure. For example, Azure Policy for Kubernetes applies specifically to AKS and is not available outside Azure. Similarly, AKS supports Managed Identities better than Managed OpenShift.

Ultimately, the advantage of Managed OpenShift over AKS is that it reduces vendor lock-in. The disadvantage is that it does not fully use the Azure platform, so advanced capabilities like Managed Identities are not supported. This has a negative effect on the security of the solutions based on it.

Problems with containers

Containers are great, but as you have seen, they do have some problems. These problems can be summarized as follows:

- Complexity
- Immaturity
- Fragmentation

Let's briefly examine each of these problems and how to cope with them.

Complexity

A complete infrastructure for containers is composed of many pieces. This might not be evident if you adopt a simpler model, like Azure App Services Web App Containers or Azure Container Instances. But when you use AKS or Managed OpenShift, it immediately becomes apparent.

Securing complex systems is hard. As an example, consider a K8s infrastructure. If you want to secure an application to be stored there, you need to cover security from many angles:

- **Development processes and deployment pipelines** Supply chain attacks are the most common in this space, so you must consider the development environment. Ask yourself:
  - How liberal is your team with rights granted to developers?
  - Is it common to grant developers local administrative rights on their machines?
  - Is it common to grant developers significant rights over the development environment?

Sometimes, developers manage resources deployed in the production environment. If you go with automation, you might assign specific rights to these pipelines. If you neglect to protect these pipelines and the artifacts they work on, it could be possible to compromise production. The SolarWinds attack is a recent example of this. You can read more about this attack here: https://azsec.tech/n9v.

- **The container registry** Containers include many components: the OS of the base image, all eventual dependencies, and third-party components. They also contain code you develop—which *for sure* contains vulnerabilities. Some of these vulnerabilities may be known; others might not be. So, it is not enough to check for vulnerabilities when you develop the solution; you also have to check for them when you upload the container to the registry, as well as afterward, on a regular basis, until you replace the container with a newer one.

- **The cluster** This relates to the infrastructure's control plane. You have seen that the CSP handles this issue. For example, Microsoft manages the control plane for AKS. Still, some risks remain, due to user error. For example, when configuring the cluster, you might assign privileges to too many users or accidentally expose private resources over the internet.

- **The nodes** These are where containers are deployed and executed. They are machines that contain an OS that must be hardened and regularly updated. On the cloud, these machines are necessarily virtual, but even if you adopt the IaaS model, the responsibility for the hosting environment is on the CSP. Therefore, you can safely ignore these. Microsoft also manages nodes for AKS. It uses images hardened with its specifications and applies most updates automatically and transparently.

- **Pods and containers** Pods and containers are the smallest units handled by the various container services. Like nodes, they are based on a lightweight OS that must be hardened and updated regularly. Sometimes they are built from public images, the assumption being they are secure, when they are not. This creates a risk. Assigning excessive rights to pods and containers is another critical factor. Depending on the configuration, you can execute the code with high privileges over the cluster, write files in the container's root file system, and much more. Therefore, it is crucial to control and limit the rights assigned to pods and containers to the minimum required for the code to work.

- **The application** The application hosted inside the container has dependencies, such as embedded third-party components. These are also affected by specific vulnerabilities.

To cope with this complexity, you must adopt a structured approach that leverages the infrastructure as much as possible, preferably taking the most straightforward approach. For example, you should use Azure App Services Web App Containers or Azure Function Containers if you do not have to build distributed or microservices applications. Similarly, if Azure Container Apps are enough, do not create a solution based on AKS simply because it might cover future scenarios. And if you do not need containers, avoid them! Remember the example of static web content.

Immaturity

Container technology is evolving fast. While some fundamental aspects are consolidated, like Docker containers, others like K8s continuously introduce breaking changes. Sometimes capabilities are deprecated even before having a clear identification of the replacement. For example, the K8s community announced the deprecation of the pod Security Policies in early 2021. Still, it took a couple of months before the identification of the pod Security Admission plugin as their replacement.

Another aspect of this problem is that breaking changes happen frequently.

How to cope with that? You are essentially required to structure your work, assuming that you have to regularly revise your solution to support the latest version. If you wait for the deprecation of the version of AKS you rely on before moving to the latest version, you may face a hard time due to the accumulated technical debt. But if you include activities to adopt the latest version every four or six months, it would be easier, and you would have more time to migrate.

Fragmentation

There is no single container technology. There are a lot of them. All of them evolve rapidly, and new ones surface daily. If you simply consider container runtimes alone, you have Docker, containerd, LXC, Podman, rkt, runC, crun, and Kata. This is just a partial list; for sure, we are missing at least a few.

Even Kubernetes is not alone. It is wildly successful—so much that most implementations of container infrastructures are based on it. Still, there are a few notable alternatives, including Docker Swarm and Hashicorp Nomad. Moreover, solutions like Kubernetes can be integrated with other open source solutions. Therefore, for each capability, you may find many alternatives.

Having choices is excellent. Having too many choices, however, is not so much. Too many choices makes it harder to choose. This is a problem, because choosing the right option is crucial. If you choose the wrong option, you might wind up with a product that is not properly maintained and becomes stale (common with open source offerings). And if you find you need to move to a different option, you could discover that doing so requires some work, as each option has its own peculiarities.

Adopting a managed solution shields you somewhat from these issues. The more managed the solution, the fewer implementation details fall under your purview, meaning you face fewer negative consequences. If you must use something like AKS or Managed OpenShift, try adopting the most common third-party components. These typically offer more guarantees than the alternatives.

Securing container services

As discussed, the most significant issues with containerized applications are complexity, immaturity, and fragmentation. With respect to complexity, you learned the six angles to consider when securing containerized applications. To review, these are as follows:

- Development and deployment

- The container registry

- The cluster

- The nodes

- The pods and containers

- The application

This section goes into more detail about securing your applications from each one of these angles.

Development and deployment

Securing development and deployment operations is not much different from securing other aspects of your application, as discussed in previous chapters—particularly in Chapter 9, "Secure coding." The main thing here is to adopt a zero-trust approach. Developers might be trustworthy, but they could be targeted, becoming attack vectors to compromise your solution. So, you should include various validation points for developed code based on automation, manual inspection, and security code reviews. Deployment pipelines are also targets for attacks and must be secured.

Adopting third-party components is also helpful from a security perspective—especially if those components are widely used, because there is a better chance that any vulnerabilities they might have will be identified and fixed. This is even more true with open source code. Compared to your own code, which will be used by a select few people, open source code is employed by millions of developers and is therefore more likely to be secure. Just remember, when you use third-party components, you are responsible for implementing processes and tools to quickly detect and fix vulnerabilities.

> **Tip** Automation can assist with this. For example, software composition analysis (SCA) tools like those available from WhiteSource, Sonatype, and Checkmarx can help you identify vulnerable code and determine how urgent it is to remediate it.

Governance plays a significant role here. If you configure Azure policies to limit what developers can do, you might be able to contain problems you might face in the event of a compromise. Given this, it may be helpful to adopt the Microsoft Cloud Adoption Framework's Azure Landing zone model. You can learn more about it here: https://azsec.tech/lgr.

Another important consideration relates to the containers themselves. You have seen that a recurring practice is to retrieve base images from repositories like Docker Hub. This is fine, particularly if you stick with official images. But you should not assume that an official image is hardened or updated with the most recent fixes. On the contrary, every image has unpatched vulnerabilities, because enough time will inevitably elapse between the preparation of the image and its release to reveal additional security issues. The bottom line is, it is your responsibility to define a pipeline that obtains the image from the chosen source, updates it, hardens it, deploys the required software, and finally pushes it to the target repository.

The container registry

When it comes to storing the actual image in a repository, the best approach is usually a private container registry like Azure Container Registry (ACR) so you can protect the images as required by your organization and apply additional checks during the image's lifetime. The repository:

- Controls who can store images and who can access or deploy them

- Validates images by checking their signature (if present) and verifying the presence of vulnerable components

- Tracks access and helps identify misuses

Verifying the source and integrity of a container is crucial. It prevents misuse by malicious actors, who might inject malicious code by deploying artfully crafted images. Using simple authentication and authorization to control access to the repository might not be enough, however, because an attacker could trick users and steal their credentials. By also relying on the signature, you adhere to the principle of separation of duties (discussed in Chapter 2), because the user who signs the container might be different from the one who uploads it to the repository.

ACR implements the Docker Content Trust (DCT) model, which is based on the concept of trusted images. Trusted images are containers signed by some user assigned the AcrTrustedSigner role. Therefore, you can achieve separation of duties by assigning the AcrTrustedSigner and the AcrPush roles to different users. This ensures that those who sign cannot upload to ACR, and vice versa.

You must also enable content trust on both the registry and the client. Suppose content trust is enabled, and you are assigned the rights to push trusted images into ACR. The first time you do so, the Docker client automatically generates the necessary signing keys, which are stored locally on the signer's machine. Clients configured to support content trust can download only trusted containers. For more information about content trust, see https://azsec.tech/r0b.

Another point concerns validation by containers to check if they contain known vulnerabilities. You might wonder why you must check for vulnerabilities at the container registry level if you have already done so while developing the application. You might also assume that applications do not decay and that everything should be OK if you did a thorough job during the previous phase. Unfortunately, it doesn't work like that. Every application has vulnerabilities, including the ones you rely on to build your applications, like the OS, third-party frameworks, and libraries. No matter how good you are, some vulnerabilities will skip your checks. For this reason, you can expect some of these vulnerabilities to be identified after you have prepared your container. So, you must regularly review the containers in the registry as well as those you have deployed to determine whether they contain vulnerable code and remediate any issues as quickly as possible. ACR provides this capability through Microsoft Defender for Containers—analyzing containers uploaded to the registry, reiterating the check after some time, and validating deployed containers.

The cluster

You address the security of the cluster primarily by considering the configuration of the control plane. You already know that with AKS, Microsoft manages the control plane. But this doesn't mean you should consider it fully hardened. Microsoft adopts a hardening approach based on the best practices available, like CIS Benchmark for Kubernetes, but still leaves some details to you.

To determine what you can do to further secure your K8s cluster, you might want to use a tool like Aqua Security's kube-bench, available at https://azsec.tech/vbq. Microsoft Defender for Containers also provides these same capabilities for AKS and other K8s managed installations on other CSPs like AWS and GCP.

The K8s cluster is not only about the control plane. You also must harden the data plane. This hardening is achieved in most K8s installations using the Pod Security Admission Controller. (Previously, developers used Pod Security Policies, but these have been deprecated since Kubernetes 1.21 and are planned for removal with version 1.25.) AKS also provides an alternative approach: Azure Policy for Kubernetes. This allows you to use the same approach you take for general Azure governance for K8s.

> **Tip** For more information about the Pod Security Admission Controller, see https://azsec.tech/a0t.

Microsoft Defender for Containers can play another role for K8s clusters: attack detection. That is, you can see events and alerts in Microsoft Defender for Cloud and on Azure Sentinel and thus respond quickly to attacks.

> **Important** Microsoft Defender for Containers should be enabled in every subscription in which you use containers.

The nodes

When securing your K8s installation, you must ensure the nodes are hardened, because their compromise could lead to the compromise of the whole cluster. Using something like the CIS Benchmark is often a good approach.

AKS deploys nodes that are already hardened and provides automatic updates out of the box. In other words, in most cases, when an update is released, you need not do anything; they are applied transparently, with no restart required. The only exception to this rule is kernel fixes, which do require a manual node restart. You can use a tool like kured to automatically restart the node for you when required; it's available here: https://azsec.tech/ydw.

> **Note** If you adopt Azure confidential containers, you also get strong hardware-based isolation.

The pods and containers

Pods and containers are other critical factors when securing your K8s configuration. They require you to consider aspects such as networking, authentication, and secrets management.

For networking, you need to ensure that flows are protected internally and externally. The first approach is simply to configure network rules so nobody can contact the inner logic directly. To achieve this, you can define an ingress and egress controller and then use network policies to force all external traffic to pass through. Common examples of ingress controllers for AKS are NGINX and the Azure Application Gateway Ingress Controller. As for network policies, they are discussed here: https://azsec.tech/oxf.

Suppose you adopt an approach like the one described in the preceding paragraph, where inner components are not reached directly but rather through an ingress controller. You might be tempted to allow cleartext communications internally to your K8s cluster because it would represent a trust boundary. While correct in principle, this could lead to problems because it allows everything inside the cluster. In other words, if an attacker manages to breach the cluster, then anything is possible! So, this approach represents a significant risk. For this reason, it might be best to require authentication and authorization at each layer. A great approach that requires minimal effort is to adopt a service mesh and enable Mutual Transport Layer Security (mTLS). Then configure the system to ensure that any container can receive requests from the authorized containers and block everything else.

Many Azure services and resources support Managed Identities. As discussed in Chapter 3, "Security patterns," adopting Managed Identities should be considered a virtuous pattern. With respect to containers, most Azure container services natively support Managed Identities, including Azure App Services Web Applications, Azure Functions Containers, Azure Container Instances, and Azure Container Apps. AKS also supports Managed Identities, but at the time of this writing, they are difficult to adopt. There is plenty of support for Managed Identity for the control plane, which you can read about here: https://azsec.tech/0ld. However, there is very little for the data plane at the time of writing. Ideally there will be more by the time you read this.

The only feasible approach to Managed Identities for the data plane nowadays is represented by Azure AD Pod Identities, an open source project to extend K8s with the ability to provide Managed Identities to pods. It's discussed here: https://azsec.tech/cj5. Unfortunately, development on this project has been stopped. So, you can expect fixes for critical bugs and security issues, but no real support for anything else. In any case, Azure AD Pod Identities never became anything more than a community-supported initiative in public preview, so its adoption for significant solutions in production was never recommended.

Microsoft is already working on an alternative approach called Azure AD Workload Identity. This project is documented at https://azsec.tech/tmc. It is in its early stages, and at the time of writing, it does not support Managed Identities yet.

So, support for Managed Identities for the data plane is still in progress. But why is this so important? To answer this, consider etcd, the distributed configuration storage for Kubernetes. etcd does not discriminate between insensitive configuration values and secrets; it encodes them all with Base64. While Base64 is a good algorithm to transfer binary values as text, it does nothing to protect those values. They are as good as in the clear. AKS's implementation does a little better than your average K8s installation because it encrypts the etcd database at rest using transparent encryption. This is because AKS uses Azure Storage Account as the backing storage. The point is that if someone steals the storage containing your etcd database, they will not get immediate access to your secrets. But this doesn't mean that it would be impossible for them to get these secrets eventually. For example, any code executed in that cluster and namespace would be able to read the content of the etcd, including the secrets. Therefore, a malicious actor could inject and execute some code to exfiltrate etcd's content.

The primary approach to address this situation is to store the credentials somewhere else, like Azure Key Vault or Hashicorp Vault, which is another solution used by containerized applications to store secrets. Now, how can you access your vault of choice? Using credentials stored on etcd would defeat the purpose of the vault. So, again, Managed Identities are the solution.

The bottom line is that this aspect of K8s security has not yet received a satisfactory answer. We have hopes for the future, but for now, you might want to adopt Azure AD Pod Identities to switch to Azure AD Workload Identities as soon as they are ready.

The application

The application is the last aspect of the K8s solution to consider, but this does not mean it is the least important. You should treat it similarly to any other type of Azure solution—that is, consider the design and implementation, use threat modeling, use automation, and perform security code reviews. In other words, to secure the application, you apply all the various practices discussed in the previous chapters.

Summary

Container security is complicated, but it should not an unreachable goal. The current technology is indeed complex and immature. Still, managed services like Azure App Services Web Applications, Azure Functions Containers, Azure Container Instances, and Azure Container Apps go a long way in obscuring this complexity and providing a much more manageable approach.

More advanced services like Azure Kubernetes Services, Azure confidential containers, and Managed OpenShift represent options you should consider only when they address needs that you cannot address otherwise. If you decide to go this route, you need to implement a development and deployment process around the chosen infrastructure to support it and guarantee an adequate level of security during the whole lifecycle of the solution.

Building an unmanaged service based on K8s is even more complicated and error prone. Therefore, you should consider this only if your organization is very structured and advanced. The creation of custom, unmanaged K8s infrastructures over IaaS or on-premises when your organization cannot manage the complexity, immaturity, and fragmentation of these infrastructures may lead to unmanageable and insecure solutions.

## CHAPTER 13

Database security

After completing this chapter, you will be able to:

- Understand how to think critically about security in general and databases in particular.

- Understand the security capabilities of Azure SQL and Azure Cosmos DB.

Why database security?

What is database security? The answer to this is simple. In fact, it's just one word: *data*.

Attackers want data. Sure, they can attack other things, but data is worth money. Data is valuable to you, and it's valuable to attackers. So, it must be protected appropriately. However, the purpose of data is to aid the business requirements. This means data must also be accessible to the appropriate people. That's why we said, "protected appropriately."

From a threat model and database perspective, the main threats are as follows:

- **Spoofing** Impersonating a database server; mitigated by authentication

- **Tampering** Maliciously changing data; mitigated by authorization and cryptographic controls

- **Repudiation** An attacker covering their tracks; mitigated by strong auditing

- **Information disclosure** Maliciously disclosing data, including malicious data exfiltration; mitigated by authorization and cryptographic controls

- **Denial of service** Degraded availability and performance; often addressed by tools like load balancing and network isolation

- **Elevation of privilege** An attacker gains more rights than they should; usually mitigated by using least privilege principles and strong authorization.

> **Note** You should always be precise with your wording when describing security. When we say, *cryptographic controls*, we mean all aspects of cryptography such as encryption, hashes, message authentication codes (MAC), and digital signatures.

Which databases?

Azure supports many database products. These include the following:

- SQL Server

- Azure SQL Server Managed Instance

- Azure SQL Database

- Cosmos DB

- Azure Database for MySQL

- Azure Database for PostgreSQL

This chapter focuses on the SQL Server family and on Cosmos DB products because of their prevalence in Azure solutions.

Thinking about database security

When you think about any service, including databases, you must consider which security-enabling technologies to use. There is a simple way to do this. First, remember that for any service, there are two planes:

- **Control plane** Also called the *management plane*, the control plane encompasses the parts of a system that administrators use to configure and manage the service. Simply put, the control plane makes the system work. It often requires elevated and privileged accounts. The control plane does not grant access to data.

- **Data plane** The data plane consists of the components of a system that normal users use to get their jobs done. The data plane allows for use of the system.

> **Important** All data plane and control operations should always use least privilege access.

Next, you need to think about the security techniques you want to use, such as the following:

- Authentication

- Authorization

- Auditing

- Data protection (cryptographic controls, masking, and others)

- Network isolation

For cryptographic controls, you can then consider these as controls for the following:

- Data at rest

- Data on the wire

- Data in use

When most people think of cryptographic controls, they think only of the first two. But Azure SQL, SQL Server and Cosmos DB support cryptographic controls (encryption and HMACs) while data is in use. This is called Always Encrypted.

With all this in mind, you end up with an empty template for each database product, like the one shown in Table 13-1. You will populate this template with various security properties later in the chapter.

TABLE 13-1 An empty template showing the Intersection of security services with control and data planes

Security Property	Control Plane	Data Plane
Authentication (AuthN)		
Authorization (AuthZ)		
Auditing		
Cryptography at rest		
Cryptography on the wire		
Cryptography in use		
Network isolation		

Tip You can use this table for any service, on any platform—not just databases on Azure. When thinking about security, this is an important table because it will help you structure your thoughts and better understand what is available in the products you're looking to use.

From a threat-modeling perspective, security services are some of the most common mitigations. For example:

- Authentication mitigates spoofing.

- Authorization mitigates tampering and elevation of privilege.

- Auditing is one way to mitigate repudiation threats.

- Cryptographic controls can mitigate both information disclosure and tampering threats.

- Network isolation is one aspect of mitigating denial of service and can extend mitigations against information disclosure and tampering.

> ### The golden rules
>
> Authentication, authorization, and auditing are important pillars of security. They are often called the *golden rules* because they start with Au, the chemical symbol for the element gold. Yes, it's a bad security pun!

Let's look at some of the databases listed in the "Which databases?" section through the lens of the blank security template in Table 13-1.

The SQL Server Family

Microsoft SQL Server has been around for a long time, with the earliest versions going as far back as SQL Server running on OS/2 and using Microsoft LAN Manager for network access.

In an Azure environment, there are three versions of SQL Server:

- SQL Server
- Azure SQL Database
- Azure SQL Managed Instance

From a security perspective, we won't discuss each product individually unless there is a need. However, here's a quick overview of each.

SQL Server

This is the "classic" SQL offering. When hosted in Azure, it runs in a Windows or Linux virtual machine (VM). It may surprise you, but yes, we said Linux! SQL Server is available on both Linux and Windows. You can read more here: https://azsec.tech/qme.

SQL Server is a common database engine for "lift and shift" solutions, where you take an existing on-premises SQL Server solution and move it into Azure. This is an example of an infrastructure as a service (IaaS) solution.

From a security standpoint, the benefit of IaaS SQL Server is you have absolute control of every security setting imaginable. The downside is you must manage every security setting imaginable!

Azure SQL Database

Azure SQL Database is the Azure platform as a service (PaaS) SQL database offering. Internally, the engine is SQL Server, but the system is managed by Azure. For example, patching and anti-malware are all addressed by Azure. Because it is a PaaS, the networking endpoints use public Azure IP addresses by default, but this can be changed using private endpoints. (More on this later.) Also, SQL Server has some features that Azure SQL Database does not—for example, linked servers.

> **Important** New features, including security features, will be made available first in Azure SQL Database, because of the agility that comes with Azure.

Azure SQL Managed Instance

Azure SQL Managed Instance is interesting. It is a fully managed PaaS offering Azure SQL Database, but with features that more closely align with SQL Server. It offers maximum compatibility with SQL Server, but it is managed by Azure, so it has all the benefits of a PaaS offering. And because it's a PaaS offering, there are no VMs to manage, nor do you need to handle anti-malware or patching.

Azure SQL Managed Instance has one feature that is important to many customers: it's a single instance solution. This means the instance is yours and shares no compute or storage resources with other Azure tenants. Therefore, it is as isolated as possible.

Security in the SQL Server family

Table 13-2 is the same as Table 13-1 but has been filled in with security controls available in the SQL Server family.

> **Note** Not all security features apply to all members of the family. (We will explain this a little later.)

TABLE 13-2 Security services in the SQL Server family

Security Property	Control Plane	Data Plane
Authentication (AuthN)	**Server**	**Server**
	TLS	TLS
	Clients	**Clients**
	Azure Active Directory (AAD)	AAD
	SQL login (IaaS only)	SQL login
	Windows authentication (IaaS only)	Windows authentication
Authorization (AuthZ)	Azure role-based access control (RBAC)	SQL RBAC
	SQL RBAC	Row-level security
Auditing	Activity Logs	SQL Audit logs
	Windows Event Logs (IaaS only)	Diagnostic settings
	Linux Logs (IaaS only)	
	SQL Audit logs	
Cryptography at rest	For data at rest, cryptography is the same for the control and data planes. SQL Server can use Transparent Data Encryption (TDE), column encryption, Always Encrypted, and Always Encrypted with secure enclaves.	
	Azure SQL Database also supports a tamper-evident Ledger feature.	

Security Property	Control Plane	Data Plane
Cryptography on the wire	TLS RPC (IaaS only) IPSec (IaaS only)	TLS RPC (IaaS only) IPSec (IaaS only)
Cryptography in use	Always Encrypted	
Network isolation	Host firewall (IaaS only) Resource management private link	Host firewall (IaaS only) Network security group (NSG; IaaS only) Private IP address ranges (IaaS only) Outbound firewall rules (Azure SQL Database) Service firewall (Azure SQL Database) Private endpoints VNet injection

> **Tip** Add the web page at https://azsec.tech/z55, titled "Security for SQL Server Database Engine and Azure SQL Database," to your web browser's favorites. It contains an updated list of resources about SQL Server security.

Let's look at each of these security controls, starting with the control plane.

Control plane authentication

Control plane authentication depends on the SQL Server product.

For authentication, we need to consider this important point:

Who is authenticating whom?

When a principal (such as a user, process, or host) connects as a client to a server, how does the principal know the server is authentic? This is server authentication.

Also, how does the server know that the client connecting to it is a valid principal?

When the client and server both authenticate one another, we often refer to this as *mutual authentication*. Authenticating both the server and the client is important because it's how you establish a level of trust. This is especially true when considering zero trust (authorize explicitly). You can never trust an unauthenticated endpoint.

Control plane server authentication

First, let's look at server authentication through the eyes of a user with administrative rights who wants to perform control plane operations such as setting up a backup policy. When a user connects to a SQL Server instance to perform administrative tasks, how do they know they are talking to the correct SQL Server endpoint and not a rogue server? The answer is generally TLS. Remember, the first and most critical service TLS provides is server authentication, and TLS is supported by all SQL Server family members.

For Azure SQL Database and SQL Managed Instance, TLS is enabled by default and cannot be disabled. The only TLS setting you have the ability to change is the protocol version, which today defaults to TLS 1.2. Unless you have valid compatibility issues, you should keep this set to TLS 1.2 or above. Configuring TLS for SQL Server on Windows and Linux is less straightforward, however, because you must install a certificate and private key and set the correct TLS configuration at the server. You can read more here: https://azsec.tech/pv6.

> **Note** This is an example of the value of PaaS solutions over IaaS solutions. With PaaS, you don't need to fiddle around with many security settings, such as TLS, as the work is all done by the platform.

Control plane client authentication

Now let's switch to how principals connecting to SQL Server products are authenticated at the control plane. For Azure SQL Database and Azure SQL Managed Instance, Azure Active Directory (AAD) accounts are used at the control plane. These accounts are subject to any Azure authentication policies you have in place, such as two-factor authentication, conditional access, and if used, privileged identity management (PIM) to restrict access on an as-needed basis. When you use https://portal.azure.com or an Azure REST API to perform control plane operations, you always authenticate using an AAD account.

Managed Instance also supports Windows authentication using AAD Kerberos. You can learn more here: https://azsec.tech/ks7.

For SQL Server in a Windows VM, you can use Active Directory (AD) accounts or local Windows accounts, and you can employ SQL authentication. SQL Server broadly refers to these as:

- **Windows authentication** This can be NTLM or Kerberos and cannot be disabled.
- **Mixed mode** This uses Windows authentication and SQL authentication.

SQL authentication is a legacy authentication mechanism that stores the credential internally in the database. It is highly recommended that SQL authentication be disabled. You can disable SQL authentication by enabling AAD authentication in Azure SQL Database using the following Azure CLI command:

```
az sql server ad-only-auth enable --resource-group <rg> --name <server>
```

or for Azure SQL Managed Instance:

```
az sql mi ad-only-auth enable --resource-group <rg> --name <server>
```

For SQL Server in a Linux VM, you can use AD authentication and SQL authentication. When using AD, you must set up a service principal name (SPN) for the SQL instance. (For more on SPNs, see https://azsec.tech/lwc.) You must also set up a Kerberos key table (keytab) file.

> **Important** When creating the keytab file, do not use RC4 to encrypt credentials. Use only AES and make sure the keytab file is protected correctly. You can read more about setting up and securing authentication here: https://azsec.tech/85f.

Recently, SQL Server added the ability to use AAD accounts. As we write this, the latest public preview release of SQL Server 2022 supports AAD authentication. (See https://azsec.tech/1eq for details.) The current public preview release is supported for SQL Server on-premises for Windows and for Windows VMs on which SQL Server is installed. With this release, Azure closes the AAD authentication gap between SQL Server and Azure SQL Database and Managed Instance, where this authentication is already supported.

How SQL Server login credentials are stored

Login credentials are stored as a salted hash using SHA-2 512. This means the password itself is not stored in SQL Server, so if an attacker gets the salted hash, they cannot use it to log on to SQL Server. This is a more secure solution than storing an encrypted password because if the encryption key is disclosed to an attacker, they could decrypt all passwords and use them to log on to SQL Server. Figure 13-1 shows where the password is stored and how it is stored. Note that the first byte is 0x02; this describes the rest of the data. In this case it's version 2, the salted SHA-2 512 hash mentioned earlier.

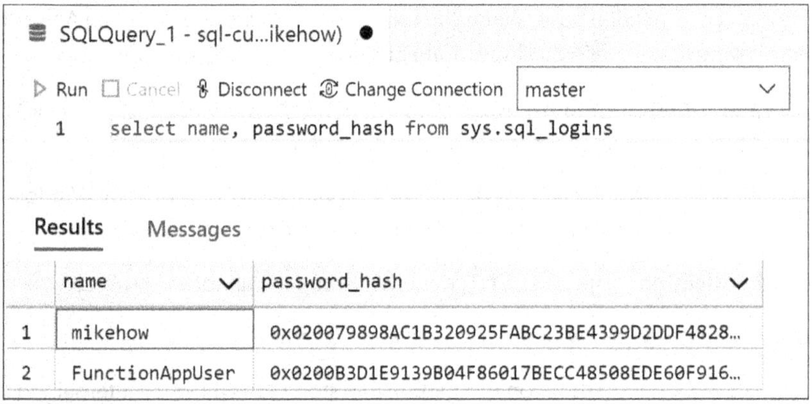

FIGURE 13-1 Querying the sys.sql_logins system table to view salted hashes of login passwords.

Control plane authorization

In SQL Server, authorization at both the control plane and the data plane uses roles and permissions. These have been in place for decades and have evolved over time as new authorization policies are needed. An entire book could easily be written on this topic.

Make sure you are familiar with the following SQL Server authorization topics:

- **Securables**   These are the resources to which the database engine can restrict access. Examples include tables and stored procedures. Some securables can be nested, which allows for security scopes—server, database, and schema. You can learn more here: https://azsec.tech/lwo.

Scopes are important because permissions can be granted at different levels and can be used to isolate access. For example, permissions could be assigned to a schema named HRDatabase that contains a collection of objects such as tables, views, and stored procedures that pertain only to people in the human resources department. Permissions could be granted at the schema level and affect all objects within that schema. Schemas make managing access to multiple objects significantly easier.

- **Permissions**   Every securable resource in SQL Server has permissions that are granted to one or more principals. This page has a list of permissions and the securable that is affected: https://azsec.tech/mzr.

- **Server-level roles**   All supported versions of SQL Server provide server-level roles to help you manage the permissions on a server. For example, any principal granted the dbcreator role can create, drop, and restore a database. You can obtain a list of each member in a server role by querying the sys.server_role_members table (https://azsec.tech/mri). You can learn more about server roles at https://azsec.tech/hov.

- **Database-level roles**   These are similar to server-level roles, but they apply at the database level only. Most database roles start with db_. For example, members of the db_securityadmin database role can modify role membership for custom roles only (not fixed roles) and manage permissions. You can learn more about database roles at https://azsec.tech/7ck.

You can get a list of the permissions effectively granted to a principal on a securable object using sys.fn_my_permissions. (See https://azsec.tech/xh6 for more information.)

In SQL Server, you can set authorization policy all the way down to individual columns using code like this:

```
DENY SELECT ON HumanResources.Employee(Salary) TO JeanV;
GRANT SELECT ON HumanResources.Employee TO MichaelH;
```

> **Note** This section applies to control plane authorization, but data plane authorization also adds row-level security. This will be covered in the "Data plane authorization" sections later in this chapter.

Control plane auditing

Control plane auditing is when a server logs details about database management, such as when a new user is added or when a new database is created.

For Azure SQL Database, control plane audit events are available from the Activity Log. You can also view this data using Log Analytics and Azure Monitor, using the following KQL as a starting point:

```
AzureActivity | where ResourceProviderValue == "MICROSOFT.SQL"
```

For SQL Server in a VM, audit logs are generated and stored by SQL Server. You must be careful to select the correct logs, however, because *audit* and *log* are both overloaded terms in SQL Server. What you're looking for are specifically security-related events.

One common way to generate and securely capture security events is to log the events to the Windows Security Log (https://azsec.tech/eb0). Alternatively, you can use the `sys.fn_get_audit_file` function. For more information, see https://azsec.tech/4ej. Finally, you can watch all events, not just security events, by using the XEvent Profiler. This is great for debugging authentication and authorization events. You can find out more here: https://azsec.tech/lpg.

> **Important** All members of the SQL family can set an audit policy at the server and database level. The prevailing practice is to set the audit policy at the server so databases will inherit it. Do *not* enable server auditing *and* database auditing at the same time, as this will create duplicate audit entries.

> **Important** Databases are optimized for availability, correctness, and performance. During periods of high activity or high network load, the auditing feature may allow transactions to proceed without recording all the events marked for auditing. When this happens, the system administrator is notified. The CAP theorem explains this situation, and IBM has a write-up on the topic at https://azsec.tech/cap.

Control plane crypto on the wire

SQL Server can support operating system–specific and other generic network security protocols. For example, SQL Server can use Windows Remote Procedure Calls (RPC). It can also use IPSec, which operates at layer 4 of the OSI network stack—well beneath the application layer (layer 7).

> **Important** You should not use RPC unless there's a pressing need, because RPC security lags behind that of TLS.

Because IPSec operates at layer 4, your applications and SQL Server don't know the network traffic is secured. We have some customers who, because they have high security requirements, use IPSec to secure communications between hosts and then use TLS to secure communications between processes—in this case, the SQL Server and the client code. With all this said, IPSec is more of an on-prem protocol than a cloud protocol. So, just use TLS.

Control plane network isolation

SQL Server in a VM has the most network isolation capabilities because a VM can easily be locked down to use only nonroutable and nonpublic IP addresses if needed. Or you could use a host-based firewall such as Windows Firewall or iptables on Linux to restrict traffic. Or you could use network security groups (NSGs) to lock traffic down further. Or you could use all these defenses!

If you need to connect to a VM running SQL Server, don't give the VM a public IP address. Instead, consider using a service like Azure Bastion to connect safely. You can and should use Azure Policy to prevent a VM that holds a database such as SQL Server from ever having a public IP address. Finally, you can disassociate a public IP address with the VM so it has only a private IP address. Then you can place other resources on the same VNet as the VM so they can communicate with one another.

Resource Management Private Link

For all Azure PaaS services, including Azure SQL Database and SQL Managed Instance, there has historically been no true network isolation *at the control plane*. However, there's a feature called Resource Management Private Link that can provide private endpoint support at the control plane!

Private links enable you to access Azure services over a private endpoint in your virtual network. When you combine private links with Azure Resource Manager's operations, you block users who aren't at specific endpoints from managing resources. Even if a malicious user gets valid credentials, they can't perform control plane operations unless they are at specific networking endpoints. This is an incredibly important defense and applies to all Azure service control plane operations as long as they use Azure Resource Manager (ARM), which is virtually everything. You can learn more here: https://azsec.tech/afy.

Now let's move our attention to the data plane, which is where users interact with the database to get their jobs done.

Data plane authentication

As noted in the "Control plane authentication" section earlier in this chapter, there is some variance among SQL Server products. We will look at both server and client authentication.

Data plane server authentication

For Azure SQL Database and SQL Managed Instance, TLS is the only option. The only control you have is the TLS protocol version, which should be TLS 1.2 and later. For SQL Server in a Linux or Windows VM, you should use TLS 1.2 and later. The control plane server authentication provides links on how to do this. Note that if you do not set a TLS protocol version policy for Azure SQL, it is possible for a client to use a non-TLS connection, so please set a minimum TLS protocol version to prevent this.

> ### A note on SQL connection strings and TLS
>
> When using TLS and SQL Server connection strings, it is common to use the following string:
>
> `Encrypt=True;TrustServerCertificate=False;`
>
> Here, `Encrypt` means "use TLS." However, `TrustServerCertificate` should not be used, because it means that any certificate used by SQL Server is trusted, regardless of where it came from, including self-signed certificates.
>
> Please do not use this option. Instead, use a real certificate issued by a certificate authority (CA) you trust. It could even be your own internal CA using, say, Microsoft Certificate Services. If you must use a self-signed certificate, then install the certificate into the root certificate store of the client making the connection.

> ### Storing SQL connection strings in Azure
>
> If you are connecting to SQL Server from a process in Azure, such as a VM or an Azure Function, you should always store a connection string in Azure Key Vault and use the Managed Identity of the caller to restrict access to the string. The best and most secure pattern is to also use the Managed Identity of the process to access SQL Server using AAD authentication.

Data plane client authentication

For Azure SQL Database and Managed Instance, you can use AAD authentication or classic SQL Server authentication. AAD is preferred because neither SQL Server nor the client need to store protected credentials. This is especially true if the client is a process and not a user. This preference for AAD authentication is not unique to Azure SQL Database; it applies for any Azure client authentication.

Azure SQL Managed Instance also supports Windows authentication using AAD Kerberos. You can learn more here: https://azsec.tech/ks7.

Finally, as noted in the "Control plane client authentication" section earlier in this chapter, SQL Server 2022 supports AAD authentication natively, too.

Data plane authorization

Data plane authorization in SQL Server is almost identical to control plane authorization, except the roles are different. For example, the db_backupoperator fixed database role is a control plane role, but db_datareader has data plane implications.

> **Warning** A column-level GRANT takes precedence over a table-level DENY. This is for backward compatibility.

Row-level authorization

One authorization mechanism that applies specifically to the data plane is row level authorization. Referred to as Row-Level Security (RLS), this authorization mechanism uses code to control access to rows of data. It is defined using the CREATE SECURITY POLICY syntax. (You can read about it here: https://azsec.tech/p6j.) It works by filtering or blocking rows within result sets. Filtering or blocking is achieved using a predicate function written in T-SQL. Conceptually, RLS is a little like a trigger, but it's called by the database engine before returning a result set. It then applies some logic to filter or even block rows.

As we have alluded to, RLS supports two types of predicates:

- Filter predicates filter read operations (SELECT, UPDATE, and DELETE).

- Block predicates block write operations (AFTER INSERT, AFTER UPDATE, BEFORE UPDATE, BEFORE DELETE).

You can learn more about RLS at https://azsec.tech/nyj. This same page has sample scenarios you can test at https://azsec.tech/vqs.

> ### Real-world experience: Limiting result sets
>
> Michael worked with a large healthcare customer helping them secure a solution handling protected health information (PHI) data in Azure. The customer chose Azure because of the agility gained from the cloud. The sticking point was the volume of PHI. Normal users of the data had access to all data going back years, and if an employee went rogue, they could potentially siphon off massive amounts of this data.
>
> Even though there were data loss prevention tools in place, users having access to so much data made the security team nervous. But the business had to do its job, and they needed access to PHI. However, the business didn't really need access to 20 years of data by default! So, an RLS policy was put in place to restrict access to data that was no more than one year old by default. This could be overridden if needed, but that event had to be given the OK, and the event details were logged. This satisfied the security team. This is a fantastic example of the security and business teams coming together to deliver a solution that meets the business needs but is secure by default, too.

Data plane auditing

For Azure SQL DB, you can enable data plane auditing at the server level and at the database level. As a rule, you should enable auditing at the server level; this is then inherited by all databases. All server and database audit events would be sent to a single log destination such as a storage account, a Log Analytics workspace, or an Event Hub.

Auditing at the server level allows you to also log events, due to Microsoft support operations. For more information, see https://azsec.tech/hw7.

If you log in to a Log Analytics workspace, the following KQL query will display all SQL interactions made against a database along with some pertinent information:

```
AzureDiagnostics
    | where Category == 'SQLSecurityAuditEvents'
    | where client_ip_s != 'Internal'
    | where strlen(statement_s) > 0
    | project TimeGenerated, client_ip_s,
            session_server_principal_name_s, database_name_s, statement_s
    | order by TimeGenerated asc
```

You can read more about auditing here: https://azsec.tech/f6e.

For SQL Server in a VM, data plane auditing involves the same mechanism as control plane auditing, referenced earlier in this chapter.

Remember, you want to get all SQL audit events at the control and data plane into a SIEM, such as Microsoft Sentinel, in real time for rapid analysis and correlation.

Data plane crypto on the wire

The options for securing data on the wire boil down to...use TLS! For Azure SQL Database and SQL Managed Instance, TLS is supported.

Data plane network isolation

Network isolation is critical for databases. They should never be exposed directly to the internet. The cloud identity boundary is critically important, too. However, do not think that just using the identity boundary is enough, because it's not. Also, focus on understanding your network defenses, too.

The first major defense built into Azure SQL Database is the firewall. Notice that we spell it with a lowercase *f*. This is because it's a simple system used to restrict inbound access to Azure SQL Database. When we use an uppercase *F*, we mean products like Azure Firewall, which are full-fledged packet-filtering stateful systems.

For IaaS SQL Server, you can use a host-based firewall on Windows (Windows Firewall) or Linux (iptables). Also, for a VM, you can use NSGs to restrict access from Azure into the VM. For example, you could restrict access to only the back-end IP address of an Azure load balancer or an Azure Function. NSGs allow restrictions by IP address, IP CIDR ranges, and Azure services by their service tag.

A service tag allows you to configure an NSG so it allows communication from, for example, Azure SQL Databases in the US West region. The service tag for that is Sql.WestUS. You can get a list of service tags using PowerShell code similar to the following, which obtains the service tag details for Sql.WestUS from East US 2:

```
$serviceTags = Get-AzNetworkServiceTag -Location eastus2
$sqlWest = $serviceTags.Values | Where-Object { $_.Name -eq "Sql.WestUS" }
```

Service tags have the benefit of removing the complexity of managing IP address ranges for Azure services because they can change often. You can learn more about service tags at https://azsec.tech/cta.

SQL Managed Instance has an option to support a public endpoint, and the default is no. SQL Managed Instance also supports a network isolation technique called VNet injection. This is the mechanism by which Azure services are deployed directly into the customer's VNet, which also allows you to further restrict access using NSGs.

You can disable Azure SQL Database public access in the Azure Portal or with PowerShell code similar to the following:

```
Set-AzSqlServer -ServerName sql-server-name -ResourceGroupName sql-server-group
-SqlAdministratorPassword $pwd -PublicNetworkAccess "Disabled"
```

The preferred method to provide strong network isolation for Azure SQL Database and, in preview at the time of this writing, SQL Managed Instance, is to use private endpoints. This is part of the Azure Private Link service. As discussed in Chapter 15, "Network security," private endpoints provide private IP addresses for PaaS offerings such as Azure SQL Database, Azure Key Vault, and Azure Storage. One of the many benefits of private endpoints is that the traffic between services on the same private network stays on the Azure backbone and never goes over the internet.

> **Tip** Microsoft offers a learning path for Azure Private Link at https://azsec.tech/vpn/ if you want to learn more.

As noted, private endpoints are for use by PaaS services only. For IaaS VMs, you can allocate any private IP address on the VM's VNet, which is similar conceptually to private endpoints. For example, you could have an Azure SQL Database using a private endpoint that uses a 10.0.0.0/24 address, such as 10.0.0.3, and you could assign a private IP address to a Linux VM, for example, 10.0.0.5. Then, because the Azure SQL Database and the VM are on the same subnet and private endpoints are unidirectional, the VM could act only as a client to the database server. Also, any other service (or attacker) that is not using that subnet can access the services. The Microsoft document at https://azsec.tech/px2 explains private endpoints and gives an example using Azure SQL Database.

Finally, Azure SQL Database supports outbound firewall rules to further restrict access to storage accounts and other databases. You can learn more here: https://azsec.tech/l49.

Cryptographic controls for data at rest

All SQL Server products support encryption of data at rest. When considering which solution is right for your application, you must understand what threat each of these technologies mitigates. This last point is important. We have encountered many architects who see the word *encryption* in the name of a technology and think they are protected. We can't stress this enough: don't fall into that trap. You need to understand how each option works. It is also critical that you understand precisely how the key structure works and when the most important keys—the root keys—are stored and protected.

Transparent Data Encryption

Transparent Data Encryption (TDE) has been available for a long time in SQL Server. The technology encrypts the database file, the backup files, and transaction logs in the background. No application changes are needed.

Now, here comes the important parts:

- TDE is designed to mitigate the threat of a stolen volume.

- TDE is *not* designed to mitigate an attacker who is able to read arbitrary tables at runtime.

> ### Real-world experience: Knowing what threats TDE does and does not mitigate
>
> Michael worked closely with a large healthcare company helping design and secure various healthcare-related workloads on Azure. One of the customer's most senior security architects has a trick question he asks anyone in a security sales or consulting capacity to gain insight into their level of security expertise: what encryption is used in their product for data at rest? If they mention only volume encryption, they fail his little test.

One benefit of TDE is automatic encryption of backups. Backups should be stored away from the main database, encrypted with the same TDE mechanism used to encrypt the database file, and restored only when brought back to the main database. This is an excellent mitigation against online and offline attacks as long as the backup is not stored with the database because the decryption key hierarchy is close by.

When using TDE with a customer-managed key (CMK) with Azure SQL Database or SQL Managed Instance, the key used to protect the TDE key is an RSA key named the TDE protector. This RSA key is stored in Azure Key Vault. Access to this key is restricted to the Managed Identity of the Azure SQL Database or SQL Managed Instance.

Important   Obviously, you must back up your TDE keys. You can use TSQL BACKUP MASTER KEY and BACKUP CERTIFICATE to do so.

Crypto shredding

Some customers manage their own keys, such as TDE CMKs. So, when deprovisioning a database, they delete all keys after they delete the database. This is called *crypto shredding* because if for some reason the database files are not deleted because of a process failure, the keys are nowhere to be found, and the data can never be recovered.

Using Managed Identities

The way TDE uses the Managed Identity associated with Azure SQL Database to access the TDE protector is a common and correct pattern in Azure. Using a Managed Identity to access sensitive data is *always* the preferred way to provide secure access. This is because the credential for the process accessing the data is secured by AAD and does not need to be protected by the application. It's also one less thing for developers to worry about.

For SQL Server in a Windows VM, the root TDE protector is protected by the Windows Data Protection API (DPAPI), which, on Windows, is the correct way to secure sensitive data. To be 100 percent correct, DPAPI encrypts data using keying material derived from the account under which the application executes or the machine account. In the case of SQL Server, a service account is used, such as NT Service\MSSQLSERVER. DPAPI does not store the data; it returns an encrypted and MAC-ed blob, which is then persisted by SQL Server. You can also use Azure Key Vault from an instance of SQL Server in a VM to store and protect the TDE key.

DPAPI protection is adequate for many environments, but it is highly recommended that you use Key Vault for the TDE key protector when storing sensitive data. See the section "SQL Server IaaS agent" in the "Miscellaneous" section later in this chapter for more information.

For SQL Server in a Linux VM, the root key is stored in /var/opt/mssql/secrets/machine-key and has the following permissions:

```
-rw------- 1 mssql mssql   44 May 24 21:45 machine-key
```

Column encryption

Column encryption has also been available in SQL Server, all versions, for a long time. It performs encryption and decryption with the database engine. Column encryption has a flexible key hierarchy, meaning you can wrap keys with other keys or certificates or use no wrapping at all.

Column encryption uses T-SQL statements to encrypt and decrypt columns in tables. This means you will need to change your query logic to encrypt and decrypt data using T-SQL statements like the following:

- OPEN SYMMETRIC KEY

- ENCRYPTBYKEY

- DECRYPTBYKEY

You can learn more about column encryption here: https://azsec.tech/gng.

Always Encrypted

We cover Always Encrypted toward the end of this chapter because it's a technical control shared by SQL Server and Cosmos DB.

Miscellaneous

What follows is brief coverage of other SQL Server technologies you should be aware of. These include the following:

- Dynamic data masking

- Data discovery and classification

- Azure SQL Ledger

- Microsoft Defender for SQL

- Azure Security Baseline

- SQL Server IaaS Agent

Let's look at each.

Dynamic data masking

Data masking is not a security defense, but it is a way to hide sensitive data from accidental disclosure. For example, in the United States, you could mask a user's Social Security number so only the last four digits are displayed. Masking is applied only when the data is presented; the data on disk is not masked. You can learn more here: https://azsec.tech/wqe.

Data discovery and classification

This is not a security defense. Data discovery and classification is a first step to protect data, but it is not a preventive, detective, corrective, recovery, or any other type of control. However, it is instrumental to implement data discovery and classification to make those other types of controls more effective.

Azure SQL Database includes tooling that allows you to discover and classify potentially sensitive data in your databases. For example, it can identify confidential data or data that could have implications due to the European Union's GDPR. (Refer to Chapter 8, "Compliance and risk programs," to learn more about GDPR.)

Data classification is a large and complex topic and is beyond the scope of this book. But Microsoft provides complete end-to-end data governance solutions using tools like Azure Information Protection (https://azsec.tech/wzq) and Azure Purview (https://azsec.tech/rh2).

Azure SQL Ledger

When people think of security, they usually think of secrecy and encryption. But if you have performed any threat modeling, you know that integrity controls are important too, to mitigate data tampering threats. In fact, one of the most important classes of threats, repudiation threats, can be mitigated by cryptographically verifiable audit logs.

A feature added to Azure SQL Database and SQL Server 2022 is Azure SQL Ledger. It is designed to provide cryptographically verifiable data. It might be best to demonstrate this by way of example. Imagine you work for an insurance company that provides discounts for safe driving. "Safe driving" can mean many things, but items you might monitor include high speed, high acceleration and deceleration, heavy braking, not using safety features like seat belts, lack of engine maintenance, and so on. Today, a driver could potentially tamper with the data on the car to cover their tracks. But using a tamper-evident logging mechanism such as Azure SQL Database Ledger would mitigate this. If a bad driver tampered with the data, this tampering event would be caught through ledger validation.

> **Note** If you're familiar with Blockchain, Ledger is a little like Blockchain, but without the distributed consensus model.

The cryptographic hash data associated with the ledger data is stored either:

- On-premises
- In a storage account
- In a new Azure service called Azure Confidential Ledger

> **Tip** Cryptographic ledger functionality is an excellent mitigation for repudiation threats. For more on repudiation threats, refer to Chapter 4, "Threat modeling."

It is critical that the hash data, which is a series of inter-connected hashes called a Merkle tree, be securely stored, because if these hashes are tampered with, then the ledger is invalid. On-prem, you can use Write-Once-Read-Many (WORM) drives. If you use an Azure Storage account, then you should use immutable storage. But the preferred approach is to use Azure Confidential Ledger. You can read more about Azure Confidential Ledger here: https://azsec.tech/5bz/.

> **Important** Protecting Ledger hash data from tampering is critical.

> ## Immutable storage
>
> Azure offers immutable storage to mitigate tampering, but it's not a cryptographic defense. Rather, it uses a write-once, read-many (WORM) model that prevents changes to data for the amount of time you define. If you're storing Azure SQL Database Ledger hashes, or log files in Azure Storage accounts, you should consider using immutable storage at least for a few weeks or months before the logs are moved to "cooler" and more cost-effective storage. You can read more about immutable storage here: https://azsec.tech/p1m.

Ledger tables are not a new table type, but rather a property on a table. Creating a table with ledger capabilities is as easy as adding the instructions inside the following WITH statement:

```
CREATE TABLE [Schema].[TableName]
(
  -- Columns
)
WITH
(
    SYSTEM_VERSIONING = ON,
    LEDGER = ON
);
GO
```

You can learn more about ledger functionality at https://azsec.tech/mar. For a technical whitepaper on the topic, see https://azsec.tech/7jn.

Microsoft Defender for SQL

Azure provides a series of Microsoft Defender products for various services, including SQL Server. You can use Microsoft Defender for SQL to protect on-premises SQL Server, IaaS SQL Server, Azure SQL Database, Azure SQL Managed Instance, and SQL Server instances in Amazon Web Services (AWS) and Google Cloud Platform (GCP).

Azure Defender for SQL constantly monitors your instances for known vulnerabilities and threats. It includes these tools:

- **Vulnerability Assessment** This is a scanning service to find, track, and repair potential database vulnerabilities. The assessment provides an overview of the security posture of your

SQL Server instances and provides detailed information about vulnerabilities discovered with potential remedies. The Vulnerability Assessment service can send a regular email that includes the results of a current scan.

- **Advanced Threat Protection**   This is a detection service that continuously monitors your SQL Server instances for threats like SQL injection, logins from suspicious or unusual locations, and password brute-force attacks. The service provides security alerts and remedies in Microsoft Defender for Cloud.

You can learn more about Microsoft Defender for SQL at https://azsec.tech/kpn.

Azure Security Baseline

The Azure Security Benchmark is a series of service-agnostic recommended security practices. Each Azure service has an Azure Security Baseline that maps to the Benchmark. You can learn more about the Azure Security Benchmark in Chapter 8. The Azure Security Baseline for Azure SQL Database is available here: https://azsec.tech/lgv.

SQL Server IaaS Agent

For SQL Server instances running in a VM, you should consider including the SQL Server IaaS Agent, as it supports better integration with Azure features such as Key Vault. You can learn more here: https://azsec.tech/7wl.

The Key Vault integration is used as an Extensible Key Management (EKM) provider to protect SQL Server keys, such as those used by TDE. You can learn more here: https://azsec.tech/yui.

Cosmos DB security

Because Cosmos DB is relatively new and was born in Azure, the database uses common Azure security controls. For the most part, it has a simpler security model than SQL Server, including Azure SQL Database. Because security is simpler in Cosmos DB, this section is considerably smaller than the previous SQL Server section.

The fact that Cosmos DB is newer is important. This means it does not have the same level of application compatibility to contend with that SQL Server does. This might seem like a harsh statement, but compatibility always means there are complexities to contend with.

> **Note** Some Cosmos DB security settings use the term DocumentDB because Cosmos DB is a document database and was previously called DocumentDB. Also, Cosmos DB uses the term *account* the same way Azure Storage uses the word: it means an instance Cosmos DB. We want to point this out because people sometimes get confused with overloaded terms, and we want to clarify that we don't mean *user account*.

Cosmos DB is a multiparadigm database. It supports multiple APIs, such as MongoDB and Cassandra. However, most of this section of the chapter refers to the SQL API.

 Important Unless otherwise stated, the rest of this chapter refers to using the SQL API.

Table 13-3 lists the security controls supported by Cosmos DB.

TABLE 13-3 The intersection of security services with control and data planes

Security Property	Control Plane	Data Plane
Authentication (AuthN)	**Server** TLS **Clients** AAD	**Server** TLS **Clients** AAD Primary keys Resource tokens
Authorization (AuthZ)	Azure RBAC	Azure RBAC Primary keys Resource tokens
Audit	Activity Log	Diagnostic settings / DataPlaneRequests
Cryptography at rest	The cryptographic controls for data at rest are the same for the control plane and the data plane. The two options are volume encryption and Always Encrypted client-side cryptography.	
Cryptography on the wire	TLS	TLS
Cryptography in use	Always Encrypted	
Network isolation	Resource Management Private Link	Private endpoints Service endpoints Service firewall

Let's look at each. You will notice the list of mitigations is smaller and simpler than that in SQL Server, especially the data plane authorization model.

Control plane authentication

When thinking about authentication, you must consider, "Who is authenticating whom?" So, we will look at a caller authenticating a server first and then the server authenticating the caller, or the client.

Control plane server authentication

When connecting to Cosmos DB to perform administrative tasks on the control plane, the connection always uses TLS for server authentication. This cannot be disabled.

With regard to who is authenticating whom, this is server authentication; the validity of the Cosmos DB instance is verified by the client. But how does the server know who the client is? That is discussed next.

Control plane client authentication

To perform administrative operations at the control plane, such as changing the way authentication works at the data plane, you must use AAD accounts. When you use https://portal.azure.com or an Azure REST API to perform control plane operations, you always authenticate using an AAD account.

Control plane authorization

Once you have connected to the server instance, authorization is performed using Azure native RBAC controls. For example, an account that has the DocumentDB Account Contributor role can manage Azure Cosmos DB accounts but not access the data within. You can read the definition of the role here: https://azsec.tech/tdt.

If you look at just the permissions, the role looks like this:

```
"description": "Lets you manage DocumentDB accounts, but not access to them.",
"permissions": [
  {
    "actions": [
      "Microsoft.Authorization/*/read",
      "Microsoft.DocumentDb/databaseAccounts/*",
      "Microsoft.Insights/alertRules/*",
      "Microsoft.ResourceHealth/availabilityStatuses/read",
      "Microsoft.Resources/deployments/*",
      "Microsoft.Resources/subscriptions/resourceGroups/read",
      "Microsoft.Support/*",
      "Microsoft.Network/virtualNetworks/subnets/joinViaServiceEndpoint/action"
    ],
    "notActions": [],
    "dataActions": [],
    "notDataActions": []
  }
],
"roleName": "DocumentDB Account Contributor",
"roleType": "BuiltInRole",
"type": "Microsoft.Authorization/roleDefinitions"
}
```

You can see that the only permissions available for this role are under actions, which describes permissions at the control plane. The dataActions section is empty, meaning this role has no ability to perform any task at the data plane, such as reading data in a container.

Managing a Cosmos DB account (that is, a server plus its databases) is a control plane activity. In contrast, reading data is a data plane activity. As such, it is protected by data plane authorization, covered a little later.

Control plane auditing

Cosmos DB offers control plane auditing using a CDBControlPlaneRequests table. For example:

CDBControlPlaneRequests

```
| project TimeGenerated, AccountName, OperationName, Result
```

Control plane crypto on the wire

There is no option other than TLS, and it cannot be disabled.

Control plane network isolation

Refer to the section "Resource Management Private Link" in the "Security in the SQL Server family" section earlier in this chapter.

Data plane authentication

Now let's switch to Cosmos DB and data plane controls. Remember, you need to consider both server and client authentication. Let's start with how a client authenticates the server.

Data plane server authentication

For server authentication when performing data plane operations, such as running a client application that uses the Cosmos DB SDK, Cosmos DB uses TLS all the time, and it cannot be disabled.

Data plane client authentication

For day-to-day data plane client authentication, Cosmos DB has three options:

- Primary keys
- Resource tokens
- AAD

If we are pedantic, primary keys and resource tokens are not *truly* authentication; rather, they are an authorization mechanism. We say this because the client using a token is not identified. If two people, Toni and Alex, have a copy of the primary key and use that key to connect to a Cosmos DB, there is no way to know if Toni or Alex made the connection. We will go over primary keys and resource tokens in the next section, "Data plane authorization."

The preferred authentication mechanism is AAD. This offers many benefits:

- Centralized control of credentials in AAD
- Strong security because you don't store credentials; rather, they are managed by AAD
- The ability to leverage AAD login policy, such as conditional access, multifactor authentication (MFA), and even certificate-based authentication

Once authentication is successful, you can use native Azure RBAC control plane authorization controls. Remember, this is the control plane, or administrative control over Cosmos DB.

Item 10 in the Azure Cloud Adoption Framework (https://azsec.tech/00p) states that

"Architecture: use identity-based access control instead of keys.

"Key-based authentication can be used to authenticate to cloud services and APIs. But it requires managing keys securely, which is challenging to do well, especially at scale. Secure key management is difficult for non-security professionals like developers and infrastructure professionals, and they often fail to do it securely, often creating major security risks for the organization.

"Identity-based authentication overcomes many of these challenges with mature capabilities. The capabilities include secret rotation, lifecycle management, administrative delegation, and more."

Data plane authorization

Earlier we mentioned that primary keys and resource tokens are not really an authentication mechanism; rather, they align more closely with an authorization technique. Data plane authorization is the topic of this section.

Cosmos DB has three data plane authorization models:

- Primary keys
- Resource tokens
- AAD data plane RBAC

Let's look at each.

Primary keys

Primary keys are accessible in the Azure Portal and can be either read-only or read-write. There is a primary and secondary key for read-only access, and a primary and secondary key for read-write access.

These keys are used in API calls. They are the original form of authorization supported by Cosmos DB. This is what some C# code might look like:

```
using (CosmosClient client = new CosmosClient(endpointUrl, authKey)) {
    // connected
}
```

The second argument to the CosmosClient() constructor is either:

- A read-only primary key
- A read-only secondary key
- A read-write primary key
- A read-write secondary key

There are a couple of problems with using primary and secondary keys:

- There is no granularity. Using the key grants read or read-write permissions to all data held in that database account.

- The keys must be protected by the client using the keys. If a key is compromised, it can be rotated at any time, but this must be done carefully to avoid causing unnecessary business interruptions.

Using this access mechanism is not recommended because there are better mechanisms available. The only real positive aspect of primary keys is that the mechanism is simple.

Resource tokens

Resource tokens are like primary keys, but they provide more flexibility. Resource tokens work a bit like Azure Storage account shared access signatures (SAS). They are a string of data that describes access information and the accessible resource; the string contents are then protected by a Base64-encoded HMAC. The secret used for the HMAC is a read-write primary key.

Here's an example of using a resource token to allow a user or a group only read access to a specific container:

```
await accountHR.CreatePermissionAsync(
    new PermissionProperties(
        id: "permissionReadOnlyHR",
        permissionMode: PermissionMode.Read,
        container: container),
    tokenExpiryInSeconds: 600);
```

By default, a resource token expires after 60 minutes. In the preceding example, it expires after 10 minutes.

When using resource tokens, a common access control model is the trusted gatekeeper model. This connects to Cosmos DB from an intermediary, which is the gatekeeper. For example, you could use an Azure Function that accepts user connections; then, based on the caller's details—for example, something associated with their AAD account—you could build a resource token for that caller and use it to access Cosmos DB.

If you must use primary keys or resource tokens, opt for the latter, as they can be constrained to specific objects such as containers. Primary keys are the keys to the kingdom and do not offer the same level of granularity.

AAD data plane RBAC

Now let's turn our attention to the preferred authorization mechanism: AAD Data Plane RBAC. Cosmos DB added data plane RBAC in 2021. This should, for most deployments, be the preferred way to authorize access to data held in a Cosmos DB database. If you are in a design meeting and someone asks, "How should we authenticate and authorize access to the Cosmos DB?" the answer should always be, "AAD and AAD RBAC."

As we write this, you cannot use the Azure Portal to configure AAD data plane RBAC. Instead, you must use either PowerShell or the Azure CLI to configure it. Here are the steps required, using Power-Shell, to grant a user account access to Cosmos DB:

1. Define a custom RBAC role that grants a principal specific access to a resource.

2. Associate the role with a principal such as Managed Identity, a service principal, or a user.

The PowerShell cmdlets to complete these steps are as follows:

- New-AzCosmosDBSqlRoleDefinition (https://azsec.tech/5dq)

- New-AzCosmosDBSqlRoleAssignment (https://azsec.tech/6c4)

The following code uses these two PowerShell cmdlets to perform the two tasks:

```
$resourceGroupName = "<ResourceGroup>"
$accountName = "<CosmosDBAccount>"

New-AzCosmosDBSqlRoleDefinition -AccountName $accountName `
    -ResourceGroupName $resourceGroupName `
    -Type CustomRole `
    -RoleName ReadOnlyRoleHR `
    -DataAction @( `
        'Microsoft.DocumentDB/databaseAccounts/readMetadata',
        'Microsoft.DocumentDB/databaseAccounts/sqlDatabases/containers/items/read', `
        'Microsoft.DocumentDB/databaseAccounts/sqlDatabases/containers/readChangeFeed') `
    -AssignableScope "/"

# GUID for the principal
$principalId = "<aadPrincipalId>"
New-AzCosmosDBSqlRoleAssignment -AccountName $accountName `
    -ResourceGroupName $resourceGroupName `
    -RoleDefinitionName ReadOnlyRoleHR `
    -Scope "/dbs/employees/colls/employee " `
    -PrincipalId $principalId
```

There are a few points of interest in this code:

- This custom role is named ReadOnlyRoleHR, and it will apply to a specified Cosmos DB account within a specified resource group.

- The DataAction argument (remember, this is data plane RBAC, not control plane) includes the individual permissions and the scope at which they will take effect—in this case, "/" or the root of the Cosmos DB instance. We're creating a custom role that encompasses three permissions.

- The second PowerShell cmdlet assigns the custom role to a principal. The principal is the GUID of the account.

- This role assignment is scoped to the employee collection within the employees database. Note the use of dbs and colls to delimit databases and collections.

Examples of permissions include the following:

- Microsoft.DocumentDB/databaseAccounts/readMetadata
- Microsoft.DocumentDB/databaseAccounts/sqlDatabases/containers/items/create
- Microsoft.DocumentDB/databaseAccounts/sqlDatabases/containers/items/delete

A full list of permissions is available here: https://azsec.tech/ed7/.

Cosmos DB always has two built-in data plane role definitions:

- Cosmos DB Built-in Data Reader
- Cosmos DB Built-in Data Contributor

You can read more about these roles, and the permissions associated with them, here: https://azsec.tech/trg.

Note that when you use data plane RBAC controls, you must explicitly grant access to users and principals. Otherwise, you will see something like this:

```
Forbidden (403); Substatus: 5301; ActivityId: ca5cbde7-0d66-4d2d-8aa0-250f823bcd6d; Reason:
(Request blocked by Auth customer: Request is blocked because principal [8afb6b88-41c2-4f1f-
9c8f-ff737af6626a] does not have required RBAC permissions to perform action [Microsoft.
DocumentDB/databaseAccounts/readMetadata]
```

You can display the data plane RBAC policy on a Cosmos DB instance by using the following PowerShell code:

```
Get-AzCosmosDBSqlRoleDefinition -AccountName $accountName -ResourceGroupName $resourceGroupName
```

If you want to use data plane RBAC only and not use primary keys or resource tokens, you can enforce this using the following:

```
az cosmosdb update --name [CosmosDBAccount] --resource-group [ResourceGroupName] --disable-key-
based-metadata-write-access true
```

Or, from PowerShell:

```
Update-AzCosmosDBAccount -ResourceGroupName [ResourceGroupName] -Name [CosmosDBAccount]
-DisableKeyBasedMetadataWriteAccess true
```

Be aware that at the time of writing, doing this prevents queries from within the Azure Portal from working.

Finally, you can assign permissions using ARM or Bicep templates. After you have set up the RBAC policy using PowerShell or the Azure CLI, you can view the results by exporting the ARM template from the Azure Portal.

> **Tip** Thomas Weiss, principal program manager in the Cosmos DB team, has an excellent video on the topic of data plane RBAC at https://azsec.tech/go1. For complete documentation on setting up data plane RBAC, see https://azsec.tech/akg.

Real-world experience: Using data plane RBAC

Michael worked with a customer using Cosmos DB. While building a threat model for the application, this question came up: "How are you authenticating and authorizing access to Cosmos DB from the Azure Function?" The answer was, "We use primary keys." The next question was, "So, where is the primary key stored, and how is it protected?" The answer was, "It's stored as a secret in Key Vault, and we use the Function's Managed Identity to restrict access to it." Michael responded, "In which case you should use Cosmos DB's data plane RBAC, because the Function already has a Managed Identity." The customer quickly started experimenting with data plane RBAC!

Important You should use data plane RBAC. It has numerous advantages over token-based authorization models. Most notably, it is more secure in that you do not need to store a secret.

Data plane auditing

You can perform data plane auditing of user interactions with your databases and collections in the Azure Portal under the Monitoring and then Diagnostic settings. (See Figure 13-2.) Note that the **Destination Table** setting is resource specific. You should use this so you can query the CDBData-PlaneRequests table rather than AzureDiagnostics. More services will support their own table in the coming months.

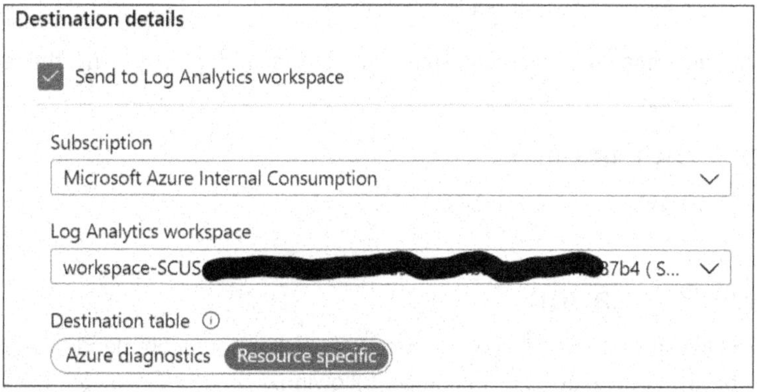

Destination details

☑ Send to Log Analytics workspace

Subscription

| Microsoft Azure Internal Consumption | ⌄ |

Log Analytics workspace

| workspace-SCUS███████████████████████87b4 (S... | ⌄ |

Destination table ⓘ

(Azure diagnostics (Resource specific))

FIGURE 13-2 Setting up a Log Analytics workspace to log data plane interactions.

The output from a log query, using KQL, looks like that shown in Figure 13-3.

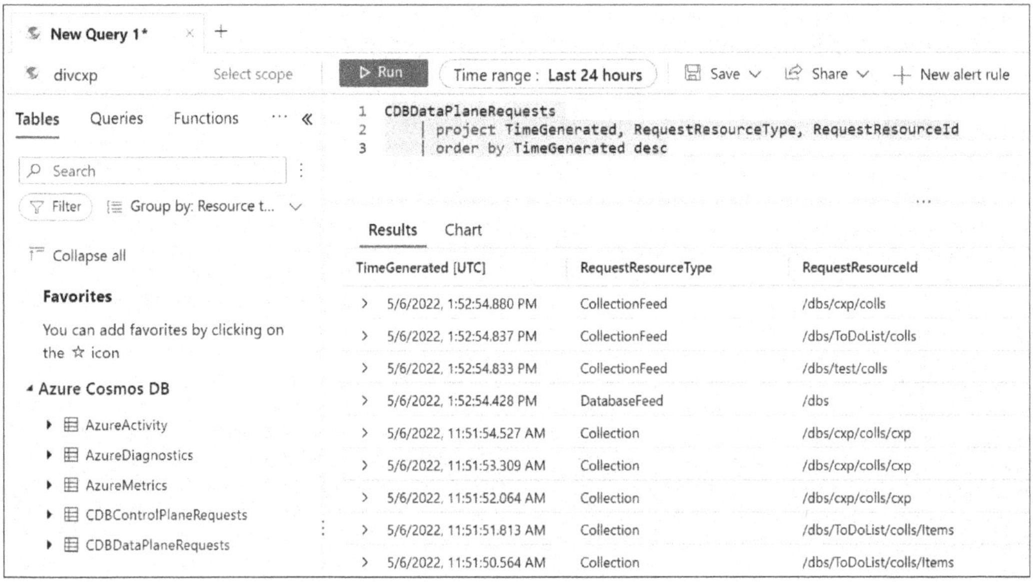

FIGURE 13-3 Using KQL to query the CDBDataPlaneRequests table to view Cosmos DB data plane interactions.

If you use resource tokens, two other properties are logged:

- **resourceTokenPermissionId** The resource token permission ID that you have specified

- **resourceTokenPermissionMode** The permission mode—all or read—that you set when creating the resource token

If you are using data plane RBAC, you will see two other logged properties:

- **aadPrincipalId** The AAD identity that made the request

- **aadAppliedRoleAssignmentId** The role assignment used to authorize (or deny) the request

Data plane crypto on the wire

Again, only TLS can be used, and it cannot be disabled.

Data plane network isolation

At the data plane, Cosmos DB can be accessed over the internet, which is not recommended. Alternatively, it can use stronger network restrictions, including the following:

- **Cosmos DB firewall** This is like the Azure SQL Database firewall. It allows access to the service from a set of IP addresses using a CIDR range or one or more single IP addresses. This is especially useful if you want to ensure the service listens only to traffic from the back end of a load balancer or Azure Function and no other IP addresses.

- **Service endpoint** You can configure Azure Cosmos DB to allow access only from a specific subnet of a virtual network (VNet) using a service endpoint. Service endpoints enable private

IP addresses in the VNet to reach the endpoint of an Azure service, such as Cosmos DB, without requiring a public IP address on the VNet. You can read more here: https://azsec.tech/vnm.

- **Private endpoint**   This is the preferred mechanism for restricting and isolating network access. Private endpoints allow users to access Azure Cosmos DB from within the VNet or from any peered virtual network. Resources mapped to private endpoints are also accessible on-premises over private peering through VPN or Azure ExpressRoute. You can learn more here: https://azsec.tech/5lh.

Cryptographic controls for data at rest

Cosmos DB offers two ways to protect data at rest with cryptographic controls. The first is essentially the same as TDE used by SQL Server. Either you can use keys managed by Azure or you can use your own customer-managed keys (CMKs) when you set up the Cosmos DB instance.

> **Note** You cannot change back to platform-managed keys if you choose to use customer-managed keys. Make sure you back up the keys if you use CMKs.

The second option for encryption of data at rest is Always Encrypted. This is new in Cosmos DB.

We also refer to Always Encrypted as encryption of data in use. We explain Always Encrypted in considerably more detail near the end of this chapter, in the section "Encryption of data in use: Always Encrypted."

> **Note** In Cosmos DB, Always Encrypted applies only to the default SQL API. However, with MongoDB API v4.2, Cosmos DB also supports MongoDB client-side field encryption. This is similar to the way Always Encrypted works in Azure SQL Database, SQL Server, and Cosmos DB. You can learn more here: https://azsec.tech/mce.

Miscellaneous

As with Azure SQL Database, there are other tools you should use or consult to help secure your Cosmos DB solutions. This section covers some of them.

Microsoft Defender for Cosmos DB

At the time of this writing, this new member of the Microsoft Defender family is in preview. Events from the Microsoft Defender for Cosmos DB are fed into Microsoft Defender for Cloud. This tool can trigger alerts for the following:

- **Potential SQL injection attacks**   Defender for Azure Cosmos DB detects both successful and failed SQL injection attempts.

- **Anomalous database access patterns** These include Cosmos DB from a TOR exit node, known suspicious IP addresses, unusual applications, or unusual locations.

- **Suspicious database activity** This includes suspicious key-listing patterns that resemble known malicious lateral movement techniques and suspicious data extraction patterns.

> **Important** Microsoft Defender for Cosmos DB works with the SQL/Core API only.

Azure Security Baseline

The Azure Security Baseline is a set of recommended security practices to help secure Azure services, including Cosmos DB. The baseline for Cosmos DB is available here: https://azsec.tech/09z.

Encryption of data in use: Always Encrypted

As noted, cryptographic controls are an effective last line of defense against compromise. When used correctly, cryptographic controls are also an element of sound zero-trust design, because in an assume-breach scenario, as long as the keys are well protected, the attacker gets nothing of value. The issue with encryption is it gets in the way of doing business! So, it often exists in tension with business needs and practices. In other words:

- Databases are designed to allow for rapid data queries so users can get business value from the data.

- Encryption is designed to prevent users from reading data!

These two goals are diametrically opposed to one another. However, Always Encrypted can help bridge the gap between them by keeping sensitive data encrypted while performing some SQL queries.

Always Encrypted is more than encryption. A better name might be Always Protected. This is because the technology includes integrity controls as well as encryption.

In SQL Server, there are two types of Always Encrypted:

- Always Encrypted

- Always Encrypted with secure enclaves

Cosmos DB supports Always Encrypted, but not Always Encrypted with secure enclaves. Always Encrypted with secure enclaves offers more flexibility than Always Encrypted when not using enclaves.

> **Note** We explain secure enclaves in more detail in Chapter 11, "Confidential computing." We explain the cryptography behind Always Encrypted in Chapter 10, "Cryptography in Azure." You might also need to review Appendix A, "Basic cryptography," as it mentions some cryptographic primitives.

Always Encrypted

Always Encrypted is supported in all current versions of SQL Server starting with SQL Server 2016. Azure SQL Database and SQL Managed Instance also support Always Encrypted.

Cosmos DB also supports Always Encrypted.

Always Encrypted is a client-side encryption and decryption mechanism. The cryptographic operations are performed by the client code. By *client code*, we mean the SQL Server or Cosmos DB driver code, such as the following:

- ODBC Driver for SQL Server

- ADO.NET

- Microsoft.Data.SqlClient

- Microsoft.Azure.Cosmos

The cryptography (key unwrapping, bulk encryption, and decryption) is not performed by SQL Server or Cosmos DB. This has some benefits:

- Neither SQL Server nor Cosmos DB take the performance hit of performing the cryptographic operations.

- Neither SQL Server nor Cosmos DB have data encryption keys.

This last point is incredibly important. In the event of a complete compromise by an attacker, there are no data encryption keys to be found at the database server. So, the attacker will only get the ciphertext for columns encrypted with Always Encrypted. As noted, this is a good design to support zero trust.

> **Note** In the interest of brevity, from here on we will focus on the use of Always Encrypted with SQL Server. The theory and practice are the same for Cosmos DB, however. There are some references to Cosmos DB and Always Encrypted at the end of this section.

When you configure Always Encrypted in a database, you must identify the following:

- Which columns you want to encrypt

- Which key you want to use for each column

- Whether you want to query the encrypted column or not

Let's look at each.

When you create a table, you can choose if zero or more columns should use Always Encrypted. When you want to encrypt columns, you reference an Azure Key Vault URI within the SQL Server configuration. (You can also use the Windows Certificate Store.) Once you do this, you can select which column master key (CMK) and column encryption key (CEK) to use. You can also use tools like SQL

Server Management Studio or PowerShell to generate the keys for you. You can choose to have one CMK wrap one CEK or have a CMK wrap two or more CEKs if you want. It's flexible.

For the sake of simplicity, we will use one CMK to wrap one CEK.

- The CMK is an RSA key and can be between 2048, 3072, or 4096 bits.

- The CEK is a 256 AES key.

This next part is important: SQL Server does *not store* the CEK. Rather, it stores the CEK wrapped in the CMK, and SQL Server does not have access to the CMK. If that didn't sink in, reread the last sentence. Only the client has access to the CMK in Key Vault.

> **Important** Make sure you have appropriate RBAC policies on the Key Vault restricting access to the CMK to only the appropriate users or processes.

You can see what SQL Server stores by querying the sys.column_encryption_key_values table. The encrypted_value column is the CEK wrapped in the CMK.

Wrapping the CEK means using the public key of the RSA key-pair to encrypt the AES CEK. To unwrap, the client will use the private key of the RSA key-pair from Key Vault to decrypt the CEK.

As shown in Figure 13-4, SQL Server cannot decrypt this blob because it does not have access to the RSA CMK. There is no code built into SQL Server to read the CMK.

```
Query 1

▷ Run   ☐ Cancel query   ↓ Save query   ↓ Export data as ∨   ▦ Show only Editor

1   select * from sys.column_encryption_key_values

Results   Messages

⌕ Search to filter items...

column_encryption_key_id   column_master_key_id   column_master_key_definiti...   encrypted_value   encryption_algorithm_name

1                          1                      1                               AagAAAFoAHQAdABwAHM...   RSA_OAEP

2                          4                      4                               AagAAAFoAHQAdABwAHMAOgAvAC8AawB2AC0AYwByAHkAcAB0AG8AdABlAHMAdAAuAH
                                                                                  awBIAHkAcwAvAGMAbQB rAGEAdQB0AG8AMQAwADcAYgAwADAAYQAzAGIAZQA1AGQQAZgA
3                          5                      5                               xADgANwA2ADQAZgB5yhucSTJycC0lTlH8ZyJ766ubVdFEfv5D6fVhQUnfaKf3a6sqvVBq7Faju5/
                                                                                  A9FixQKcEkzmIHolBLk1wJCNZqRyPUlY8zRAvxhXvPUoSJkqFQV1trpb/CRKLdgKg5C3uaGHxnA,
4                          6                      6                               eP3qzp7M0JcdKNhtxlo3BOVCMZjimLkNvdaOB5/s5zmM0X/19mM/nmlE1+Ps0OOm/HiLp3ALd
                                                                                  wQSpRzveHwN3KAdim7D2lI2Clo85PBenss0HrmWQHYMGzaMMbCVNpR9c/D1Qs67XQTH6xf
                                                                                  o6EGatBqbxBdfHqDXtYZzdMfM9vyWvAipcd+Ewx+9VN+wPdM3Gska6xi9rIAvL6PbVWaoEEev,

Query succeeded | 0s
```

FIGURE 13-4 Querying the sys.column_encryption_key_values table to see the encrypted column encryption keys.

The next decision is, do you want to query any encrypted columns? This will determine which mode you use to encrypt the column. You have two options:

- **Deterministic** If you select this option, the initialization vector (IV) for the data is the plaintext to be encrypted. This means that two plaintexts will have the same ciphertext, but this is crucial to allow your code to query the encrypted data. Deterministic encryption allows you to perform equality and inequality queries over the encrypted column.

- **Randomized** When you use this option, the IV is cryptographically random, and the cipher-text data cannot be queried.

The randomized versus deterministic decision changes dramatically with enclaves, as does the key management. We'll discuss this in a moment.

So how does this all work? Let's look at the lifecycle of a database connection and insert and fetch a row of data using Always Encrypted. The client code must indicate when it connects to SQL Server that it wishes to take advantage of Always Encrypted. This is a key-value pair added to the connection string:

```
Column Encryption Setting=enabled
```

The connection string can be built using code like this:

```
SqlConnectionStringBuilder builder = new SqlConnectionStringBuilder();
builder.DataSource = <servername>;
builder.InitialCatalog = <dbname>;
// Other settings
builder.ColumnEncryptionSetting = SqlConnectionColumnEncryptionSetting.Enabled;
SqlConnection conn = new SqlConnection(builder.ConnectionString);
conn.Open();
```

When your code connects to SQL Server configured for Always Encrypted, various metadata is sent to the client, including the following:

- The location of the RSA key-wrapping key (for example, a Key Vault URI)

- Details about which columns are encrypted

- The deterministic or randomized data

- The blob that contains the wrapped AES column encryption key

The account configuring Always Encrypted keys must have Alter Any Column Master Key and Alter Any Column Encryption Key permissions to create and delete a column master key and column encryption key, respectively.

As long as the client can access SQL Server and the Key Vault to get the CMK and then decrypt the wrapped AES key, it will have the 256-bit AES key in memory that can be used to encrypt and decrypt data columns. Remember, there might be more than one set of keys, but we're going to just focus on one CMK and one CEK. Also, when using Key Vault, the key-unwrapping is performed within the confines of Key Vault, and the RSA CMK can be a hardware key of type RSA-HSM.

Recall that in Chapter 4, we introduced a COVID vaccination clinic scenario. We'll return to that scenario here, in this case using a table named Clinic that has a small number of columns:

```
CREATE TABLE Clinic
(
    ID int NOT NULL,
    LastName varchar(64),
    FirstName varchar(64),
    Address varchar(255),
    City varchar(64),
    State char(2),
    ZIP varchar(12),
    TaxID char(11)
);
```

We will also create an index on the TaxID column:

```
CREATE INDEX taxIdIndex on [dbo].[Clinic] (TaxID)
```

Of these columns, only the last one, TaxID, will use Always Encrypted with deterministic encryption because we want to search on that field. There is no extra syntax required on the TaxID column because Always Encrypted configuration is performed outside the table and handled by the SQL Server (or Cosmos DB) engine.

If you want, you can use T-SQL to configure tables for Always Encrypted, using syntax like this:

```
CREATE TABLE Clinic
(
    -- Other columns
        TaxID var (11)
            ENCRYPTED WITH (COLUMN_ENCRYPTION_KEY = ClinicCEK,
            ENCRYPTION_TYPE = DETERMINISTIC,
            ALGORITHM = 'AEAD_AES_256_CBC_HMAC_SHA_256'),
);
```

SSN or NIN?

In the United States, a user's Social Security number would be the TaxID. This might sound cynical, but in the United States, *Social Security number* should really be renamed to *national identity number* (NIN), because a person's SSN is used for much more than access to Social Security. Because it really is a national identity number, it is a valued target for bad actors.

Our code inserts a row into SQL Server, such as this:

```
INSERT dbo.Lender
VALUES (1001, 'Andrews', 'Lisa', '909 Catherine St, 'Brandon', 'FL', '33509', '123-45-6789')
```

This is where the magic begins. Right before the SQL driver sends the row to SQL Server, it checks to see if any columns require encryption. In this example, the TaxID column is to be encrypted using deterministic encryption. The driver has the 256-bit AES key and uses it to encrypt the TaxID. It is more than encryption, though; the driver code also creates an HMAC to verify the data is not tampered with. The driver converts the original INSERT statement to something that looks like this:

```
INSERT dbo.Clinic
VALUES (1001, 'Andrews', 'Lisa', '909 Catherine St, 'Brandon', 'FL', '33509',
'MDFvdS9rb21 --snip-- FqTQzNBLOdj093PQ==')
```

The TaxID is no longer in plaintext; it is now ciphertext and an HMAC.

SQL Server accepts the row, inserts it into the table, and updates the index. Note that the index is *not* plaintext, even though we set it up as an index on a plaintext TaxID. The index now becomes an index over ciphertext.

Suppose that at some point in the future, someone wants to query the table to find a specific TaxID. Be aware that just having access to the database and the appropriate keys is not enough. Your users need the View Any Column Master Key Definition and View Any Column Encryption Key Definition permissions in the database, too. To query the data, we can use the following T-SQL:

```
DECLARE @TaxID CHAR(11) = '123-45-6789'
SELECT Lastname, Firstname from Clinic where TaxID=@TaxID
```

> **Important** You must use declared variables to perform a query on an Always Encrypted column. You cannot use a string literal, such as where TaxID='123-45-678'.

The SQL driver at the client recognizes that the TaxID is an encrypted column, so it encrypts the data using the AES key that is in memory at the client. So, the query becomes as follows:

```
SELECT Lastname, Firstname from Clinic where TaxID='MDFvdS9rb21--snip--FqTQzNBLOdj093PQ=='
```

When the server gets the request, it performs the query against the encrypted TaxID, which includes using the index if determined by the execution plan. So, rather than answer this question:

Does '123-45-6789' equal '123-45-6789'?

the server asks this question:

Does 'MDFvdS9rb21--snip--FqTQzNBLOdj093PQ==' equal 'MDFvdS9rb21--snip--FqTQzNBLOdj093PQ=='?

The database query engine compares the two sets of ciphertext—the one in the database and the other that came in as a query argument. This is so important to understand. Nothing is encrypted or decrypted by SQL Server; the actual comparison operation is performed by comparing two sets of ciphertext. If you have a table that includes more than one encrypted column and the column is returned to the client, it too is decrypted at the client.

There is a big limitation with Always Encrypted: you can only perform equality or inequality operations over encrypted columns, and only if they are configured to use deterministic encryption. For example, the following operators will work:

- =

- <>

However, the following operators will not work, because they are not equals or does not equal operations:

- >=
- like

Also, this works only with columns marked to use deterministic encryption, which uses the plaintext (in this case '123-45-6789') as the IV. Randomized encryption uses a random IV and does not support queries over encrypted columns that use randomized encryption. Randomized columns can still be returned in the result set and decrypted by the client driver; you just cannot query on a randomized column.

Real-world experience: Randomized vs. deterministic

Michael worked with a large finance customer who wanted to use Always Encrypted, but there was a big problem. The customer required data items like SSNs to be "correctly encrypted," which meant using a random IV when encrypting the data. But they also wanted to query on that column, which you cannot do with randomized columns.

To solve this, the company kept the SSN column and added a Last4SSN column. The SSN column used randomized encryption, and the Last4SSN column used deterministic encryption. So, a query like this:

```
DECLARE @last4 = '1234'
SELECT Surname, Firstname, SSN from Customer where Last4SSN=@last4
```

might return something like this:

Surname	Firstname	SSN	Last4SSN
Hill	Andrew	123-37-1234	1234
Lidman	Anna	872-65-1234	1234
Ruivo	Pedro	611-88-1234	1234
Misiec	Anna	872-65-1234	1234

At no point is the SSN decrypted until the data is decrypted by the client and then displayed.

Also, notice that two Annas have the same SSN: Anna Misiec and Anna Lidman. Perhaps Anna changed her name at some point in her life, but her SSN stayed the same. In this case, because the SSN is encrypted with randomized encryption, the ciphertext is different. This would not be the case if SSN used deterministic encryption; they would have the same IV (the plaintext, in this case the SSN itself), and the ciphertext would be the same.

Tip You can learn more about Always Encrypted using the ADO.NET SQL client here: https://azsec.tech/b1z.

As we discussed Always Encrypted, you might have noticed a few limitations, including the following:

- The requirement to use deterministic encryption to query an encrypted column

- An inability to use any SQL statement beyond = and <>

Some of these limitations are removed when you use Always Encrypted with secure enclaves, so let's cover that next.

Always Encrypted with secure enclaves

Secure enclaves are a specially protected region of memory designed to withstand attack from rogue administrators and rogue cloud operators. This is important. In a zero-trust environment, you trust no one, and that includes administrators and people hosting your applications. Secure enclaves are an important solution for some zero-trust scenarios. We explain secure enclaves in considerably more detail in Chapter 11.

Note SQL Server runs part of its query engine in a secure enclave.

Always Encrypted with secure enclaves is a little different from Always Encrypted in that it performs encryption and decryption of data at the server, but only within a secure enclave. Plaintext is not viewable at all by anyone at the server. Just like Always Encrypted without secure enclaves, the final decryption is performed at the client as long as it has access to the data in the database and it has access to the key encryption key in Key Vault.

Azure SQL Database supports Always Encrypted with secure enclaves, but to use it, you must choose specific compute hardware. To deploy an Azure SQL Database that uses secure enclaves, you deploy as you normally would, but choose DC-series compute hardware. You can then select a DC-series VM. These VMs have CPUs with Software Guard Extensions (SGX), which provide the secure enclave support.

Note SQL Server on-prem and SQL Server in a Windows VM do not use SGX. They use another enclave technology named virtualization-based security (VBS). Chapter 11 touches on this.

When you configure your Azure SQL Database, you can set the underlying hardware on the Compute and Storage page, as shown in Figure 13-5.

FIGURE 13-5 Selecting the Azure SQL Database hardware configuration to support secure enclaves.

> ⚠ **Important** DC-series VMs are not available in all Azure regions, so make sure you deploy your Azure SQL Database in a supported region if you want to use Always Encrypted with secure enclaves. You can search for VM availability at https://azsec.tech/lzy; look up DCsv2-series VMs.

> 💡 **Tip** Here's a little tip if you're just starting out with secure enclaves. The cost for DCsv2-series VMs is more than many other VM types. If you're learning using a limited Azure subscription, you can save money by moving the compute from a DCsv2-series VM to a smaller VM type when you are not using the database. Remember to move the compute back to DCsv2 when you want to restart your Always Encrypted testing.

Designing solutions using Always Encrypted

You can't take an existing system, enable Always Encrypted, and expect it to work. It won't. Many SQL statements will raise exceptions. The only way to use Always Encrypted effectively is to design your solution from the start with Always Encrypted in mind. You will probably need to make changes to your table configurations and change SQL statements so they work correctly with Always Encrypted. But the effort is well worth it for the security benefits gained.

To use Always Encrypted with secure enclaves, you must use the Provisioned compute tier. Serverless is not supported.

The main reason to use Always Encrypted with secure enclaves over Always Encrypted without them is the extra capability and functionality you get from secure enclaves because the ciphertext is decrypted within the enclave where it is queried. The benefits include better support for more SQL statements, such as comparison operators (LIKE, BETWEEN), joins (GROUP BY, ORDER BY), and more. Even better, these operators can be performed over columns using randomized encryption. However, equality (equals and not equals) operations are performed over deterministic columns because the comparison is over the ciphertext, just like Always Encrypted without secure enclaves.

> **Attestation and secure enclaves**
>
> Attestation is an important part of secure enclaves. Attestation means verifying the code loaded into a secure enclave environment is the correct code and is not malicious. The SQL Server code handles sensitive data in the enclave, and it's imperative that the code is valid. Azure SQL Database uses Microsoft Azure Attestation; for SQL Server in a VM or on-prem, attestation is performed by the Host Guardian Service. For SQL Server and Azure SQL Database, the code loaded into the enclave is part of the SQL query engine. We explain attestation in more detail in Chapter 11.

Cosmos DB and Always Encrypted

In early 2022, Cosmos DB released support for Always Encrypted. The technology is equivalent to Always Encrypted in SQL Server, but Cosmos DB does not support secure enclaves.

To use Always Encrypted, you need to call REST APIs either directly or using a Cosmos DB client SDK.

The two packages that support Always Encrypted are as follows:

- **.NET** Microsoft.Azure.Cosmos.Encryption
- **Java** azure.cosmos.encryption

The process to enable and then use Always Encrypted involves the following steps:

1. Set up a Key Vault.
2. Connect to Cosmos DB.
3. Create a data encryption key.
4. Set the container cryptographic policy.

We discuss each of these steps next.

Set up a Key Vault

First, you need to set up a Key Vault and create an RSA key. It can be 2048, 3072, or 4096 bits and either a software (of type RSA) or hardware (of type RSA-HSM) key.

Cosmos DB requires you to know the key name and the version number. You can get the full key identifier in the Azure Portal by clicking the key name and then the version number. The full key identifier will look like this:

https://kv-xxxxxxx-tst.vault.azure.net/keys/CMKAuto1/d78590f4ee3f4277b55b17c7c5ae595d

You will also need to make sure the client using this system has access to Key Vault. As described in Chapter 10, "Cryptography in Azure," Key Vault supports two authorization models: vault access policy and Azure RBAC.

If you are using the classic vault access policy, then the account accessing the Key Vault will need the following permissions:

- get and list

- sign and verify

- wrapKey and unwrapKey

If you are using the newer Azure RBAC model, you simply grant the account the Key Vault Crypto User role. (See https://azsec.tech/cur for more information.)

> **Important** Remember, Cosmos DB does not access Key Vault. Your users and application Managed Identities access Key Vault to get the RSA key-wrapping key. If any environment using Cosmos DB is compromised, the RSA key cannot be accessed through Cosmos DB. This is an example of plausible deniability.

Connect to Cosmos DB

To connect to Cosmos DB, you create a `CosmosClient()` instance that uses `WithEncryption()`. For example:

```
using Azure.Identity;
using Microsoft.Azure.Cosmos;
using Microsoft.Azure.Cosmos.Encryption;
using Azure.Security.KeyVault.Keys.Cryptography;

var tokenCredential = new DefaultAzureCredential();
var keyResolver = new KeyResolver(tokenCredential);
var client = new CosmosClient(<Connection String>)
    .WithEncryption(keyResolver, KeyEncryptionKeyResolverName.AzureKeyVault);
```

Create a data encryption key

Next, you need to create a data encryption key. You can do so using code like this:

```
var database = client.GetDatabase(<db name>);
await database.CreateClientEncryptionKeyAsync(
    "keyDEK",
    DataEncryptionAlgorithm.AeadAes256CbcHmacSha256,
```

```
new EncryptionKeyWrapMetadata(
    KeyEncryptionKeyResolverName.AzureKeyVault,
    "keyCMK",   // a friendly name
    akvUrl,
    EncryptionAlgorithm.RsaOaep.ToString()));
```

There are two references to ciphers in this code:

- AeadAes256CbcHmacSha256 is the algorithm used to protect (encrypt and MAC) your data. It uses the data encryption key to perform bulk data cryptographic operations.

- RsaOaep is the algorithm used to wrap the data encryption key.

Set the container cryptographic Policy

Finally, you set the cryptographic policy for the container. To do so, you can use code like this:

> **Important** Once the cryptographic policy is set, it cannot be changed.

```
var pathSsn4Digits = new ClientEncryptionIncludedPath {
    Path = "/ssn4digits",
    ClientEncryptionKeyId = "keyDEK",
    EncryptionType = EncryptionType.Deterministic.ToString(),
    EncryptionAlgorithm = DataEncryptionAlgorithm.AeadAes256CbcHmacSha256
};
var pathSsn = new ClientEncryptionIncludedPath {
    Path = "/ssn",
    ClientEncryptionKeyId = "keyDEK",
    EncryptionType = EncryptionType.Randomized.ToString(),
    EncryptionAlgorithm = DataEncryptionAlgorithm.AeadAes256CbcHmacSha256
};
await database.DefineContainer("clinic", "/partition-key")
    .WithClientEncryptionPolicy()
    .WithIncludedPath(pathSsn4Digits)
    .WithIncludedPath(pathSsn)
    .Attach()
    .CreateAsync();
```

> **Tip** There is a full C# and Java sample available here: https://azsec.tech/ccs.

SQL injection

We want to wrap up this chapter by making sure you understand that SQL Server, Azure SQL Database, SQL Server Managed Instance, and Cosmos DB are all subject to SQL injection attacks. Chapter 9, "Secure coding," explains injection issues in detail, but we want to discuss it briefly here, too.

SQL injection is not a server vulnerability. Instead, it is a weakness in the way the caller constructs SQL statements. It is imperative that the code you write that creates SQL statements uses correct coding constructs. This usually means:

- Don't use string concatenation to build SQL statements.

- Use parameterized queries to build SQL statements.

For Cosmos DB client code, you can use code like this in C#:

```
var queryDefinition = container.CreateQueryDefinition(
    "SELECT * FROM c where c.id = @ID");
await queryDefinition.AddParameterAsync(
    "@ID",
    id,
    "/id");
```

Or in Java:

```
SqlQuerySpecWithEncryption = new SqlQuerySpecWithEncryption(
    new SqlQuerySpec("SELECT * FROM c where c.id = @ID"));
sqlQuerySpecWithEncryption.addEncryptionParameter(
    "/id", new SqlParameter("@ID", id));
```

In these examples, the variable id is untrusted but rendered safe because we're using parameters.

For SQL Server, you can use code like this C#:

```
var sqlCmd = "select SalesPerson from Sales where mon = @month";
var cmd = new SqlCommand(sqlCmd, conn);
cmd.Parameters.Add("@month", System.Data.SqlDbType.Int);
cmd.Parameters["@month"].Value = month;
```

In this example, month is the untrusted variable.

Summary

Azure stores immeasurable amounts of sensitive data in databases, and that data must be protected at all costs. Using the strategies outlined in this chapter, and with the aid of a good threat model, you can ensure you have the appropriate mitigations in place to protect your data.

SQL Server, Azure SQL Database, Azure SQL Managed Instance, and Cosmos DB all offer extensive defenses, and you should use as many of these defenses as possible to secure your data.

## CHAPTER 14

CI/CD security

After completing this chapter, you will be able to:

- Secure the pipeline, deployment agent, and targeted resources.

- Articulate and apply pull request (PR) and PROD deployment approvals.

- Handle service principals during the deployment process.

What is CI/CD?

Continuous integration and continuous deployment—CI/CD for short—is the current best practice for developing and deploying an application into production environments. CI/CD involves a series of automated workflows to continually build, test, and integrate code changes (continuous integration) and to deploy those changes (continuous deployment). Together these workflows comprise a CI/CD pipeline.

> **Tip** If you are unfamiliar with CI/CD, read more about it here: https://resources.github.com/ci-cd/.

CI/CD tools

There are many tools available that support various stages of the CI/CD pipeline. Some of these tools integrate with a source repository, others manage work items, and still others include plug-ins with all types of useful and configurable features.

Azure DevOps and GitHub pipelines are two examples of CI/CD tools. Both are integrated with their own repository and offer management of work items (called *issues* in GitHub). Both also offer manual deployment approvals for environments (such as PROD) independent of the pipeline definition and separately controlled through RBAC. Another CI/CD tool is Jenkins. It is built completely on extensible plug-ins to integrate with multiple external repository providers, work-item tracking systems, and approval processes. The advantage of using Jenkins is its flexibility, but this flexibility can be a security risk, too. For example, if the pipeline definition is not carefully maintained, crafty attackers can skip many standard practices, such as requiring deployment gate approval, with write access to that pipeline definition.

> **Note** Choosing a CI/CD tool is an individual choice and often involves a trade-off between infinite configurability and some imposed structure. We prefer Azure DevOps or GitHub due to their more structured approach because it reduces the risk of a misconfigured pipeline and allows for greater segregation of duties.

Source control systems and supply chain attacks

Source control systems provide repositories for source code. In a public cloud or a private cloud (in other words, an on-prem datacenter), everything is software defined—including infrastructure, governance, policies, networking, traditional code, and so on. In addition, all modern application development processes use components to accelerate development under commercial or open source licensing models.

As you might imagine, source code repositories are a common target for bad actors; attacks on source control systems are called *supply chain attacks*. It's up to you to try to prevent or remediate these attacks. This includes using security tools, protecting your developers, using good pull-request hygiene, and restricting access to source code.

Security tooling

Protecting your source control systems requires the use of software component analysis (SCA) tools and other security tools. These are covered in Chapter 9, "Secure coding."

When these tools identify a vulnerability or a breach, rapid remediation is key to keeping your security risks low. The remediations required vary by case. Some strategies are:

- Updating to a known good version of an external component.

- Replacing a vulnerable component with a different technology. Just remember that the grass isn't always greener on the other side of the fence!

- Adding an intermediary to block the attacker—for example, a web application firewall (WAF). Just be aware that using such an intermediary does not constitute a permanent fix.

Protecting your developers

An adversary might steal the credentials of one of your developers or use malware to assume control of their workstation to impersonate them. So, you must implement strong defenses against credential theft, lateral movement, and malware attacks. At a bare minimum, you need zero-trust identity measures, such as multifactor authentication (MFA), conditional access, cloud access security brokers, and malware protection. You should also increase developers' privileged access security level from enterprise security (typical today) to specialized security. For more information about specialized security, see https://azsec.tech/a6l and https://azsec.tech/m39.

Pull request approvals and PR hygiene

A pull request (PR) occurs when a developer is ready to add new code to the source code repository. Before this code is added, however, the PR must be approved using a tool-based and/or human security review. (Human reviews are still better at detecting anomalies in content than automated ones.)

To prevent the insertion of malicious code, both the developer and the reviewer should practice good PR hygiene. On the developer side, practicing good PR hygiene involves these best practices:

- Executing work in the branch tied to the work item, such as user stories, product backlog items (PBI), issues, and so on

- Linking the PR to the same work item

- Adding comments and PR descriptions to explain how the change was implemented and which files were modified (that is, do not rely on the version control system alone)

- Linking the "why" of the change to the work item

For the reviewer, practicing good PR hygiene means:

- Reading the work item, committing comments and PR descriptions, and cross-checking them with the file changes to make sure they match

- Looking for code changes not justified by the linked PBI

- Talking to the developer to clear up any issues you're unsure about

Reviewers should apply special care for changes in the following areas:

- Changing the pipeline definition

- Changing deployment scripts

- Using new third-party packages in the code

- Consuming additional external (web) services

Separation of duties, least privilege overview

Access to source code must be strictly controlled with RBAC. Be sure to apply special care when assigning rights for the following activities:

- Editing secrets (such as creating or updating service connections in Azure DevOps or GitHub)

- Configuring branch policies

- Configuring PR policies

- Configuring PROD environment deployment approvals

- Changing the pipeline definition

- Changing deployment scripts

Secrets and service connections

Securing secrets and service connections is critical in a CI/CD pipeline. There are a few ways to do this:

- **Managed Identity for Azure DevOps (AzDO) CI/CD pipelines** In an ideal world, all secrets would be stored in an Azure Key Vault accessed through an Azure Active Directory Managed Identity. Unfortunately, this approach, while doable, is not practical due to its inherent complexity. (See https://azsec.tech/8qu for more information.)

- **Protecting Azure DevOps service connections** Azure DevOps encrypts and protects service connection credentials. Service connections that use Azure Active Directory service principals need a secret. This secret is write-only, meaning you cannot read it back in the user interface. The key to protecting this secret relates to how it is handled from the time it is created in Azure Active Directory until it enters Azure DevOps. It is a process issue. For more on how Azure DevOps encrypts and protects service connection credentials, see https://azsec.tech/ufz. You can learn more about securing service connection secrets here: https://azsec.tech/tf8.

- **Protecting service principal secrets in GitHub** GitHub has secrets protection built in. Azure login is a GitHub action that can and should use the secrets store variables to pass the credentials. For more information, see https://azsec.tech/dd4.

Protecting the main branch in Azure DevOps and GitHub

As you no doubt know, software developers use code branching to work on different parts (or branches) of the same project without affecting each other. The code as a whole is often called the *trunk* or *main branch*. Protecting the main branch in any project is obviously critical. Fortunately, it's also easy.

> **Note** While many branching strategies are possible, most teams use short-term feature branches. One of the most common of these is GitHub Flow.

To do this in Azure DevOps:

- Configure a branch policy for the main branch that, at a minimum, requires two reviewers for each PR and does not allow requestors to approve their own changes. To learn more about configuring a policy for the main branch, see https://azsec.tech/ik3. To find out how to require a minimum number of reviewers for PRs, see https://azsec.tech/w9r.

- Do not grant anyone the Bypass Policies When Completing Pull Requests and Bypass Policies When Pushing branch permissions for the main branch. This is discussed in more detail here: https://azsec.tech/w9f.

- Require all branches to be created in folders. See https://azsec.tech/cgs for more information.

In GitHub, you protect the main branch by configuring a branch protection rule with the following parameters:

- Require a PR before merging.

- Require multiple approvers. For most solutions, two is an acceptable number, but for highly sensitive solutions, additional approvers might be appropriate.

- Dismiss stale PRs.

- Optionally, require review from code owners.

- Do not allow specific actors to bypass required PRs.

- Restrict who can dismiss PR reviews.

> **Tip** To find out how to create a branch protection rule in GitHub, see https://azsec.tech/3ha.

Protecting the PROD deployment in Azure DevOps and GitHub

You can use Azure DevOps environments for each type of environment, from DEV to PROD. Approvals for DEV and other non-PROD environments are optional. However, PROD environment deployments should require at least one approver. For more information, see https://azsec.tech/zln.

In GitHub, you can use GitHub workflow environments for each type of environment, from DEV to PROD. As with Azure DevOps, approvals for DEV and other non-PROD environments in GitHub are optional. However, PROD environments should be protected with the following environment protection rules:

- Require at least one approver.

- Limit the environment to a specific protected branch (in most cases, the main branch).

- Store secrets, such as credentials, in the environment.

Tip For more information about GitHub environment protection rules, see https://azsec.tech/mrx.

Securing deployment agents

CI/CD pipelines use agents, or runners, to run automated jobs. Microsoft describes agents as follows:

> With Microsoft-hosted agents, maintenance and upgrades are taken care of for you. Each time you run a pipeline, you get a fresh virtual machine for each job in the pipeline. The virtual machine is discarded after one job (which means any change that a job makes to the virtual machine file system, such as checking out code, will be unavailable for the next job).

In addition to using Microsoft-hosted agents, you can use self-hosted agents as well as GitHub agents.

Here are a few key points about agents:

- Microsoft-hosted agents cannot access private endpoints and private IP addresses on VMs to execute deployments.

- You can collect a group of agents into an agent pool. That way, instead of managing each agent individually, you can manage them as a group.

- Microsoft- and GitHub-hosted agents and agent pools automatically destroy the VM executing a job when the job is complete. With self-hosted agents and agent pools, however, this is not the case. You must take steps to ensure the VM is destroyed (preferred) or at least cleansed of pipeline-specific data and, most importantly, execution credentials before it is used again. This prevents one pipeline using another pipeline's secrets (for example, credentials).

- Do not install multiple agents on a single VM or container. Otherwise, secrets could be leaked between agents.

- Agents should use outbound connections only. Azure DevOps agents and GitHub agents adhere to this principle, and we suspect this is true for all agents. If your deployment system does not follow this principle, switch brands immediately.

Securing Azure DevOps agents

To secure Azure DevOps agents, use one of the following approaches:

- **Use Azure virtual machine scale set (VMSS) agents** With this approach, Azure DevOps takes a used agent instance offline and re-images the agent. For more information, see https://azsec.tech/nks and https://azsec.tech/48l.

- **Run a self-hosted agent in Docker** You can require a fresh container instance for each run by passing the --once flag. See https://azsec.tech/s1d and https://azsec.tech/ebd for more details.

Securing GitHub agents

GitHub cannot create single-use self-hosted runners. Mitigation attempts at destroying the agent after each use depend on timing and are therefore not guaranteed to work; so, such a mitigation must be considered partial. For more information, see the GitHub documentation here: https://azsec.tech/q9j. The only full mitigation against secret leakage is single-purpose (for a specific pipeline) runners. While managing access to self-hosted runners using groups is a feasible solution (see https://azsec.tech/cju), it is still difficult to manage at scale.

> **Warning** GitHub public repos should never use private agents. Any fork of the GitHub public repo can launch an attack against the agent itself or the VMs or containers hosting the agent. It can also launch an attack on any resource to which the agent's identity or service connection(s) has modify access. For example, Enterprise Policy as Code (see https://azsec.tech/q6p) has User Administrator privileges in your Azure Active Directory tenant. This public repo has no pipeline configured.

Summary

CI/CD environments are attack vectors, and as such, they should be protected. Securing CI/CD environments requires security tooling, protecting developers, diligent PR reviews, separation of duties, protecting pipeline secrets, protecting the main branch, PROD environment deployment approvals, and protecting the agent/runners.

## CHAPTER 15

Network security

After completing this chapter, you will be able to:

- Understand Azure network basics, including VNets, CIDR blocks, and routing.

- Understand UDRs and NSGs.

- Understand basic network topology, environment restrictions, and ingress/egress control objectives.

- Develop solutions protected by network virtual appliances.

- Implement PaaS services without public IP endpoints.

Network threats are related to either large attack surfaces or denial-of-service (DoS) attacks. This is the reason for using network defenses in the age of zero trust and identity as the new primary perimeter. In a holistic zero-trust approach, network security provides an important secondary defensive perimeter.

Azure networking primer

In a cloud environment and in some on-premises environments, networking is defined through code that is often referred to as *Infrastructure as Code* (IaC). For Azure, that code is written as an ARM template, Bicep file, or Terraform module.

Azure uses virtual networks (VNets) and subnets within each VNet to segment your solution's network. VNets are independent of each other, and communication is possible only to public IP addresses or to peered VNets. VNet peering is most often done through a hub-and-spoke model, as shown in Figure 15-1.

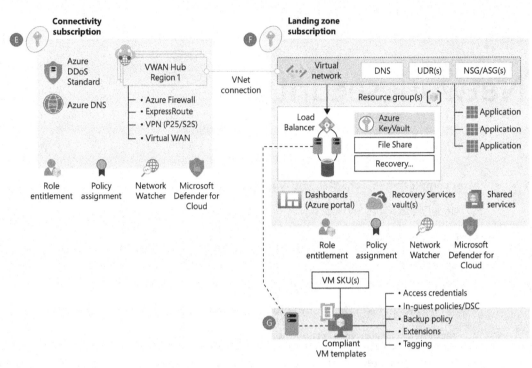

FIGURE 15-1 Virtual WAN network topology.

In Bicep, the simplest VNet and subnet deployment is as follows:

```
resource my_vnet_001 'Microsoft.Network/virtualNetworks@2020-06-01' = {
  name: 'my-vnet-001'
  location: 'eastus2'
  properties: {
    addressSpace: {
      addressPrefixes: [
        '10.0.0.0/24'
      ]
    }
    subnets: [
      {
        name: 'subnet-main'
        properties: {
          addressPrefix: '10.0.0.0/26'
        }
      }
      {
        name: 'subnet-private-endpoints'
        properties: {
          addressPrefix: '10.0.0.64/26'
        }
      }
    ]
  }
}
```

This Bicep file defines the following:

- A VNet named my_vnet_001

- An address space of 256 IP addresses, starting at 10.0.0.0, through a CIDR notation

  - A subnet named subnet-main, specifying 59 IP addresses, starting at 10.0.0.0

  - A subnet named subnet-private-endpoints, specifying 59 IP addresses, starting at 10.0.0.64

This leaves 128 IP addresses usable for future subnets.

Let's learn more about VNet networking.

IPv4, IPv6 in Azure

Although the end of IPv4 has been predicted for the last 15 years, it is still the dominant addressing schema, despite "running out" of address space. Technologies such as network address translation (NAT) have extended IPv4's life. VNets and subnets in Azure predominately use IPv4; however, Azure does support IPv6.

> ### Real-world experience: Do customers use IPv6?
>
> None of us have ever seen IPv6 in any of our engagements or heard of anybody using IPv6. Therefore, this chapter focuses on IPv4.

IPv4 concepts

IPv4 uses 4 bytes of addressing, written as decimals between 0 and 255, and separated by dots. The IPv4 address space (2^{32}) is subdivided into subnets. This subdivision is achieved with subnet masks.

A subnet mask specifies which bits are fixed by the subnet and which bits are available for resource addressing—for example, 11111111.11111111.11111111.11000000, or written as decimals, 255.255.255.192.

The starting address, called a *network prefix*, must fit into the subnet mask. Also, the subnet mask may not truncate the network prefix. In other words, the starting address must align correctly on the power of 2 subnet masks. The 0-bits part of the subnet mask can be used for the host part or, in the case of a VNet, to create subnets.

IPv4 addresses in Azure and CIDR

When specifying address prefixes in ARM, we use a Classless Inter-Domain Routing (CIDR) notation—for example, 10.0.5.0/24. CIDR notations specify the starting address, called a *network prefix* (in this example, 10.5.0.0), and the subnet mask size (here, /24), indicating how many leading ones are in the subnet mask. The number of addresses available for your use is calculated as follows:

addresses = $2^{32-maskSize} - 5$

The 5 in the formula is used by Azure itself, specifying the first five addresses in a subnet.

The smallest block is a /29, which gives three available addresses. A block of /30 would have fewer than zero available addresses. See Table 15-1 for examples.

TABLE 15-1 CIDR definition examples

CIDR	Subnet Mask	Network Prefix	Host Part	IP address	Available Addresses
10.0.1.8/29	255.255.255.248	10.0.1.8	0.0.0.6	10.0.1.14	3
10.2.4.0/24	255.255.255.0	10.2.4.0	0.0.0.129	10.2.4.129	250
10.3.0.0/16	255.255.0.0	10.3.0.0	0.0.17.15	10.3.17.15	65,530

Routing and user-defined routes

Azure uses standard IPv4 (and IPv6) routing. User-defined routes (UDRs) are used to inject routing through intermediaries. This capability is essential to route outbound traffic to the internet or to an on-premises environment through network virtual appliances (NVAs). It is common to use a UDR that routes all outgoing traffic from your solution to an NVA to perform packet inspection for the purposes of detecting data leakage. This is often called *data egress filtering*.

UDRs are attached to subnets (best practice) or individual NICs (not recommended). Each UDR has a unique name and can be reused across multiple subnets and VNets. Governance enforces the use of the correct per-region UDR.

Network security groups

Network security groups (NSGs) and UDRs are associated to subnets (best practice) or individual network interface cards (NICs), but this is not recommended. Both UDRs and NSGs can be reused for multiple subnets or NICs.

NSGs specify IP address–based access control through rules for inbound and/or outbound connectivity. These rules are ordered, meaning that once a rule is satisfied, no additional rules are processed. The last rule is a default rule denying all inbound and outbound traffic on any port and any protocol. This last rule enforces an allow-listing approach to grant communication.

> **Note** Not using an NSG will allow all traffic.

NSGs are named and have an evaluation order priority, a port number, a protocol source, a source IP address, a destination IP address, and an action (allow or deny). These values can be set to Any. The IP addresses can contain IP ranges, service tags, or application security groups (ASGs). Figure 15-1 shows an example.

Priority ↑	Name ↑↓	Port ↑↓	Protocol ↑↓	Source ↑↓	Destination ↑↓	Action ↑↓	
⌄ Inbound Security Rules							
1001	GatewayManager	443	Tcp	GatewayManager	Any	✅ Allow	🗑
1002	Internet-Bastion-PublicIP	443	Tcp	Any	Any	✅ Allow	🗑
65000	AllowVnetInBound	Any	Any	VirtualNetwork	VirtualNetwork	✅ Allow	🗑
65001	AllowAzureLoadBalancerIn...	Any	Any	AzureLoadBalancer	Any	✅ Allow	🗑
65500	DenyAllInBound	Any	Any	Any	Any	❌ Deny	🗑
⌄ Outbound Security Rules							
1001	OutboundVirtualNetwork	22,3389	Tcp	Any	VirtualNetwork	✅ Allow	🗑
1002	OutboundToAzureCloud	443	Tcp	Any	AzureCloud	✅ Allow	🗑
65000	AllowVnetOutBound	Any	Any	VirtualNetwork	VirtualNetwork	✅ Allow	🗑
65001	AllowInternetOutBound	Any	Any	Any	Internet	✅ Allow	🗑
65500	DenyAllOutBound	Any	Any	Any	Any	❌ Deny	🗑

FIGURE 15-1 NSG definition.

It is recommended that you always keep one high-priority NSG spot unused (for example, a spot with a priority of 100) so that if an attack occurs, you can block incoming traffic using a Deny/All IPs/All Ports/All Protocols rule.

Application security groups

Application security groups (ASGs) simplify the assignment of multiple network interface cards (NICs) to a network security group (NSG). We discourage defining network security at the NIC level because it tends to be hard to maintain at scale. It is better to define NSGs for subnets. However, in certain lift-and-shift scenarios, assigning NSGs to NICs can replicate existing micro-segmentation from the on-premises solution without creating lots of subnets. For this use case, group every NIC in a micro-segment to an ASG and use that ASG in the NSG to achieve significantly simpler NSG definitions.

Landing zones, hubs, and spokes

Well-governed Azure tenants implement enterprise-scale landing zones and use a hub-and-spoke networking model—either a traditional model or a newer virtual WAN model. When designing the landing zones and spokes, enterprise architects typically place security and other shared services in the hub and/or in specialized spokes.

Hub and spoke and segmentation

A spoke is often created for each business solution area, with subnets subdividing for more segmentation when desired. It is important to avoid getting too fine-grained, because "nano-segmentation," as this practice is often called, is both fragile and difficult to manage. Using any number of technologies, the hub can limit which VNets are allowed to communicate with each other.

Environment segregation, VNets, and allowed communications

A core tenet is to only allow landing zones of the same environment to communicate between their VNets. This leads to the rules shown in Table 15-2.

TABLE 15-2 Matrix defining allowed communications between resources in different environments

From -> To	SANDBOX	DEV	DEVINT	QA	PROD	ONPREM
SANDBOX	Yes	Forbidden	Forbidden	Forbidden	Forbidden	Forbidden
DEV	Forbidden	Yes	Yes	Forbidden	Forbidden	Exception
DEVINT	Forbidden	Forbidden	Yes	Forbidden	Forbidden	Exception
QA	Forbidden	Forbidden	Forbidden	Yes	Forbidden	Exception
PROD	Forbidden	Forbidden	Forbidden	Forbidden	Yes	Approval
ONPREM	Forbidden	Approval	Approval	Approval	Approval	n/a

To summarize:

- **SANDBOX** SANDBOX environments are used for experiments. These environments should be completely isolated, with no connection to other environments, including the on-premises environment. Although PaaS services may use public endpoints, VMs should not be exposed directly to the internet through a public IP address. Use VPNs or the Azure Bastion Service to reach such VMs.

- **DEV** DEV environments are used in continuous integration (CI) to test the code before merging them into the main branch. These environments can communicate with other DEV environments. A DEV might also need to communicate with a DEVINT environment for development-time testing, since DEVINT environments contain reasonably stable versions of code from other teams.

- **DEVINT** DEVINT environments are used to verify changes after a PR merge into the main branch. They are used to test for dependency problems between different developments.

- **NONPROD environments** The remaining NONPROD environments (including DEVINT) can communicate only with solutions in the same environment type—for example, DEVINT to DEVINT, QA to QA, PERF to PERF, and so on.

- **PROD environments** These must communicate only with other PROD environments. On a related note:

  - Traditional CI/CD deployment strategies commonly use one VNet per region for each landing zone.

  - In blue/green CI/CD deployment strategies, green environments must not communicate with blue environments, or vice versa. Although this is not a security issue, such communication patterns violate the concept of blue/green.

Ingress and egress controls

Every organization will want to control connections between VNets in the same region or across regions. This is also known as east/west traffic. East/west traffic belonging to the same landing zone can be allowed without extra restrictions.

Inbound and outbound internet connections are always routed through the network hub(s) via firewalls and other security devices such as Azure Application Gateways, Azure API Management Gateways, Azure Front Door, and/or Azure Firewall. Inbound restrictions are enforced by preventing public IP addresses in the spokes, while outbound restrictions are enforced through the application of UDRs on every subnet not containing security appliances.

On-premises traffic (to/from) is routed through firewalls, NAT devices, and VPNs over the public internet or through an ExpressRoute (dedicated) connection.

VMs and PaaS components in the spokes may not contain any public IP addresses unless required due to technical limitations or special circumstances. Any such requirement will necessitate a thorough threat model and approved exception. An Azure Function App handling an Event Grid trigger is an example of a technical limitation requiring such an exception.

NVAs and gateways

As discussed, NVAs are implemented in the hub network to guard trust boundary transitions, whether ingress or egress. Depending on the direction, this is also known as *north/south* or *east/west* traffic, as shown in Table 15-3.

TABLE 15-3 Traffic directions

Source	Destination	Direction
Internet	Azure services	North/south
Azure services in one solution	Azure services in another solution	East/west
Azure services	On-premises services	North/south

> **Note** This book discusses Azure native services. However, many third-party NVAs are available for use within Azure. Their usage patterns parallel those of the native services.

Azure Firewall

Firewalls analyze transiting traffic at OSI layers 3 through 7 (see https://en.wikipedia.org/wiki/OSI_model), providing audit, traffic filtering, and threat intelligence capabilities. For example, a firewall can identify the following:

- Source and destination IP addresses, either directly (through an IP range) or indirectly (through IP tags and reverse FQDN lookups)

- Destination URL patterns

- The destination URL's web category, such as liability (bad sites), high-bandwidth, business use, and so on

- The protocol used, and optionally, the enforcement of security protocols such as TLS

- Port numbers

- Intrusion patterns

- And much more

Azure Firewall Premium SKU

The Azure Firewall Premium SKU goes beyond the basic firewall capabilities implemented with the Standard SKU by adding the following features:

- **TLS Inspection**   This is somewhat auxiliary to the other capabilities because it enables you to unencrypt requests to inspect them. This allows them to use more information than the servers or ports involved.

- **Intrusion Detection and Prevention**   This enables you to inspect packages in detail to identify, report, and even block potential malicious activity.

- **URL Filtering**   This enables you to define extensive rules to block requests. For example, you might want to allow requests from https://www.contoso.com but block requests from https://www.contoso.com/mymaliciousapp.

- **Web Categories**   These enable you to block specific targets based on their category, like gambling, social media, and so on.

The Azure Firewall Standard SKU also includes advanced capabilities such as threat intelligence.

Azure web application firewalls

Web application firewalls (WAFs) inspect HTTP/HTTPS traffic to audit or filter common malicious payloads. The Azure WAF can be applied on Azure CDN, Azure Front Door, or an Azure Application Gateway.

OWASP ModSecurity CRS is the source for many of the attack patterns covered by WAFs. You can find further details here: https://owasp.org/www-project-modsecurity-core-rule-set/. Many of these categories should be defended through secure coding practices; the WAF simply adds one more defensive layer and centralizes logging of attempted attacks.

It is important to understand that WAFs are based on heuristics determined over the years through observation of attacks. This provides a lot of value, because it allows them to recognize those attacks and to prevent them from occurring again. Unfortunately, however, there is no guarantee that the next attacker will use one of those techniques. For example, it has happened in the past that penetration testers learned of the presence of WAFs after having completed their exercise. In that case, the WAF was ineffective, so much so that the penetration tester didn't even notice it! Moreover, WAFs are not unknown to knowledgeable attackers. If your adversary knows their business, you can assume that it may take them anywhere from just a few minutes to a couple of hours to circumvent it.

Another shortcoming of WAFs is that they do not know anything about your solution. Therefore, they cannot apply more stringent controls. For example, if you have a text field that accepts a phone number, the WAF may not be able to determine attacks where the phone number has been tweaked. But your application can detect them, and it should.

To summarize, WAFs play a very important role when used correctly, because they allow you to identify common attacks and to act, but you should not believe that they can do magic.

API Management Gateway

As its name clearly indicates, the primary purpose of an API Management (APIM) Gateway is API management. However, it also provides security-related capabilities in addition to its core capabilities. For example, an APIM gateway:

- Accepts API calls and routes them to your back ends

- Verifies API keys, JWT tokens, certificates, and other credentials

- Enforces usage quotas and rate limits

- Transforms your API on the fly without code modifications

- Caches back-end responses

- Logs call metadata for analytics purposes

Because the APIM gateway is not primarily a security NVA and therefore lacks WAF capability, it must be combined with a WAF-capable front end, such as Azure Front Door or Application Gateway.

Azure Application Proxy

Azure Application Proxy is intended for publishing on-premises and IaaS-based solutions on the internet. Application Proxy exposes the (private) app to a public endpoint and protects it by requiring valid authentication with Azure AD.

PaaS and private networking

PaaS was intended to rely exclusively on the identity perimeter. However, this was roundly rejected by horrified security teams. (This author experienced only one exception to this as a cybersecurity consultant.) Although some aspects of this widespread rejection can be traced to outdated network-perimeter thinking, there are many reasons to keep a PaaS private:

- Layered defenses are better than single-layer defenses (see the section "Defense in depth" in Chapter 2, "Secure design").

- The attack surface can be reduced for internal services.

- All internet ingress can be routed through a single place for logging, inspection, and intrusion detection.

- All internet and on-premises egress can be routed through a single place for a data-loss prevention (DLP) system.

The solution is to inject PaaS endpoints and, if applicable, the outgoing implied NIC into a VNet. In addition, any such technology must disable public endpoints. Azure uses myriad approaches to solve this problem.

> **Important** PaaS public endpoint traffic originating in Azure is routed within Azure's internal network. Therefore, this traffic does not go over the open internet and is better protected.

Private shared PaaS

PaaS services may have any combination of the following, which need to be made private:

- Endpoints for the data plane

- Endpoints for the control plane for complex services, such as Databricks, Synapse, and AKS

- Egress calls requiring routing via a UDR to an egress control network virtual appliance

- The consumption of data sources directly through private networking

Service endpoints and private endpoints

Service endpoints were an early technology to solve the problem of protecting shared PaaS in a private VNet. Service endpoints can be thought of as automanaged firewalls. The public DNS entry and IP address still exist, but connection requests for them are rejected by the firewall, except from the subnet containing the service endpoint. (See Figure 15-2.) Many services support service endpoints.

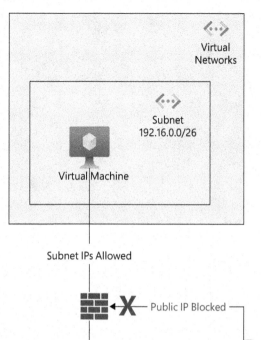

Virtual Networks

Subnet
192.16.0.0/26

Virtual Machine

Subnet IPs Allowed

Public IP Blocked

Public IP

Internet

Storage Accounts

FIGURE 15-2 Visualization of a service endpoint.

Private endpoints have replaced service endpoints. They project a virtual NIC into the VNet of your choosing. Private endpoints hide the public IP address of the service instance. Each PaaS service can have multiple private endpoints in different VNets and subnets. (See Figure 15-3.)

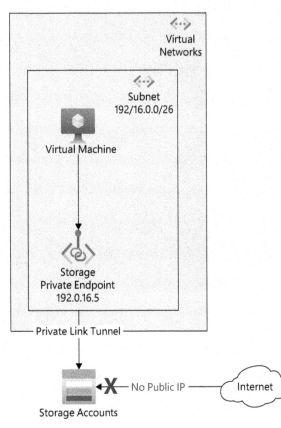

FIGURE 15-3 Visualization of a private endpoint.

> **Recommendation** In new environments, use private endpoints instead of service endpoints. Additionally, migrate existing PaaS solutions with service endpoints to private endpoints.

A note on names

The terms *private endpoint* and *private link* are often used interchangeably, but they are two different things. A private link is the underlying tunneling technology, and a private endpoint is the manifestation of a PaaS endpoint in your VNet and subnet.

Private endpoints and the private DNS problem

The Domain Name System (DNS) translates a host name, called a *fully qualified domain name* (FQDN), into an IPv4 or IPv6 address. In a traditional Active Directory environment, this is often handled by the server hosting the domain controller (DC) role. For public endpoints in Azure, the resolution is forwarded by the DC to Azure's DNS service.

> **Note** When one of your services fails to communicate with another service, the likely culprit is a DNS lookup problem.

DNS resolution for private endpoints within the same VNet is handled by Azure DNS. In any nontrivial system, the FQDN for private endpoints also needs to be resolved by DNS in peered VNets. Fortunately, Microsoft's documentation has a solution for this problem, located here: https://azsec.tech/rf1.

Shared App Service plans

Integration of shared App Service plans for API, Web, and Function Apps in your VNet requires the following:

- Private endpoint for ingress

- VNet integration for egress

In addition, to enable outbound connections for all communications to pass through the VNet, making them subject to UDR, you must enable the `WEBSITE_VNET_ROUTE_ALL` setting. This may seem confusing, so let's tease out the concept. The sample Function App in Figure 15-4 uses a Key Vault for secret storage and needs a storage account for itself. You can also add databases and other services to consume from the Function App.

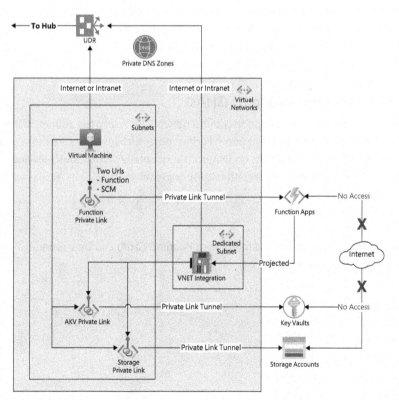

FIGURE 15-4 VM accessing Function App privately and Function App protected within the same VNet.

Dedicated PaaS instances

Dedicated PaaS instances provide another path to private PaaS services. Examples of such dedicated instances include the following:

- **Azure App Service Environment (ASE) hosting an isolated SKU App Service plan** This provides some of the same easy deployment and management as a shared App Service plan while running on a dedicated scale set.

- **Integration Service Environment (ISE)** This provides the same level of isolation for Logic Apps. ISE are being deprecated - do not use in new solutions.

- **Databricks clusters with No Public IP (NPIP)** These are isolated, but the control plane is public and must instead be protected with strong Azure Active Directory authentication.

Managed VNets

Services that provide managed VNets and private link hubs, such as Synapse, create VNets in your subscription. This exposes any ingress through private link hubs (Synapse provides three public endpoints) and managed private endpoints to connect to other services.

Agent-based network participation

SaaS-like services such as Azure DevOps and Purview provide IaaS-based agents. These are hosted on-premises in a VM or VM Scale Set (VMSS). They do not accept inbound connections and receive all their instructions from outgoing requests, reducing the risk. Unfortunately, you still need to manage the VMs increasing the risk; therefore, if available, use PaaS-based approaches, such as Managed VNets.

Azure DevOps (ADO) self-hosted agents (SHAs)

ADO SHAs are often hosted in a shared subscription within a network hub (separate subnet). Using the SHA scale set capability, you can scale your agent pools. Furthermore, such instances are destroyed after completing a job. This destruction prevents an SHA from accidentally or maliciously leaving information behind or having an altered state that affects the next job.

> ### Other agents
>
> Other names for such agents are Self-Hosted Integration Runtime (SHIR) and Data Gateway (DGW). They behave similarly to ADO SHAs.

Azure Kubernetes Service networking

Azure Kubernetes Service (AKS) networking is a complex topic beyond the scope of this book. However, this section provides a brief overview of the two networking options supported by AKS:

- **Kubenet**   Native to Kubernetes, Kubenet is created as part of the cluster deployment. It manages IP addresses and provides access to AKS elements through load balancers and network address translation (NAT) requiring smaller IP address spaces. Kubenet is available only on Linux clusters. You can find more information about Kubenet here: https://azsec.tech/6ga.

- **Azure Container Networking Interface (CNI)**   The CNI provides more control over the network layout; however, it requires more IP addresses, because pods get full connectivity. It supports both Linux and Windows clusters. You can find more information about it here: https://azsec.tech/hk6.

Ingress controls

AKS can deploy an internal load balancer (ILB) or an external load balancer (ELB) for your cluster. An ILB does not expose a public IP address, allowing you to control ingress through a firewall. If you decide to use an ELB with a public IP address, you can use an Azure Application Gateway with WAF as an ingress controller to protect your cluster. Alternatively, you can use Nginx as the ingress controller. It is recommended to keep the ingress controller in a separate subnet within the VNet. For more information, see https://azsec.tech/9qe.

Egress controls with UDR

Like the previously discussed shared App Service plans, egress from an AKS cluster can call any IP address. You can prevent this, however, by first routing egress traffic through a firewall using UDRs. For more information, see https://azsec.tech/a6y.

Private endpoints for Kubernetes API server

The cluster itself is always in a VNet. However, the Kubernetes API server is a PaaS with a public IP address. As with other shared PaaS resources, using a Private Endpoint removes the public IP address.

Cluster network policies

AKS can use a network policy engine for a cluster. Network policies require CNI networking and must be specified when the cluster is created. (See https://azsec.tech/iml for more information.)

Clusters can use one of two network policy solutions:

- **AKS with Azure network policies created via Azure CLI**   To apply this solution, use the following code:

```
az aks create \
    --resource-group $rg \
    --name $name \
    --node-count 5 \
    --generate-ssh-keys \
    --service-cidr 10.5.0.0/24 \
    --dns-service-ip 10.0.0.10 \
    --docker-bridge-address 172.17.0.1/16 \
    --vnet-subnet-id $subnet \
    --service-principal $sp \
    --client-secret $pwd \
    --network-plugin azure \
    --network-policy azure
```

- **AKS with Calico network policies created via Azure CLI**   To apply this solution, use the following code:

```
az aks create \
    --resource-group $rg \
    --name $name \
    --node-count 5 \
    --generate-ssh-keys \
    --service-cidr 10.5.0.0/24 \
    --dns-service-ip 10.0.0.10 \
    --docker-bridge-address 172.17.0.1/16 \
    --vnet-subnet-id $subnet \
    --service-principal $sp \
    --client-secret $pwd \
    --windows-admin-username $winusername \
    --vm-set-type VirtualMachineScaleSets \
    --kubernetes-version 1.20.2 \
    --network-plugin azure \
    --network-policy calico
```

You can now define network policies. Network policies can be based on pod attributes, such as labels. They are similar to NSGs and can control traffic within a cluster as well as external communication. Here's an example of a network-policy definition in YAML:

```
kind: NetworkPolicy
apiVersion: networking.k8s.io/v1
metadata:
  name: backend-policy
  namespace: development
spec:
  podSelector:
    matchLabels:
      app: webapp
      role: backend
  ingress: []
```

These policies can be deployed with the kubectl command:

```
kubectl apply -f backend-policy.yaml
```

The dangling DNS problem

One key benefit of cloud-based solutions is agility. It is possible to quickly spool up and tear down resources. As a result, applications that might have taken months to deploy on-premises can be deployed in minutes in Azure. This ability to spool up and tear down resources has a dark side, however. The most notable issue is called the *dangling DNS problem*, which enables attackers to hijack your resources. This is often referred to as a *subdomain takeover*, and yes, it's as bad as the name suggests.

Here's what happens: when you map to a DNS canonical name (CNAME) record (an alias) for an Azure resource that is no longer provisioned, it leaves the associated domain "dangling." This subdomain then becomes subject to takeover. This issue is not new; people have known about it for years. But the issue is exacerbated in the cloud.

> ## CNAME records
>
> A CNAME record maps one domain name to a canonical name. For example, when you develop an application in Azure, you might decide to map an easy-to-remember DNS name to another, not-so-easy-to-remember DNS name that is provided by Azure.

An example

Here's an example of the effects of a dangling DNS. Suppose that in Azure, you register a "nice" DNS name, app.contoso.com, to point to app-contoso-prod-002.azurewebsites.net. Then, at some point, you remove app-contoso-prod-002.azurewebsites.net. This leaves app.contoso.com dangling—that is, pointing to something that does not exist. Now suppose a bad actor, using tools that are well understood, discovers your dangling DNS (because DNS names and hierarchies are public information) and then creates an Azure resource that has the old not-so-easy-to-remember DNS name, app-contoso-prod-002.azurewebsites.net. Now, all traffic meant for app.contoso.com goes to app-contoso-prod-002.azurewebsites.net, which is controlled by the bad actor. The potential impact of this vulnerability ranges from cookie harvesting to phishing and beyond.

> ## Spelunking CNAMEs
>
> If you're interested in understanding the DNS entries that have a CNAME entry, you can use the `Get-DnsClientCache` PowerShell cmdlet. (Type 5 is a CNAME.) The example in Figure 15-5 is from within Windows Server 2022 right after startup. As you can see, ocsp.digicert.com has an alias named cs9.wac.phicdn.net. This is the endpoint used for DigiCert's certificate revocation using Online Certificate Status Protocol (OCSP).

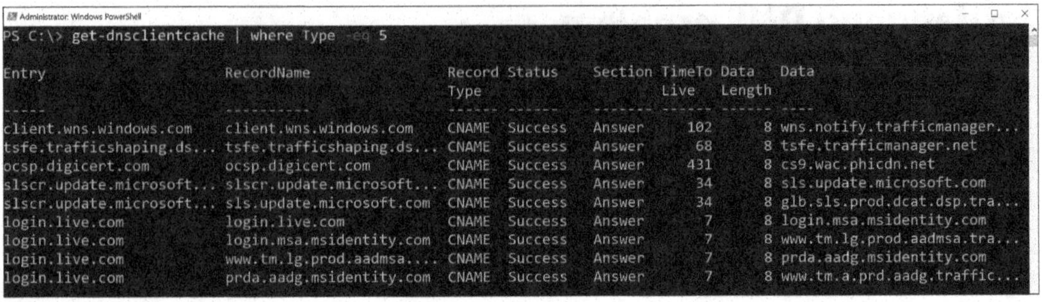

FIGURE 15-5 Looking at DNS CNAME records using PowerShell.

Fixing dangling DNS

At the time of this writing, a new capability named DNS reservations has been added to Azure to help mitigate dangling DNS issues. You can read more about DNS reservations here: https://azsec.tech/tfw.

Another way to mitigate dangling DNS is to use Microsoft Defender for DNS, which will detect and inform you of this issue.

There are yet more ways to mitigate dangling DNS, but they are more complex and require DNS knowledge. These include using DNS alias records and removing CNAME records when they are no longer used.

Summary

In this chapter, you were introduced to several important networking concepts. It then fleshed out how to reduce the attack surface on a PaaS by hiding the public endpoints in favor of private networking. The available approaches for private networking vary by PaaS type. They include service endpoints, private endpoints, VNet integration, dedicated PaaS instances, Managed VNets, and agent-based network participation.

This chapter also covered Kubernetes networking. Although the Kubernetes networking discussion is not sufficient to understand all the intricacies of Kubernetes networking, it should provide you with sufficient understanding of how to get started with AKS networking.

Finally, this chapter discussed the dangling DNS problem and how to mitigate it using a special capability within Azure.

Core cryptographic techniques

After reading this appendix, you will be able to:

- Grasp core cryptographic constructs.

- Better understand common cryptographic terms.

Why this appendix?

Originally, we didn't think we needed this appendix. But as we wrote more text, we realized that for the book to be well-rounded, we were wrong.

This appendix is designed to give a layperson a brief introduction to the cornerstones of modern cryptographic solutions. It is not designed to replace extensive books on the topic of cryptography—and there are plenty of good ones. Here are just a few:

- *Cryptography Engineering: Design Principles and Practical Applications* by Niels Ferguson, Bruce Schneier, and Tadayoshi Kohno (Wiley)

- *Practical Cryptography* by Niels Ferguson and Bruce Schneier (Wiley)

- *Serious Cryptography: A Practical Introduction to Modern Encryption* by Jean-Philippe Aumasson (No Starch Press)

- *The Manga Guide to Cryptography* by Masaaki Mitani, Shinichi Sato, and Idero Hinoki (No Starch Press)

> **Note** You may think that the last book is a tongue-in-cheek suggestion, and perhaps it is. But there's no denying it's an excellent book if you're new to cryptography and enjoy manga!

Thinking about cryptography

At a high level, much of cryptography can be carved up into two major areas:

- Secrecy and integrity/authentication

- Symmetric and asymmetric algorithms

These two groups lead to a combination of four cryptographic solutions and associated techniques (see Table A-1):

- Symmetric secrecy

- Asymmetric secrecy

- Symmetric integrity/authentication

- Asymmetric integrity/authentication

TABLE A-1 Cryptographic solutions and associated techniques

	Symmetric	**Asymmetric**
Secrecy	Symmetric ciphers	Asymmetric ciphers
Integrity and Authentication	Hashes Message authentication codes	Digital signatures

The rest of this appendix covers these four areas and associated cryptographic techniques. After that, it covers other topics of importance, such as certificates and key derivation.

Symmetric ciphers

When most people think about cryptography, they're thinking of symmetric ciphers. The most common of these today is the Advanced Encryption Standard (AES) algorithm. AES is a block cipher, which means it encrypts and decrypts one block at a time. The standard block size for AES is 128 bits. With AES, the same key is used to encrypt and decrypt data and must be known to all communicating parties.

> **Note** Today, most TLS sessions use AES for bulk-encryption of data.

Symmetric ciphers operate in various cipher modes, such as the following:

- **Electronic code book (ECB)**   This is rarely used because two sets of identical plaintext yield the same ciphertext, when using the same key. This helps attackers because if two ciphertexts are the same, then the two plaintexts are the same. So, don't use it.

- **Cipher block chaining (CBC)**   This is the default for many libraries. When a block is encrypted, the resulting single block of ciphertext is XORed with the next block of plaintext before it is encrypted—and hence the name! For many situations, this is a good default mode to use, as it does not suffer from "same key, same plaintext, same ciphertext" weakness of ECB.

- **Galois Counter Mode (GCM)**   GCM is becoming an important mode. It is complex to explain and certainly beyond the scope of this appendix. GCM not only encrypts, but it also produces a tag. This is like a message authentication code (MAC), which we will cover later in this appendix.

Block ciphers also require a padding mode. Because plaintext might not carve up nicely into 64-bit or 128-bit blocks, the last block is usually padded. Examples of padding modes include the following:

- **ANSIX923** A sequence of bytes filled with zeros before the length

- **ISO10126** Random data before the length

- **None** No padding

- **PKCS7** A sequence of bytes, each of which is equal to the total number of padding bytes added

- **Zeros** Consists of bytes set to zero

.NET defaults to using PKCS7 padding, as does the Always Encrypted cipher suite used by SQL Server and Cosmos DB and the Microsoft Data Encryption SDK.

Some block modes, such as CBC and GCM, need an initialization vector (IV), which is fed into the first encryption block. An IV must be unique and unencrypted. An IV is usually appended to the ciphertext so the decryption process has access to the IV. The role of an IV is to create different ciphertext if an encryption key is reused—which is why it needs to be unique. An IV does not need to be random.

There are many other well-known and no-longer-secure symmetric block ciphers, such as DES and TripleDES. There also exist stream ciphers that encrypt and decrypt one byte at a time. Currently, AES is the go-to symmetric cipher, however.

Please also note that AES is derived from the Rijndael algorithm, but Rijndael is not AES, so please do not use Rijndael.

The major advantage of symmetric ciphers is they are quick and well understood. The major disadvantage is all communicating parties must share the same key to encrypt and decrypt the data.

Asymmetric ciphers

Unlike symmetric ciphers, asymmetric ciphers use key pairs: a private key and a public key. These keys are generated using math. You cannot deduce one key just by knowing the other. If software performs a cryptographic operation using one key, the inverse cryptographic operation must be performed using the other key.

The public portion is, as its name suggests, public, and can be shared with anyone. The private key is just that: private, so must remain protected and are never shared, but they should still be backed up.

The most well-known asymmetric algorithms in widespread use today are as follows:

- Rivest-Shamir-Adleman (RSA)

- Elliptic curve (EC)

- Diffie-Hellman (DH)

The following are the core asymmetric cryptographic operations:

- Encrypt and decrypt

- Sign and verify (for digital signatures)

- Wrap and unwrap (to protect and unprotect other keys, such as symmetric keys)

Each of these use the public and private key differently. For example:

- Encrypt with public, decrypt with private.

- Sign with private, verify with public.

- Wrap with public, unwrap with private.

This means if you know someone's public key, you could send them an encrypted message, and only the valid recipient can decrypt it because only they have the private key associated with the public key. Or someone could digitally sign a document with their private key, and anyone could verify it came from them using their public key.

Not all asymmetric algorithms support all cryptographic operations, however. RSA can perform all six of the aforementioned operations, but EC can only sign and verify. You cannot encrypt using EC.

The advantage of asymmetric ciphers is they don't require key sharing among all parties the way symmetric cryptography does. The downside is performance. RSA and DH are both incredibly slow. EC, while slower than symmetric operations, is significantly faster than RSA and DH.

Hashes

A hash is a data fingerprint. A person's fingerprint identifies them, but it does not tell you anything about them. A hash is the same way. The result of a hash function is often called a fingerprint, thumbprint, or digest.

The most common hash algorithms today are the SHA-2 suite of algorithms:

- SHA-2 224

- SHA-2 256

- SHA-2 384

- SHA-2 512

SHA-3 is new and still not commonly used. Currently, TLS does not use SHA-3. It is our opinion that you should still use SHA-2 until SHA-3 has had a little more time in the market and because SHA-2 is not broken. SHA-2 has been a standard since 2001 and SHA-3 since 2015. Also, NIST is not presently replacing SHA-2 with SHA-3.

Back to SHA-2. You'll notice that each hash function in the preceding list has a number at the end. This is the bit size of the resulting digest. So, if you have a 2 MB Word document and you hash the contents using SHA-2 256, you get a 256-bit digest that identifies the document (that is, a fingerprint).

A property of a good hash function is that it resists collisions, so you should not be able to find two documents that have the same digest. Some older hash functions—such as MD4, MD5, and SHA-1—have been demonstrated to have collisions and as such should no longer be used.

Fun fact #1: SHA-2 224 is a full SHA-2 256 with some bits thrown away, and SHA-2 384 is a full SHA-512 with some bits thrown away.

Fun fact #2: There is a well-known but esoteric attack against hash functions called a *length extension attack*. SHA-2 256 and SHA-2 512 are potentially subject to these attacks, but the truncated versions, SHA-2 224 and SHA-2 384, are not.

Hash functions are often called an integrity check, and it's not uncommon to see, for example, a list of files with their SHA-2 hash. You can see an example at https://azsec.tech/gp7 when you click the Updated Packages tab. When you download the file updates, you can verify they have not been tampered with by recalculating the hash yourself.

Hash functions are lightning fast. For most solutions, you will want to use SHA-2 256. It's a good middle ground of speed and security. Always Encrypted uses SHA-2 256. The problem with hashes is that the document and its hash cannot travel with each other. This is because an attacker could change the document and recalculate the hash at any stage, and no one would know. There is nothing secret, like a key, to protect the hash from alteration. Hashes work in the sample link in the preceding paragraph because the hash information is on the website and cannot be tampered with.

Message authentication codes

We need to look at another option: message authentication code (MAC). A MAC is used to provide tamper detection and authentication. It does this by using a shared key called a MAC key.

The most prevalent MAC today is the hashed MAC (HMAC), which uses a hash function as its base. An easy way to think about an HMAC is it's a hash function, but instead of hashing only a message, it stirs in a secret key, also.

If you prefer a more precise definition, if a hash function can be represented as:

$h = H(m)$

where h is the resulting digest, H is the hash algorithm, and m is the message, then an (incredibly simplified) HMAC could be represented as:

$hmac = H(\ K\ ||\ H(\ K\ ||\ m\ )\ )$

where hmac is the resulting HMAC, H is the hash algorithm, K is a MAC key, and m is the message. (The || symbol means concatenation.)

This construct yields an interesting property: if a user creates a document and derives its HMAC using an HMAC key, an attacker will need to modify the document and then re-create the HMAC. But doing so would mean having access to the key (K), which is a secret known only to all communicating parties.

> **Note** In the previous section, we said Always Encrypted uses SHA-2 256. This is technically not correct, however. In fact, Always Encrypted uses HMAC SHA-2 256.

HMACs are fast, but they have one major problem: verifying an HMAC means you must know the MAC key (K), and that is the same for all parties. This means there is no way to know who *actually* created the document and created the HMAC, because if 10 entities have access to the same MAC key, it could have been any of those 10 entities that performed the work.

There is a way to solve the problem associated with HMACs, gain the benefits of asymmetric keys, and use them rather than shared, symmetric MAC keys: digital signatures, covered in the next section.

Digital signatures

From a practical perspective, the big difference between an HMAC and a digital signature is the key. Sure, there are other differences, like the algorithms used and such, but let's ignore those details in this 100-level introduction.

A common digital signature algorithm used today is Elliptic Curve Digital Signature Algorithm (ECDSA). Ethereum uses ECDSA to sign blockchain transactions.

When your code digitally signs something, it uses your private key on a document hash. This offers an advantage over an HMAC: if you sign something, anyone with your public key can verify it came from you. There is no need to disseminate sensitive HMAC keys; all they need is your public key. And because the key is public, anyone can gain access to it to verify your digitally signed documents. Also, because only you have the private key used to sign the hash, then the signed document must have come from you.

But there's a nagging problem. How do you know to whom the public key belongs? That's where certificates come in. They're discussed next.

Certificates

Certificates are designed to do one thing: to cryptographically bind a name, such as an email address or a DNS name, to a public key. To understand how certificates work, you must understand their lifecycle. To explain this, we will use a real example: the certificate used for the Azure Security Podcast website at https://azsecuritypodcast.net. This website contains the show notes for all episodes and is hosted on Azure as an App Service. Here's how it works:

1. We need a certificate so we can use TLS on the site. Some software on Azure App Service creates an RSA key pair. (It could have been EC, but we chose RSA.)

2. The private key is stored securely in Azure.

3. The public key is wrapped into a certificate signing request (CSR) along with the site's name and contact information, and the entire request is signed with the private key. Note that the private key does not leave its source. It's used to sign the request, but nothing more.

4. The CSR is sent to a certificate authority (CA)—in our case, GoDaddy.

5. GoDaddy verifies that the CSR came from someone with administrative access to the azsecuritypodcast.net site. (There are multiple ways to do this; we won't cover all the possibilities here.)

6. Assuming the verification is OK, GoDaddy creates the certificate. In it they include a serial number, valid from and valid to fields, the name of the website, the public key, and a few other critical items.

7. The entire blob is digitally signed by the private key associated with a GoDaddy certificate. This certificate is usually an intermediate certificate, which is perhaps signed by another intermediate certificate, which in turn is signed by a root certificate.

The result is the App Service has a digitally signed certificate we can use for TLS using the private key created in step 1.

> **Note** The current certificate standard is X.509 version 3.

Key derivation

We want to cover one final topic that's not represented in Table A-1: key derivation. Humans generally use passwords and passphrases as credentials, but human language makes for lousy cryptographic keys because human language is low entropy. A better way to use passphrases as a starting point for keys is to use key derivation functions. By the way, the best solution is to never use anything but cryptographically random keys!

The most well-known derivation function is defined in RFC 2898 and is referred to as a *password-based key derivation function* (PBKDF). This function takes a few arguments:

- A hash algorithm

- A salt (a unique value)

- An iteration count

- The starting passphrase

On the first iteration, the function hashes the passphrase, the iteration count (zero), and the salt. Let's call this k_0. On subsequent iterations, the function hashes the output from the previous iteration, with the iteration count and the salt. This continues until the iterations are complete. This is often called *salting and stretching*. The output from the final step could be used as an AES key or an HMAC key. Microsoft internally uses iteration counts of 100,000.

PBKDFs are also used in environments that need to prove a user possesses a password. In this scenario, you don't need the password; you just need to store something that can be used to prove they know the password. So, when a user presents their password, you pass it through the same PBKDF function and compare it with the stored PBKDF result; if they are the same, then the user knows the password. This is better than storing the password or even an encrypted password, because if an attacker gets the list of PBKDF-derived passwords, they can do nothing with the data other than attempt a brute-force attack. In this scenario, you also need to store the salt and the iteration count with the resulting PBKDF data.

The salt and the iteration count protect against online and offline attacks. This includes resistance to rainbow tables, which are precomputed tables of password hashes. So, rather than calculate hashes from passwords, an attacker takes the hash, looks it up in a rainbow table, and gets the password directly! You can read more about rainbow tables here: https://azsec.tech/x8c/.

You can also think of the iteration count as a "Moore's law compensator." Like an IV, the salt does not need to be random or encrypted, but it must be unique.

Other derivation functions include Argon2 and scrypt. These are both memory hard, which means they are inefficient when used on massively parallel hardware like custom chips and GPU cards—a favorite tool for attackers who perform brute-force attacks.

Cryptographic vulnerabilities

Over the decades, numerous weaknesses have been found in cryptographic algorithms and solutions, so it's important to stay ahead of new research in this area. A common issue is the combination of AES, CBC, and PKCS7 padding.

There's a known weakness called the Padding Oracle attack, discussed here: https://azsec.tech/74a. What's interesting about this is a recent issue affected the Azure SDK and the code used to encrypt data at the client. The fix was to move to use AES-GCM (identified as version 2) rather than AES-CBC (identified as version 1). But because the SDK uses cryptographic agility by adding a 1-byte version number at the start of the protected blob, the code can easily decrypt older data encrypted with AES-CBC but can encrypt and write out using the more secure AES-GCM.

Index

H

I

W

X - Y - Z

Plug into learning at

MicrosoftPressStore.com

The Microsoft Press Store by Pearson offers:

- Free U.S. shipping

- Buy an eBook, get three formats – Includes PDF, EPUB, and MOBI to use with your computer, tablet, and mobile devices

- Print & eBook Best Value Packs

- eBook Deal of the Week – Save up to 50% on featured title

- Newsletter – Be the first to hear about new releases, announcements, special offers, and more

- Register your book – Find companion files, errata, and product updates, plus receive a special coupon* to save on your next purchase

 Pearson